THE HISTORY OF ENGLISH LAW
Centenary Essays on
'Pollock and Maitland'

FREDERIC WILLIAM MAITLAND, 1850–1906
Painting by Beatrice Lock
Reproduced by permission of Downing College, Cambridge

PROCEEDINGS OF THE BRITISH ACADEMY · 89

THE HISTORY OF ENGLISH LAW
Centenary Essays on 'Pollock and Maitland'

Edited by
JOHN HUDSON

Published for THE BRITISH ACADEMY
by OXFORD UNIVERSITY PRESS

Oxford University Press, Great Clarendon Street, Oxford OX2 6DP

Oxford   New York
Athens Auckland Bangkok Bogota Bombay
Buenos Aires Calcutta Cape Town Dar es Salaam
Delhi Florence Hong Kong Istanbul Karachi
Kuala Lumpur Madras Madrid Melbourne
Mexico City Nairobi Paris Singapore
Taipei Tokyo Toronto Warsaw

and associated companies in
Berlin Ibadan

Published in the United States by
Oxford University Press Inc., New York

First published 1996
Reprinted 1997

British Library Cataloguing in Publication Data
Data available

ISBN 0–19–726165–5
ISSN 0068–1202

Printed in Great Britain
on acid-free paper by
Bookcraft (Bath) Ltd.
Midsomer Norton, Somerset

Contents

Notes on Contributors   vii

Preface   ix

Abbreviations   xi

Maitland and Anglo-Saxon Law: Beyond Domesday Book   1
PATRICK WORMALD

Maitland and Anglo-Norman Law   21
JOHN HUDSON

The Writs of Henry II   47
J. C. HOLT

'The Age of Bracton'   65
PAUL BRAND

Maitland on Family and Kinship   91
STEPHEN D. WHITE

Maitland and the Criminal Law in the Age of *Bracton*   115
HENRY SUMMERSON

The Learned Laws in 'Pollock and Maitland'   145
R. H. HELMHOLZ

The Origins of the Crown   171
GEORGE GARNETT

Maitland and the Rest of Us   215
PAUL R. HYAMS

'Pollock and Maitland': a Lawyer's Retrospect   243
S. F. C. MILSOM

Bibliography of the Writings of F. W. Maitland   261
MARK PHILPOTT

Index   279

List of Plates

Frontispiece: Frederic William Maitland, 1850–1906

Between page 148 and page 149

1. Sir Frederick Pollock, Bart., 1845–1937

2. A poster attacking Maitland for his views on women students (CUL, UA, CUR 61, no. 154)

3. The Oxford message of condolence on Maitland's death (CUL, UA, CUR 39 (21); *Cambridge University Reporter*, 37 (1906–7), 526)

4. The page of the manuscript of *The History of English Law* in which Maitland celebrates finishing the book (CUL, Add MS 6994, p. 303)

Notes on Contributors

Dr Paul Brand is a Research Fellow of the Institute of Historical Research, London. He is the author of *The Origins of the English Legal Profession* (1992) and *The Making of the Common Law* (1992). His Selden Society edition of volumes I and II of *The Earliest English Law Reports* is currently in press.

Dr George Garnett is Fellow and Tutor of St Hugh's College, Oxford. His publications include an edition of the *Vindiciae, contra tyrannos* (1994), and he was co-editor of *Law and Government in Medieval England and Normandy* (1994). He is currently working on a study of royal succession in England, 1066–1154.

R. H. Helmholz is Ruth Wyatt Rosenson Professor of Law in the University of Chicago. He is author of *Roman Canon Law in Reformation England* (Cambridge, 1990), and his *The Spirit of Classical Canon Law* will be published in 1996 by University of Georgia Press, as part of its series on the Spirit of the Laws.

Sir James Holt is Professor Emeritus of Medieval History in the University of Cambridge, and a Fellow of the British Academy. He is best known for his *Magna Carta* (2nd edn, Cambridge, 1992). His interests in legal history concern society and law, politics and law, and, above all, the rule of law. He has come to place more trust in writs and charters than in texts. This is expressed in his contribution to this volume which is derived from his present work on the acta of the Angevin kings.

Dr John Hudson is a Lecturer in Mediaeval History at the University of St Andrews. He is author of *Land, Law, and Lordship in Anglo-Norman England* (1994) and co-editor of *Law and Government in Medieval England and Normandy* (1994). His *Formation of the English Common Law* is currently in press.

Paul R. Hyams is Associate Professor of History at Cornell University, Ithaca, NY, having been a Fellow of Pembroke College, Oxford. He is author of *King, Lords and Peasants in Medieval England* (1980), and of articles including 'The Common Law and the French Connection', 'Warranty and good lordship in twelfth-century England', and 'The Jews as an immigrant minority, 1066–1290'. He is now working on a book *Rancor and Reconciliation in Medieval England*.

S. F. C. Milsom is Professor Emeritus of Law in the University of Cambridge and a Fellow of the British Academy and was formerly Professor of Legal History in London. Relevant writings are: an introduction to the 1968 reissue of Pollock and Maitland; a lecture on Maitland printed in vol. 66 of the Academy's Proceedings; *The Legal Framework of English Feudalism* (1976); and *Historical Foundations of the Common Law* (2nd edn 1981).

Dr Mark Philpott is currently College Lecturer in Medieval History at St John's and Brasenose Colleges, Oxford. Educated at Worcester College, Oxford, he has held posts at Birkbeck College, London; the Queen's University of Belfast; Christ Church, Oxford, and Worcester College. His research centres on the Anglo-Norman Church and its law, in which area he has published several articles.

Dr Henry Summerson is currently medieval Research Editor with the *New Dictionary of National Biography*. He has published several articles on thirteenth-century law enforcement, and an edition of *Crown Pleas of the Devon Eyre of 1238* (1985). He has also worked extensively on the north of England in the Middle Ages — his two volume history of medieval Carlisle appeared in 1993.

Stephen D. White is Asa G. Candler Professor of Medieval History at Emory University and has taught at St Andrews University, Wesleyan University, and Harvard University. He is the author of *Custom, Kinship, and Gifts to Saints* (1988), *Sir Edward Coke and the Grievances of the Commonwealth* (1979), and various articles and reviews.

Dr Patrick Wormald is a Lecturer in Modern History at the University of Oxford, and a Student of Christ Church, Oxford. He was co-author of *The Anglo-Saxons* (ed. J. Campbell, 1982), and edited *Ideal and Reality in Frankish and Anglo-Saxon Society* (1983). He has written numerous papers on kingship, law, conversion and monasticism in the British Isles and western Europe from the fifth to the twelfth centuries. He is currently finishing his long-term project on *The Making of English Law: King Alfred to the Norman Conquest*.

Preface

An 'OPUS MIRABILE', 'that work which has superseded all that went before it'; thus did J. H. Round refer to Pollock and Maitland's *History of English Law*.[1] The present volume is a celebration of the *History*, a study of the writing of legal history in the late nineteenth century, and a contribution to present day scholarship on medieval law. The focus is almost entirely upon Maitland. Pollock's contribution to the *History* was very limited, as he himself admitted.[2] Contributors have looked at Maitland's working methods and style; his reaction to his predecessors and contemporaries; the sources he used and did not use; his concentration upon England as opposed to the wider assemblages of lands ruled by the kings of England. And as Maitland would have wished, they have also analysed topics and issues to which he devoted only limited attention. In turn, they have revealed the scope for further scholarship, in legal history and in the study of Maitland. The manuscript copy of the *History* remains little exploited, despite being a vital source for those concerned with his style. The relationship of that style to other literature of the day, and perhaps to other arts, most notably music, also requires investigation.[3] A full intellectual biography will one day deal with these aspects of Maitland, as well as his attitude to law, history, and other disciplines such as statistics.

This future biographer will no doubt comment upon the speed at which Maitland worked, and upon the late-nineteenth century circumstances that allowed him to write the history in roughly five years. By the time the current volume appears, a similar period will have passed from when, in the distinctly late twentieth-century circumstances of Fitzwilliam College car park, I first raised with Professor Holt the idea

[1] Letter of Round to Maitland, 28 March 1895; Maitland's reply is *Letters*, i no. 154. *The King's Serjeants and Officers of State* (London, 1911), p. 1.

[2] M. DeWolfe Howe, ed., *The Pollock-Holmes Letters* (2 vols, Cambridge, 1942), i 60–1; Pollock's calculation of the division of labour, Cambridge University Library, Add. MS 2766/16/18.

[3] Note that both Helmholz and Hyams, below, pp. 157, 239, use the word *leitmotiv* in discussing the style of this devotee of Wagner's music. One also wonders, for example, whether in Maitland's circle discussions concerning England as a 'land without music' accompanied those concerning England as a land without editors of its ancient law-codes.

of a symposium to celebrate 'Pollock and Maitland'. In that time many have helped both with the symposium[4] and the production of this volume. Thanks are due to the organising committee — Sir James Holt, Professors Milsom and Baker, Patrick Wormald, myself, and in particular Rosemary Lambeth of the British Academy; to the contributors for their exemplary punctuality; to Henry Summerson and Mark Philpott for contributions not presented at the original symposium; to James Rivington and Janet English for guidance with publication; and to Nora Bartlett for her indexing.

John Hudson

---

[4] Held at Downing College, Cambridge, on 7–8 July 1995.

Abbreviations

ANS — *Proceedings of the Battle Conference on Anglo-Norman Studies.*
ASC — *Anglo-Saxon Chronicle.*
ASE — *Anglo-Saxon England.*
(BI)HR — *(Bulletin of the Institute of) Historical Research.*
BL — British Library
BN — Bibliothèque Nationale.
Bracton, Thorne – *Bracton De Legibus et Consuetudinibus Angliae*, ed. & trans
    S. E. Thorne (4 vols, Cambridge, Mass., 1968–77).
BNB — *Bracton's Note Book*, ed. F. W. Maitland (3 vols, London, 1887).
CLJ — *Cambridge Law Journal*
CMA — *Chronicon Monasterii de Abingdon*, ed. J. Stevenson (2 vols, London,
    1858).
Collected Papers – H. A. L. Fisher, ed., *The Collected Papers of Frederic William
    Maitland* (3 vols, Cambridge, 1911).
CRR — *Curia Regis Rolls* (HMSO, 1922–).
DB — *Domesday Book seu Liber Censualis Wilhelmi Primi Regis Angliae*, ed.
    A. Farley and H. Ellis (4 vols, London, 1783, 1816).
Dialogus — Richard FitzNigel, *Dialogus de Scaccario*, ed. & trans C. Johnson, rev.
    F. E. L. Carter & D. E. Greenway (Oxford, 1983).
Domesday Book and Beyond — F. W. Maitland, *Domesday Book and Beyond*
    (repr. with Foreword by J. C. Holt, Cambridge, 1987).
EHR — *English Historical Review*
Elton, *Maitland* — G. R. Elton, *F. W. Maitland* (London, 1985)
English Lawsuits — *English Lawsuits from William I to Richard I*, ed. R. C. van
    Caenegem (2 vols, Selden Soc., 106, 107, 1990–1).
EYC — *Early Yorkshire Charters*, vols. I–III, ed. W. Farrer (Edinburgh, 1914–16);
    index to vols. I–III, ed. C. T. & E. M. Clay; vols. IV–XII, ed. C. T. Clay (Yorks.
    Arch. Soc. Rec. Ser. Extra Ser., 1935–65).
Fauroux, *Recueil* — *Recueil des actes des ducs de Normandie*, ed. M. Fauroux
    (Mémoires de la société des antiquaires de Normandie, 26, Caen, 1961).
Fifoot, *Life* — C. H. S. Fifoot, *Frederic William Maitland: a Life* (Cambridge,
    Mass., 1971).
Garnett and Hudson, *Law and Government* — G. S. Garnett and J. G. H. Hudson,
    eds, *Law and Government in Medieval England and Normandy: Essays in
    Honour of Sir James Holt* (Cambridge, 1994).
Gervase — Gervase of Canterbury, *The Historical Works of Gervase of Canterbury*,
    ed. W. Stubbs (2 vols, London, 1879–80).
Gesetze — *Die Gesetze der Angelsachsen*, ed. F. Liebermann, (3 vols, Halle,
    1903–16).

Gierke — F. W. Maitland, trans, *Political Theories of the Middle Age, by Otto Gierke* (Cambridge, 1900).

Glanvill, Hall — *Tractatus de Legibus et Consuetudinibus Regni Anglie qui Glanvilla vocatur*, ed. and trans G. D. G. Hall (Edinburgh, 1965).

Holt, *Magna Carta* — J. C. Holt, *Magna Carta* (2nd edn, Cambridge, 1992).

JMH — *Journal of Medieval History.*

Letters, i — C. H. S. Fifoot, ed., *The Letters of Frederic William Maitland*, vol. i (Selden Soc., Supplementary Ser., 1, 1965).

Letters, ii — P. N. R. Zutshi, ed., *The Letters of Frederic William Maitland*, vol. ii (Selden Soc., Supplementary Ser., 11, 1995).

Letters to George Neilson — *F. W. Maitland. Letters to George Neilson*, ed. E. L. G. Stones (Glasgow, 1976).

LHP, Downer — *Leges Henrici Primi*, ed. & trans L. J. Downer (Oxford, 1972).

LQR — *Law Quarterly Review*

Maitland, *Constitutional History* — F. W. Maitland, *The Constitutional History of England* (Cambridge, 1908).

MGH — Monumenta Germaniae Historica.

Milsom, *Legal Framework* — S. F. C. Milsom, *The Legal Framework of English Feudalism* (Cambridge, 1976).

ns — New Series

PBA — *Proceedings of the British Academy.*

PKJ — *Pleas before the King or his Justices, 1198–1202*, ed. D. M. Stenton (4 vols, Selden Soc., 67, 68, 83, 84, 1952–67).

Pollock and Maitland — Sir Frederick Pollock and F. W. Maitland, *The History of English Law before the Time of Edward I* (2 vols, 2nd edn reissued with a new introduction and select bibliography by S. F. C. Milsom, Cambridge, 1968).

PP — *Past and Present.*

PR — *Pipe Rolls*

PRO — Public Record Office

PRS — Pipe Roll Society

RCR — *Rotuli Curiae Regis. Rolls and Records of the Court held before the King's Justiciars or Justices*, ed. F. Palgrave (2 vols, Record Commission, 1835).

Reading Cartularies — *Reading Abbey Cartularies*, ed. B. R. Kemp, (2 vols, Camden Soc., 4th Ser. 31, 33, 1986, 1987).

Reg. Ant. Linc. — *The Registrum Antiquissimum of the Cathedral Church of Lincoln*, ed. C. W. Foster and K. Major (10 vols, Lincoln Rec. Soc., 1931–73).

RRAN — *Regesta Regum Anglo-Normannorum, 1066–1154*, ed. H. W. C. Davis *et al.* (4 vols, Oxford, 1913–69).

S — P. H. Sawyer, *Anglo-Saxon Charters: an Annotated List and Bibliography* (London, 1968).

Stenton, *English Feudalism* — F. M. Stenton, *The First Century of English Feudalism 1066–1166* (2nd edn, Oxford, 1961).

Stubbs, *Charters* — *Select Charters and other Illustrations of English Constitutional History*, ed. W. Stubbs (9th edn, Oxford, 1913).

TRHS — *Transactions of the Royal Historical Society*

VCH — *Victoria County History*

Proceedings of the British Academy, **89**, 1–20

RALEIGH LECTURE ON HISTORY

Maitland and Anglo-Saxon Law: Beyond Domesday Book

PATRICK WORMALD

WE ARE OF COURSE HERE to praise famous men; and certainly not to bury them under the rubble of the learning that has accumulated over the century since the first publication of the *History of English Law*.[1] At the same time, my idea of what makes a worthy tribute comes from two remarks of Maitland's own. 'I try', he wrote (of his anxiety about the shortcomings of *Domesday Book and Beyond*), 'to cheer myself up by saying that I have given others a lot to contradict'; and (from his illuminating inaugural, 'Why the History of English Law is not written'), 'the lawyer must be orthodox, otherwise he is no lawyer; an orthodox history seems to me a contradiction in terms.'[2] We owe this first and greatest of professional medievalists the compliment of arguing with him as one would with a contemporary colleague. Yet the *History of English Law* is also a monument. It deserves something of the attention that we give to works whose greatness we readily admit, yet do not regard as being in quite the idiom of modern histories: Gibbon, Macaulay, even Stubbs. It demands, that is to say, to be explained. To put it another way, I am a 'heretic', like the eminent scholar who concludes these proceedings. I take it for granted that Maitland (and Pollock) made mistakes, even laboured under serious misconceptions. But it is not enough to say that they were wrong; we

---

© The British Academy 1996

[1] Read at Cambridge 7 July 1995. A fuller and somewhat differently balanced version of this Raleigh Lecture was read at Birmingham on 28 November 1995, under the title 'Frederic William Maitland and the Earliest English Law'. For many of the more substantial points of legal history (e.g. nn. 26, 43–5, 56–61, 69–70, 76), recourse must regrettably be had to my *The Making of English Law* (Oxford, forthcoming), where there is scope to discuss them at greater length.

[2] *Letters*, i no. 200; *Collected Papers*, i 491.

must know why. Historians of this class are not wrong without good reason; we must find those reasons. I shall not, then, spend much of this lecture celebrating Maitland's virtues. That would be preaching to the converted. Nor shall I dwell for long on where, whether in my view or that of others, he was in error. That would be a pygmy's dance on a titan's shoulders. What I wish to try to do is to understand how, for better for worse, he took the lines that he did.

I start at something of a disadvantage compared to the other contributors to this series. As we all know (as one of us should have known before he first presumed to comment on Maitland and Anglo-Saxon law), the *History of English Law*'s chapter on the Anglo-Saxons was not written by Maitland. Chapter 1 (as it was in the first edition) was Pollock's work, and Maitland's reaction was never to let him write another. The evidence on this seems unambiguous. Letters are extant from both men which say as much.[3] But this may not justify us in transferring responsibility for all flaws in the Anglo-Saxon chapter from the hero of our proceedings to their other walk-on character.[4] This chapter may not be unadulterated Pollock. Pollock could write with flair and insight, but not of course with Maitland's inimitable effervescence. The Anglo-Saxon law chapter *is* lifeless by comparison with the preceding one on the 'Dark Ages', which Maitland introduced to the second edition, or almost all the fourteen that follow. There are few if any arresting images. There is little or no wit. This chapter also bears a marked similarity in wording and content to a later essay of Pollock's on the subject; whereas Maitland's own short surveys for *Social England* and for *Encyclopaedia Britannica*, dated two years before and nine years after the *History of English Law*, are in the palpable idiom of the rest of the book.[5] It may be possible to detect

[3] *Letters*, i no. 109, p. 103 (1892), and cf. no. 138 (1894); M. deW. Howe, ed., *The Pollock-Holmes Letters* (2 vols, Cambridge, 1942), i 60–1. Dr Zutshi tells me that the whole of the original MS (CUL Add MS 6987) is in Maitland's hand, *but* the first (Anglo-Saxon) chapter is not included.

[4] Heinrich Brunner, whose review found the Anglo-Saxon chapter, 'not on a level with the other chapters of this excellent work', politely declined to develop the point that he detected, 'with some degree of precision the authorship of portions of this work': *Political Science Quarterly*, xi (1896), 535–6, (cf. *Zeitschrift der Savigny-Stiftung für Rechtsgeschichte, germanistische Abtheilung*, xvii (1896), 126–7).

[5] Sir F. Pollock, 'English Law before the Norman Conquest', *LQR*, 14 (1898), 291–306, repr. in *Essays in Anglo-American Legal History* (3 vols, Boston/Cambridge), pp. 88–107; F. W. Maitland, 'Outlines of English legal history', in H. D. Traill, ed., *Social England* (London, 1893), repr. in *Collected Papers*, ii esp. 418–35; and 'History of English Law', in *Encyclopaedia Britannica* (10th edn, XXVIII supplement, 1902), repr. in H. M. Cam, ed., *Selected Historical Essays of F. W. Maitland* (Cambridge, 1957), esp. pp. 97–102. To give two potentially revealing examples: Pollock is fond of the word 'archaic' and its derivatives ('English Law', 88, 92, 103, 105, and cf. Pollock and Maitland, i 38, 43–4, 47, 55, 57, etc.), but it is notably rarer

traces of differences of opinion between the two.[6] Yet some passages seem to bear the Maitland touch. A final sentence, new to the second edition ('the king's lordship and the hands that gather the king's dues are everywhere; and where they have come the king's law will soon follow'), recalls Round's dry observation that 'the hand of Esau was less distinctive than the pen of the Downing Professor'.[7] If Maitland intervened at this stage, he could presumably have done so in the first edition; and the relative rarity of changes between the two editions suggests that Pollock's views generally had his endorsement.[8]

It is no surprise that they should. Maitland's summaries of 1893 and 1902 may be livelier than Pollock's chapter, but they are similar enough in content to leave an impression that Pollock wrote with a draft of the first of them at his elbow. Here too is the formalism generated by 'doomsmen's' law (though with a sympathetic *aperçu* of its rationale); here are feud and 'pecuniary mulct' slowly — all too slowly — making way for punishment.[9] Given his vision, already crys-tallised in his inaugural lecture, of the social history that 'lies concealed within the hard rind of legal history', we can well believe that Maitland regretted Pollock's relegation of sundry topics to the realm of 'social

in Pollock and Maitland's introductory chapter or wherever else it might have been expected, as also in the *Social England* and *Britannica* essays; preferred terms are 'ancient', 'old', even 'rude' or 'barbarous', and there may here be a further reaction against Maine's schematic thought (below, p. 16). Again, Pollock and Maitland's introductory chapter (2nd edn) strik-ingly (and justly) refers to the legislation of Alfred's successors as 'capitularies', 19; the same idea recurs in *Collected Papers*, ii 422, and *Selected Historical Essays*, p. 98; but it is absent from the Pollock and Maitland chapter on 'Anglo-Saxon law', or from Pollock's acknowledged works.

[6] Thus, outlawry is said to have 'developed in the Danish period as a definite part of English legal process' (i 43), and, in the first edition (i 26–7) to have been 'used *in or very soon after Alfred's time* — as a substantive penalty'; but the italicized phrase is absent from the second edition, and there seems to be little evidence of the idea in Maitland's later discussion (ii 449–53, etc.), or in his other writings. See also below, n. 23, on private jurisdiction.

[7] Quoted by H. E. Bell, *Maitland* (London, 1965), p. 62.

[8] The sentences added to the chapter's opening paragraph in the second edition express the philosophy of *Domesday Book and Beyond* which is now cited. Other changes are: on the relationship between royal and other forms of lordship (i 30/6); kindred is 'not yielding precedence to', rather than 'prior to' the State (i 31/7); the critique of Kemble is modified (i 33/9, 62/39–40), giving pause as to the remarks on i 28/4; Brunner's criticism (p. 536) of the first edition's point about the 'fore-oath' (i 16) is taken on board (i 40 and n. 1), as also his schoolmasterly reproof (ibid.) about penal slavery (i 56/33); secular and ecclesiastical courts are no longer 'sharply' separated (i 40/16); above all, the double-edged discussion of private justice is dropped (i 43/20–1) in favour of the much more categorical *Domesday Book and Beyond* account (see below). In this light, and without wishing to deny Pollock all claims to humour, one ponders such phrases, already in the first edition, as 'worshipful company of the Statutes of the Realm', and 'Clovesho that "famous place" whose situation is now a matter of mere conjecture' (i 27/3, 42/18). See also below, Hudson, n. 43.

[9] 'Outlines of English legal history', pp. 424–8.

antiquities'.[10] But part at least of what he said that he disliked about this chapter was that 'it will make it very difficult for me to say anything about Anglo-Saxon law in any later part of the book'.[11] This was a defect he was in a position to remedy, and so are we. He contrived to return to the pre-Conquest period in later sections of the *History of English Law*, as well as in part II of *Domesday Book and Beyond*, the self-confessed repository for much of what he had felt precluded from incorporating in 1895. Then, on top of the brief 'encyclopedic' accounts already mentioned, there are three notable early papers, one early Selden Society introduction, his review of Liebermann, and a variety of *obiter dicta* in his letters.[12] We can hardly plead ignorance of Maitland's views on Anglo-Saxon law.

Nor are we left in much doubt that for him, as for Pollock, its role in the story of English law was merely marginal. The first words of the second edition's new introduction speak of history's 'seamless web' (displaying Maitland's Johnsonian capacity to launch clichés). But this 'historian of situations, [not] development' saw the primary need as 'a fairly full statement of the English law of the Angevin time'.[13] As will be obvious by the time I finish — as will scarcely be news to some — it is here that I think his cardinal error lay. It is therefore appropriate to begin by stressing that Maitland had three perfectly good reasons for it. In the first place, he could not get out of his mind the glaring contrast between the *Leges Henrici Primi* at one end of the twelfth century and *Glanvill* at the other.[14] He was entirely aware of the reasons why the *Leges* might not be taken at face value.[15] What never seems to have occurred to him is that it might have misrepresented the nature of pre-Conquest English justice. We shall return to this point more than once. Meanwhile, a second factor was that Pollock and Maitland wrote, as we shall see, in the Salad Days of the Germanic

---

[10] Pollock and Maitland, i 56, 62, and cf. i 34, 49; *Collected Papers* i 485–6.

[11] See n. 3; and below, Hudson, p. 29.

[12] See especially Pollock and Maitland, i 296–305, 568–82; ii 240–60, 314–23, 449–58, 503–4, 514–15, 598–603; *Domesday Book and Beyond*, pp. 220–356; *Collected Papers*, i 202–46, 304–28, iii 447–73; *Selected Historical Essays*, pp. 41–51; and *Letters*, i nos 87, 96, 238, 271, 305; *Letters*, ii nos 37, 175, 311, etc.

[13] Pollock and Maitland, i p. ci; cf. pp. 225, ii 672–3, and 'Outlines of English legal history', p. 418; but note *Letters*, i no. 285 (to Poole, referring to Stubbs's introduction to the final edition of his *Select Charters*): 'Are not all men continuationers?' For Maitland 'as historian of situation', see R. W. Southern, review of *Letters*, i, *History and Theory*, 6 (1967), 111.

[14] E.g. Pollock and Maitland, i 165, ii 448; *Collected Papers*, i 332 (1885), ii 28–30, 36 (1889), 443–4 (1893), iii 451 (1904); *Selected Historical Essays*, p. 102 (1902).

[15] Pollock and Maitland, i 32 (Pollock?), 100–1; *Domesday Book and Beyond*, pp. 80–7; *Collected Papers*, ii 433 (1893); *Letters*, ii no. 37, p. 53 (to Rashdall, 1892); cf. Hudson, pp. 44–5.

Historische Rechtsschule, whose birth Maitland admiringly recalled when introducing his translation of part of Gierke's *Genossenschaft* For this school, the value of the Anglo-Saxon codes, couched as they uniquely were in the vernacular, was that they axiomatically repre-sented 'an especially pure type of Germanic archaism' (as Pollock put it).[16] Not only did this rule out *a priori* any important link with the dynamic force of the emergent Common Law; it is also meant that there was little point in repeating a story that the *Rechtsschule* itself had already told.[17]

Thirdly, and in any case, Maitland clearly felt out of his depth in Anglo-Saxon materials, as well he might. Though the 'satisfactory edition of the land-books' that he thought 'a long way off' in 1897 is still advancing at glacial speed, we have an infinitely better idea than he could ever have of what constitutes an acceptable document.[18] He lacked the benefit of Liebermann's *Gesetze* until three years before he died, and then only had the texts volume, whose interest (as he noted when declining to review it a second time) 'lies quite as much within the linguistic as within the legal department'. Another letter of the next year to W. H. Stevenson about the young H. M. Chadwick's *Studies on Anglo-Saxon Institutions* says that 'it is full five years since I had a look at Anglo-Saxondom', and continues, with habitually ludi-crous modesty, that his 'knowledge of it was always superficial', and he 'could hardly tell "wer" from "wite".'[19] A. L. Smith shrewdly observed that the scope of the *History of English Law* was fixed by the extent to which it related (in its own words) to 'a luminous age . . . an age of good books . . .'.[20] To either side lay the Anglo-Saxon evi-

[16] *Gierke*, pp. xv–xvii; Pollock and Maitland, i 44, echoing 'Outlines of English legal history', p. 429, 'purest specimens of pure Germanic law'.

[17] *Collected Papers*, ii 12–13 ('Materials for English legal history', 1889): if beginning before the late-eleventh century, 'we shall have to eke out our scanty knowledge with inferences drawn from foreign documents . . . in that case the outcome will be much rather an account of German law in general than an account of that slip of German law which was planted in England: a very desirable introduction to a history of English law it may be, *but hardly part of that history*' (my emphasis).

[18] Above all from P. H. Sawyer, *Anglo-Saxon Charters: An Annotated List and Bibliography* (London, Royal Historical Society Handbooks, 1968), now being revised by Dr Susan Kelly.

[19] *Letters*, i no. 395 (1904); *Letters*, ii no. 311 (1905).

[20] A. L. Smith, *Frederic William Maitland: Two Lectures and a Bibliography* (Oxford, 1908), pp. 39–40; Pollock and Maitland, ii 672–3. Note that Maitland looked to be overridden by Liebermann's eventual publication of the Anglo-Saxon and Anglo-Norman laws, Pollock and Maitland, i 97 n. 3; while controversies about the origin of proprietary right 'are better left to those who have more copious materials for the history of very remote ages than England can produce', Pollock and Maitland, ii 77 (with reference in n. 2 to Brunner's review of the first edition). Cf. too the remark about the Anglo-Saxon dooms in *Domesday Book and Beyond*, p. 226; and the pessimism about Anglo-Saxon law preceding the passage quoted in n. 17 above.

dence and the Year Books; and in devoting what turned out to be his last years to elucidating the latter, he effectively forsook the former. His verdict on Stubbs's (as he thought) relatively tentative coverage of the period before 1066 could very well express his own hesitation: 'many an investigator will leave his bones to bleach in that desert before it is accurately mapped.'[21] As a 1901 forecast of Anglo-Saxon studies in the century to come, it was not wholly off beam.

In these lights, the marvel of Maitland is that he was so seldom wrong. But wrong he could be, sometimes by what now amounts to common consent. Merely to catalogue the post-Maitland heresies of modern Anglo-Saxonists would be distasteful in this (or any) setting.[22] I shall thus say little, and then only towards the end, of Maitland's misconceptions about bloodfeud. I shall spare you 'bookland' with all its appurtenances. I shall (of course) give 'feudalism' a wide berth. Instead, I wish to highlight three issues, which boil down in the end to one; so far as law was concerned, Maitland, in common with nearly all commentators until now, drastically underestimated the power and the aggression of the Old English state.

My first issue is one where heresy is now unanimous, if espoused (as heresies should be) to varying extremes, from wildly sectarian to *via media*. The case argued by Part II of *Domesday Book and Beyond*, that, in Maitland's own irresistibly quotable words, 'the well-endowed immunist of St Edward's day has jurisdiction as high as that which any palatinate earl of after ages enjoyed': that case has, in effect, collapsed.[23] Julius Goebel powerfully restated Henry Adams's thesis, attacked by Maitland, that Anglo-Saxon grants of judicial privilege conceded only the fines and forfeitures that came of doing justice; why, otherwise, should the lord's court appear in Henry I's short writ on shire and hundred courts, but not in the entire corpus of pre-Conquest legislation?[24] Naomi Hurnard demonstrated with measureless erudition

---

[21] *Collected Papers*, iii 506. This was doubtless one reason why, 'of all that I have written, [*Domesday Book and Beyond*] makes me most uncomfortable': *Letters*, i no. 271.

[22] For a critique of some specifics in Pollock's chapter, especially its allegations of 'archaism', and of the king's non-intervention, see P. Wormald, 'Charters, Law and the settlement of disputes in Anglo-Saxon England', in W. Davies and P. Fouracre, eds, *The Settlement of Disputes in Early Medieval Europe* (Cambridge, 1986), pp. 149–68.

[23] *Domesday Book and Beyond*, pp. 258–92, quoted at p. 283; cf. ibid., pp. 80–107; Pollock and Maitland, i 43 (the more hesitant formulation of the first edition's pp. 20–1, omitted from the second in favour of *Domesday Book and Beyond*, perhaps hinting that Pollock and Maitland did not see eye to eye); also ibid., i 73, 576–80, ii 453–5.

[24] Hn com 3, *Gesetze*, i 524; H. Adams, 'The Anglo-Saxon courts of law', in *Essays in Anglo-Saxon Law* (Boston, 1876), pp. 27–54; J. Goebel, *Felony and Misdemeanor* (repr., Philadelphia, 1976), pp. 339–78.

that the 'pleas of the Crown', which Cnut professed to reserve but actually anticipated the Confessor in his readiness to alienate, were not the major pleas that Maitland had thought them, but redeemable, hence minor; it was just because they were petty enough for lords to think that they could take their profits for granted that Cnut found it necessary to remind them that they could not.[25] It is thus unnecessary to go as far as my own (positively Muggletonian) position, which holds that lords' courts are as evanescent in the not inconsiderable body of recorded lawsuits before 1066 as they are in legislation (but thereafter as evident in case-law as in prescriptive texts); and that even our one apparently solid instance of Oswaldslow resulted from 'bent' evidence laid before the 1086 commissioners by the sainted Wulfstan.[26] Even Helen Cam, playing Wiglaf to Maitland's Beowulf, fell back on the redoubt that lords' jurisdiction was limited to the hundred level, with those possessing whole hundreds privatising their courts *de facto*; she thought government was anyway so much less active before 1066 that immunity from its intrusions was redundant.[27]

How can Maitland have got it so wrong? In part, he was victim of his priceless common sense. 'No one in the middle ages does justice for nothing'; in other words, kings and their officials would lose interest in administering justice once they no longer harvested its fruits. Yet Maitland himself knew from Domesday Book of instances where courts whose revenues had been alienated were still run by royal officials, and he can have found few where the logic of his position was visibly worked out.[28] Of other considerations playing on his mind, some have been met already. Here above all, he was vulnerable to bogus charters. Even his safety-net, that 'the traditions . . . legends current in later times, cannot be altogether neglected', is lost once we appreciate that the manufacture of so many fraudulently ancient franchises implies that something in the

---

[25] II Cn 12, *Gesetze*, i 316–17; N. Hurnard, 'The Anglo-Norman Franchises', *EHR*, 64 (1949), 289–323, 433–60.

[26] P. Wormald, 'A handlist of Anglo-Saxon Lawsuits', *ASE*, 17 (1988), 247–81; 'Charters, Law', 163; 'Lordship and justice in the early English kingdom: Oswaldslow revisited', in W. Davies and P. Fouracre, eds, *Property and Power in The Early Middle Ages* (Cambridge, 1995), pp. 114–36.

[27] H. M. Cam, 'The "Private" Hundred in England before the Norman Conquest', and 'The Evolution of the medieval English franchise', both repr. in id., *Law-Finders and Law-Makers in Medieval England* (London, 1962), pp. 59–70, 22–43.

[28] *Domesday Book and Beyond*, pp. 277; and pp. 87, 92, 95–6; this point is argued in detail by D. Roffe in chapter 5 of his unpublished 1987 Leicester Ph.D. thesis, 'Nottinghamshire and the North: a Domesday Study', and in 'Brought to Book: lordship and land in Anglo-Saxon England', another unpublished paper that he has kindly shown me.

post-Conquest climate was creating a new demand for them.[29] The *Leges Henrici* was probably again a decisively malign influence. 'If that book has any plan at all', wrote Maitland, 'it is a treatise on the law of jurisdiction, a treatise on "soke" ' and it has plenty to say about the jurisdiction of lord's courts.[30] Maitland was hindered from seeing that private justice might be a function of lordship that reached England only with its conquerors, by the suggestive if hardly conclusive fact that its vocabulary, unlike that of so much of the law, remained English.[31] In any case, his jurisdictional analysis was only part of the case that Anglo-Saxon law had escaped the 'archaic' straitjacket in which Pollock enfolded it, to the extent that 'tribalism was giving place to feudalism'; a case which, depending how one defines that much-defined word (and no one, of course, ever defined it more wittily or wisely), he went far towards making.[32] He had long come to see 'jurisdiction in private hands' as 'that most essential element of feudalism'.[33]

This point re-introduces the question of Maitland's sense of his place in European scholarship. To a degree unmatched by any English medievalist before Powicke and his disciples, Maitland was intensely cosmopolitan. Kemble and Stubbs were *au fait* with the main currents of continental thought. But so far as I know, neither they nor anyone else (nor many before quite recent times) paid such close attention to what foreign historians were saying about subjects which interested them.[34] One of the most striking features of his correspondence and papers is the constantly sounded note of fury at the failure of his fellow-countrymen to measure up to the standards of scholars overseas, even as regards texts or topics which were an Englishman's birthright.

[29] *Domesday Book and Beyond*, p. 267; two of the earlier charters that mattered most to his argument, S 183, 278, are deeply problematic; while few of the writs he cited on pp. 260–1 have withstood later scrutiny: Wormald, 'Oswaldslow', pp. 128–9.

[30] *Domesday Book and Beyond*, p. 80; *LHP*, 20–23, 25–33, Downer, pp. 122–37, etc.

[31] Pollock and Maitland, i 73, 576; cf. the justly famous passage on the Frenchification of English legal terminology, Pollock and Maitland, i 80–7.

[32] 'Outlines', *Collected Papers*, ii 423; *Domesday Book and Beyond*, pp. 295–6; to judge from *Letters*, i no. 96 (to Pollock, 1891), the work which became *Domesday Book and Beyond*'s 'England before the Conquest' first germinated as 'Origins of Feudalism'; cf. Hudson, below, p. 31. For Maitland's definitions, see Pollock and Maitland, i 66–7, 'an unfortunate word', etc.; *Collected Papers*, i 175 (1879), 'a good word [which] will cover a multitude of ignorances'; above all the immortal 'squib' in *Constitutional History*, p. 142, echoed in the 1889 inaugural lecture, *Collected Papers*, i 489.

[33] Pollock and Maitland, i 68 and (e.g.) 527.

[34] It would be interesting to know how many other twentieth-century English medievalists sent copies of their latest work to counterparts of Meyer, Petit-Dutaillis, Brunner, Gierke and Liebermann: *Letters*, ii no. 306 (cf. no. 295, 'debts of a very personal kind' to Gierke, Brunner, Stutz, Hübner and Liebermann); and how often has the death of a scholar from these islands been marked by the sort of international accolade published in *LQR*, 23 (1907), 137–50?

His Liebermann review is an astonishing extended metaphor of the race for colonies, which concludes starkly, 'we have lost the Anglo-Saxon laws'. To use that image for a German's work at a time of escalating Anglo-German African rivalry, must have been meant to hurt — to hurt not the revered 'little man' of course, but Englishmen who had left him the field.[35] The primary clue to Maitland's theory of Anglo-Saxon jurisdiction is thus contained in a letter to Pollock of 1891, when the *History of English Law* was under way: 'As to the A-S "immunities" . . . I don't think we can dissociate the English from the Frankish question. Adams's essay represents the school of Roth. Against this there has been a marked reaction both in France and Germany'. It is quite true that Adams had followed Roth's line, and that this had been largely discredited by the 1890s.[36] The last thing Maitland was prepared to be was insular or out-of-date. The discussion in *Domesday Book and Beyond* features repeated analogies between the experience of the late Old English polity and the dying Carolingian empire.[37] Which brings us to the last and surely decisive point. Maitland evidently had half an eye on the apparently lethal results of the lavish outlay of Frankish immunities, and was drawing appropriate conclusions about the events of 1066. It is hard enough for today's historians to think away the implications of its overwhelming defeat for the health of the pre-Conquest state. In the 1890s, the decade of '*the* battle*'*, as Maitland characterized it with waning amusement to J. H. Round, one of its two protagonists, it must have been utterly impossible.[38] And Maitland in fact makes the lineage in his mind perfectly clear, when summing up his survey of Domesday 'Sake and Soke': seignorial control of courts would not have been a matter of indiffer-

[35] *Collected Papers*, iii 447–73, at p. 472. Examples are easily multiplied: Pollock and Maitland, i cv; *Letters*, i no. 14 (to Bigelow, 1885 'constant fear that some German or Russian or Turk will edit Bracton and shame the nation which has produced six volumes of rubbish'; — targeting the wretched Sir Travers Twiss); *Collected Papers*, i 485 (1889, 'who else [than Liebermann] should publish the stupid things?'); iii 424 (1901, 'terror lest the Savigny Stift or the École des Chartes should undertake an edition' of the Year Books); cf. too the introduction to *Bracton's Note Book* of 1887, quoted by H. A. L. Fisher, *Frederick William Maitland* (Cambridge, 1910), p. 34 (with the personal comment of this brother-in-law of Maitland, p. 53); and another diatribe from the first of his Selden Society Year Book series (vol. 17, 1903, pp. xxxii-xxxiii), climaxing on the characteristically Biblical note, 'Lo! they turn unto the Gentiles'.

[36] *Letters*, i no. 95. See the discussion by Fustel de Coulanges, *L'Origine de la système féodale* (Paris, 1890), pp. 336–425, to which Maitland refers. It is appropriate to add that the long-established reaction against Maitland's views for England is now being matched by a marked minimalization of the consequences of Frankish immunities, for which it is enough to refer to the discussion and bibliography of Paul Fouracre, in Davies and Fouracre, eds, *Property and Power*, pp. 53–81.

[37] *Domesday Book and Beyond*, pp. 263–5, 278–9, 280, 282–4.

[38] *Letters*, i no. 134.

ence to 'far-sighted men . . . but it has not been proved to our satisfaction that the men who ruled England in the age before the Conquest were far-sighted. Their work ended in stupendous failure'.[39]

My second heresy has had adherents at times but has on the whole been banished to windswept hillsides by Maitlandian orthodoxy. There were few things of which he felt more sure than that the introduction of the jury of presentment by the Assize of Clarendon in 1166 was a watershed in English law. Nor did he seriously hesitate to accept Brunner's famous thesis that its origins lay in the Frankish royal inquest, and that it was brought to England by Norman and then Angevin kings.[40] He admitted an element of doubt, and never really accounted (any more than had Brunner) for the phenomenon's apparent presence in Ethelred's third code. More to my point, he accepted, indeed did much to establish, that there was some connection between presentments by juries and the obligations of Frankpledges.[41] He still remained fairly certain that the denunciatory functions of the frankpledge were introduced by Henry II's edict.

This is hardly the place for a detailed analysis of the issue. I shall keep it as simple and close to Maitland as I can by focusing on the frankpledge question. Did neighbourhood sureties, tithings, already have the duty of exposing their erring members to the king's justice as well as indemnifying their misdeeds before 1166, or indeed 1066? If so, the 'Angevin breakthrough' might be a change of tactics but scarcely a new strategy. I believe that Anglo-Saxon evidence does allow us to say this. Maitland thought that it did not. The villain of the piece (from my angle) is again the *Leges Henrici Primi*. 'In the days of (the "Leges" of) Henry I . . . there is no talk of presentment of offences'.[42] Yet the *Leges* is perceptibly referring in the relevant passage to Cnut's law obliging all aged twelve and over to be in 'hundred and tithing'. It

---

[39] *Domesday Book and Beyond*, pp. 102–3.

[40] Pollock and Maitland, i 138–44; 'Outlines', *Collected Papers*, ii 454; 'History,' *Selected Historical Essays*, p. 101; but cf. also Pollock and Maitland, i 151–2 ('puzzling'), ii 642–3 ('a matter of doubt'). The literature on this subject is of course vast: enough to say that one of the most recent and authoritative treatments, R. C. van Caenegem, 'Public prosecution of crime in twelfth-century England', in C. N. L. Brooke, *et al.*, eds, *Church and Government in the Middle Ages. Essays presented to C. R. Cheney on his 70th Birthday* (Cambridge, 1976), pp. 41–76, is a vindication of Maitlandian first principles.

[41] Pollock and Maitland, i 568–71, 580. There is an even clearer account of the linkage in 'Leet and Tourn', part of Maitland's introduction to *Select Pleas in Manorial Courts* (Selden Soc., 2, 1888), pp. xxvii–xxxviii, excerpted in *Selected Historical Essays*, pp. 41–51; and not to be ignored is his remarkable 1881 paper, 'The criminal liability of the Hundred', *Collected Papers*, i 230–46, which left regrettably little trace in either Pollock and Maitland or any of Maitland's later writings.

[42] *Selected Historical Essays*, pp. 49, 46.

goes on at once to echo Cnut's clauses about lords' responsibility to go surety for their men. These clauses are based in turn on Ethelred's Woodstock code, whose closely related equivalent for the Five Boroughs area was the Wantage code; and this Wantage code has the notorious reference to the duty of the wapentake's 'twelve leading thegns' under oath to accuse and to arrest the '*tihtbysig*' (i.e. 'charge-laden'): the provision of its Woodstock counterpart is that the king's reeve is to place in surety those seen as 'untrustworthy to all people', or else to execute them.[43] In that light, the Wantage twelve are neither isolated nor necessarily Scandinavian. They are one cog in machinery designed to develop local liability for the persistently deviant. So was the 1166 jury. To take this mode of argument further: Cnut goes on to demand in almost the same breath that twelve-year-olds swear an oath to eschew robbery. Frankpledge recruits swore such an oath in *Bracton*'s time. The oath of loyalty previously specified by Edmund had imposed a duty not to conceal its breach by neighbours; and his next law had ordered steps to be taken against thieves. Alfred had already decreed an 'oath and pledge', which, according to his son, was 'taken by the whole people', and meant non-compliance with crime.[44] To take an oath not to cover up for criminals is not a lot different from swearing to denounce them. To clinch the point, the measure adduced by Brunner in tracing the criminal inquest to Carolingian roots was a stipulation by Charles the Bald of a general oath binding on *all* subjects, and applying to theft as well as loyalty itself.[45]

One can readily grant that this is not a discourse of empanelled twelve and itinerant justice such as Henry II laid down; but we can now more easily see how the Wantage Code comes so close. It is clear that we already have an idea of communal responsibility to take action about behaviour that harms all, not merely of injury redressed between parties concerned; and if justice is not done yet by specialist journeymen, we still have officials who act in the name of established authority. If you will allow me a Maitland parody (as Maitland's shade surely will): Ælfric is an inveterate rustler; Wulfric and the other nine members of his tithing have made good his depredations once too often. To them he is now *tihtbysig*; they surrender him to Ælfstan, king's reeve, who

[43] *LHP*, 8: 1–3, Downer, pp. 102–3, II Cn 20–20a, 31–31:1, *Gesetze*, i 322–3, 334–5; I Atr 1:10–11, pp. 218–19; III Atr 3:1–2, pp. 228–9; I Atr 4–4:1, pp. 220–1.
[44] II Cn 21, *Gesetze*, pp. 324–5; *Bracton*, f. 124, Thorne, ii 350–2; III Em 1, *Gesetze*, i 190; Af 1, pp. 46–7; II Ew 5, pp. 142–3.
[45] A. Boretius, ed., *Capitularia Regum Francorum* (MGH, Legum Sectio II, 2 vols, 1883) 260: 4 + Addit. 1, II, pp. 272, 274; H. Brunner, *Die Entstehung der Schwurgerichte* (Berlin, 1872), pp. 458–63 (the Italian capitularies cited by Brunner (*Capitularia* 91:8, 213:3, I, pp. 192–3, II, pp. 86–7) do not materially strengthen his case).

has a short way with such miscreants. A perfunctory effort to find him
new sureties is of no avail. Ælfric is soon at the end of a rope. But there
is a taint in this blood. Ælfric's great-grandson, William, has the ancestral
light fingers with others' stock. Earl Robert of Leicester is in the vicin-
ity; William is duly denounced as '*rettatus vel publicatus*' by Giles and
eleven of the hundred's other heads of frankpledges. As William dangles on
his gibbet, we beg leave to doubt that he is much consoled to contem-
plate the enhanced dignity of the men and the process that put him there.

Some of these things Maitland could well have seen. Some he very
nearly did. But readiness to take Brunner's word for it (and, we must
add, reluctance to go beyond German experts to continental sources)
is now compounded by another trait in Maitland's intellectual psy-
chology. Sir Richard Southern insists that 'anyone who wishes to understand his historical starting-point ... must read his essay on Real
Property'.[46] This greatest of legal historians bursts into view with a
dazzling display of verbal pyrotechnics at the expense of the legal
profession. A decade later, his Inaugural suspected (in what must be
more disguised autobiography) that legal history's future can only lie
with failed lawyers. In the last year of his life, he lauds the emergence
of a rational code of German law, with more sidelong glances at the
English approach, crediting this in part to the labours of the German
scholars he so admired.[47] His extraordinary sense of the need to 'liber-
ate' both past and present from their intellectually constricting embrace
was a mainspring of his enduring modernity.[48] It was born of disgust

---

[46] Southern, review of *Letters*, i, 107; *Collected Papers*, i 162–201 (1879). Plucknett also spotted
its relevance, 'Maitland's view of Law and History', *LQR*, 67 (1951), 184–5; as indeed had
Pollock himself, *Quarterly Review*, 206 (1907), 406.

[47] *Collected Papers*, i 493–6; iii 474–88. For the autobiographical side of the inaugural, see S.
F. C. Milsom, 'F. W. Maitland', *PBA*, 66 (1980), 273. Plucknett's dismay, 187–91, might have
been tempered by considering the likely impact on Maitland of the employment of most
German legal historians as '*Juristen*', then as now — the requirement of 'failure' in England
presumably arising from the far lower academic salaries west of the North Sea (then as
now): cf. *Letters*, ii no. 135.

[48] *Collected Papers*, i 493: 'it is to the interest of the Middle Ages that they be not brought
into court any more'; *Collected Papers*, iii 486: 'anyone who really possesses what has been
called the historic sense must, so it seems to me, dislike to see a rule or an idea unfitly
surviving in a changed environment'; while (p. 487) the Germans are 'pioneers — masters'
of legal history, which 'encouraged them to believe that every age should be mistress of its
own law'. Compare *Letters*, ii no. 116, pp. 104–5, an important letter to (significantly, perhaps)
Dicey: 'The only direct utility of legal history (I say nothing of its thrilling interest) lies in
the lesson that each generation has an enormous power of shaping its own law ... I am sure
that [its study] would free [men] from superstitions ... the only justification that I ever urge
in foro conscientiae is that if history is to do its liberating work it must be as true to fact as
it can possibly make itself, and true to fact it will not be if it begins to think what lessons it
can teach'; cf. too the observation that 'there is nothing strange in the coincidence' that 'the
great years of the Record Commission, 1830 to 1840' were those of ' "radical reform" ':

at the entrapment of his fellow-lawyers in history blended of illusion and anachronism. He loved to catch Coke or Blackstone in the toils of a historical *trompe-l'œil*.[49] Such is the voice of the *History of English Law* on the jury: 'the prevailing opinion ... has triumphed over the natural disinclination of Englishmen to admit that this "palladium of our liberties" is in its origin not English but Frankish, not popular but royal'.[50] Maitland would bend over backwards to disabuse Englishmen of misplaced faith in the uniqueness of their Island Story. But Anglo-Saxon frankpledge carried an extra handicap: William of Malmesbury had attributed it to King Alfred. He may have known what he was talking about: he was the only twelfth-century historian who certainly read Anglo-Saxon law-codes; his Old English was better than Maitland's or ours; and he could have worked out the correct meaning of texts so elliptical as to elude us. But Maitland went right along with Stubbs's and Morris's contempt for the idea.[51] He had a special reason to do so. All through the time that the *History of English Law* was being written, he was wrestling with *The Mirror of Justices*, whose mischiefs included high regard for Alfred's legal ways.[52] Whatever left the taste of legal legend could not be objective legal history.

In my third and (for now) last heresy, I stand alone, though of course in hope of converts. Like most commentators on early law to date, Pollock included, Maitland believed that its dominant notion was one of tort rather than crime.[53] Each was ready to admit that the concept of punishment was making 'progress' before 1066.[54] Not, however, enough: 'on the eve of the conquest many bad crimes could still be paid for with money'; 'the great need of the time was that the ancient system of money compositions ... should give way before ...

'the desire to reform the law went hand in hand with the desire to know its history', *Collected Papers*, ii 9–10; and *Collected Papers*, iii 438–9: 'strenuous endeavours to improve the law were not impeded, but forwarded by a zealous study of legal history ... Now-a-days we may see the office of historical research as that of *explaining, and therefore lightening*, the pressure that the past must exercise upon the present, and the present on the future. To-day we study the day before yesterday, in order that *yesterday may not paralyse to-day, and to-day may not paralyse tomorrow*' [my emphasis].

[49] Thus, his demolition of the 'Common Law tradition' that the Year Books had originated as an 'official' record: (Selden Soc., 17, 1903), pp. xi–xiv; and see below, n. 52, on *The Mirror of Justices*.

[50] Pollock and Maitland, i 141–2; cf. 'Outlines', *Collected Papers*, ii 445.

[51] *Gesta Regum*, ed. W. Stubbs (2 vols, London, 1887–9), ii 122, i 129–30; Introduction, ii, p. li; W. A. Morris, *The Frankpledge System* (Harvard Historical Monographs XIV, 1910), p. 6; Pollock and Maitland, i pp. xcviii, 65; *Collected Papers*, ii 422.

[52] W. J. Whittaker and F. W. Maitland, eds, *The Mirror of Justices* (Selden Soc., 7, 1895), pp. ix–x, xxvi–xxvii, 8, 54, 166–71; and cf. *Letters*, i nos. 112, 171.

[53] Pollock and Maitland, i 46, ii 449.

[54] Pollock and Maitland, i 48, ii 451–2; *Collected Papers*, i 225–6, ii 428.

true punishments'; if Henry I's charter promised a 'return to the old English system of pre-appointed wites', 'we may be glad that he did not keep it'; 'a scheme of *wer* and bloodfeud, of *bót* and *wite*' 'disappears with marvellous suddenness'.[55] Maitland thus missed the pronounced switch in later Anglo-Saxon law from amendment to penalty. The best summary indication of this is the very sense of the word '*bót*'. From Edward the Elder's time, with few and explicable exceptions, it means compensation to God, Church, king or community at large. In other words, it in effect meant the same as '*wite*'. It was the price of mercy, which was high. Many offences were penalized by the 'king's disobedience' of 120 shillings (£2 or £2.50); several of the more serious by the royal '*mund*' of £5; some of the worst of all, defiance of written law among them, by *wergeld* itself, the cost of life.[56] In short, *mund* that had once been the value of the king's protection was now the premium on his commands; *bót*, once redress of a tort to an injured kin, was now a fine for harming the whole people.

Nor was Maitland alert to all implications of the scope of later Anglo-Saxon punishment. Abingdon's chronicle called the death penalty '*more iudicii Angliae*'; and it has recently been shown that this was an Anglo-Saxon, not a Norman, inheritance.[57] The point may even be upheld by archaeological evidence from 'execution cemeteries', which had opened for business before, but not much more than a century and a half before, 1066.[58] The large number of forfeitures to the king recorded throughout the southumbrian area from Alfred's reign to the Confessor's are unlike equivalent sanctions under the Ottonians and Salians in often relating to lesser crimes than treason.[59] All this bears on the crucial question of the origins of the concept of felony. Maitland was in good company in deciding that the conversion of a word whose basic meaning is 'broken faith' into a term for 'crime of any considerable gravity', was a process whose 'details are

---

[55] Pollock and Maitland, ii 451–2, i 74, ii 514, 448, 458; cf. i 106, ii 522–3.

[56] E.g. II Cn 83–83:1, *Gesetze*, i pp. 366–7 (cf. 63, pp. 352–3, 73:1, pp. 360–1(!)). Note that the £5 and £2 fines that are much more widespread in the 'shire customs' of Domesday Book than any local variations correspond respectively to the king's 'protection money' and to the 120 shillings (480 Mercian pence) 'disobedience money'.

[57] *CMA*, ii 104 (the crime was theft); J. Gillingham, '1066 and the introduction of chivalry into England', in Garnett and Hudson, eds, *Law and Government*, pp. 31–56, especially pp. 38–46.

[58] E.g. N. Gray Hill, 'Excavations on Stockbridge Down, 1935–6', *Papers and Proceedings of the Hampshire Field Club and Archaeological Society*, 13 (1937), 246–59.

[59] E.g. Wormald, 'Handlist', nos 23, 25, 31, 37–9, 41, 45, 56, 60, 100, 102, 124, 127, 129, 132, (theft); 40, 50, 54, 58, 61, 71, 145, 148 (homicide and mayhem); 29, 53, 68, 78 (sexual offences); compare K. Leyser, *Rule and Conflict in an Early Medieval Society. Ottonian Saxony* (London, 1979), pp. 36–8, 153 (n. 33).

obscure'.[60] He hesitantly thought that the link lay 'in the rule that the felon's fee should escheat to his lord'. But we are still left with the question why larceny should be treated as severely as treason itself or nearly so. An explanation is to hand in a feature of later Anglo-Saxon jurisprudence that we have already observed: the 'oath and pledge' taken by twelve-year-olds extended fidelity to disavowal of theft, just like its close Carolingian counterpart.[61] An elasticated conception of the 'king's enemy' was stretched to cover serious but conventional crimes against the community as a whole. In these terms, conventional crime was indeed a breach of faith, one that imperilled a whole people in so far as it unleashed the anger of God. Such a theory could come — gradually of course — to colour the mind-set and vocabulary of the post-Conquest ruling establishment.

Now, we must again recognize that Maitland was not unconscious of these possibilities: he had in full measure the great scholar's maddening tendency to have noticed what one thought one had been first to notice oneself. Never mind the number of times he (and Pollock) commended the law-making of kings from Alfred to Cnut; a remarkable footnote in his chapter on 'Crime and Tort' observes the 'increasing frequency' of late Saxon forfeitures for 'grave crimes', the spread of amercements for 'king's disobedience', and the relevance of Frankish 'forfeiture of goods for the elastic offence of *infidelitas*'.[62] His work for *Domesday Book and Beyond* must have increased his respect for the capacities of the Old English state, whose ability to tax at a 'monstrous' level he set the fashion for crediting.[63] But this merely resurrects the question

[60] Pollock and Maitland, i 303–4, cf. ii 464–70, 478–502. Compare S. F. C. Milsom, *Historical Foundations of the Common Law* (London, 1969), p. 355: 'a mystery'.

[61] See W. Kienast, *Unternaneneid und Treuvorbehalt in Frankreich und England* (Weimar, 1952), pp. 15–27; Kienast mostly missed the evidence from pre-Conquest England, pp. 173–4, but made a strong case that such an oath was unknown in Normandy before 1066 — a point which may well be thought to carry more weight than the question whether Carolingian inquests are better attested in Normandy than England, as Brunner made Maitland think, Pollock and Maitland, i 141–4.

[62] Pollock and Maitland, i 515 (n. 4) (already in the first edition, p. 514): endorsements of later Anglo-Saxon royal legislation often extend to a scouting of possible Frankish influence: Pollock and Maitland, i pp. c–ci, 19–20, 44, 51, 94, 142, ii 451–2; *Collected Papers*, i 204, 225–6, ii 14, 20, 423; *Selected Historical Essays*, p. 98. At *Collected Papers*, i 316–17 is an alternative suggestion about the origins of felony which is notably closer to the one adopted above; and also to be noted are the implications of *Collected Papers*, i 230–46, on 'The criminal liability of the Hundred'.

[63] *Domesday Book and Beyond*, pp. 3–8, 446–75; see the debate between John Gillingham and Ken Lawson, *EHR*, 104–5 (1989–90), with J. Campbell, 'The Anglo-Saxon State: a maximum view', *PBA*, 87 (1994), 39–65. There may even be hints of a change in Maitland's view of Anglo-Saxon law itself, in 'History', *Selected Essays*, pp. 99, 102: this is notably less inclined to make so much of the 'three laws', as opposed to the pre-eminent king's law, than Pollock and Maitland i 106–7 (or *Collected Papers*, ii 20–1 (1889)), and the gulf between the

why he went no further. He often said that kings of England made law at a time when there was elsewhere silence (or worse); even more often that they were strong enough to build up their own law in the age first exposed to the stimulus of the Learned Laws. He knew that it was in England rather than their overseas lands that Angevin initiative bore fruit.[64] It is not *prima facie* audacious to see a connection between these facts. Maitland did not. Why not?

A first point relates to '*bót*' rather than punishment. Maitland naturally lacked an ear for the rhythms of blood-feud. As ever, it is remarkable how much he did understand. His very first paper after his 'Real Property' polemic latched on to the possible significance of female kin for compensation and feud in Welsh law.[65] 'The traveller who has studied the uncorrupted savage can often tell the historian of medieval Europe what to look for, never what to find'. The drift of this quotation shows Maitland battling with the insidious temptations of Maine's evolutionary schemes of human law.[66] But he might well have responded to the insights of modern anthropology as warmly as today's historians of early medieval society, few of whom would dissent from his *caveat*. Even if he was preoccupied by 'the many bad features of the system of pecuniary mulcts', the word 'marvellous' can as well mean 'remarkable' as 'admirable'; there may be a hint of Maitlandian irony in the 'marvellous revolution' that 'the kinsfolk of the slain lose their right to a *wer* [with] A modern statute ... required to give the *parentes occisi* a claim for damages in any English court'. All of that said, there is no denying that he had the traditional lawyer's preference

---

Leges Henrici Primi and *Glanvill* is (only) 'at first sight very wide' — though that point is not developed. Note too the implications of the final sentence added *in the second edition* to the chapter on Anglo-Saxon law, above, p. 3.

[64] Pollock and Maitland i 19, 105; *Collected Papers*, ii 20, 316, 422–3; *Selected Historical Essays*, pp. 97–8; Pollock and Maitland, i 167–8, 302–3 (n. 3), and see below, n. 77; cf. M. T. Clanchy, *England and its Rulers (1066–1272)* (London, 1983), p. 145; also Holt, below, pp. 47–64, and Helmholz, below, pp. 145–69.

[65] *Collected Papers*, i 226: 'nice questions might arise from the mutual interference of family obligations'; cf. Pollock and Maitland, ii 240–5; and also *Letters*, ii nos 54. 84. For modern appreciation of this aspect of Welsh law, see now T. M. Charles-Edwards, *Early Irish and Welsh Kinship* (Oxford, 1993), pp. 181–200; and for the anthropological dimension (of course) M. Gluckman, 'The peace in the feud', *Custom and Conflict in Africa* (Oxford, 1956), pp. 1–26.

[66] *Collected Papers*, iii 300: part of a notable essay on 'The Body Politic' which represents Maitland's most considered (albeit otherwise unpublished?) critique of the school of Maine. To be set against the warmth of his inaugural's remarks about Maine, *Collected Papers*, i 486–7, see (e.g.) *Collected Papers*, iii 460 (from his review of Liebermann), *Letters*, ii nos 97, 146 (extending even to Sidgwick), 279, 370, together with the comments of Fisher, *Maitland*, p. 27; also Pollock and Maitland, i pp. xciii–xcv, ii 240, and *Domesday Book and Beyond*, pp. 344–6; see also White, below, pp. 91–113.

for punishing the crime over compensating its victim.[67] To that extent, he was himself trapped in the lawyerly time-warp from which he had sought to escape through historical study.

As we might by now have guessed, Maitland was led to accept the ongoing relevance of '*bót*' down to and after the Conquest by his usual incubus, the *Leges Henrici Primi*.[68] He perceived some of the problems that the *Leges* author faced. But he failed to see the effect of its dependence on Anglo-Saxon codes, which the same man had Latinized (not without difficulty) in his '*Quadripartitus*'; nor did he realize that this author's knowledge of the realities of Anglo-Saxon law could have been as limited as his command of Old English language.[69] He was apt to see the *Leges* muddle as the mirror of a confused mind, itself the product of a confused situation. So it was, in each respect; yet not quite as Maitland meant. In an age that was coming to expect fuller and more systematic statements of law, the *Leges* writer was trying to reconstruct English law from memorials that misled him inasmuch as they were inspired by other priorities; from a background in French 'feudal' lordship, he struggled to understand the system of a state whose old ruling class had been displaced by conquest.[70] It was not that the Old English kingdom was hidebound by '*bót* and *wite*', any more than it was crippled by private jurisdiction. Rather, a regime with a well developed sense of 'royal rights', but with an abiding regard for its ancestral codes for no other reason than that they *were* ancestral, was now overrun by a political culture which put a premium on lordship and had a tendency to codify everything in sight.

Maitland's forensic intuition here dovetailed with his historical professionalism.[71] His inaugural claims that, though 'our patience of centennial celebrations has been somewhat severely tasked this year' (another modern note), the ensuing 3 September would 'see the seven-

---

[67] Pollock and Maitland, ii 459. For ways in which bewigged perspectives blinkered understanding of feud in a different, but not necessarily dissimilar, context, see J. Wormald, 'Bloodfeud, kindred and government in early modern Scotland', *PP*, 87 (1980), 90–7.

[68] Pollock and Maitland, i 106, ii 448, 458; 'Outlines', *Collected Papers*, ii 428.

[69] Pollock and Maitland, i 100–1; *Collected Papers*, iii 470–1 (reviewing Liebermann); and the letter above, n. 15. On the *Leges*, see Hudson below, p. 44–5; and P. Wormald, '*Quadripartitus*', in Garnett and Hudson, *Law and Government*, pp. 133–47.

[70] As to the sort of priorities that would encourage King Alfred and his heirs to preserve a minutely detailed tariff of compensations for bodily injuries, while leaving everyone bar William of Malmesbury in ignorance of all that they envisaged by 'oath and pledge', see P. Wormald, '*Lex Scripta* and *Verbum Regis*: legislation and Germanic kingship from Euric to Cnut', in P. H. Sawyer and I. N. Wood, eds, *Early Medieval Kingship* (Leeds, 1977), pp. 105–38.

[71] For Maitland's professionalism, see above all G. R. Elton, *F. W. Maitland* (London, 1985), pp. 19–34, 98–102, with the review by S. F. C. Milsom, *Times Literary Supplement* 28 February 1986, 225–6; but Elton's case was in part anticipated as early as A. L. Smith's tribute, *Maitland*, pp. 5–6.

hundredth birthday of English legal memory'; *Glanvill's* completion is
the moment when 'English law becomes articulate [and] we become the
nation whose law may be intimately known'. 'I would not for one
moment speak slightingly of the memorials of an earlier time'; but
those of the twelfth century were more audible and must be heard
first. Much of this lecture is a hymn to the matchless resources of the
Public Record Office; one of its most 'modern' themes is its harping
on all there remains to do.[72] The materials to which he gave most of
the rest of his life were dauntingly intractable but they were recognis-
ably legal records. Whether from his grandfather, whose histories he
praises for that quality in a letter to his sister, from his life at the Bar, or
from the model of his German peers, he had acquired an overpowering
feeling for the primacy of 'hard' evidence.[73] It was not a spirit calculated
to develop empathy towards evidence which was 'soft' precisely
because it was spawned by an age that knew not professional law.
Whatever else they were, the *Leges Henrici Primi*, and the Anglo-
Saxon codes beyond, were not law such as could be 'intimately known'.

   The problem that neither Maitland nor any later legal historians
have been able to solve is how we are to conceive of law or law-making
under a vigorous regime, with an as yet rudimentary bureaucracy, and
nothing easily recognisable as a legal profession. Maitland took it for
granted that the alternative to written law was *'Alleinherrschaft des
Gewohnheitsrechtes'*.[74] But if custom is not a constant; if it can be
moulded by social pressures or manipulated to political ends, as we
now know that it can, then presumably it can also be shaped by
legislative design, in a process that is largely shielded from the historian's gaze. Law can be dynamic without lawyers or systematic law-
giving. Maitland was predisposed by both historical skills and legal
training to equate the beginnings of state intervention with the birth
of legal professionalism.[75] His commitment to PRO-style records made
him see the same gulf in England as his German counterparts saw on
the continent, between the 'learned' laws and the 'folk' law which the
Leges Henrici had artificially respirated. It was as though the legislation

---

[72] *Collected Papers*, i 480–6; cf. *Collected Papers*, ii 8–12. Though Maitland appears to have
garbled his memory of Vinogradoff's introducing him to the PRO (*Letters*, i no. 374; Fisher,
Maitland, pp. 24–5; Plucknett, 'Maitland's place', 186–7; Fifoot, *Life*, p. 60), it is significant
that he thought back to this moment in the spirit of the typical Victorian 'conversion'.
[73] *Letters*, i no. 98; the importance of Maitland's opinion of his grandfather as a guide to his
own values is noted by Fisher, pp. 2–3, by his sister herself, *CLJ*, 11 (1951–3), 67–8, and by
Fifoot, *Life*, pp. 10–11; cf. also Southern, review of *Letters*, i, 108.
[74] Pollock and Maitland, i 19 27.
[75] Cf. *Collected Papers*, ii 37; 'towards the end of the [Angevin] period the history of law
begins to be . . . a history of professional learning'.

of kings from Alfred to Cnut had never been. If, instead of contrasting the worlds of *Glanvill* and the *Leges*, Maitland had dwelt on what Rannulf de Glanville *fils*, chief justiciar, could have learned from Hervey de Glanville *père*, knight of the shire, he might have seen how the Angevin legal establishment could inherit structures erected by the first kings of the English on a customary base.[76]

I hope it is clear from what I have said that the weaknesses of Maitland's account of Anglo-Saxon law were in a real sense the effects of his strengths: his lack of insularity, his scorn for unsupported tradition, his respect for raw evidence. It is thus appropriate that I should conclude by stressing that one outcome of what I am arguing would be to buttress a central plank in Maitland's case. Time and again, he returned to the point that the history of law in England and in other European countries differed because the king of England was in command of his courts, whereas the lack of such control abroad splintered law into provincial customs to which the ultimate response of frustrated rulers was resort to the law of Rome.[77] To me that seems an essential truth, however much nuanced by criticism of some of its more vigorous expressions. I would add that this need not be as incompatible as it at first looks with the major modern heresies. If, in the first place, 'state' power was an inheritance from pre-Conquest kings, initially only partly glimpsed and grasped by their successors, then the contradictions and hesitations of twelfth-century kings in face of 'feudal' priorities become readily intelligible, without our having to reckon that they somehow blundered into amercing every disseisin, every failed pleas.[78] To agree, secondly, that the justice of the 'state' was the most powerful force in play is not to deny that it might be as greedy, cruel and inept as the justice of any lord — if more so, perhaps, than a Victorian instinct could easily accept.[79]

[76] Cf. R. Mortimer, 'The family of Rannulf de Glanville', *BIHR*, 54 (1981), 1–16; H. M. Cam, 'An East Anglian Shirt Moot of Stephen's reign', *EHR*, 39 (1924), 568–71 Cf. Hudson, below, p. 39–46.
[77] Pollock and Maitland, i 24, 84, 111, 131–4, ii 5, 36, 313, 558–9, 632, 673; *Collected Papers*, i 482, ii 64, 434–45; *Selected Historical Essays*, p. 104; also *Justice and Police* (1885), p. 32; *Select Pleas*, pp. lxxii–lxxiii; and *Gierke*, p. xiii; cf. too *Letters*, i nos. 50 (to Vinogradoff, 1888), 202 (1897?), 449 (1905). For part of the trouble that this view got Maitland into, see Fifoot, *Life*, pp. 227–31; and Elton, *Maitland*, pp. 79–88.
[78] See Elton's very pertinent version of the Milsom critique, in his *Maitland*, pp. 44–8, especially pp. 47–8: Maitland 'does overlook the likelihood that it took more than one king, even a Conqueror, to triumph over the social structure and world of ideas within which had been able to conquer England in the first place'. On punishment of disseisin or false claims, see Pollock and Maitland, ii 41–5, 519, 539, 572–3.
[79] Cf., e.g., M. T. Clanchy, 'Law and love in the Middle Ages', in J. Bossy, ed., *Disputes and Settlements. Law and Human Relations in the West* (Cambridge, 1983), pp. 47–67; also his 'A medieval realist: interpreting the rules at Barnwell Priory Cambridge', in E. Attwooll, ed.,

The difficulty of critically assessing a historiographical giant, even one who would have welcomed it as much as Maitland, is the risk of lapsing into absurd and impertinent patronisation. I therefore end by claiming that Maitland was in one respect totally wrong. I am quite unable to understand how this near-exact contemporary of W. G. Grace, whose last 'Golden Summer' was also in 1895, could have had no more to say of cricket than that there was 'too much sitting about'.[80]

Perspectives in Jurisprudence (Glasgow, 1977), pp. 176–94, where he points out (p. 179) that the introduction to the edition by J. Willis Clark, *Liber Memorandorum Ecclesie de Bernew-elle* (Cambridge, 1907), pp. xliii–lxiii, with all its potential for a revisionist view, was ironically the last thing Maitland ever wrote. See also Hudson, below, pp. 34–9.
[80] W. W. Buckland, 'F. W. Maitland', *CLJ*, 1 (1923), 282. I am grateful to the other participants in this symposium for their criticism and advice, notably to the editor, to Professor van Caenegem, to Dr Magnus Ryan and above all to Dr Jenny Wormald.

Proceedings of the British Academy, **89**, 21–46

Maitland and Anglo-Norman Law

JOHN HUDSON

Maitland's work

WHEN RALPH VAUGHAN WILLIAMS DIED in 1958, there were just two photographs in his bedroom: those of Gustav Holst and F. W. Maitland. In 1907, Vaughan Williams had commemorated Maitland with a song for chorus and orchestra, entitled *Toward the Unknown Region* — 'no map there, nor guide, nor voice sounding, nor touch of human hand . . . that inaccessible land.' The title, text, and theme clearly were suited to Maitland's somewhat agnostic religious views. One wonders, though, whether Maitland's historical interests and approaches, at the very least the meaning of the 'Beyond' in *Domesday Book and Beyond*, were not sufficiently familiar to the composer for him to realise how appropriate was the piece's title.[1]

The working back from the known into the unknown region is the most famous aspect of Maitland's historical technique:

> if the age of Glanvill and Bracton throws light forward, it throws light backward also. Our one hope of interpreting the *Leges Henrici*, that almost unique memorial of the really feudal stage of legal history, our one hope of coercing Domesday Book to deliver up its hoarded secrets, our one hope of making an Anglo-Saxon land-book mean something definite, seem to lie in an effort to understand the law of the Angevin time, to understand it thoroughly as though we ourselves lived under it.[2]

[1] M. Kennedy, *The Works of Ralph Vaughan Williams* (Oxford, 1964), pp. 112–13, 241, 431; Fifoot, *Life*, pp. 168, 179–81, 296 n. 7. The piece is based upon Walt Whitman's poem 'Darest Thou now O Soul', from 'Whispers of heavenly death', and was dedicated to Maitland's widow, Florence, sister of Vaughan William's first wife. Vaughan Williams later set four poems by Maitland's daughter, Fredegond.

[2] Pollock and Maitland, ii 673; see also *Domesday Book and Beyond*, p. xix; in *Letters*, i no. 36, to Pollock, 7 April 1888, Maitland wondered whether his contemplated history of the manor should 'begin by describing the situation as it was at the end of cent. XIII, and then to go back to earlier times.' Maitland's scepticism about natural sequences of political and historical development also may well underlie his desire to base his discussion upon specific sources of 'the known', rather than upon preconceived stages of assumed evolution; see e.g. S. Collini, D. Winch, and J. Burrow, *That Noble Science of Politics* (Cambridge, 1983), p. 300

Maitland's assessment of the Anglo-Norman period

The Anglo-Norman period, with the partial exception of the Conqueror's reign,[3] was not central to any of Maitland's works. *Domesday Book and Beyond* focused upon the centuries before 1086, the *History of English Law* upon the years between 1154 and 1272. Let us nevertheless try to assess Maitland's overall view of the period. One might start (like a lazy and fortunate student) with an old copy of the *Encyclopaedia Britannica*, and find that the entry on 'English Law (History)' was by Maitland: 'We may regard the Norman conquest of England as marking the confluence of two streams of law. The one we may call French or Frankish. . . . The other rivulet we may call Anglo-Saxon.' However, the student's laziness will be revealed, for in the *History of English Law*, Maitland wrote that

> the problem to which the historian must address himself should not be stated as though it were a simple ethnical question between what is English and what is French. The picture of two rivulets of law meeting to form one river would deceive us, even could we measure the volume and analyze the waters of each of these fancied streams.[4]

He went on to emphasise the complexities of causation, the difficulties of analysis. In particular, he stressed that developments *after* the Conquest did not necessarily occur *because of* the Conquest: rather, 'a concurrence of many causes was requisite to produce some of those effects which are usually ascribed to the simple fact that the Normans conquered England.'[5]

Maitland regarded the Conquest's direct impact on legal change as slow and limited. This was typified by the history of legal language. If French-based words now dominate legal language, 'this is no immediate and no necessary effect of the Norman Conquest. . . . The destiny of our legal language was not irrevocably determined until Henry of Anjou was king.'[6] The slow pace and limited extent of legal change reflected the small number of conquerors; there was no folk migration. In addition, William did not impose a foreign code on the conquered.

There is no Norman code. Norman law does not exist in a portable trans-

---

for possible discussion between Maitland and his mentor, Sidgwick, concerning such natural sequences.

[3] See e.g. *Letters*, i no. 211 (22 March 1898) to J. H. Round: 'I feel sorry for any one who has to read Domesday and Beyond unless he is one of the small number of the Elect, who were predestined to fall under the Conqueror's spell.'

[4] *Encyclopaedia Britannica* (11th ed., Cambridge, 1910), ix 600, Pollock and Maitland, i 79; see also i pp. c–ci.

[5] Pollock and Maitland, i 87; see also i 89.

[6] Pollock and Maitland, i 80–7, quotation at 84.

plantable shape. English law will have this advantage in the struggle: — a good deal of it is in writing.

We may safely say that William did not intend to sweep away English law and to put Norman law in its stead. On the contrary, he decreed that all men were to have and hold the law of King Edward — that is to say, the old English law — but with certain additions which he, William, had made to it.[7]

Moreover, 'there were good reasons why the technical terms of the old English law should be preserved if the king could preserve them. They were the terms that defined his royal rights.' William was aware of the disruptive effects of lordly power, and sought that 'a combination might be made of all that was favourable to the duke in the Norman, with all that was favourable to the king in the English system.'[8]

Maitland also argued that there were similarities between pre-1066 English and Norman law,[9] and between ancient customs more generally: 'all ancient procedure is formal enough, and in all probability neither the victors nor the vanquished on the field at Hastings knew any one legal formula or legal formality that was not well known throughout many lands.'[10] Such similarities help to explain why no system of personal law developed in Norman England.[11] Rather, developments favoured a unified law for all the king's subjects, a vital precondition for the later emergence of a common law.

The need for unity was central to Maitland's view of royal law and justice. The last Anglo-Saxon kings had been, in Maitland's eyes, all too profligate in their grants of jurisdiction, and their regime displayed marked weaknesses.[12] The Norman kings may not have stopped the former, but until 1135 they had reversed the latter. Like many of his contemporaries, Maitland saw king and lords as naturally opposed: 'the chief result of the Norman Conquest in the history of law is to be found not so much in the subjection of race to race as in the establishment of

[7] Pollock and Maitland, i 79, 88.

[8] Pollock and Maitland, i 82, 92. When, at i 92, Maitland wrote of William I 'bringing even the Norman barons under English land law', he was referring to the obligations they owed the king for their lands, not what he would have called 'private law'.

[9] See e.g. Pollock and Maitland, ii 455, although note i 456 on English custom becoming unintelligible.

[10] Pollock and Maitland, ii 558.

[11] Pollock and Maitland, i 90–2.

[12] Note Maitland, *Constitutional History*, pp. 59–60; *Domesday Book and Beyond*, pp. 282–3. For similarities between Maitland and Stubbs' interpretations of the Norman Conquest, see W. Stubbs, *The Constitutional History of England* (3 vols, Oxford, 1874), i 247–8 (firm government), 256–7 (opposition of king and barons), 275 (limited legal change), 278 (amalgamation of Norman and English: 'the strongest elements of both were brought together'); cf. E. A. Freeman, *The Norman Conquest* (6 vols, Oxford, 1867–79), i 1–2, 4–5, v 364–404, 441–60.

an exceedingly strong kingship which proves its strength by outliving three dispute successions and crushing a rebellious baronage.'[13] First, then, amongst the period's contributions to the development of law was powerful kingship, the smack of firm of government — famously translated in the *Leges Henrici Primi*, 6.2a, as 'tremendum regie maiestatis . . . imperium'.

One aspect of such firm Norman government was the Inquest. Derived from Frankish practice, this involved a question being put on behalf of the king or duke to a sworn body of neighbours. 'That the Norman duke brought [the Inquest] with him as one of his prerogatives can hardly be disputed . . . Under Henry II. the exceptional becomes normal. The king concedes to his subjects as a royal boon his own prerogative procedure.'[14] Also introduced by the Conquest was 'the general theory of tenure', that 'all land is held of the king.' This too reinforced royal power.[15]

Yet if the regime of the Norman kings was powerful, it was also restricted and *ad hoc*. In their court, business was primarily limited to 'the great men and the great causes'; its jurisdiction 'was of necessity a flexible, occasional jurisprudence, . . . meeting new facts by new expedients, wavering as wavered the balance of power between him and his barons.'[16] Elsewhere, Anglo-Norman law and judicial administration were singly lacking in organisation: 'If [the *Leges Henrici*] paint English law as a wonderful confusion, they may yet be painting it correctly.' 'The picture that these law-books set before us is that of an ancient system which has received a rude shock from without while within it was rapidly decaying.' An influx of Frenchmen into the English local courts did not help, and meanwhile 'everywhere in western Europe new principles of social and political order were emerging; new classes were being formed; the old laws, the only written laws, were becoming obsolete; the state was taking a new shape.'[17]

The cure which Maitland prescribed was still greater activity by the royal court and justices, and this would be provided by Henry II, the hero of Maitland's narrative. The account for his reign helps to

---

[13] Pollock and Maitland, i 94. For such opposition generating legal change, see e.g. Pollock and Maitland, i 80; he did not write in the same way about tensions between lords and their men.

[14] Pollock and Maitland, i 143–4.

[15] The most useful statement of Maitland's views is *Constitutional History*, pp. 152ff.

[16] Pollock and Maitland, i 108. Maitland said little of Henry I's activities — perhaps because of the lack of legislation and other written records; Pollock and Maitland, i 95–6, 109.

[17] Pollock and Maitland, i 100, 104–5, 105. The picture of the Anglo-Norman period as one of confusion survives e.g. in R. C. van Caenegem, *The Birth of the English Common Law* (2nd ed., Cambridge, 1988).

reveal what Maitland believed lacking in the Anglo-Norman period: 'the reign of Henry II. is of supreme importance in the history of our law, and its importance is due to the action of the central power, to reforms ordained by the king.' Key elements of Henry's reforms were that 'the whole of English law is centralized and unified by the institution of a permanent court of professional judges, by the frequent mission of itinerant judges throughout the land, by the introduction of the "inquest" or "recognition" and the "original writ" as normal parts of the machinery of justice.'[18]

In Maitland's overall scheme, therefore, the Conqueror and his sons were most important for correcting the weaknesses of the Anglo-Saxon state and then maintaining their power sufficiently for Henry II to undertake his work. This achievement relates to another of Maitland's preoccupations: why England developed its own Common Law, rather than succumbing to Roman Law. A lack of firm government might have led to localism and hence the triumph of Romanism. He asked whether eventually 'English law would have capitulated and made way for Roman jurisprudence' had Harold won at Hastings. Then, 'in the woful days of Stephen, the future of English law looks very uncertain. If English law survives at all, it may break into a hundred local customs, and if it does so, the ultimate triumph of Roman law is assured.' Instead, Henry II succeeded and 'in England the new learning found a small, homogeneous, well conquered, much governed kingdom, a strong, a legislating kingship. It came to us soon; it taught us much; and then there was healthy resistance to foreign dogma.'[19]

The Anglo-Norman period in The History of English Law

Because the *History of English Law* is concerned primarily with the years 1154–1272, it is not always easy to use with reference to the Anglo-Norman period.[20] One certainly cannot just concentrate upon Book I, Chapter IV, entitled 'England under the Norman Kings.' This is a relatively brief chapter, of only thirty-two pages, compared with the thirty-eight on 'The Age of Glanvill' and fifty-two on 'The Age of Bracton'. Moreover, these thirty-two pages range widely outside

---

[18] Pollock and Maitland, i 136, 138; see also e.g. i 144, 150, 153.

[19] Pollock and Maitland, i 79, 110, 24. Yet Maitland still could refer to the Angevin period as 'a perilous moment', ii 673. The perilous moments start to become so numerous as to constitute perilous centuries. See also F. W. Maitland, *English Law and the Renaissance* (Cambridge, 1901); *Gierke*, pp. xiii–xiv; Helmholz, below. Note J. W. Burrow, *A Liberal Descent* (Cambridge, 1981), pp. 134–5, on Stubbs and Roman Law.

[20] Cross references, for example between Books I and II are few; for one example, see i 328 n. 2, referring back to i 71 on *beneficia* and fiefs in Normandy.

the Anglo-Norman period, in particular the seven and a half pages dealing with legal language. Of the remainder, five treat the legislation of the Anglo-Norman kings, almost eleven the *Leges*. This leaves a mere eight and a half pages for the following sub-headings: 'Effects of the Norman Conquest'; 'No mere mixture of two national laws'; 'Personal or national law'; 'Maintenance of English land law'; 'The English in court'; 'Norman ideas and institutions'; 'Custom of the king's court'; 'Royal justice'.

Treatment of elements of land law had appeared in Book I, Chapter III, on 'Norman Law', the background of the inquest waited until Chapter VI, 'The Age of Glanvill'. However, most matters of substantive law and procedure were left to Book II, 'The Doctrines of English Law in the Early Middle Ages.' There, the Anglo-Norman period was sometimes simply excluded. The *History* did not examine the origin of frankpledge. Discussion of aids did not go back before *Glanvill*, nor that of the duties of townships before Henry II.[21] For some other subjects, Maitland did give 'earlier' or Anglo-Norman law its own section or sub-section, but even these did not constitute thorough surveys of the evidence.[22] Discussion is included sometimes because of the light which later evidence casts upon it, but more often in order to explain later developments.

The positioning of such discussions is also of interest. A reverse chronological order might be seen as reflecting Maitland's 'Domesday Book and Beyond' approach. Thus the treatment of 'Wardship' deals in turn with 'Bracton's rules'; 'The law in Glanvill'; 'Earlier law'; 'Norman law'; 'Origin of these rights'.[23] However, such a reverse structure is untypical. More common is a forward arrangement, although sometimes preceded by a brief sub-section on the Bractonian Common Law position. With or without such an introduction, quite short sub-sections arranged chronologically forwards are followed by a considerably longer discussion of the thirteenth-century situation.[24] The analysis can contain flashbacks and flash-forwards. The overall chronological pattern of a chapter, such as that on 'Conveyance', tends therefore to a series of zigzags, not a constant forward or backward direction.[25]

Some other sections are particularly abstract in their discussion, giving no indication of chronological change. In general, as with the

---

[21] Pollock and Maitland, i 349–51, 565; see also e.g. ii 46–7 on the protection of seisin.
[22] See e.g. Pollock and Maitland, i 460 on aliens.
[23] Pollock and Maitland, i 319–27; the evidence on Norman law is not chronologically earlier, but the pattern of Maitland's thought is clear.
[24] Note e.g. the arrangement of sections and sub-sections in Book II, Chapter VI, 'Inheritance'.
[25] Pollock and Maitland, ii 80–106.

analysis of ownership and possession or of incorporeal things, these are basically Bractonian. Others contain more examples and footnote citations but concentrate on the thirteenth century, with only occasional chronological shifts backwards and forwards. Thus the chapter on juris-diction, with the exception of the section on the borough, relies heavily on citations from *Bracton, Bracton's Note Book*, the *Hundred Rolls*, and the *Placita Quo Warranto*.[26] Treatment of aspects particularly important in Norman England, such as seignorial jurisdiction, is there-fore very brief, and draws on very limited evidence.[27] Elsewhere the Anglo-Norman period is amalgamated in discussion of the thirteenth century, for example with citations from *c.* 1066–1154 being used to support a general point in the text.[28]

Thus one cannot simply single out the sub-sections with titles such as 'Earlier law' or 'Vassalism in the Norman age', add them to the chapter on 'England under the Norman Kings', and hope to arrive at a complete picture of Anglo-Norman law. Much material and discussion relevant to the Norman reigns is present in the bulk of the book devoted to the later twelfth and the thirteenth century. Maitland's analysis is too carefully integrated to allow easy excerpting.

The History of English Law *and* Domesday Book and Beyond

Maitland recognised at least some of the limitations of his treatment of the Anglo-Norman period, even before they were brought into sharper focus by Brunner's review of the first edition.[29] In the fair copy manuscript of the *History*, Maitland deleted a long section at the end of the Anglo-Norman chapter's final footnote. In it, he had protested

---

[26] See Pollock and Maitland, i 538–9, 545–6, for shifts backwards.

[27] See esp. Pollock and Maitland, i 584–94. Nor does *Domesday Book and Beyond* analyse in depth the 'feudal justice' (p. 80) deriving from lordship and tenure, or exploit the charter sources concerning such justice.

[28] E.g. Pollock and Maitland, i 271 n. 3, 306–7, 352 n. 2.

[29] Pollock and Maitland, i 94 n. 2, and see below, p. 39; Maitland, of course, did not significantly modify his interpretation in the second edition. His sole response to Brunner's criticism that his treatment of gage began with Domesday Book, and of forms of gage with *Glanvill*, was to add two sentences referring to Anglo-Saxon landbooks to his brief paragraph on 'Antiquity of gages', and to footnote Brunner's review, a charter cited there by Brunner, and another of Brunner's works; Pollock and Maitland, ii 118. Other new footnote references, and occasional modifications to the text, in the second edition reflect publications too recent to be included in the first edition, notably works by Liebermann; e.g. i 89 and n. 6, cf. (1895) i 67 and n. 7; 101 n. 4, 103 nn. 1 and 3, 104 n. 3. Other changes in the second edition relating to the Anglo-Norman period include i 94, reference to Stevenson; i 95, a new passage concerning Westminster Hall; also occasional minor verbal changes, e.g. i 92 'capital', replaces (1895) i 70 'great'; see also below, n. 43, p. 30.

that his attitude to the influence of Norman law was made 'unbiased by any misplace patriotism', and admitted that

> the law which prevails in England at the end of the twelfth century, more especially the private law, is in a certain sense very French. It is law evolved by French speaking men, many of whom are of French race, many of whom have but begun to think of themselves as Englishmen; in many respects it is closely similar to that which prevailed in France. But we do not believe that the conquering Normans brought much legal doctrine with them, or tried to impose what they did upon the English.[30]

Maitland's view of what constituted legal doctrine, his preference for written law,[31] and his tendency to omit 'private law' from Book I all contributed to his underestimating of Norman influence.

However, the limited treatment of the Anglo-Norman period also stemmed from the way in which the *History* evolved during its writing. The 'Introduction' to the first but not the second edition included the following passage:

> Our purpose at one time was to have turned back from the Angevin to the Norman time for the purpose of setting before our readers in a Third Book some speculations as to the true intent and meaning of the Domesday Survey, for we hold with Mr Seebohm that the study of that enigmatical record should come after and not before the study of less obscure texts. But our work grew in our hands and has become all too bulky. Divers other reasons also have persuaded us that what we had schemed and even written about Domesday Book had better wait for a while.[32]

Let us try to construct a chronology. Between late 1889 and early 1891 Maitland was writing chapters on 'Tenure', 'Status', and 'Jurisdiction', and Pollock his chapter on Anglo-Saxon law.[33] Then in April 1891 Maitland wrote to Bigelow that 'at present I am up to my eyes in Domesday and I hope to get some theory out of it that will enable me to attack the A-S land books. But studying Domesday involves a great

---

[30] Cambridge University Library, Add. MS 6987, f. 124.
[31] See above, p. 23.
[32] Pollock and Maitland (1895), i pp. xxxv–vi. The plan of the Third Book, apparently to be placed at the end of the existing work, is uncertain. It may have been intended to contain work by both Pollock and Maitland, for appended to the above passage is a section of a footnote initialed by Pollock: 'My own contributions in the shape of a paper in the Transactions of the Devonshire Association for 1893, and the Presidential address which opens the volume for 1894, are published for what they are worth, but must be taken as provisional. — F.P.' The decision to publish these elsewhere may indicate the early abandonment of the projected third book, leaving as its main relic a chapter by Maitland on Domesday Book. Pollock's article 'A brief survey of Domesday', *EHR* 11 (1896), 209–30 may also have used material he had assembled whilst the third book was still proposed.
[33] *Letters*, i nos. 78, 83, 86, 87; M. DeWolfe Howe, ed., *The Pollock-Holmes Letters* (2 vols, Cambridge, 1942), i 34.

deal of drudgery.'[34] On 1 November 1891 he told Pollock that 'I have now written in rough five big chapters — Tenure — Status — Jurisdiction — Domesday — Origins of Feudalism. My next task will be the general history from 1066 to 1272. Then the way will be clear for "private law".'[35] 'Tenure', 'Status', and 'Jurisdiction' appeared as the first three chapters of Book II of the *History*, but 'Domesday' and the 'Origins of Feudalism' came to be excluded.

In April 1892 Maitland wrote to J. H. Round that 'D. B. "intrigues" me the more one reads it. I lectured on it for a whole term and wrote all that I said; but I have no intention of publishing anything, at any rate for a long time to come.' This presumably refers to his lectures in the Michaelmas term of 1891 on 'English land law in and before 1086', and these must have been related to the draft chapters on 'Domesday' and 'Origins of Feudalism', the latter of which I take to have primarily concerned the Anglo-Saxon period.[36] In May, Maitland wrote the following to Vinogradoff:

> F. P[ollock]. . . . has written an Anglo-Saxon chapter. *Between ourselves* I do not like it very much, partly because it will make it very difficult for me to say anything about A-S law in any later part of the book. My effort now is to shove on with the general sketch of the Norman and Angevin periods so that my collaborator may have little to do before we reach the Year Book period — if we ever reach it. So I am half inclined to throw aside all that I have written — it is a pretty heavy mass — about Domesday and the A-S books. Perhaps when you have got out your folk land papers I may publish in some separate form a few things I want to say about A-S conveyancing — always supposing that you have neither said them nor wished to say them.[37]

In November 1893 the minutes of the Syndicate of Cambridge University Press and a letter from Maitland to Gross shows that he was still contemplating three volumes, but the relationship of these to a possible Book III concerning Domesday is unclear.[38] Neither the 'Domesday' nor the 'Origins of Feudalism' chapters survive in the fair copy manuscript of the *History*, but at a date which I have been unable to ascertain Maitland did submit at least his 'Domesday' chapter to the Press; in

---

[34] *Letters*, i no. 93; see also no. 95.

[35] *Letters*, i no. 96.

[36] *Letters*, i no. 106; Fifoot, *Life*, p. 96; on the contents of the 'Origins of Feudalism' chapter, see below, p. 31. Maitland published short pieces on Domesday before 1895: 'Domesday measures of land', *Archaeological Review*, 4 (1889–90), 391–2, and 'Domesday Book', in R. H. I. Palgrave, ed., *Dictionary of Political Economy* (London, 1893), pp. 629–30 (I owe these references to Mark Philpott). The first of these is a brief letter, but the latter shows that at least some of his ideas were already fully formed, for example that 'Domesday Book is a geld book, a tax book. Geldability, actual or potential, this is its main theme.'

[37] *Letters*, i no. 109.

[38] Cambridge University Library, UA, Pr. V. 12; *Letters*, i no. 130.

July 1894 he wrote to Round concerning Domesday matters, and stated that 'I am reconsidering my position which is complicated by the existence in irretrievably printed sheets of a supposed chapter on D. B.'.[39] It is uncertain whether the 'Origins of Feudalism' chapter had also been submitted to the Press. Nor is it clear quite when the final decision on the 'Domesday' chapter was taken. Even as late as December 1894, after he had finished the *History*, Maitland wrote to Round that 'I am meditating a postponement of all my Domesday stuff in order to avoid collision.' However, this may only mean that Maitland, having already decided to exclude the 'Domesday' chapter and other material from the *History*, was contemplating what to do with it.[40] In July 1895 he wrote of submitting two or three essays on Domesday to the *English Historical Review*,[41] but these instead became *Domesday Book and Beyond*, published in 1897.

There is no indication that the problems arising from Pollock's Anglo-Saxon chapter, from the omission of the 'Domesday' or the 'Origins of Feudalism' chapters, or from the abandonment of 'Book III' led to major changes in the plan for or content of the rest of the *History*.[42] Can we establish a definite relationship between the content of *Domesday Book and Beyond* and the material excluded from the *History*?[43] The third essay, on the hide, certainly involved work under-

---

[39] *Letters*, i no. 137.

[40] *Letters*, i no. 147. Maitland may have completed his fair copy manuscript at the beginning of November 1894; Cambridge University Library, Add. MS 6994, f. 303; 'Explicit 2 Nov' 1894 In festo animarum.'

[41] *Letters*, i no. 164.

[42] Conceivably Pollock's Anglo-Saxon chapter may have led Maitland to limit the amount of early, in particular Anglo-Saxon, material in the thematic chapters written after the middle of 1892.

[43] Comparison of the first and second editions of the *History* shows that only limited changes were made relating to the appearance of *Domesday Book and Beyond*. Pollock and Maitland (1895), i p. xxxvi n. 1, the latter part of which is cited above, n. 32, began 'Our readers must therefore be asked to forgive a few phrases which seem to promise a discourse on Domesday'; for such phrases and their replacement in the second edition by references to *Domesday Book and Beyond*, see Pollock and Maitland, i 293, 579 = (1895) i 274, 566; see also i 25, two sentences added to what was the first paragraph of the first edition ('Much of . . . this kind'). In general, most changes involving *Domesday Book and Beyond* were simply additions to footnotes, referring the reader to *Domesday Book and Beyond*; e.g. Pollock and Maitland, i 38, 42, 82, 235, 362, 619, ii 12. On other occasions the reference is preceded by an explanatory statement, e.g. i 187, 259 ('as to the old English army, see . . .'), 297 ('for the use of this word before the Conquest, see . . .'). Reference to *Domesday Book and Beyond* could replace other citations: Pollock and Maitland, i 289 n. 7. On other occasions both text and notes were modified; Pollock and Maitland, i 558 (hundred and communal property), 603 (small manor), 633 (complete re-working of section linking village and borough). Work relating to *Domesday Book and Beyond* produced a new paragraph on 'Vill and village', i 562–3; also an important addition (i 595) on the legal sense of the manor, qualified by reference to Tait's review of *Domesday Book and Beyond*. Modifications were also made to Pollock's Anglo-

taken after the completion of the *History*.[44] Otherwise, the preface to *Domesday Book and Beyond*, in words rather similar to those of the 'Introduction' to the first edition of the *History*, suggests a very close relationship:

> The greater part of what is in this book was written in order that it might be included in the *History of English Law before the Time of Edward I*.... Divers reasons dictated a change of plan. Of one only need I speak [that Round's *Feudal England* had been forthcoming]. In its light I have suppressed, corrected, added much.[45]

Essay, I, 'Domesday Book', must be very closely related to the 'Domesday' chapter of the *History*, of which Maitland had received proofs.[46] Particularly the opening pages of Essay II, 'England before the Conquest', show it to have derived from the chapter on the 'Origins of Feudalism'. Whether the original chapter would have included other material, for example on Normandy, must remain uncertain.[47]

Domesday Book and Beyond thus complements the *History*. However, its form and content do not suggest that Maitland ever had detailed plans for a treatment of the Anglo-Norman period as complete as that of the 'Age of Bracton'. The focus of *Domesday Book and Beyond* left uncovered topics discussed at length for a later period in the *History*. There is little or nothing about the king's court, procedure, the classification of offences, or much else which appeared in the second volume of the *History*.[48] Maitland wished to treat Domesday Book as above all a geld book, and therefore consciously left many aspects of its legal interpretation to others: 'some future historian may be able to reconstruct the land-law which obtained in the conquered England of 1086, and (for our records frequently speak of the *tempus*

Saxon chapter, including sections on the post-Conquest period: cf. i 34 and (1895) i 10 on the five hide unit and the knight's fee; i 43 omits a long passage from (1895) i 20 in a discussion of private jurisdiction. References to Domesday material in the first edition survive unchanged in the second: e.g. i 241–2, 313.

[44] In June 1896 Maitland wrote to R. L. Poole (*Letters*, i no. 177) that 'I am off to Horsepools in order that I may count "hides" in Domesday'. See also *Domesday Book and Beyond*, p. xx.

[45] *Domesday Book and Beyond*, p. xix.

[46] If, after the abandonment of Book III, Maitland ever seriously thought of retaining the 'Domesday' chapter, its position would have been slightly anomalous. It presumably would have been intended as part of Book II. However, unlike the other chapters of that book, it treated a wide range of themes within a confined historical period, material which otherwise might have been slotted into Chapters II and III of Book II of the *History*, on 'The Sorts and Conditions of Men' and 'Jurisdiction and the Communities of the Land'.

[47] *Constitutional History*, pp. 141–64.

[48] Conceivably Maitland restricted his discussion of some of these matters because he felt they had been treated, at least provisionally, by M. M. Bigelow, *History of Procedure in England* (London, 1880); see Pollock and Maitland, i p. cvii.

Regis Edwardi) the unconquered England of 1065.'[49] A combined reading of *Domesday Book and Beyond* and the *History* still does not provide a full analysis of Anglo-Norman law.

After Maitland

How then can historians develop Maitland's achievement? Many subjects, such as the legal position of women, the extent of regional variation in law, comparison with other realms or principalities, must here be left aside. Rather, I shall concentrate on three areas: language; disputing and the scope of legal history; the significance of the Norman Conquest and Anglo-Norman law. Throughout I look to Maitland to provide a 'map, guide, voice, and human hand.'

Language

Maitland wrote that 'language is no mere instrument which we can control at will; it controls us.'[50] It is hard to deny that a serious problem of language has arisen in writing about legal history, a problem related to wider questions of historical language, but also in particular to the use of terms of art associated with a technical modern discipline, law. The most obvious example from the former category is 'feudalism': 'Every one now-a-days can pick holes in "the feudal system" and some great writers can hardly mention it without loss of temper.'[51] That again is Maitland, who went on to justify the word feudalism as useful for comparative purposes. Although Maitland himself certainly used problematic modern words and concepts concerning medieval law, he was very aware of the linguistic and interpretative difficulties.[52] It was the desire to avoid anachronism, the misapplication of modern assumptions, that underlay his preference for the 'Domesday Book and

---

[49] *Domesday Book and Beyond*, p. 2.

[50] Pollock and Maitland, i 87.

[51] 'Why the history of English law is not written', *Collected Papers*, i 488–9. See also 'The law of real property', ibid., i 175: ' "Feudalism" is a good word, and will cover a multitude of ignorances.'

[52] See e.g. Pollock and Maitland, i 68, 230 for sovereignty and public and private law; Book II, Chapter VIII, 'Crime and Tort'. Note also Pollock and Maitland, i 229 on the arrangement and categorisations to be used in Book II; i 2–6, his initial discussion of 'Ownership and Possession', reveals a highly sensitive approach to thirteenth-century terminology, the relation of these terms to thirteenth-century concepts, and the relation of both to modern terms and concepts; see also ii 153 n. 1.

Beyond' approach.[53] What further possible solutions are there to these problems, what else might Maitland suggest were he here?

First, he would say that the use of modern categorisations, and hence language, is necessary to identify what is of interest to us; sheer amounts of evidence need not be the best indication of a matter's historical importance.[54] Secondly, he no doubt would argue that the proscription of certain words as historically incorrect is not a sufficient, nor perhaps a necessary, solution to the problem of language. Rather, proscription produces two other dangers: either one can use no modern language to discuss the past, and historical discourse collapses, or one resorts to other words which soon turn out to carry almost as much modern mental baggage: the two obvious examples for the legal historian are 'property/ownership' and 'rights'.

Thirdly, he would probably say that a linguistic problem was no bad thing. There should be no orthodox, correct way to tackle it. Rather a variety of intelligent approaches will bear fruit. Such is the burden of comments like the following: 'we shall, for example, pass backwards and forwards between civil and criminal procedure, just because most modern writers have sedulously kept them apart.'[55] Fourthly, it is necessary to question and criticise one's own categories, and to be aware of their history. Thus he wrote in the context of the law of descent that 'the main fault to be found in Blackstone's classical exposition is the tendency to treat the Lombard *Libri Feudorum* as a model to which all feudal law ought to correspond.'[56] Likewise, he rejected as simplistic or inappropriate any rigid positivist definition of 'right', requiring enforcement by a single sovereign body. Thus he wrote to Vinogradoff that 'the point that I should like emphasized — but perhaps you are coming to this — is that not having remedies in the King's own court is not equivalent to not having rights.'[57] In general, Maitland sought to tease meaning from language (and with Maitland's wit his teasing is in both senses). This is a key characteristic of his style. One of his tasks was to work out meaning when people had difficulties in saying what they meant; hence both his interest in specific

[53] Cf. the form of some of his notable work from the 1880s, such as 'The mystery of seisin', which, at least rhetorically, links the law of the first half of the nineteenth century more directly to that of the middle ages; *Collected Papers*, i 358–84.

[54] See e.g. Pollock and Maitland, i 229.

[55] Pollock and Maitland, ii 573 n. 7.

[56] Pollock and Maitland, ii 260 n. 1; see also ii 289 n. 1. Unfortunately Susan Reynolds in her *Fiefs and Vassals* (Oxford, 1994), does not discuss Blackstone; Maitland receives praise for his critique of the 'severe feudalists', *Fiefs and Vassals*, p. 347.

[57] *Letters*, i no. 50; see also no. 38, and *Domesday Book and Beyond*, pp. 42–3. Such concern may be connected with his worries about Austin's jurisprudence; see below, n. 62.

words, and his use of analogy where direct explanation seemed insufficient.[58]

The linguistic problem, for Maitland as for us, involved minimising anachronism whilst still speaking to the modern reader. The logical conclusion of his approaches was the provision of extensive portions of original texts, explicated in detail and with considerable care by a modern commentator. Terminology can be analysed, Latin words compared with the vernacular. Real cases can be dissected and compared, imaginary cases constructed to illustrate key points.[59] The tactics of the parties can be scrutinized, the impact of norms assessed. Such an approach is not obvious from his survey treatment of the Anglo-Norman material in the *History of English Law*. However, it is more apparent in his immersion in *Bracton* and the *Note Book* which underlies the greater part of the *History*, and is clearest in his emphasis upon editing, translating, and introducing mediaeval texts. This method provided the greatest possible chance of accurate, comprehensible, and meaningful dialogue between past and present. Only in such ways could 'by slow degrees the thoughts of our forefathers, their common thoughts about common things, ... become thinkable once more.'[60]

Law, Legal History, and Disputing

It seems likely that Maitland had, at least by the standards of his time, a fairly broad view of law's domain.[61] Excessively rigid views of law were subjected to his characteristic irony: 'tenure in villeinage is protected, and if we choose to say that it is protected by "positive morality" rather than by "law properly so called," we are bound to add that it is protected by a morality which keeps a court, which uses legal forms, which is conceived as law, or as something akin to law.'[62] He

---

[58] *Domesday Book and Beyond*, p. 226: 'Men are learning to say what they really mean.'

[59] On Maitland's use of imaginary, ideal cases, see S. F. C. Milsom, review of G. R. Elton, *F. W. Maitland*, *Times Literary Supplement* 28 February 1986, 225–6.

[60] *Domesday Book and Beyond*, p. 520.

[61] Note, however, that he excluded certain matters as, for instance, 'political' or 'constitutional' rather than legal: see e.g. Pollock and Maitland, i 80, 297, ii 462; also ii 603 n. 4 which sends the reader to pages in Book I for the constitutional and political aspects of the history of the Inquest. On use of the category legal, see further, J. G. H. Hudson, *The Formation of the English Common Law* (London, 1996), ch. 1, and White, below.

[62] Pollock and Maitland, i 361. The 'Introduction' to the *History*, which might seem the best source for Maitland's general thoughts on law and legal history, was largely Pollock's work; *Pollock-Holmes Letters*, i 60–1. Some of Maitland's ideas are apparent in his essays or suggested by his letters. Note his doubts concerning Austin's jurisprudence; e.g. *Letters*, i nos. 239, 253, and *Encyclopaedia Britannica*, ix 606 on Austin: 'though he was at times an acute dissector of confused thought, he was too ignorant of the English, the Roman and every other system of law to make considerable addition to the sum of knowledge; and when

was well aware that courts could be used to exact vengeance; the fair copy manuscript of the *History* shows him spicing up a text which first spoke of peasants who 'impleaded each other in the village courts' by replacing the word 'impleaded' with 'assailed'.[63] However, his emphasis remained upon substantive law and formal procedure leading to and during court cases.

Influenced in part by developments in jurisprudence and in the social sciences, legal historians since Maitland have broadened their scope, particularly to the more general category of disputing.[64] Rather than concentrating on court proceedings, analysis may stretch from the origins of the dispute to its termination, not just in court but also by methods such as a marriage alliance between the parties. A greater number of dispute descriptions have become available, and in addition historians have grown interested in literary accounts of disputes, particularly those in the vernacular literature designed for aristocratic audiences. Whatever the clerical influence upon them, however stylised they may be, they still provide our best written indication of aristocratic thinking.[65] They allow us to see in play, both in and out of court, the variety of norms and perceptions which constituted legal thought.[66]

Studies of disputing have analysed causation, conduct, and settlement. They have asked, for example, whether disputes typically arose in certain circumstances. For the Anglo-Norman period, insufficient evidence survives to give any worthwhile detailed answers concerning offences against the person or moveable goods, but concerning land disputes some suggestions may be made. Re-marriage seems to have been a particular cause of inheritance disputes. The ending of grants

---

Savigny, the herald of evolution, was already in the field, the day for a "Nature-Right" — and Austin's projected "general jurisprudence" would have been a Nature-Right — was past beyond recall.'

[63] Cambridge University Library, Add. MS 6987, f. 56; Pollock and Maitland, i 85.

[64] On 30 March 1895 Maitland wrote to Bigelow: 'I hope that you have received a copy of the book that Pollock and I have just published. With my share of the gift go pleasant memories of hours spent over the Placita Anglo-Normannica and of pleasant talks with its author'; *Letters*, i no. 153. However, Maitland expounded very few cases, real or imaginary, with specific reference to the Anglo-Norman period: see Pollock and Maitland, i 106–7 (imaginary case), 450–2; for briefer mentions of cases, see e.g. i 91, 93, 110 n. 1, ii 599 n. 2; cf. the lengthy expositions of real later cases at i 156–60, 549–51. Even the case of Modbert and the priory of Bath, which he described in a review as 'perhaps the best of all the "Placita Anglo-Normannica" that have come down to us', received only a footnote reference: *Collected Papers*, iii 19, Pollock and Maitland, ii 602 n. 2.

[65] They also present our best chance of discovering the spoken words behind the Latin of documents.

[66] See e.g. P. R. Hyams, 'Henry II and Ganelon', *Syracuse Scholar*, 4 (1983), 22–35; S. D. White, 'The discourse of inheritance in twelfth-century France: alternative models of the fief in *Raoul de Cambrai*', in Garnett and Hudson, eds, *Law and Government*, pp. 173–97.

for limited terms often produced strife, whilst the succession of a new lord, particularly one who was not the simple heir of the decedent, might also bring a flurry of conflicts.[67] Further study might confirm other hypotheses, for example as to whether disputes tended to arise over lands distant from a lord's centre of power.

In studies of the conduct of disputes, power, relationships, and honour have taken over the prominence enjoyed by rules and courts in Maitland's model. In particular, behaviour outside court is analysed.[68] Private war, or 'high level inter-personal violence', was not common in Anglo-Norman England, except during Stephen's reign, but instances from the decades soon after the Conquest continue to come to light. A saint's life of the first half of the twelfth-century recounted the following incident from 1086 × 1094. Two men living under the abbot of Burton's authority (*sub iure*) fled to a neighbouring village, to live under the power (*sub potestate*) of Count Roger the Poitevin. The abbot's first action was aimed against the men's goods. He ordered the seizure of the crops still in the men's barns, 'hoping in this way to induce them to return to their dwelling.' Such action merely led to an escalation of the dispute. The men looked to the count for protection, perhaps suggesting that an attack on them was now an affront to his honour. Roger threatened to kill the abbot wherever he was found.

> Violently angry, the count gathered a great troop of peasants and knights with carts and weapons and sent them to the monks' barns at Stapenhill and had them seize by force all the crops stored there . . . Not content with this, Count Roger sent his men and knights to lay waste the abbey's fields at Blackpool, encouraging them especially to lure into battle the ten knights whom the abbot had recruited as a retinue from among his relatives.

The abbot tried to calm his men, and sought divine help. However, his more martially inclined relatives ignored his requests, and engaged the count's men in battle, 'few against many'. One of the count's knights had his leg broken, another was flung into a muddy stream, and the remainder took flight.[69] Military means, perhaps backed by divine help, brought this stage of the dispute to an end, but the subsequent finale lies more fully in the realm of the supernatural. The peasants who were the cause of the trouble died suddenly. On the day when they were

[67] See e.g. J. G. H. Hudson, *Land, Law, and Lordship in Anglo-Norman England* (Oxford, 1994), pp. 61–2 (Nigel d'Aubigny's actions as a new lord), 97–101, 116–17.
[68] Pollock and Maitland, ii 574 ff. generally plays down the role of self-help.
[69] Reference and translation courtesy of Professor Bartlett, whose edition and translation of the *Life* will appear in *Oxford Medieval Texts*. Maitland would have been pleased to find such an account; he wrote to Neilson concerning the Saints Lives attributed to Barbour that 'I often wish that in the *Vitae Sanctorum* we had fewer miracles and more mortgages'; *Letters*, ii no. 30.

buried, they appeared carrying their wooden coffins on their shoulders. Not surprisingly, this led the count to repent, and submit.

Such events, military and supernatural, were an infrequent element of disputes. However, the case also reveals more common ones, such as the importance of supporters, and appeal to higher authority not for judgment but for aid.[70] Gifts were made to officials for their help in future disputes.[71] When the abbot of Abingdon made a settlement with Nigel d'Oilly, the following condition was imposed: 'whenever the abbot has a plea in the king's court, Nigel will be present on the abbot's side, unless the plea is against the king, and when the abbot goes to that court, Nigel shall provide lodgings for him and if nothing appropriate can be found, he shall give up his own lodgings for his accommodation.'[72]

As for practice in court, compared with modern or even thirteenth-century law, a smaller proportion of Anglo-Norman cases may have been decided by rational evidence or knock-down argument. Criteria of relevance and proper procedure may have been laxer than those later enforced by royal justices who might well be strangers to local politics, and who were used to processing, even deciding, large numbers of cases.[73] The less clear the case or the more irreconcilable the parties, the more likely that other factors, power, friendship, eloquence and so on, would become involved.

However, there is a danger here of moving too far from Maitland's picture of more regular procedures. Many of the trials in vernacular literature are treason trials, wherein political elements were long to remain unusually prominent. Even other judicial hearings in literary texts, and perhaps a large proportion of those extensively recorded in more traditional sources, were in some sense hard cases: otherwise they would not have been worth writing about. Here too, the play of power, friendship, and eloquence may have enjoyed unusually wide scope. Generalising from such accounts may lead to a model which overemphasizes the play of power, friendship, and eloquence. Hearings could and did turn more narrowly on matters of fact or matters of law. In land cases, witnesses or documents might be brought, in cases of violence and theft, alibis stated, pleas of self-defence made, incriminating physical marks on the accused shown. Or arguments might rest on

---

[70] See e.g. *English Lawsuits*, no. 246. Later, the more plentiful sources give evidence of violence entering into land disputes, see e.g. *CRR*, i 101.

[71] See e.g. P. A. Brand, *The Origins of the English Legal Profession* (Oxford, 1992), pp. 9–10; note also *English Lawsuits*, no. 317. Twelfth-century perceptions of the distinctions between bribery and such grants merit extended study.

[72] *English Lawsuits*, no. 206.

[73] See Brand, *Legal Profession*, chs 1 and 2.

implicit or explicit appeal to norms, and their relationship to the facts
of the dispute. Thus both parties might agree on the implications of
certain classifications of land-holding, but disagree over the categoriz-
ation of the disputed land.[74] Or if both parties accepted the existence
of a norm, the defendant might choose to argue that the case was an
exception to that norm.

If problems in deciding the case or reconciling the parties proved
great, resort might be had to ordeal.[75] If it failed to scare the subjected
party into confession, ordeal was meant to bring a supernatural and
spectacular end to a dispute. Other aspects of settlement had similar
purposes. For example, in a world where few offenders were caught
and still fewer punished to the full, the rhetoric and ritual of execution
must have played a large part, only occasionally hinted at in the
sources.[76]

However, it is a preference for compromise which has gained most
attention in studies of dispute settlement.[77] In the Anglo-Norman
period, settlements are best studied in monastic charter chronicles,
which combine documents and narrative. They reveal considerable
variety. There are clear decisions, either following a court judgment or
after one party had admitted that it was in the wrong.[78] There are also
obvious compromises.[79] In other cases still, however, there is a clear
judgment that one party is in the right, the opponent being allowed
only a minor sweetener which in no way conceals that they had been
defeated.[80] These three types of settlement mark points on a con-
tinuum, rather than being the sole discrete categories. Comparisons
can be attempted between types of dispute: were compromises more
common in land disputes than those involving offences against the
person? Further comparisons can be made with other realms at
the same period, or with other periods of English history. It seems
increasingly likely that a prevalence of settlements involving at least
an element of compromise remained common throughout the Middle

---

[74] See e.g. *English Lawsuits*, no. 226.
[75] See P. R. Hyams, 'Trial by ordeal: the key to proof in the early Common Law', in M. S.
Arnold *et al.*, eds., *On the Laws and Customs of England* (Chapel Hill, NC, 1981), pp. 90–126;
R. J. Bartlett, *Trial by Fire and Water: the Medieval Judicial Ordeal* (Oxford, 1986). Maitland's
emphasis when dealing with early forms of proof is very much on the supernatural and
ordeal; Pollock and Maitland, esp. i 74, ii 598–603.
[76] See e.g. *English Lawsuits*, no. 471.
[77] See e.g. M. T. Clanchy, 'Law and love in the middle ages', in J. Bossy, ed., *Disputes and
Settlements: Law and Human Relations in the West* (Cambridge, 1983), pp. 47–67.
[78] E.g. *CMA*, ii 116 (concerning jurisdiction), 129, 206. Note also occasions when redress is
unavailable, for examples against royal officials; *CMA*, ii 7.
[79] E.g. *CMA*, ii 18–19; 20; 166–8.
[80] E.g. *CMA*, ii 118, 140; 188–90 (receipt of friendship).

Ages. This has many implications, of which just two can be mentioned
here. It warns against simple association of compromise with any one
form of judicial or social organization. And it suggest that the wide
range of methods of pursuing disputes discussed above were not just
a feature of the pre-Common Law period.[81]

Law in Anglo-Norman England

As Maitland argued, one of the main contributions of the Anglo-
Norman reigns before 1135 to the formation of Common Law was
the strength of kingship. Underlying this strength were Anglo-Saxon
powers, particularly as it is now clear that Maitland exaggerated the
Anglo-Saxon kings' dispersal of major jurisdictional rights.[82] The Conquest not only preserved such powers, but also countered some of the
political weaknesses apparent particularly in the Confessor's reign by
extending the landed base of monarchy and strengthening royal
lordship.

Brunner was otherwise surely right to criticize the *History* for
underestimating Norman influence after 1066.[83] Certainly there were
similarities between Anglo-Saxon and Norman law, certainly William
I and his successors confirmed the *Laga Edwardi*, and certainly their
own legislative innovations were limited. However, by 1086 England
had a new, French aristocracy. These men brought their customs with
them to England not in writing but in their heads.[84]

Prominent therein were ideas concerning lordship. As Maitland
argued, lordship was not absent from Anglo-Saxon England, but
Norman ideas, together with the consequences of Conquest and settlement, gathered more closely the elements of personal lordship, land-
holding and jurisdiction.[85] The honour was one unit through which
parties could pursue their aims and manage their affairs: 'Each feudal

---

[81] For a study which implies considerable similarities between Anglo-Norman and Common
Law disputing, see M. T. Clanchy, 'A medieval realist: interpreting the rules at Barnwell
Priory, Cambridge' in E. A. G. Attwooll, ed., *Perspectives in Jurisprudence* (Glasgow, 1977),
pp. 176–94. Most civil cases still today, of course, are settled out of court.

[82] See e.g. N. D. Hurnard, 'The Anglo-Norman franchises', *EHR* 64 (1949), 289–327, 433–60;
above, Wormald.

[83] *Political Science Quarterly*, 11 (1896), 534–44 at 535; see also above, p. 27. Maitland's
treatment of Norman law had of course been limited, in part because of the scarcity of
available sources.

[84] See esp. P. R. Hyams, 'The Common Law and the French connection', *ANS* 4 (1982),
77–92, 196–202; J. C. Holt, 'Feudal society and the family in early medieval England: (i) the
revolution of 1066', *TRHS*, 5th Ser. 32 (1982), 193–212; also above, p. 28, for Maitland's
opinion formulated in the manuscript of the *History*.

[85] For Maitland's views, see e.g. *Domesday Book and Beyond*, pp. 67, 294, 311.

group strives to be a little state; its ruler and his subjects alike have an interest in all that concerns its territory.'[86]

However, like Stubbs and Bigelow, Maitland wrote little about lords' courts, except concerning their jurisdiction derived from royal grants of sake and soke. Yet seignorial courts clearly were very important in Anglo-Norman England. As well as dealing with a wide range of non-legal business, they were places in which grants were made and witnessed. Kings recognized their importance in litigation. In 1108 Henry I decreed that land disputes between the vassals of any baron of his honour should be dealt with in the court of their common lord. Likewise, in 1164, Henry II laid down that if a dispute arose between a layman and a cleric as to whether land was alms or lay fee, and both litigants vouched the same bishop or baron concerning the holding, the plea was to be held in the bishop or baron's court.[87] Accounts of disputes and private charters show even relatively unimportant lords holding courts. A mid-twelfth-century grant by Walter of Bolbec to the abbot of Ramsey is peculiarly revealing since it seeks to spell out the obligations of a lay fee:

> If the abbot does wrong in any matter towards lord Walter so that Walter wishes to implead him, the abbot shall come to his court and shall do him right as for a lay fee ... And if the lord, Walter of Bolbec, shall hold a plea in his court and shall desire the abbot to attend, the abbot shall come if he can, or send worthy representatives of his men in the aforesaid shires, and this by the usual summons and without dispute.[88]

Nevertheless, even if seignorial groups strove to be little states, this did not mean that they always resisted outside contact. Lords' courts were not just composed of their tenants, or even of their men. The presence of neighbours, sheriffs, or even royal justices is not uncommon in recorded instances of meetings of lords' courts.[89] The more powerful and prestigious those attending the court, the more effective it would be, the greater the honour which the lord assimilated. Effectiveness not autonomy was the essential aim.

Moreover, seignorial courts did not replace the local courts of Anglo-Saxon England, the hundred and the shire. The survival of these was a vital legacy to later legal development. Whilst, as suggested

[86] Pollock and Maitland, i 346.
[87] Stubbs, *Charters*, pp. 122, 166 (Constitutions of Clarendon, c. 9). See also e.g. *English Lawsuits*, no. 227.
[88] *Chronicon Abbatiae Rameseiensis*, ed. W. D. Macray (London, 1886), p. 275.
[89] See e.g. *English Lawsuits*, no. 164. Overlords' courts may also have had an important role, as places where grants might be made, or for the hearing of cases, including cases already heard in a lesser lord's court; see e.g. Stenton, *First Century*, no. 41; Hudson, *Land, Law, and Lordship*, pp. 35, 38, 140–1.

above, the process of Conquest and settlement strengthened the influence of lordship, scattered patterns of settlement restricted the numbers of areas dominated by one lord. A county such as Oxfordshire lacked one dominant magnate, and the most influential people in the county court might be men of very limited national significance.[90] This also meant that in the county court Englishmen and English practices continued to have some important influence, for example upon procedure. Changes in practice were likely to be gradual rather than revolutionary. This was still more true of the hundred court. The lower down one passes in society, the more limited may have been the impact of Conquest upon law.

Does this multiplicity of courts indicate confusion, as Maitland suggested? There is little sign that contemporaries were confused. In fact, in matters of law as well as others, lords and king can often be seen to cooperate. Lords' courts were part of the Norman regime for ruling a conquered country. Moreover, if one takes the view-point of disputants, the existence of a choice between a variety of courts, lacking strict jurisdictional boundaries, may have created not confusion but distinct advantages. If conflicts over jurisdiction did arise, or if one party felt that it had suffered a wrongful decision which it could reverse, the king's courts sometimes heard cases of 'defect of justice'.[91] When Henry II looked back to his grandfather's reign, he surely did not see it as a time of confusion, but as one of justice, closely connected to strong kingship and good lordship.

A complicated mixture of clear change and continuing developments can also be seen with regard to land-holding. Again, lordship entered more fully into the creation and conceptualization of land-holding relationships. Most Anglo-Norman charters chose the lord's officers, barons, and men as the appropriate audience to which to announce his grants. A ceremony of seising of the man by the lord initiated the tenurial relationship, and lordship continued to play a noteworthy part especially between the two initial parties to the relationship.[92] A single piece of land might descend by a series of grants

[90] R. V. Lennard, *Rural England* (Oxford, 1959), ch. 3, esp. pp. 61–2.
[91] M. G. Cheney, 'A decree of King Henry II on defect of justice', in D. E. Greenway *et al.*, eds, *Tradition and Change* (Cambridge, 1985), pp. 183–93; on Henry I see also Hudson, *Land, Law, and Lordship*, e.g. pp. 136–8, and more generally J. A. Green, *The Government of England under Henry I* (Cambridge, 1986), esp. chs 4 and 5.
[92] Milsom, *Legal Framework*, goes furthest in integrating lordship and land-holding. See also Hudson, *Land, Law and Lordship*, esp. pp. 16–21, chs 5, 7. Cf. Maitland, 'Mystery of seisin', *Collected Papers*, i 365, 'unless we are to suppose a time when seisin meant not mere possession but possession given, or at least recognized, by the lord of the fee. But for imagining any such time we have no warrant.'

through various levels of lord and tenant, and the very arrangement of Domesday Book reflects such a hierarchy of land-holding relationships.[93]

Change in the form of land-holding was clearest in the upper levels of society. Terminological evidence here supports a conclusion which might be reached *a priori* from the replacement of an Anglo-Saxon aristocracy with a French one. The word *feudum* — fief or fee — achieved predominance. In the period 1066–1100 it came to be used not only to mean the actual tenement, but also to classify certain lands as held 'in fee', that is heritably and by secular service, often, but not always, military.[94] The Anglo-Saxon word *bocland*, meanwhile, all but disappeared. When, during the first half of the twelfth century, men sought to translate *bocland*, they adopted a variety of words. They knew that *bocland* and *feudum* were not easy alternatives, for the terminological shift reflected changes in substantive law.[95]

Since Maitland's time, there has been a considerable increase in the number of charters available for the study of land law.[96] In particular, there are more complete collections, and more documents relating to lay grantees. These, taken with other evidence, allow a more complete, more nuanced assessment.[97] Various perceptions of rights in land

---

[93] Reynolds, *Fiefs and Vassals*, pp. 336–7, 345–6, where it is suggested that Domesday Book itself may have greatly sharpened perceptions of such a hierarchy.

[94] Hudson, *Land, Law, and Lordship*, pp. 94–7; see also Pollock and Maitland, i 234–5.

[95] Cf. the arguments of D. Roffe, 'From thegnage to barony', *ANS*, 12 (1990), 157–76, and Reynolds, *Fiefs and Vassals*, ch. 8.

[96] On Maitland's desire for the editing of such charters, see E. J. King, 'John Horace Round and the *Calendar of Documents preserved in France*', *ANS*, 4 (1982), 93–103, 202–4.

[97] For this paragraph, see Hudson, *Land, Law, and Lordship*; also White, '*Raoul de Cambrai*', and J. G. H. Hudson, 'The origins of property', in Garnett and Hudson, eds, *Law and Government*, pp. 198–222. Maitland's treatment e.g. of alienability reflects in part the sources available to him. (For other factors, see below, White, pp. 101–12). The lack of complete charter collections, except some ecclesiastical cartularies, helps to explain why Maitland did not adopt a statistical approach. His statements concerning the frequency of appearance of certain phrases in charters are sometimes vague and not always trustworthy; inevitably he tended to cite charters which did use a certain phrase, and not to deal with those which omitted it: e.g. ii 309 'the charters of the twelfth century afford numerous examples of expectant heirs joining in the gifts of their ancestors', and he took this as supporting 'the necessity for the heir's concurrence.' Cf. his treatment of lords' consent (i 340–1): 'For the period between 1066 and 1217 we have hundreds of English charters, and at first sight they seem to go the full length of proving that from the Conquest onward no tenant could alienate his land without his lord's consent .... But considerable care is necessary in drawing inferences from these documents. [For example, m]ost of the very early charters that we possess relate to gifts in frankalmoin, and, when examined, they will often appear to be confirmations and something more.' In fact, it is simply not the case that most charters recording grants even to the Church record either the lord's or the heir's consent to the donation. Various explanations are possible, some specific, some general. Each transaction involves a piece of land with its own history, and if it was the donor's own acquisition not

co-existed in Anglo-Norman England, differing for example with the order of those concerned — lay or ecclesiastical — or their position in a relationship — lord or tenant. The variety of perceptions could produce disputes, but also helped to sharpen thinking about land-holding. At least by 1135, the tenant in fee, particularly if he had inherited his lands rather than recently acquired them from a lord, generally enjoyed a position approaching that of a tenant in *Bracton*'s England. He had considerable security of tenure within his life-time, provided he fulfilled the services which he owed his lord. His heir, particularly if a close relative, would normally succeed him.[98] The tenant could also make grants from his lands, although his family or lord might challenge his actions on the grounds that they were unreasonable; their success in so doing would depend on a court's view of what constituted a reasonable grant. He himself, his heirs, and his grantees all enjoyed protection from a variety of sources. Royal intervention was at least a possibility which needed to be considered by lords when dealing with their tenants. Clearly the situation was not identical to that in the thirteenth century. In the Anglo-Norman period, a greater variety of non-legal factors might more seriously affect land-holding relationships, the hard cases which custom might allow to arise were more numerous, reliance on royal remedies was less. However, particularly because tenure in fee spread down society, Anglo-Norman land law made a notable contribution to later Common Law, both in its apparent lack of regional variation and in the very substance of its customs.

Land tenures other than holding in fee may owe much to Anglo-Saxon practice, and many tenants would have been of English descent.[99] Socage, which was to be the great residuary tenure of later Common Law, may well have preserved characteristics of some of the tenures which Domesday Book simply described as 'holding freely'. Lands which in the Anglo-Saxon period were thegnages may quite

---

his inheritance, his heir's consent may not have been necessary; even now, let alone in Maitland's day, it is often very hard to discover whether land was inheritance or acquisition, and hence to interpret the absence of consents from land grants. Also, silence may be a sign that consent was so necessary that it was assumed, or may indicate a real lack of consent. It is indeed over the interpretation of silences, and the assumptions they hide and reveal, that Professor Milsom has diverged furthest from Maitland.

[98] Cf. Maitland's views on the development of primogeniture, Pollock and Maitland, ii esp. 266, 274, 309, and White, below, pp. 108–10.

[99] There may also have been greater continuity in the forms of holding lands from churches, notably by lease; see e.g. Roffe, 'Thegnage', 172. One reason why there may have been greater continuity with regard to land-holding lower in society and offences against the person and moveables as opposed to aristocratic land-holding is that matters concerning the former would have been dealt with largely in the local shire or hundred courts.

often have re-emerged later in sergeanties. Connections can rarely be proved, but they receive strong support when one necessarily adopts Maitland's method of working backwards to the scraps of pre-Conquest information.[100]

Likewise, there was probably considerable continuity across the Conquest in law dealing with wrong-doing against the person or moveable goods.[101] Pollock and Maitland saw the Anglo-Saxon response to such offences as characterized by fixed monetary scales of payments to the king (*wites*) and compensations to the victim or kin (*wer* and *bót*). The death penalty was largely reserved for those unable to make such payments, and for a few, very serious, 'unemendable' offences. Maitland believed such a system continued beyond the Conquest.[102] Here, as elsewhere in Anglo-Norman sections of the *History*, he relied heavily on the *Leges*: 'the writer of the *Leges Henrici* represents the criminal law of his time as being in the main the old law, and we have no reason to doubt the truth of what he tells us.'[103] In general, Maitland was willing to treat the *Leges* with some trust if they were not contradicted by other evidence. However, there are signs in the second edition of the *History* that Maitland's distrust of at least some of the *Leges* was growing, encouraged by Liebermann's recent work.[104] Such caution is no doubt justified. Take the *Leges Henrici Primi*. Certain sections reveal what to us is one of the author's greatest weaknesses.

---

[100] See J. Campbell, 'Some agents and agencies of the late Anglo-Saxon state', in J. C. Holt, ed., *Domesday Studies* (Woodbridge, 1987), 210–12; Roffe, 'Thegnage', 171–2; note also F. W. Maitland, 'Northumbrian Tenures', in his *Collected Papers*, ii 96–109; G. W. S. Barrow, 'Northern English society in the twelfth and thirteenth centuries', *Northern History* 4 (1969), 1–28. Note also the social relegation of the heriot, owed by the aristocracy in Anglo-Saxon England, but only by the peasantry in thirteenth-century Common Law.

[101] See also Wormald, above.

[102] See Pollock and Maitland, i 105–7, ii 449–62, 514.

[103] Pollock and Maitland, ii 457; see also i 97ff., 300, cf. i 312, and also 'The law of real property', *Collected Papers*, i 176–7, which stated with reference to land law that the compiler's 'work is bad and untrustworthy'. Apart from Domesday Book itself, the *Leges* are the main source for Essay I in *Domesday Book and Beyond*. However, in the Anglo-Saxon chapter of the *History* it is stated, presumably by Pollock, that 'some details we find on the subject [of kinship] in the so-called laws of Henry I. fall under grave suspicion, not merely of an antiquary's pedantic exaggeration, but of deliberate copying from other Germanic law-texts', Pollock and Maitland, i 32.

[104] See Pollock and Maitland, i 100 n. 1 ('literary vanity'), cf. (1895) i 78 n. 1. In the second edition, i 104, the man responsible for the *Leges Edwardi* was called a 'romancer', in the first edition, i 81, he was the 'writer'. Note also the change made at i 27 where the *Leges Willelmi/Leis Willelmi* are demoted from a position at the end of the tradition of Anglo-Saxon laws — (1895) i 3 — to a 'second class of documents, namely, compilations of customs and formulas which are not known ever to have had any positive authority.' The change presumably was made by Maitland. The manuscript of the *History* shows Maitland already struggling with the *Leges* in the early 1890s: *Cambridge University Library*, Add. MS 6987, f. 101 (= 1st ed., i 79), displays an almost unique amount of re-adjustment on the fair copy.

He drew on books, and he drew on personal experience. However, when written sources and personal experience clashed, his inclination was always to go by the book. This must reduce our willingness to use his text whenever it rests upon, or seeks to take into account, a written text. Like his inclusion of reliefs based upon Cnut's laws, his inclusion of *wergilds* and *bóts* based upon Alfred's tells us very little about the law of his own day.[105]

Other historians have contrasted the Anglo-Saxon period, characterised by a system of fixed *wer*, *bót*, and *wite*, with the Norman period, characterized by arbitrary amercements to the king and wider use of the death penalty and mutilation.[106] However, the distinctions are perhaps too sharp. Use of the death penalty and mutilation for serious offences were characteristic of Anglo-Saxon as well as Anglo-Norman law.[107] In addition, *wites* and amercements may have been very similar. Presumably it was the desire to avoid punishment which lay behind the payment of *wite*. As to their fixed amounts, it may be a peculiarity of the relevant sources that emphasizes precision. What the Anglo-Saxon laws, the post-Conquest *Leges*, and the Domesday customs may intend to indicate by their scales of payment is good practice, the equivalent of post-Conquest statements that the emendation or amercement should fit the offence.[108] Other evidence, for example relating to heriots, shows that scales of payment provided by law-codes were not rigidly followed in practice in Anglo-Saxon England. And whilst *wites* were less fixed than the codes suggest, readers of the plea rolls will know how standardised the supposedly arbitrary amercement could become.

The codes' precise statements of *wers* and *bóts* should be treated with the same caution as those of *wites*. Compensations may have been negotiated according to circumstances. For serious and intentional offences, any regular use of compensations enforced in court — as opposed to negotiated in out-of-court settlements — may have been disappearing by Henry I's reign at the latest, if not already in the Anglo-Saxon period. For lesser offences, such flexible payments of compensation survived into thirteenth-century law regarding trespass.[109]

Assessment of the Anglo-Norman period, both its innovations and

[105] *LHP*, 14, 93, Downer, pp. 118, 292–8. See also e.g. *LHP*, 70.20, Downer, p. 224 on parents inheriting; comment in Hudson, *Land, Law, and Lordship*, p. 115.
[106] Note esp. J. Goebel, *Felony and Misdemeanor* (New York, 1937).
[107] See above, Wormald, p. 14.
[108] See e.g. Magna Carta, c. 20. I take Henry I Coronation Charter, c. 8, to be such a statement, not a restoration of an old system of absolutely fixed *wites*; cf. e.g. Goebel, *Felony*, p. 384.
[109] Cf. Pollock and Maitland, ii 523. Likewise, proof by oath continued for lesser offences.

its continuations from the Anglo-Saxon past, thus suggests a more gradualist explanation of the formation of the Common Law than might be gained from some readings of Maitland, and especially from his chapter on the 'Age of Glanvill'. However, Maitland's main distinction between Anglo-Norman law and early Common Law was not concerned, for example, with the substance of inheritance patterns. Rather, it emphasized Common Law's widespread use of standardized royal remedies, the forms of action characterized by their writs and their juries. Such a distinction, now framed in terms of classification, routinization, and bureaucratization, still largely holds good. Developments were certainly under way before 1135, and a wide range of underlying factors, for example increasingly literate government, continued to work in this direction. However — paradoxically perhaps — it is in relation to the timing and speed of the shift towards new administrative forms that the events of Stephen's reign provided a great stimulus to Common Law's development. They brought an end to an extremely powerful regime, dating back into the Anglo-Saxon period, a regime notable for its simplicity, in which royal contact tended to be with areas and key local officials, not the great mass of individual subjects.[110] The accession of Henry II was accompanied by the need for reconstruction. In some cases, this took the form of more routine royal enforcement of existing customs and procedures. It is in this context that many requirements in the Assizes of Clarendon and Northampton can best be understood.[111] At the same time, royal government took new directions, notably in the extent of its contact with individuals in the localities, particularly through the eyre. The combination and inter-reaction of such administration with existing customs and practices produced Maitland and *Bracton*'s Common Law.

---

[110] See generally J. Campbell, 'Obervations on English government from the tenth to the twelfth century', *TRHS*, 5th Ser. 25 (1975), 39–54.

[111] In this sense, royal perceptions of good custom would underlie the assizes just as they explicitly appear in the Constitutions of Clarendon. For further discussion, see e.g. Hudson, *Land, Law, and Lordship*, p. 69 on Assize of Northampton, c. 4; cf. e.g. Pollock and Maitland, i 571 on presentment by frankpledge as an innovation from the Assize of Clarendon. I would like to thank Rob Bartlett, George Garnett, and Patrick Wormald for their help with this essay.

Proceedings of the British Academy, **89**, 47–64

The Writs of Henry II

J. C. HOLT

THIS PAPER ORIGINATED in something between an invitation and a challenge 'to tell us about all those charters you've collected'. By some mysterious process it subsequently acquired a formidable title which you will all recognize — 'The Age of Glanvill', and it was in something like panic that I had it reduced to the present topic. But even that is too large, and I shall restrict myself to a small number of matters — first, the collection of *acta* which is now housed in the Faculty of History at Cambridge, the state of the archive, its management, and the prospects of completion. I shall then discuss some of the problems which the work has brought to mind, and I shall focus attention in the end on the writs of Henry II, particularly those which belong to the first years of his reign.

But we are here to celebrate the *History of English Law*, and it is well to begin with Maitland's chapter, 'The Age of Glanvill'. The wonder of it is that he could construct so intricate a fabric with so little material. Admittedly, this included all the larger building blocks — the Assizes of Henry II and Richard I, the texts of *Glanvill*, the *Dialogus de Scaccario*, and Magna Carta, with which he ends the chapter. But for filling the spaces in between these major items he had to make do with selections from Bigelow's *Placita Anglo-Normannica*[1] and Palgrave[2], and with documents and related narratives recorded in the chronicles of Abingdon, Battle, St. Albans and elsewhere, evidence which in these cliometric days we are inclined to classify as anecdotal. His insight did the rest, first and foremost perhaps his appreciation that justice was a commodity. 'Thus', he writes,

> before the end of Henry's reign we must already begin to think of royal justice — and this is becoming by far the most important kind of justice — as consisting of many various commodities each of which is kept in a different

[1] M. M. Bigelow, *Placita Anglo-Normannica, Law Cases from William I to Richard I* (Boston, 1881).
[2] Francis Palgrave, *The Rise and Progress of the English Commonwealth* (London, 1832).

receptacle. Between these the would-be litigant must make his choice; he must choose an appropriate writ and with it an appropriate form of action. These wares are exposed for sale; perhaps some of them may already be had at fixed prices, for others a bargain must be struck. As yet the king is no mere vendor, he is a manufacturer and can make goods to order.[3]

And again in his concluding remarks on the Anstey case:

[The king] no doubt sold his aid; he would take gifts with both hands; he expected to be paid for his trouble. He sold justice, but it was a better article than was to be had elsewhere.[4]

These are remarkable passages, at once imaginative and down to earth. They stand in sharp contrast to the somewhat flat account given by Stubbs.[5] They are a measure of the enormous advance which Maitland achieved. Stubbs's approach was institutional. Maitland, in contrast, got inside the litigant.

Now note what Maitland did not do. He did not pursue the speciation of writs or the pedigree of particular writs. He could have done so. He had to hand the precedent of Bigelow, for the Introduction to *Placita Anglo-Normannica* (which had been in print for fourteen years when the *History of English Law* appeared), time and again takes such a line. Take Bigelow's comment on writs of Henry I — 'The next writ gives promise, though vaguely, of the writ of novel disseisin of Glanvill'[6] . . . 'Another writ to the same party points more directly to the writ of Glanvill'[7] . . . 'The next writ in order in the reign of Henry I, to which, however, no date is assigned, indicates a fluctuation, if the writ be later in time, receding to the unsettled state of the earlier writs referred to'[8] — a deviant writ, that one, a throwback to the primordial Anglo-Norman form. Then — 'The promise of Glanvill, as above indicated, disappears again in the times of Stephen' . . . and finally, almost safely harboured after its long voyage — 'The form of the later writ reappears more distinctly than ever at the beginning of the reign of Henry II'.[9]

Now Bigelow was not alone in following this line. Round's researches into the earliest fines led him in the same direction. He talked of the emergence of the 'true' final concord by 1175 from earlier inchoate forms and he was disposed to correlate the diplomatic to the dating.

[3] Pollock and Maitland, i 151.
[4] Ibid., 159.
[5] Stubbs's comments also suffer from being fragmented. See *Constitutional History of England* (3 vols, Oxford, 1897), i 506–9, 522–3, 614–8, 638–67.
[6] Bigelow, p. xxiv.
[7] Ibid.
[8] Ibid., pp. xxiv–v.
[9] Ibid., p. xxv.

Dealing with an early fine of 1163, different in form from his first 'true' fine of 1175, he commented:

> It may fairly be presumed that if, at the date of this fine, the fully developed form existed it would have been duly employed at Westminster on this occasion. We may therefore safely assert, at least, that it came into use between the dates of these two transactions.[10]

And since those early days the efforts of Bigelow and Round have developed into a major industry. In 1959 Professor van Caenegem rightly warned against a teleological approach in which historians 'tended to work against the stream of history and to focus on the classic period [*Glanvill* and *Bracton*] and to throw glances back for "early examples" of certain writs and certain institutions'.[11] Nevertheless, his *Royal Writs* is a monument, not to the error as he saw it, but to the basic method, ordered as his book is, writ by writ and action by action.

The effect has been to create a vast phylogeny of writs necessarily subject to all the limitations which such an approach involves. Difficulties were apparent within a few years of the appearance of *Royal Writs*. In 1963 Doris Stenton contended that the writs which van Caenegem there saw as precedents for novel disseisin were in fact examples of the *justicies* and viscontiel writs.[12] So there have been difficulties of inter-specific definition. There are other problems. There are large assumptions in the supposition that there was some kind of logical development in the form and definition of writs over half a century or more, assumptions about the transmission of administrative practices now very difficult to determine, a transmission which in some way has to traverse the reign of Stephen.[13] Then again it is obvious that the approach looks at the evidence vertically, over time, each stage of development resting on its predecessor. Lifting the writs from their immediate context, it steers us away from a lateral or panoramic view of all the evidence at a particular point in time, and this has some

---

[10] J. H. Round, *Feudal England* (London, 1895), p. 515. Two years after the appearance of the *History of English Law* Round pursued the matter further in 'The earliest fines', *EHR*, 12 (1897), 293–302. See also F. W. Maitland, *Select Pleas of the Crown* (Selden Society, 1, 1888), pp. xxvii–xxviii. Both Maitland and Round commented on the need to collect and publish the early fines (Pollock and Maitland, ii 97n.; *EHR*, 12, 296). It has yet to be done. All fines earlier than 1216 discovered in pursuing the *acta* have been copied and await filing.
[11] R. C. van Caenegem, *Royal Writs in England from the Conquest to Glanvill*, (Selden Society, 77, 1959), p. 14.
[12] Doris M. Stenton, *English Justice between the Norman Conquest and the Great Charter* (Philadelphia, 1964), pp. 80–2.
[13] Some of the continuities are apparent from T. A. M. Bishop, *Scriptores Regis* (Oxford, 1961).

importance when considering the terms of the Treaty of Winchester of 1153 and the circumstances of the accession of Henry II. Finally, it is concerned almost entirely with the supply of justice and says nothing at all about the demand for justice.

Now Maitland has none of this. He came closest to it, very briefly, in his discussion of final concords,[14] but in examining forms of action, where above all one might expect him to resort to such an approach, he was remarkably cautious, expressing his caution in characteristically nuanced phrases:

> We do indeed come upon writs which seem as it were to foretell the fixed formulas of a later age; we are sometimes inclined to say 'This is a writ of right, that a writ of debt, that a writ of trespass'; but we have little reason to suppose that the work of issuing writs had as yet become a matter of routine entrusted to subordinate officers whose duty was to copy from models. Perhaps no writ went out without the approval of the king himself or the express direction of his justiciar or chancellor, and probably every writ was a purchaseable favour.[15]

We can look for continuities with greater confidence now after the work of van Caenegem and Bishop, but Maitland's doubts help to explain why there is no resort to phylogenetic methods in the chapter on the 'Age of Glanvill'. There was also a more powerful reason. Maitland throughout was conscious that justice was a matter of both supply and demand [though he never put it so crudely]. The interplay of the two runs through the passages which have already been quoted and is revealed most clearly of all in his comment on the Anstey case:

> Many comments might be made upon this story. It will not escape us that in these early years of Henry's reign royal justice is still very royal indeed. Though the king has left his justiciar in England, there is no one here who can issue what we might have supposed to be ordinary writs. A great change in this most important particular must soon have taken place. The judicial rolls of Richard I's reign were largely occupied by accounts of law-suits about very small pieces of ground between men of humble station, men who could not have laboured as Anstey laboured or spent money as he spent it.[16]

That may leave us with doubts and queries. Was there really no-one

---

[14] 'After some tentative experiments a fixed form of putting compromises on parchment seems to have been evolved late in Henry II's reign . . .' (Pollock and Maitland, ii 96–7). Maitland was influenced here by Round.

[15] F. W. Maitland, *Equity, also The Forms of Action at Common Law* (Cambridge, 1909), p. 315.

[16] Pollock and Maitland, i 159. For a full account of the Anstey case see Patricia M. Barnes, 'The Anstey Case' in *A Medieval Miscellany for Doris Mary Stenton* (PRS, ns 36, 1962), pp. 1–24.

in England in Anstey's time to issue ordinary writs in the king's absence? Or was it that Richard of Anstey sought something special? Is the great change which Maitland imagined partly to be explained by the fact that the plea rolls are the first source to give us evidence of the legal actions of the humble? And in any case were litigants all that humble? These are legitimate doubts, not all of which can be resolved. But they are minor qualifications to the main point. Between 1154 and 1200 there was a vast increase in the demand for justice, and if we are to talk about the supply, we first have to understand the demand.

Now let me turn to the *acta*. The project was launched with two entirely new resources. The first was the photocopier, or, as it was the first known, the xerox machine. The arrival of this in universities and libraries in the late 1950s transformed the enormous labour of transcription which had dogged earlier scholars, Salter, Galbraith and Doris Stenton, all of whom attempted a collection of the acts and then sensibly turned away from it. Of these Salter made the most serious effort. His photographs descended to Galbraith, then to Pierre Chaplais, and they have been used in the present project. The difference between Salter's day and ours lies in this: of all the documents which are now on file not more than a dozen or so have been transcribed by hand; manual transcription is used only when camera or copier prove inadequate. In the last resort there is nothing quite like the human eye, but eye and hand are unacceptably slow for a task of this dimension.

The second resource was quite accidental. It is quite impossible for a University teacher to undertake the task alone; it requires an office and an assistant. Few now will remember 'the March windfall', the occasion when the University Grants Committee found that it was approaching the end of the Quinquennium of 1967–72 underspent, with vast sums still in hand. Panic ensued — pleasurable panic, it must be said; it is the only occasion when I can recall being asked whether I could possibly *increase* my bid for new appointments. Out of this flash flood of funds the University of Reading was able to provide money — £1000 a year, no less! — for a part-time assistantship for which I had originally submitted a somewhat hopeless bid. So the work started unexpectedly. Since then it has gone steadily forward, supported regularly by the British Academy and from time to time by the Leverhulme Trust and other sources. It was housed in the University of Reading up to 1978, and since then in the Faculty of History at Cambridge. It is not very impressive visually — a very small room, three filing cabinets, eight card index boses, and a research assistant surrounded by works of reference and copies of documents in process. It began before the personal computer came on the scene. Of that more in a moment.

The operation has a two-fold purpose: first to provide a collection of source material, an archive, ultimately open to all scholars, of the acts of Henry II, Richard I, Eleanor of Aquitaine, John count of Mortain, and other members of the family, to fill the gap, in short, between the existing *Regesta Regum Anglo-Normannorum* and the first surviving chancery enrolments of 1199–1201; and secondly, to prepare the acts for publication, starting, for obvious reasons, with the acts of Henry II. To this end a database was planned a year or so ago. It is restricted to Henry II and will remain so confined until the work on Henry is completed. So far it has advanced to a skeletal structure for all the writs; that is to say it does not yet include texts. Hence I can talk with greater assurance about writs than charters; hence also my unreadiness to engage in serious questions of diplomatic.

So the work began in October 1972. Twenty years on (for there have been occasional interludes) we have nearly 4000 documents on file, most of them in multiple copies — original, *inspeximus*, cartulary, transcript, and print. I say 'we'. In the beginning I had the staunch support of Barbara Dodwell, and, in all, five research assistants have played their part. It is a co-operative work, and it can be done in no other way. So 'we' means a team, which has lost old, and taken on new, members from time to time.

Despite the compression into three filing cabinets, there is an awesome impression of bulk; *in toto*, taking into account all the copies, the archive probably comprises somewhere between 20 and 30,000 documents; we have never counted accurately because we could see no point in doing so. On the other hand the number of distinct *acta* is important. Several estimates have hitherto been made of the total surviving royal acts of the monarchs of the twelfth century. The most frequently quoted is that of Bishop who guessed at 'about 5000' acts for the period between 1100 and 1189.[17] This is an underestimate. In rough arithmetic, based on the volumes of the *Regesta*, Henry I accounts for just under 1500, Stephen and Matilda for just under 1000, leaving 2500 for Henry II. In fact our holdings for Henry II are already approaching 2500, with more to come. My guess is that the total for him will end at about 3000. This is a healthy increase on Bishop. Even so, his guess was a good one in his circumstances. Barbara Dodwell and I began by estimating that Henry II and Richard I together would

---

[17] *Scriptores Regis*, p. 32. Bishop's figure includes both English and continental *acta*.

yield 10,000 plus: we were wrong, and I am very glad that we were wrong and Bishop more nearly right.[18]

The collection includes some rich finds: some twenty original documents of Henry II not known to Bishop,[19] fifty acts of Henry II from continental repositories which were unknown to Delisle and Berger, and perhaps 200 acts of Richard, both as king and count of Poitou, and of Eleanor of Aquitaine not known to modern scholarship. Most remarkable of all has been the discovery of a mammoth edition of some 500 folios of the acts of Richard, both as count and king, complete with itineraries and indices, the forgotten life-work of Achille Déville. This survives only in manuscript in the Bibliothèque Nationale.[20] It has been by-passed by all modern scholars, both editors and biographers. Landon has one reference to it but clearly did not inspect it. It contains some 150 documents not in his *Itinerary of Richard I*.[21] Practically all this continental work has been done by Dr Nicholas Vincent. He has demonstrated what was already obvious: Landon's work on Richard I is hopelessly inadequate. More unnerving, he has shown that some of Delisle's texts of acts of Henry II are unsatisfactory. So also are parts of his apparatus. So ground hitherto regarded as firm is shifting alarmingly. We once thought that Delisle did not need reworking. Now we know that he does.[22]

The task will never be complete. Short cuts will be necessary. Not all the endless antiquarian collections in the Bibliothèque Nationale can be examined. At the Public Record Office it is unlikely that we shall be able to work systematically through the class of Ancient Petitions or the exchequer Memoranda Rolls; and only the insanely fanatic would pursue Henry II and Richard I through the unprinted records of the courts of King's Bench and Common Pleas. So lines have to be drawn. But, even so, something can be said of the state of the archive. First, work on continental repositories is almost concluded and the holdings of material referring to the continental possessions of the Angevins is more than 95 per cent complete. Britain is not so

---

[18] Van Caenegem reports rather different totals for Bishop (*Royal Writs*, p. 4 and n.), but he relied on Bishop's thesis, where Bishop went for a higher figure of *c.* 750 originals and 5000–6000 copies for the period 1100–1189. Curiously these are closer to the truth. It is not clear why Bishop reduced them in *Scriptores*.

[19] J. C. Holt and Richard Mortimer, *Acta of Henry II and Richard I: hand-list of documents surviving in the original in repositories in the United Kingdom*, (List and Index Society, special series, 21, 1986), p. 1.

[20] Paris, BN, NAL, 1244.

[21] L. Landon, *Itinerary of Richard I* (PRS, ns 17, 1937). The solitary reference is at p. 157, no. 225.

[22] The above figures are based on Dr Nicholas Vincent's 'Angevin Acta in France: Final Report', October 1994.

far advanced. It is probable that 20 per cent of the English material still has to be collected. Now this necessarily affects the force of the conclusions and suggestions which I intend to advance. Those concerning the continental lands, even where negative, are for all practical purposes certain. Those concerning England depend on a balance of probabilities, though strong probabilities. More important perhaps, there are questions concerning dating, diplomatic and other matters which are not worth attempting to answer until the collection is complete. So on a number of interesting matters — I am thinking of the use of diplomatic evidence to determine dating — I shall not even try to be tentative. I shall simply say nothing at all.[23]

On the most important conclusion of all I shall be very brief. It is simply this: there was no such thing as an Angevin Empire stretching in a homogenous *regimen* from the Cheviots to the Pyrenees. Some seven years ago I hazarded a guess that very few acts of Henry II would be found for the southern provinces of the Plantagenet lands.[24] This is now certain. There is an *acta* frontier following the southern border of the *comté* of Anjou. South of that Henry II acted in and for a number of obvious centres. Poitiers, Fontevrault, Bordeaux: these apart, very few acts, certainly less than 50 of the total collection of 2500, concern beneficiaries of any kind, monastery or church, town or tenants, throughout the vast reaches of Aquitaine. Here such acts as survive derive from Eleanor of Aquitaine and Richard count of Poitou. They chiefly comprise confirmations of earlier grants and alienations by the dukes of Aquitaine, along with letters of protection and privileges of toll. They reflect a somewhat different authority and a very different ducal function from Henry's in the north, not to mention his role as king of England. Eleanor sums the matter up. As queen of England, acting as regent in Henry's absence, she issued writs in no way different from those of her husband. As duchess of Aquitaine she issued charters and mandates little different from those of the dukes her predecessors. Administratively she was a split personality working within two quite distinct administrative matrices. The one does not seem to have affected the other to any great degree.

[23] Meanwhile, in addition to Bishop, see Pierre Chaplais, *English Royal Documents King John — Henry VI 1199–1461* (Oxford, 1971), which includes some invaluable comments on the twelfth century, and Norbert Friedrich, *Die Diplomatische und Rechtshistorische Entwicklung der Insularen Writs unter König Heinrich II von England (1154–1189) und ihr Verhältnis zu der Kontinentalen Urkunden*, (Inauguraldissertation, Ruhr-Universität, Bochum, 1977).

[24] J. C. Holt, 'The *acta* of Henry II and Richard I 1154–1199: the archive and its historical implications' in Peter Ruck, ed., *Fotografische Sammlungen mittelalterlicher Urkunden in Europa*, (Marburg, 1989), pp. 137–40.

I have dealt with the southern provinces in summary fashion because they are now in the hands of Dr Vincent from whom we can expect a major paper on the subject.

Yet I intend to deal with one matter here and now because it is part of a larger picture which includes all the Plantagenet lands. At the time of writing (April, 1995) we have collected 2452 acts of Henry II. Those familiar with the collection of Delisle and Berger of acts concerning France will recall that they total 768, in short 31 per cent of the total. But in fact they included many acts concerning Britain and the proportion of English acts is much higher than 69 per cent — it is probably nearer 80 per cent, if not more.[25] Now Alison Cawley made similar calculations for Richard I.[26] In his case, using figures based on Landon's collection, she showed that of 590 acts (including reseals), 433 (73 per cent) concern England, 117 (22 per cent) concern Normandy, 15 (2·5 per cent) concern Anjou, and 25 (4 per cent) Aquitaine. And even these figures underestimate English preponderance. They are dependent on the preservation of documents by beneficiaries and on the survival of beneficiaries' records. These were probably roughly constant factors throughout the Plantagenet realm. But they necessarily exclude documents, especially writs, which beneficiaries had no reason to preserve, and hence all the vast number of letters which were sealed close and circulated within the offices of government and increasingly from 1166 onwards in many civil actions in the English royal courts. Almost none of these survive. If we had a proportionate selection of them to hand the preponderance of England, and to a lesser extent Normandy, would be even greater, for the two Exchequers generated business and used written instruments out of all proportion to any other institutions elsewhere within the dominion. They also developed new forms of document which now survive only in the kingdom and the duchy; the final concord is an obvious example.

Now this broad count bypasses the functions of the seneschal and other officers of the count/duke in the southern provinces. Beginning with Powicke, English scholars have revelled in the evidence which points to a centralized system of control operated by seneschals exercising vice-regal jurisdiction.[27] And to be sure, in Anjou for example,

---

[25] Delisle and Berger included documents of all kinds. My calculations at this point are approximate because so far only the writs have been entered on the database.

[26] Alison Cawley, 'The King and his Vassals: a study of the chancery of Richard I', BA dissertation, University of Cambridge, 1982.

[27] *The Loss of Normandy* (Manchester, 1961), especially pp. 18–35. See also John Le Patourel, 'The Plantagenet Dominions', *History*, (1965), 289–308, reprinted in John Le Patourel, *Feudal Empires* (London, 1984); W. L. Warren, *Henry II* (London, 1973), especially pp. 561–2; and John Gillingham, *The Angevin Empire* (London, 1984), pp. 54–9.

we find the seneschal exercising judgment with the prévôt and other witnesses in a civil action in a court of Anjou, *curia Andegavensis*, which is also described as a *curia regis*.[28] I do not intend to get tangled in this well established approach. We badly need a comparative study of the activity of these officials which assembles all the documents in full. We have not attempted to embody such material in the *acta* (enough is enough!) except where it includes a specific mention of direct royal authorization. In any case my concern is not with provincial processes, whether centralized or local, but with the frequency to which recourse was made to them.

On this surviving writs shed a harsh light. However we cast the figures English documents and English interests are massively predominant. From this point on I am dealing not with the total collection but with the writs; I have no reason to believe that they are not representative of the whole. Of the total of 887 writs at present on file 719 (81 per cent) concern England, 131 (15 per cent) concern Normandy, and 32 (4 per cent) the rest of France (including Clairvaux). Of the 602 writs issued in England 570 (95 per cent) concern England, 20 (3.5 per cent) concern Normandy, and 10 (2 per cent) concern the rest of France. Of the 180 writs issued in Normandy, 69 (38 per cent) concern England, 100 (56 per cent) concern Normandy, and 9 (5 per cent) the rest of France. Of the 34 writs issued in Anjou and provinces west and south 19 (56 per cent) concern England, 3 (9 per cent) concern Normandy, and 12 (35 per cent) concern the rest of France.[29] Alison Cawley provides equally startling figures for Richard I, totalling all the *acta* from Landon. She showed that in every year of his reign, except 1190, wherever Richard was, Normandy, Anjou, Aquitaine, Germany or the Holy Land, English acts exceeded, or in one year matched, *all* the rest.[30] I leave the defenders of the 'Angevin Empire' to embody this evidence in their arguments. A repair job may be possible. It could be that in the case of Aquitaine the void is filled by the acts of Eleanor and Richard as count of Poitou. That must await on Dr Vincent. But such a saving operation would not apply to Anjou where there is a similar void; perhaps there the void is filled by acts of the seneschals. But even if all this rejigging fell nicely into place we should end not so much with a building restored as with a series of semidetached and detached

---

[28] Jacques Boussard, *Le Comté d'Anjou sous Henri Plantagenet et ses Fils*, Bibliothèque de L'École des Hautes Études, fasc. 261 (1938), pp. 178–9. This is one of several possible interpretations of a somewhat enigmatic record.

[29] The reader will note a reduced overall total at this point. It occurs chiefly because some documents cannot be given a secure place-date.

[30] In 1190 England was preponderant everywhere except in Anjou where the largest number of acts was directed to Normandy.

properties, their owners and managers each jealous of his enclave. For our present purposes it is apparent that in the case of both Henry and Richard, the figures are only marginally affected by the king's itinerary. Under Henry Norman acts predominated in Normandy; elsewhere the predominance of England comes through strong and clear. And it is worth noting that this seems to contravene the evidence from England itself, where it becomes apparent, as the information becomes more and more detailed, that local men and institutions came in to seek privileges and judgment from the king as he moved about the country, so that the record of these dealings, the Fine roll, reflects the itinerary.

Now every writ or charter has to be triggered by something. They do not spring in the total chronological disorder in which they survive from the royal mind or from impenetrable bureaucracy. In almost every case they are responses to requests — petitions from the beneficiary. This is the only possible explanation of the haphazard order in which they appear.[31] It is also very probable, though less subject to systematic proof, that they were handed over to the petitioner — the beneficiary or his agent — and taken by him to whatever authority was addressed or seemed most appropriate.[32] We have to imagine an almost infinite multiplicity of cases like Richard of Anstey, a traffic of monks, clerks, knights, stewards, all seeking this or that privilege or protection or support.

It is probable that the system was much less cumbersome than it seemed to Maitland in the light of the Anstey case. At its best communication was rapid and efficient. Consider the following example. On 17 April 1199 at Harcourt in Anjou John as lord of England issued a writ in favour of the canons of Wells — an original document, one of the most valued in the whole collection.[33] On 29 April at Westminster Geoffrey fitz Peter, King Richard's justiciar, issued a writ executing John's writ *de ultra mare*. That is an interval of 12 days, exactly the same as the maximum time allowed by today's Parcel Force for packages within the United Kingdom. The matter was entirely

[31] I have dealt with this in greater detail in 'The end of the Anglo-Norman realm', *PBA*, 61 (1975), 3–45, and in 'Ricardus Rex Anglorum et Dux Normannorum', *Accademia Nazionale dei Lincei*, 253 (1981), 17–33, reprinted in J. C. Holt, *Magna Carta and Medieval Government* (London, 1985). See pp. 30–2. 70–3.

[32] Bishop, pp. 2–3, referring to *Reg. Ant. Linc.*, i no. 57 — 'H. rex Anglorum Osberti vicecomiti salutem. Precipio tibi ut permittas ita habere huic Roberto de Grainvilla prebendam suam de Lincolnia ...' where 'huic' is the indicative word. This is a rare documentary example; there are many others in chronicle narratives. See, for example, *CMA* ii 226.

[33] Dean and Chapter of Wells, charter 14. The writ was issued before John had even been acclaimed as duke of Normandy. Nevertheless he adopted the style of lord of England, Normandy, Anjou and Aquitaine. He was moving fast: Richard died on 6 April; John was acclaimed as duke of Normandy on the 26th.

routine, confirming earlier grants and confirmations from Richard and John of the manor, hundred, and church of North Curry. The documents reveal what happened. John's writ was addressed to the knights and free tenants of the hundred of North Curry. But it was not sent or taken directly to them. Someone one took it instead to Geoffrey fitz Peter who then issued his writ. Then the same agent or another bore the two writs off to Wells where they remain lodged in the diocesan archives. The procedure was an informed one for it was designed to circumvent the fact that John was not yet king of England, and there can be little doubt as to who the agent was. Simon archdeacon of Wells was a clerk to the chamber of Richard Lionheart and he served in the same role in the early years of John. The most likely explanation of this expedited writ is that Simon himself obtained it in Anjou and may even have taken it himself to London along with other official business. At all events it almost certainly went from Harcourt to Westminster in what we would now call the official bag, and this at a time when John and his agents had very pressing business to do with the succession. There was a skilled and influential operator at work here. The private litigant and petitioner would be unlikely to match such speed. Nevertheless this evidence is concrete, the dates of both time and place are beyond challenge, and the case is well worth bearing in mind as a contrast to the extended itinerary of Richard of Anstey.

If now we accept the premise — no petition, no writ (and indeed no charter), the import of the evidence is quite clear. More English men and more English institutions were ready to seek out the king in his continental lands than were his continental vassals in England and even in their homelands. The figures preclude any easy explanation that kings were more powerful than dukes (although of course they were), or that there was less documentation and less surviving documentation in the southern provinces of the dominion. There is nothing to suggest that feudal and royal warranty was as yet in competition with the public notary and the practical application of Roman Law. The alternative argument of Professor van Caenegem, that the enclave of Common Law in England and Normandy survived because it antedated the spread of Roman Law may shed light on the general European scene.[34] But it cannot explain the confinement of the Common Law to England and Normandy within the Plantagenet lands. In 1154 general resort to the public notary in southern France lay perhaps a century or more into the future. It is simply that south of Normandy and even more south of Anjou, demand faded, demand for royal

---

[34] R. C. van Caenegem, *The Birth of the English Common Law* (Cambridge, 1973), pp. 85–92.

confirmation, royal warranty, royal jurisdiction. It is demand itself which varies as we traverse the provinces of the Plantagenet realm. The whole system as it is reflected in the surviving charters and writs was demand-led.

It is necessary now to deal with a possible reservation. It is this: it could be that the picture is distorted in some way by its entire dependence on the beneficiary. Every writ which we have on file was preserved by the immediate beneficiary or by a secondary beneficiary to whose archive it was transferred. It would be possible to argue that the preponderance of England reflects a special need to preserve documents as protective instruments in litigation — litigation necessarily determined by the structure and procedure of the courts, and this would bring us back in full circle to the supply-side and to the unique features of the Common Law. There is some truth in this: if demand created supply, supply shaped demand. But whether it affects the preservation of the documents is another matter. If a document is not going to be of much use in litigation it is unlikely that it will be obtained and then not preserved; it is more likely that it will not be sought in the first place. But there is a more telling argument than this simple one of common sense. The figures for both Henry II and Richard I depend, as we have seen, on preservation by beneficiaries. With King John it is a different matter, for the Chancery enrolments allow us to examine documents at the point of issue; preservation by beneficiaries is thereby made irrelevant.

Consider now the Charter roll for 1 John. That it was a Charter roll rather than a roll of letters patent does not matter for the present purpose; in fact it contains both charters and letters patent, though not many of the latter. It runs from May 1199 to May 1200. For nine months of the year, from July 1199 to February 1200, John was on the continent, mainly in Normandy and for a short period further south at Chinon, Poitiers and Niort. Hence his itinerary had a continental focus; it might well have been his father's. For the present purposes it is a peculiar year. Anjou was out of the count; under the seneschal, William des Roches, the Angevins had received Arthur of Brittany as Richard's successor. By contrast, the crisis in the succession generated more than normal business in Poitou and areas further south where John was hastily mending fences and securing loyalty and support. Ireland comes into the picture too — an element wholly absent at the accession of Henry II. But all these are very minor impediments in the way of a comparison. Of the total of 493 acts recorded on the roll, 347 (70 per cent) concern England, 65 (13 per cent) concern Normandy, and 53 (11 per cent) concern the rest of France. Wales and Ireland account for 28 (6 per cent). These are remarkable figures given that, from the brief visit to England for his coronation onwards, John's major concern was for the security of his continental possessions and the defeat of Arthur. The figures are equally decisive when related to the itinerary. Of the total of 205 acts issued in England all but 4 concern the British Isles; the total for Ireland and Wales (10) exceeds the total for the continent (4). Of the 276 documents issued in Normandy 156 (57 per cent) concern England, 62 (22 per cent) concern Normandy, and 44 (16 per cent) concern the rest of France. In Normandy John still found time for 14 acts (5 per cent) for Wales and Ireland. Finally, during John's brief visits to Chinon, Niort and Poitiers, 12 documents were issued of which 7 concerned the southern provinces. All in all, these figures, figures of issue remember, provide overwhelming confirmation of the calculations for Henry II and Richard. The somewhat higher figure (16 per cent) for documents for the southern provinces issued in Normandy is to be explained by the fact that many of these acts were at John's initiative. They were a response to the crisis caused by Arthur. That apart (and it is not a large divergence), the distribution of the acts of John as preserved in this chancery enrolment, is no different from the distribution of the writs of Henry II, as preserved by beneficiaries. We have to conclude that the geographic distribution of Henry's writs is accurately reflected in those which survive.

In another matter, however, this is very far from the case. I turn now to the social distribution of the writs. It is common ground that the church preserved its archives better than the layman. It is nevertheless surprising how dramatically this is revealed in the general social balance of the *acta*. Of the 887 writs, 653 were issued for monastic institutions (including the military orders and hospitals), 131 for cathedral churches, 64 for individuals, most, but not all, laymen, 21 for towns, and 18 of a miscellaneous nature. In short 88 per cent for the church, and fewer than 7 per cent for the laity. If all acts, charters as well as writs, are taken into account, it makes little difference — still less than 10 per cent for the laity. It is an emphatic difference, and it is given even greater emphasis by the charter roll of 1 John. Of the 493 documents there preserved 121 were for monastic institutions, 32 for cathedral churches, 270 for individuals, 33 for towns and 36 miscellanea. In short, 33 per cent for the church, 59 per cent for the laity — compared with Henry II, twice as many charters and writs for individuals than for monasteries, 8 times as many than for cathedral churches. Now admittedly in 1199–1200 King John was buying political support variously and lavishly. Even so, it is impossible to compare the

record for Henry's reign with that for John's first year without concluding that in Henry's case a vast number of acts in favour of the laity
have been lost, and a far higher proportion, perhaps 80 per cent of the
total issued, than anyone has imagined hitherto. By contrast is is very
likely that a really good ecclesiastical archive, Lincoln or Durham, for
example, preserves most if not all the acts issued in its church's favour.
The result is that the *acta* have a very strong ecclesiastical bias, accentu-
ated by the fact that lay documents are often preserved because they
became of interest to the church; ecclesiastical cartularies are one of
the main sources for them.

I turn finally to the chronology of the writs. For the purposes of
the database they have been divided into three chronological blocks.
The divisions occur at 1162, where the termination of Thomas Becket's
chancellorship provides a precise *terminus ante quem*, and at 1172/3
determined by the introduction of the *die gratia* formula with all its
well known difficulties.[35] Other, more precise methods have been used
for individual documents and much remains to be done, but within the
database even a precisely dated document has to be categorized; we
cannot work with a clutter of individual dates. Allowing for this rough
and ready method the preliminary calculations are not without interest.
Of our 887 writs 58 cannot be categorized; these consist of summaries
or 'mentions' to which no date can be attached other than 1154–89.
Of the remaining 829, 662 (80 per cent) belong to the period before
1172/3 and perhaps as many as 450 (54 per cent) to the period
before 1162. Within that the proportion of early (pre-1162) writs issued
for monasteries and cathedral churches is somewhat higher — 61 per
cent. The database does not yet extend to charters, but I expect them
to yield closely similar results for ecclesiastical beneficiaries. The total
of writs for individuals is too small to yield significant results, but the
total of all documents for individuals is interesting. Out of 256 the same
proportion was issued after 1172/3 as before 1162, *c*. 95 documents (37
per cent) in each case. The burst of activity after 1172/3 was probably
a result of the rebellion of 1173/4, but it is a very minor blip in
the figures compared with the very large numbers of writs issued to
ecclesiastical beneficiaries in the early years of the reign and especially
prior to 1162. In the years immediately following the accession there
was a wide and vigorous market in which the king was displaying his
wares and selling them with enthusiasm. The Church bought greedily.
Whether the laity were equally pressing we shall never know, but my

[35] R. L. Poole, 'The dates of Henry II's charters', in his *Studies in Chronology and History*,
(Oxford, 1934), pp. 302–7, reprinted from *EHR*, 23 (1908).

guess is probably not. There were very few requirements of the church which as yet Henry was not prepared to meet. After a civil war laymen were a different matter. The Church had standard demands: each lay petition was *sui generis*.

The market was defined by English circumstances. The proportion of the total number of writs issued for Normandy which belong to this early period up to 1162 is lower — 33 per cent, and a considerable number of these concern properties in England. The figures for the rest of France are too small to be used. There is an easy enough explanation of this distribution. Henry had succeeded to Normandy in 1150, to Anjou in 1151 and to Aquitaine *iure uxoris* on his marriage to Eleanor in 1152. In all these provinces the succession was over and done with. Moreover, of all these areas, only Normandy had undergone anything like the crisis which England had suffered during the Anarchy, and in Normandy it had largely come to an end with the submission to Geoffrey of Anjou in 1145. The year 1154, therefore, was not a great dividing line on the continent, except in the settlement of a number of claims and counter-claims in Normandy. Elsewhere there are enough general charters of confirmation to suggest that the approval of a crowned king was worth having. But that is all.

In England, in contrast, title itself was in question. The Treaty of Winchester of 1153 put all lands and rights acquired during Stephen's reign in doubt. Nearly 120 monasteries had been founded during the reign. We have charters of confirmation and supporting writs for nearly all of them. Quite apart from that, church after church, great cathedral, ancient monastery or minster, queued up to obtain confirmation of real or alleged rights and privileges. Henry quickly found, or was provided with, a standard formula for such grants — tenure as in the time of king Henry I.[36] By 1162 the Church comprised enclosures great and small, all fenced in with charters and writs provided by the brave new king. All parties benefited — the Church immediately, but the king also because the more he confirmed the greater his presence grew, for every charter and writ brought attendant actions into the king's court:[37] all parties, that is, except for the church's tenants who had to defend their real or alleged hereditary right — at Abingdon, St. Albans, Battle, and of course ultimately at Canterbury against Becket, who as

---

[36] J. C. Holt, 'The Treaty of Winchester' in Edmund King, ed., *The Anarchy of Stephen's Reign* (Oxford, 1994), pp. 291–316, esp. 297, 312–15. See also the comments in R. R. Darlington, ed., *The Cartulary of Worcester Cathedral Priory* (PRS, ns 38, 1968), p. xxiii.

[37] For the specific instance of Kirkstall see Holt 'Treaty of Winchester', pp. 314–5.

Chancellor had managed the settlement in the first place.[38] There is some irony in that this holy alliance of king and Church collapsed in mutually inflicted injuries in 1164. But before that happened the interlocking effect of the Treaty of Winchester and the immediate demand for protection and confirmation which followed from it had enhanced the function of the written word by renewing and extending the documentary basis on which property and rights were held and defended. And written instruments bred yet more written instruments.

In this paper many problems have been left by the wayside. It is plain that after Henry himself, the architects of the settlement of 1154–62 were Becket and Richard de Lucy, first and foremost, then Robert de Beaumont, earl of Leicester, and Geoffrey de Mandeville, earl of Essex, and a number of *curiales*. Witness-lists will allow us in time to say more about this inner group in government. Then again there is little indication of payment by beneficiaries, and nothing about accounting procedures, except for the charge later levied against Becket that he had misappropriated funds which he had received as Chancellor. And if we have found yet more writs, the bulk of them warns us that many of them play little part in the emergence of the Common Law — writs of protection, for example, and of freedom from toll. These, like the purely legal writs, were being reduced to common form. And we may wonder whether many writs which seem to spring from or lead on to judicial proceedings — writs *ne vexes*, for example — were anything more than precautionary defences against a rainy day. We have nicely detailed stories of such litigation, at Abingdon, Battle and St. Albans, in particular, but we have no indication of its overall bulk. And again, in what ways, if any, did the flood of documentation after 1154 contribute to the establishment of the rule embodied in *nemo tenetur*? Over the years we have had much speculation on these and other matters. In time the *acta* may take us a little further towards firmer solutions. My task has been more mundane. Rather than speculate, I have tried to describe the political and social geography of one portion of the acts, the writs. It has not been

---

[38] For Abingdon see *CMA*, ii 183–90, concerning Marcham and elsewhere. For St. Albans see *Gesta Abbatum Monasterii S. Albani*, ed. H. T. Riley (3 vols, London, 1867–9), i 159–66, 166–74, concerning the wood of Northawe and the priory of Walsingham. For Battle see *The Chronicle of Battle Abbey*, ed. Eleanor Searle, (Oxford, 1980), pp. 212–18, concerning Barnhorn, and for comment J. C. Holt, 'More battle forgeries', in M. W. Barber, P. McNulty, P. Noble, eds, *East Anglian and other studies present to Barbara Dodwell, Reading Medieval Studies*, 11 (1984), 75–86. For Canterbury see Mary Cheney, 'The litigation between John Marshal and Archbishop Thomas Becket in 1164' in J. A. Guy and H. G. Beale, eds, *Law and Social Change in British History* (London, 1984), pp. 9–26.

attempted before. That is my excuse for presenting it to you in a preliminary form. A more cogent reason is that it will come to be the foundation on which speculation must henceforth be based.

Proceedings of the British Academy, **89**, 65–89

'The Age of Bracton'

PAUL BRAND

Maitland and *Bracton*

WHEN MAITLAND HAD WRITTEN the chapter in the first book of the *History of English Law* which provided an overall survey of English law and the English legal system during the rein of Henry III, 'The Age of Bracton' must have seemed a natural title. *Bracton*, the work which Maitland characterized as the 'crown and flower of English medieval jurisprudence', had of course been written during the reign of Henry III. Nor was Maitland, although he was properly sceptical about the supposed connexion of Rannulph de Glanville with the treatise which bore his name,[1] in any doubt that *Bracton* had been the work of the Devonshire clerk and royal justice whose name it bears, Henry of Bratton.[2] Henry III's reign was also for Maitland the 'Age of Bracton' in at least two other senses. Although he believed that the main part of *Bracton* had been 'written between 1250 and 1258' and that the author had gone on 'glossing and annotating it at a later time' (by implication down to the time of his death, in 1268),[3] its heavy reliance on judicial decisions from the first half of the reign meant that virtually the whole of the reign could be seen in legal terms as having been the 'Age of Bracton'. The second, and connected, sense lies in what seems for Maitland to have been the relatively unproblematic nature of the relationship between the law stated in the treatise and that followed in the king's courts. *Bracton* provided an accurate guide to English law in practice during Henry III's reign. Although Bracton had assumed 'a much larger liberty of picking and choosing his 'authorities' than would be conceded now-a-days to an English text-writer', 'whenever we compare his treatise with the

[1] Pollock and Maitland, i 163.
[2] Pollock and Maitland, i 206. 'Bracton' is, of course, simply an incorrect version of the surname 'Bratton'.
[3] Pollock and Maitland, i 207.

records' the treatise did indeed seem 'to be fairly stating the practice of the king's court'.[4] Maitland did not suppose that Henry of Bracton had been a dominant figure in the judicial administration of the period. It was therefore not 'The Age of Bracton' in the same way as the previous period had been 'The Age of Glanvill'. Bracton had, nonetheless, been one of the major royal justices of the period and also a figure whose background was typical of that of a majority of his fellow justices.[5] He was thus, if not a dominant, yet still a characteristic, judicial figure of his period.

Many of Maitland's views and assumptions about *Bracton* have come in the last twenty years to look much less secure. The most radical challenge to the existing consensus about the treatise was that posed by the late Professor S. E. Thorne in his modestly, but misleadingly, entitled 'Translator's Introduction' to volume III of his translation and revision of Woodbine's text of *Bracton*, published in 1977. Maitland's views have now found an able and eloquent defender in J. L. Barton in what amounts to an extended review of Thorne's 'Translator's Introduction', published in 1993.[6] However, even as he defended Maitland's views on the date and authorship of the treatise, Barton implicitly cast doubt on something which even Thorne had not really challenged: Maitland's view of the relationship between the text of *Bracton* and English law in practice. This paper will re-examine Maitland's views of *Bracton* in the light of the work of Thorne and Barton. It will also question Maitland's picture of the position of Henry of Bracton within the judiciary of his period.

The Date of *Bracton*

Before we can turn to the question of the authorship of *Bracton* it will be necessary first to establish when the treatise was composed. It was Maitland's belief that most of *Bracton* had been written between 1250 and 1258.[7] Thorne's arguments in favour of an earlier date were of two kinds: general, and external, ones, and much more specific, internal ones. The general arguments are not a major part of the overall thesis and are less than wholly persuasive. They will not be rehearsed in

---

[4] Pollock and Maitland, i 209.
[5] Pollock and Maitland, i 205.
[6] J. L. Barton, 'The mystery of Bracton', *Journal of Legal History*, 14 (1993), 1–142.
[7] Pollock and Maitland, i 207. Earlier, in *Bracton's Note Book*, he had placed most of its composition within slightly narrower limits, between about 1250 and 1256: *BNB*, i p. 44.

detail here.[8] The internal arguments are much stronger. The strongest of these will be restated here, albeit sometimes in modified form. Some further internal evidence will also be adduced in support of the proposed redating.

Thorne argued that parts of *Bracton* must have been written prior to the 'provisions' of Merton of 1236[9] since a number of passages relating to changes made by that legislation give every appearance of being additions to a text that was originally complete without them.[10] A passage referring to the new rule of Merton, c. 2, allowing a widow to dispose in her will of the unharvested crops on her dower lands, for example, reads like an awkward addition to what had once been a simple argument explaining why neither heir nor executors got any allowance for the value of the unharvested crops on lands assigned to a widow in dower.[11] This was that the widow herself (or rather, her executors) likewise got no allowance for unharvested crops on her dower lands when they reverted to the heir at her death. While the addition correctly states the law as it had now become it removes the whole point of the original argument. The brief section on redisseisin, the action created by c. 3 of the provisions of Merton, in the tractate on novel disseisin, also looks like an addition.[12] This is not just because of its placing in a miscellaneous section at the end of the tractate but also because of the sparsity of comment and exposition devoted to it. This is in marked contrast with most of the rest of the tractate. Although there is little direct evidence to indicate that the references to the awarding of damages to a doweress under c. 1 of the provisions in the tractate on dower are a later insertion[13] it must surely be significant that the text gives two quite different formulas for the clause instructing the sheriff to levy those damages.[14] It is difficult to believe that both were ever in use and it seems most likely that the two forms represent alternative possibilities under consideration

[8] *Bracton*, ed. Thorne, iii pp. xxxiii, xxxvi. For some criticisms see Barton, 'Mystery of Bracton', 5, 123–4.
[9] Thorne does not say that all of the treatise had necessarily been written prior to 1236: 'When the text itself was written is a question to which there is no simple answer, for the tractates were composed at different times, but since the innovations introduced by the provisions of Merton in 1236 appear as insertions, much of the *De Legibus* must already have been in existence by that date . . .' (*Bracton*, iii p. xiv). Barton is therefore wrong to suggest that he is combatting the view that 'a first version of the whole of the text which we now have was written before 1236': Barton, 'Mystery of Bracton', 9.
[10] *Bracton*, iii pp. xiii–xiv.
[11] *Bracton*, f. 96, Thorne, ii 276.
[12] *Bracton*, f. 236b, Thorne, iii 201–2.
[13] *Bracton*, f. 312b, Thorne, iii 398–9.
[14] This does not seem to have been noticed by Thorne.

shortly before or after the provision's enactment. Further evidence for composition of at least two of what Thorne took to be additional passages relating to the provisions of Merton not long after 1236 is to be found in the way that these passages refer to those provisions as the 'nova ... gracia et provisione' or 'nova constitucione..'.[15] Neither look plausible ways of referring to legislation which by 1250 was already fourteen years old.[16]

Thorne also mentions as evidently inserted and readily dateable the brief passage included in the replevin section at the end of the tractate on pleas of the crown relating to the writ of recaption,[17] a remedy which he believed could be dated to c. 1237 and to have been closely connected with the invention of the writ of redisseisin by the provisions of Merton.[18] While the closeness of that particular connexion may be open to question, there is early authority for ascribing the invention of this remedy to William Raleigh and thus dating it to the period between 1234 and 1239 when Raleigh was senior justice of the court *coram rege* and responsible for various legal innovations.[19] Nor can there be much doubt that it is an insertion, for it interrupts the final section of a discussion of the different kinds of avowry which could be made in replevin.[20] The treatise gives two versions of the writ. One envisages the action being heard before the justices in eyre, the other before the county court, though both writs suppose the prior (and still pending) replevin litigation to have been heard in the county court. These are evidently two alternative drafts, of which only one (that authorizing a hearing in the county court) was eventually adopted.[21] It thus seems probable that this material itself dates to the later 1230s, and that it was added precisely because the section on replevin as originally written had no reference to recaption for the good reason that its writing preceded the invention of the remedy.

As Thorne also noted, there were at a number of different places in

---

[15] *Bracton*, ff. 96, 312b, Thorne, ii 276, iii 398–9.

[16] *Bracton*, iii p. xxxi.

[17] *Bracton*, f. 159, Thorne, ii 447–8.

[18] *Bracton*, iii p. xiv.

[19] Maitland, *Collected Papers*, ii 147 (CB 95).

[20] Either the person who inserted the passage or a subsequent editor seems also to have been responsible for inserting '*secundam*' in the immediately succeeding passage to make it appear as though it was referring to the pleading of recaption. However, the subsequent reference to a decision made by Raleigh in his 1232 Leicestershire eyre makes it clear that it is really about the action of replevin and continues the discussion which precedes the inserted material: *Bracton*, f. 159b, Thorne, ii 448.

[21] It was later possible to bring an action of recaption before royal justices but only if the original action of replevin had itself already been removed before them. This is not the situation presupposed by this writ.

the treatise texts of writs whose limitation dates correspond to those in use before the changes made by legislation of 1237 or at still earlier dates or which could best be understood as crudely and inaccurately altered versions of writs containing such limitation dates.[22] Examples of the former were two writs of attaint (for reversing the verdict of assizes of novel disseisin and mort d'ancestor) of which the first contained a limitation date ('after our first coronation at Westminster') appropriate only between 1229 and 1237; the second a limitation date ('after the first coronation of our uncle Richard') appropriate at any date between 1218/20 and 1237.[23] A third example is the limitation date for the writ of nuisance. This is abbreviated to being 'after the last return etc.'.[24] Thorne plausibly suggests that this represents the limitation date in use between 1218 and 1229 ('after the last return of King John from Ireland into England') rather than that used after 1229 ('after our first coronation') or that used after 1237 ('after our first crossing into Brittany'). Examples of crudely altered limitation dates are provided by the two limitation dates given for the writ of novel disseisin ('after the last return of the lord king from Brittany into England' and 'after the last return of King Henry') and a third given for the related writ of nuisance ('after our last return from Brittany into England').[25] As Thorne notes, this is not a limitation date which was ever in use but it does look like a botched attempt by someone working after 1237 to update the limitation date in use between 1218 and 1229 ('after the last return of King John from Ireland') 'by someone who knew that Henry's name should appear, not John's, and that the place should be Brittany, not Ireland'.[26] Barton's suggestion that the author was using an out of date register of writs and may have been intending to return later to correct his errors seems particularly implausible if we are really to believe that the treatise was written during the 1250s by someone currently active as an assize justice.[27]

Thorne also argues convincingly that the treatise originally held that the assize *utrum* could only be brought by clerks (the position established by Pateshull in a 1227 decision) but that it had been supplemented soon after 1236 by a reviser who noted that today (*hodie*) it could be brought by either a clerk or a layman.[28] Since there seems

[22] *Bracton*, iii p. xxviii.
[23] *Bracton*, f. 291, Thorne, iii 343.
[24] *Bracton*, f. 233b, Thorne, iii 194.
[25] *Bracton*, ff. 179, 185b, 233, Thorne, iii 57, 72, 192.
[26] *Bracton*, iii p. xxviii.
[27] Barton, 'Mystery of Bracton', 19–20.
[28] *Bracton*, iii p. xvii; *Bracton*, f. 285b, Thorne, iii 329.

to be no evidence of the assize actually being brought by laymen after *c.* 1240 this in turn suggests (even if Thorne does not note this fact) that the passage had been added by that date but not revised thereafter for the way in which the statement is phrased indicates that the reviser was talking specifically about current practice (*obtinet hodie*), not about what the law ought to be, but no longer is.[29] Further evidence (again not noted by Thorne) to suggest composition of this part of the treatise not later than the early 1230s comes from the passage restricting the use of the assize to lay rectors of parish churches instituted by the ordinary.[30] Legislation of 1234 specifically extended the use of the assize to religious holding churches to their own use.[31]

Although Barton may well be right to reject Thorne's assertion that the whole section of 'formed' writs of prohibition is a later addition to a discussion of prohibitions written before this kind of prohibition came into use,[32] it must be significant that so many of these 'formed' writs can themselves be dated to the 1230s as such prohibitions certainly went on being drafted at later dates.[33] The most economical explanation is surely that the author was writing this section no later than *c.* 1240.

There is also other, independent evidence to support Thorne's general hypothesis of an earlier date for the composition of the treatise. Passages concerned with procedure and practice provide particularly good evidence for the date of composition since in general they read as though they are describing procedure and practice current at the time of the writing of the treatise. The forms of judicial commission which the treatise contains include a variant on the writ patent of commission to the justices of the general eyre covering justices appointed with power solely to take assizes of novel disseisin and mort d'ancestor and to deliver gaols.[34] This is a form apparently last used in 1226.[35] It is difficult to believe that anyone compiling such a treatise

---

[29] A Nicol, 'Changes in the assize utrum between the constitutions of Clarendon and Bracton' in J. B. Post and R. F. Hunnisett, eds, *Medieval Legal Records edited in Memory of C. A. F. Meekings* (London, 1978), pp. 18–24 at p. 21.

[30] *Bracton*, ff. 285b–6, Thorne, iii 330.

[31] *CRR*, xv nos 1173, 1178.

[32] *Bracton*, ff. 402b–5, Thorne, iv 253–61; *Bracton*, iii pp. xix–xx; Barton, 'Mystery of Bracton', 24–5.

[33] *Bracton*, iii p. xx; *Bracton*, f. 403b, Thorne, iv 256–7 (November 1236); f. 404, Thorne, iv 257 (prior to 1240); f. 404b, Thorne, iv 258–9 (1240 or earlier); ff. 404b–5, Thorne, iv 259–60 (after 1236); f. 405, Thorne, iv 261 (case of 1235–6). To these might be added *Bracton*, f. 405, Thorne, iv 260–1 which seems to be related to litigation of 1228.

[34] *Bracton*, f. 109, Thorne, ii 309.

[35] C. A. F. Meekings, 'Introduction', in *Calendar of the General and Special Assize and General Gaol Delivery Commissions on the Dorse of the Patent Rolls, Richard II (1377–1399)* (Nedeln, Liechtenstein, 1977), pp. 1–2.

in the 1250s would have bothered to include it or even necessarily have known of its existence. Nor is it easy to see why someone writing in the 1250s should have wanted, or even been able, to include a writ of summons and list of articles from the 1227 Shipway session of the Kent eyre and a related mandate just after giving a much more up to date version of the same articles plus elsewhere a separate writ of summons.[36] It is much easier to see how a treatise which had originally included the 1227 summons and articles (perhaps as an interesting variant on the standard type) might have been imperfectly updated by incorporating the later set but without discarding the earlier variants. Other evidence pointing to composition in the late 1220s or early 1230s is the author's mention in passing, and without a hint that it was at the time of composition no longer in use, of the essoin of the common summons at the general eyre, a type of essoin still allowed in 1232 but which had ceased to be allowed by the time of the general eyre visitation of 1234–6.[37]

Other evidence points less specifically only to composition prior to the mid-1240s. The forms of appointment of justices for the hearing of individual assizes and related writs envisage only two possible alternatives: the appointment of four knights of the county and the appointment of a justice of the Common Bench with power to choose his own associates.[38] The first form was in use only up to c. 1242–3.[39] The presence of only these two forms in the treatise also incidentally provides strong negative evidence against composition of this part of the treatise by Henry of Bratton during the 1250s. Had he been composing the treatise then, his own assize commissions (which do not belong to either of these two types) would surely have been much more readily to hand than either of these. The author also appears to be describing the current practice of the courts in the passage about mesne process in personal actions in the tractate 'Of exceptions'.[40] For him the next stage in that process after initial summons and two attachments is *habeas corpus*.[41] *Habeas corpus* was indeed commonly part of mesne process in such actions as late as Trinity term 1243, though often

[36] *Bracton*, ff. 117b–18, Thorne, ii 333–4.
[37] *Bracton*, f. 110, Thorne, ii 312; *Crown Pleas of the Wiltshire Eyre, 1249*, ed. C. A. F. Meekings (Wiltshire Archaeological and Natural History Society, Records Branch, 16, 1961), p. 45.
[38] *Bracton*, ff. 110b–11b, Thorne, ii 313–16.
[39] Meekings, *Calendar of Assize and Gaol Delivery Commissions*, p. 3.
[40] *Bracton*, ff. 439–44b, Thorne, iv 363–78.
[41] *Bracton*, f. 440, Thorne, iv 367.

bypassed.[42] By Hilary and Easter terms of 1244 it had disappeared.[43] It is difficult to believe that this portion of the text could possibly have been written after 1243, though it might well have been written some years earlier. At first sight, the reference in the treatise to the writ of grand distress provides a contrary indication.[44] The grand distress only became a regular part of the mesne process in personal actions in the late 1240s.[45] There are, however, isolated instances of its use in cases going back as early as 1207 and it was in intermittent use thereafter.[46] It is probably significant that while the author gives the actual formulas of writs up to and including that of the first writ of simple distraint he does not give any formulas for the other writs of distraint which he mentions including the writ of grand distress.[47] This is probably because he knows of these writs only from plea roll references to them and not from the writ formulary from which he took the other writs, which presumably represents the judicial writs in common use at the time this part of the treatise was composed. This suggests that at the time of writing the writ of grand distress was not yet part of the normal mesne process.[48]

A more substantive point concerns the treatise's mention in passing of the use of the action of warranty of charter as a substitute for the action of mesne where the tenant seeking acquittance had a charter from the mesne lord or his ancestor or (though the treatise notes that there is some dispute about this) in place of the action of *ne vexes* where the tenant was seeking to prevent his lord claiming more services than were contained in his charter of feoffment.[49] Plea roll evidence does, indeed, indicate that warranty of charter was used as a substitute for mesne but not after 1236.[50] No legal writer writing in the 1250s

---

[42] cf. PRO, KB 26/130, mm. 6d, 19d, 20, 20d, 22; cf. KB 26/130, mm. 3(1) d, 17.

[43] KB 26/132, KB 26/133, KB 26/134A *passim*.

[44] *Bracton*, f. 440b, Thorne, iv 368.

[45] The grand distress was not yet part of mesne process in the Bench in Easter term 1244 (PRO, KB 26/133 and 134A *passim*) but was in use by 1249/50 e.g. KB 26/135, m. 31 (Mich. 1249), KB 26/138 mm. 7, 12d, 16d, 17d (Hil. 1250) etc..

[46] *CRR*, v p. 7 and cf. *CRR*, v p. 141. For its use in later cases see *CRR*, xiv no. 386 (1230); *CRR*, xv no. 719 (1233); PRO, KB 26/129, m. 8 and KB 26/130, m. 19d (1243).

[47] *Bracton*, f. 440b, Thorne, iv 367–8.

[48] It may also be this second-hand knowledge of writs which explains why he thinks that the writ of distraint *'quod sis securus habendi corpus ejus'* is distinct from the initial writ of simple distraint. The evidence of the plea rolls suggests that they are simply two variant forms of the first writ of distraint: see Paul Brand, *Contribution of the Period of Baronial Reform (1258–1267) to the Development of the Common Law in England*, D.Phil thesis (Oxford, 1974), p. 311.

[49] *Bracton*, f. 399, Thorne, iv 243, 244. But note that at *Bracton*, f. 38, Thorne, ii 119, the treatise specifically says it cannot be used in place of *ne vexes*.

[50] The latest example of its use is *CRR*, xv no. 1682.

would have referred to it as though it were uncontested current practice. Its use in place of *ne vexes* is likewise attested only between 1220 and 1234.[51] A reference to its use being contested but supportable fits the mid or even early 1230s much better than the 1250s.

A date prior to *c*. 1240 is also suggested by the author's doctrine that lords are generally only justified in demanding the services specified in their charters of feoffment.[52] The courts seem to have followed the same line down to that date. Thereafter, they came to accept that lords might be entitled to additional services provided they could show seisin of them subsequent to the making of the tenant's charter.[53] While it is plausible that this was a change of which the author of the treatise did not approve he is unlikely to have simply passed it over in silence, without even arguing against it. The most likely explanation is that he was writing before it had occurred. This is also the most likely explanation for a related feature of his discussion, his assertion that three kinds of suit of court (for the hearing of pleas by writ of right, for the judgment of thieves and for the afforcement of the lord's court) could be claimed by lords even without any specific stipulation for them in the tenant's charter of feoffment.[54] Again, this is a doctrine which was followed in a series of cases decided between 1223 and 1241 but which disappeared thereafter.[55] It is impossible to believe that, had the author been writing in the 1250s, he would have written as though this was still current law.

The Authorship of *Bracton*

Maitland believed that the whole treatise, as originally written, was the work of Henry of Bracton. In Thorne's view, however, Bracton must have played a much smaller part in its composition. The treatise had probably been in Henry of Bracton's possession from some time in the mid-1230s.[56] He had been responsible for adding various passages connected with William of Raleigh's activities in the later 1230s and relating to the provisions of Merton plus a relatively small number of passages reflecting his own judicial career and experience during the

[51] *CRR*, viii p. 193 (1220); *CRR*, xi nos 1018, 1215 (1223); *BNB*, pl. 1000 (1224); *CRR*, xii no. 2524 (1226); *BNB*, pl. 1771 (1227); *CRR*, xiii no. 717 (1228); *BNB*, pl. 531 (1231); *CRR*, xiv no. 1768 (1231); *BNB*, pl. 837 (1234).
[52] *Bracton*, ff. 35, 38, Thorne, ii 112, 119.
[53] Brand, *Contribution of the Period of Baronial Reform*, pp. 70–1.
[54] *Bracton*, f. 35, Thorne, ii 112.
[55] Brand, *Contribution of the Period of Baronial Reform*, p. 73.
[56] *Bracton*, iii p. v.

1240s and 1250s.[57] He could not have written the major part of
the treatise since much of it had been written before the earliest
probable date for Bracton's entry into clerical service in the courts, the
earliest date when he became even a potential author for such a
treatise.[58] These parts of the treatise had been written by a clerk
sufficiently close to the great justice Martin of Pateshull, who had
retired from the Bench in 1229, to refer to him as 'Martin' and to
know what the great man used to do and say in court.[59] This pointed
to the most distinguished of Pateshull's clerks, William of Raleigh,
whom Henry of Bracton had himself served as a clerk. Thorne was,
however, surprisingly reluctant to give Raleigh full credit and preferred
to characterize him as no more than 'the prime mover behind the *De
Legibus*'.[60]

Within a few years of Henry of Bracton's death in 1268 it was
clearly believed that he had been the author of the treatise which still
bears his name. The first folio of one of the earliest surviving MSS. of
Bracton (OA) has an inscription noting that this is '*principium libri
domini H. de Bratona*'.[61] There also survives a copy of the letters issued
early in 1278 by Robert of Scarborough acknowledging the receipt of
'*librum quem dominus Henricus de Breton*' composuit' on loan until
the following June from master Thomas Bek archdeacon of Dorset,
acting as agent for Robert Burnel, bishop of Bath and Wells.[62] This
may simply have been because a manuscript, perhaps at this stage the
only manuscript, of the treatise was found among Bracton's possessions
after his death, possibly among the property he had left at Wells, which
might explain how Burnel obtained his copy of the manuscript. It would
have been natural under these circumstances to ascribe authorship of
the treatise to Bracton without any detailed examination of its contents.
Ascription to Bracton may, however, have come from, or been confirmed by, a reading of the treatise. In certain manuscripts the authorial
ego of a passage at the beginning of the treatise is extended to '*ego
Henricus de Brattone*' ('*ego Henricus de Brattone animum erexi ad*

---

[57] *Bracton*, iii pp. xxx–xxxi, xliii. Thorne thought it just possible that Bracton had entered
Raleigh's service earlier than the mid-1230s and was therefore responsible for material
relating to William of Raleigh dating from c. 1232 onwards: *Bracton*, iii pp. xxxi, xxxii.
[58] *Bracton*, iii pp. v, xxxi.
[59] *Bracton*, iii pp. xxxii–xxxiii.
[60] *Bracton*, iii p. xxxvi. His formulation is that 'it flourished during his years as clerk and
judge, began to falter when he exchanged the Bench for the court *coram rege* and was drawn,
as the king's chief legal adviser, into the political events of the reign, and all but ceased
when he left the law for a bishopric in 1239'.
[61] *Bracton*, iii p. li.
[62] PRO, E 36/275, f. 175. It is printed in D. Ogg, ed., *Johannis Seldeni ad Fletam Dissertatio*
(Cambridge, 1925), p. 11.

vetera judicia justorum . . .').[63] A more subtle suggestion of Bracton's authorship is also to be found in that section of the tractate on the assize of novel disseisin which deals with errors in the names included in writs.[64] His is the first name used as an exemplar to demonstrate possible errors in first names (where 'William' is put in error for 'Henry'); his first name and surname are used to illustrate errors in syllable (*'Henricus de Brothtona'* for *'Henricus de Brattona'*) and letter (*'Henricus de Brettona'* for *'Henricus de Brattona'*). His too is the name used to illustrate an error in the dignity held by the plaintiff ('Henry de Bratton precentor' for 'Henry de Bratton dean').

Yet there are good reasons for doubting with Thorne whether Henry of Bracton could have been the author of all or even a major part of the treatise. The first, as Barton himself recognizes, is the difficulty in explaining why he should have abandoned work on the treatise in 1256, some twelve years before his own death, at exactly the time when his retirement from the bench meant that he had more leisure and despite the fact that he remained perfectly capable of other kinds of activity.[65] The political circumstances of the mid-1250s were surely not enough to have daunted an author who had already invested much time and effort in his work from completing it. Abandonment of the treatise is much more plausible as the act of a man in despair at ever bringing suitably up to date or even imposing any real order on a treatise which was mainly the work of another author writing several decades earlier.

A second argument depends on the dating of substantial portions of the treatise. Parts of the treatise must have been written during the later 1220s or early 1230s. While there is no real hard evidence to support Richardson's hypothesis that Henry of Bracton was only born as late as *c.* 1210 and was therefore too young to have become a clerk much before the mid-1230s, the total absence of references to Bracton on the Bench plea rolls or in other contemporary official sources before the mid-1230s indicates that he did not become a court clerk much before then.[66] Nor can he immediately have acquired the degree of legal knowledge and expertise that was required for the composition of a major legal treatise. He must therefore remain an unlikely candidate for authorship of the major part of the treatise which was composed prior to the late 1230s.

---

[63] It only appears, however, in two of the MSS. collated by Woodbine and both Barton ('Mystery of Bracton', 1) and Thorne (*Bracton*, iii p. li) consider it to be a later addition.
[64] *Bracton*, f. 188b, Thorne, iii 79.
[65] Barton, 'Mystery of Bracton', 125–6.
[66] Barton, 'Mystery of Bracton', 2–3.

There are, in any case, strong arguments for supposing that the treatise as we now have it is the work of more than one author or at the least of an author and an independent reviser. Maitland himself noted some of this evidence, though he attempted to explain it away as the consequence of a single author having second thoughts without undertaking a full revision of his text.[67] Take, for example, the treatise's discussion of the question of the validity of legacies of freehold land made by grantees who have been granted land to hold to themselves, their heirs, assigns and legatees. The view originally taken (and stated at two different points in the treatise) was that such a bequest was valid. A legatee in possession could plead the bequest in his defence. A legatee out of possession could (or at least should be able to) sue for the enforcement of the bequest in the king's court, though such a writ was not currently in use.[68] In a third passage, however, the treatise comes down firmly against validity.[69] It seems clear, however, that this passage too originally agreed with the others for in introducing what now stands as the argument against validity the author says that '*Videtur prima facie quod haec dictio "legare" supervacua sit et haberi debeat pro non adjecta . . .*' All that has happened is the striking out of the answering (and originally more convincing) counter-argument. This is surely the work of a reviser in a hurry who disagreed with the original author but could not be bothered to formulate his own arguments. It does not look like the work of a man who had simply changed his own mind but did not find it necessary to refute his own original arguments for holding in favour of devises. An original author who had changed his mind would surely also have remembered to revise the other passages where he discussed the same question.

A second area where it seems clear that a second author with a diametrically opposed view-point has been at work revising what the first author said is in two passages which discuss whether courts christian may exercise jurisdiction over bequests of freehold land in boroughs and towns where local custom allowed such legacies.[70] In the first, the original author gave all the good reasons for allowing court christian jurisdiction over such cases. A reviser then came along and added the comment 'These things are true, according to R. and the others' ('*Hec vera sunt, secundum R. et alios*'), a distancing remark which does not answer the arguments but does ascribe them to the unspecific 'R. and the others' rather than the author himself. He then notes a single

[67] *BNB*, i pp. 36–7.
[68] *Bracton*, ff. 18b, 412b, Thorne, ii 70, iv 283.
[69] *Bracton*, f. 49, Thorne, ii 149.
[70] *Bracton*, ff. 409b, 412, Thorne, iv 273, 282.

contrary decision from 1218 as authority for the opposite view but without any supporting rationale for that decision. He has made a similar change in a second passage which is illustrating how matters once subject to secular jurisdiction can become subject to ecclesiastical jurisdiction. One example used is that of tenements left by will in boroughs and cities. Again it is surely a clumsy reviser rather than an author who has changed his mind who has distanced himself from the original view-point of the text by adding '*secundum quosdam*' to it and then goes on to give the contrary view. The new view robs the whole passage of its value as illustrating the point it is meant to demonstrate and the distancing phrase '*secundum quosdam*' is surely a very strange one for an author to use about what had once been his own view.

Evidence of a rather different kind for at least two authors having been at work on the treatise is also to be found in the opening pages of the treatise. The first author is to be heard in the *prohemium auctoris*.[71] He describes the work as a whole as a *tractatus*. He tells us that the *intencio . . . auctoris* is to treat of 'the matters and cases which occur and are found each day in the kingdom of England' and to 'instruct and teach all who wish to know how lawsuits and pleas are decided according to the laws and customs of England . . .'. There is nothing here to suggest any criticism of the current judiciary; nothing to suggest that the author's material will not be taken from current cases and procedure. We hear a very different voice in the immediately preceding passage.[72] This author describes the treatise not as a *tractatus* but as a *summa* divided up into *paragrapha* and *tituli*. He also gives as his purpose in writing the rather different one of writing for 'the instruction at least of lesser men' ('*ad instructionem saltem minorum*') and talks of greater men who are 'foolish and insufficiently instructed, who climb the seat of judgment before learning the laws' and of how they pervert laws and customs by deciding cases more by their own will than by the authority of the laws. It is this author who talks of going back to the 'ancient judgments of just men (*vetera judicia justorum*), searching through . . . their deeds, their *consilia* and *responsa*'. Here again, then, we have two very different authorial voices, or rather the voice of an author and of his reviser. The first author was writing when the cases in the treatise were still current cases; the second at a time when their appearance in the treatise required justification.

There may even be some evidence of the existence of two authors (or an author and a reviser) in the passage already discussed about

---

[71] *Bracton*, f. 1b, Thorne, ii 20.
[72] *Bracton*, f. 1, Thorne, ii 19.

errors in names.[73] In the very same passage the example of an error in *cognomen* used is that of '*Hubertus Roberti*' where '*Hubertus Walteri*' was the proper name. The name of the great archbishop of Canterbury and royal justiciar (who had died in 1205) is hardly likely to have been the first name that came to mind to someone of Henry of Bracton's generation. It would have been much more obvious to a legal author of a previous generation. The example of an error in the identification of the dignity held by the plaintiff as 'Henry de Bratton precentor' when the plaintiff is 'Henry de Bratton dean' may be even more revealing. Here, Bracton has indeed again used his own name but he has not given himself any of the dignities he is known ever to have held (prebendary, archdeacon, chancellor). He may, of course, have been dreaming about what his future career might bring him, but it seems more probable that here (as elsewhere) he has simply substituted his own name for that of the individual whose name originally stood there. If so, it is tempting to suggest that this might have been one of the two judges whose judgments are cited so heavily in the treatise: the Martin of Pateshull whom Raleigh served as clerk and who had been dean of St Paul's cathedral in London.

There is no reason for doubting that Henry of Bracton was responsible for the addition to the treatise of material directly connected with his own career as a royal justice. It also seems likely, as Thorne suggested, that he was responsible for adding to the treatise material connected with William of Raleigh's period as senior justice of the court *coram rege* and to which he had access as one of William of Raleigh's clerks. We are almost certainly hearing Henry of Bracton (even if his name was not in the original manuscript) speaking as the *ego* of the '*ego ... animum erexi ad vetera judicia justorum ...*' for it was surely Bracton who was faced with the problem of justifying a book full of references to long-dead and long-retired judges and their judgments and we also know from Bracton's own references in the treatise that he was critical of the judgments of his contemporaries on the bench.

We can also be reasonably certain that William of Raleigh played a major part in the production of the treatise. Another of Martin of Pateshull's clerks could have written the passages recounting what the great justice used to say and do in court and referring to the great man by his first name, but the fact that the treatise subsequently passed into the hands of Henry of Bracton, who was one of Raleigh's clerks, strongly suggests that it was Raleigh who wrote these passages. Raleigh

---

[73] Above, p. 75.

is, indeed, a plausible author for most, if not all, of the various constituent parts of the treatise, for the writing of those parts of the treatise which can be dated would coincide with his period as a senior clerk in Pateshull's service and as a justice of the Common Bench.

'Bracton's Note Book'

Vinogradoff's discovery in 1884 of a manuscript in the British Museum (Additional MS. 12269) containing around 2000 transcripts of entries on the plea rolls of the Common Bench, Eyres and King's Bench from the period between 1217 and 1239/40 when Martin of Pateshull and William of Raleigh were justices of those courts (and only from those courts where they were acting as justices) provided for Maitland essential evidence of how it had been possible for an author writing in the 1250s to make such extensive use of the judicial decisions of that earlier period. It had been known since the time of Madox that Bracton had possessed plea rolls belonging to Pateshull and Raleigh and had been made to surrender them in 1258,[74] but it was in this manuscript (which Maitland, following a hint from Vinogradoff, christened 'Bracton's Note Book') that Maitland thought he had found the evidence of how Bracton had actually set to work to select and copy material from the earlier rolls to be used in the writing of the treatise. 'Even with the aid of a note book, his feat of citing some five hundred cases scattered about in some fifty rolls was a gigantic feat of patience, industry, memory' but, Maitland considered, 'without some such aid the feat would have been impossible' since 'to have transplanted five hundred cases directly out of this disorderly mass into their proper places in a systematic exposition of the law, would have been beyond the power of any man.'[75] It was true, he admitted, that no more than 200 of the cases Bracton cited could actually be found in 'Bracton's Note Book' but he conjectured that the 'Note Book' was the sole and fortunate survivor of the two or more such 'Note Books' compiled and used by Bracton.[76]

Thorne's discussion of 'Bracton's Note Book' is not one of the more lucid parts of his 'Translator's Introduction'.[77] He does not, it seems, deny that the 'Note Book' had been in the possession of Henry of Bracton: indeed, it is difficult to see how he could have done so,

---

[74] *BNB*, i p. 25.
[75] *BNB*, i p. 79.
[76] *BNB*, i p. 79.
[77] *Bracton*, iii pp. xxxiv–xxxix.

given the strength of the evidence Maitland had adduced to demonstrate precisely this point.[78] Nor does he deny that Bracton was responsible for at least part of the 'Note Book' (the transcripts of *coram rege*
cases of the period 1234/5–1239/40 which it contains).[79] It was his belief,
however, that these had been added to an original nucleus of transcripts
of enrolments from twenty-eight consecutive terms (running from
Easter term 1227 to Easter term 1234) for which Bracton had not been
responsible.[80] Copies of enrolments from still earlier terms had been
derived from existing collections of such enrolments which were
'copied as the maker of the book came upon them . . .'.[81] Thus the
'Note Book', just like the treatise itself, was, for Thorne, mainly a work
of the 1220s and 1230s rather than of the 1250s and was, again like the
treatise, mainly produced by someone other than Henry of Bracton.

Thorne also argued that the 'Note Book' had in fact played no
significant role in the composition of the treatise. In the absence of an
index, he suggests, it would have been difficult to find cases dealing
with any particular subject and thus to make use of a 'Note Book'
arranged chronologically.[82] Even where cases were transcribed into the
'Note Book' they were sometimes cited in such a way as to show
the author was citing them directly from the plea roll or from personal
knowledge. Sometimes the author of the treatise mentions the location
of a case on the relevant plea roll, or cites a case under the correct year
and term where the 'Note Book' misascribes it or shows knowledge of
facts or names that are only found in the plea roll entry and not in the
'Note Book' version of that entry.[83] Sometimes the author demonstrates
personal knowledge of circumstances connected with a case that cannot
have been derived either from the original plea roll entry or from the
'Note Book' version of that entry.[84] A majority of the 500 cases cited
in the treatise were not, in any case, to be found in the 'Note Book'.[85]
These, Thorne suggested, must have been cited directly from the rolls
themselves. He does not consider Maitland's suggestion that they might
have been cited from other 'Note Books' now lost. Thorne did not
wholly exclude the possibility that the 'Note Book' had been compiled

---

[78] *Bracton*, iii p. xxxix: 'Bracton, who, to all appearances, was with Raleigh during those years
and into whose possession the Note Book may already have come . . .' Maitland's evidence
for connecting the Note Book specifically with Henry of Bratton and not just with the author
of the treatise is given in *BNB*, i pp. 93–104.

[79] *Bracton*, iii p. xxxix.

[80] *Bracton*, iii pp. xxxviii–xxxix.

[81] *Bracton*, iii pp. xxxvi–xxxviii.

[82] *Bracton*, iii p. xxxiv.

[83] *Bracton*, iii p. xxxiv.

[84] *Bracton*, iii pp. xxxi–xxxiii.

[85] *Bracton*, iii p. xxxiv.

with the writing of the treatise in mind. But if so it was, he suggested, curious that so few of the cases transcribed were then cited in the treatise (no more than 150 out of 2000 entries copied);[86] and if the author had indeed set about creating a law-book from the record of the decisions of the courts all he would really have needed was a summary of the legal rule that the case embodied 'similar to the short annotations in the margins of the Note Book and the paragraphs of the *Casus et Judicia*', not full transcripts of individual enrolments. It would have been much easier and more convenient for him to have noted the relevant point as he read through the rolls than for him to read them and then have his clerks go through and transcribe each relevant entry in full. Thus the 'Note Book' made very little sense as a compositional aid.[87] Indeed, if Thorne's arguments about the date and authorship of the treatise were correct, an aide-memoire such as the 'Note Book' would in any case have been much less essential for the writing of the treatise than Maitland had supposed it to be, for on Thorne's view of the treatise's date and authorship, it would not have been too difficult for the author to cite cases from memory from the rolls (with perhaps some subsequent checking of those citations). It is less clear what Thorne did suppose the purpose of the compilation to have been. The originally independent collections of enrolments of the 1220s he seems to have seen as a by-product of the education of junior clerks of the Bench, giving them practice in copying enrolments and becoming acquainted with their formulae; the collections of the 1230s as by-products intended for the instruction not just of clerks but also of professional lawyers.[88] The general alternative purpose of the whole collection at which he seems to be hinting is an educational one.

It is clear that Maitland must be wrong about the date when the enrolments now found in 'Bracton's Note Book' were first selected and copied from the rolls. Many of the cases might have been selected and copied at any time up to and including the 1250s for they are unannotated or given annotations which are no help in dating when those annotations were made. But some do contain unmistakable clues about when the processes of copying and annotation took place. It is impossible, for example, to believe that someone working in the 1250s would have bothered to have copied cases about rights of common only to mark them as rendered obsolete by the provisions of Merton.[89]

[86] *Bracton*, iii p. xxxiv.
[87] *Bracton*, iii p. xxxviii.
[88] *Bracton*, iii p. xxxviii.
[89] *BNB*, pll. 1883, 1975.

It must also have been a selector and copyist working before the enactment of the provisions and an annotator working not long afterwards who were responsible for copying an entry which raises the question of the doweress's right to the crops on her dower land beside which an annotator (working surely within a few years of the enactment of the provisions) has noted that this has now been altered by the '*nova gracia*'.[90] Probable evidence of a copyist and an annotator both working as early as the 1220s is to be found in the annotation to an enrolment of a case of Trinity term 1222 which notes an opinion of the royal justice William Briwerre holding for an analagous (but even more extensive) limitation on the obligation of warranty in such a way as to suggest that at the time of the annotation Briwerre (who died in 1226) was still alive or only just dead.[91] It is less clear that Thorne has definitively established those portions of the text of the 'Note Book' for which Henry of Bracton is responsible and those for which others were responsible; or indeed those portions which are direct copies from the plea rolls and those portions which were taken at second hand from existing collections, and further work still needs to be done on this.

The absence of an index from the volume as we now have it does not, of course, prove that one never existed. Thorne's evidence that some of the cases which are found in the 'Note Book' are in fact cited in ways that show the 'Note Book' was not being used is hardly conclusive. It only applies to a relatively limited number of citations and goes to show not that the 'Note Book' was of no use but rather that the author(s) of the treatise had more than one source of information for the cases cited in the work: recollection and direct access to the rolls as well as consultation of the 'Note Book'. A much more potent objection to the notion that the 'Note Book' was used in the composition of the treatise is the presence in the 'Note Book' of only a minority of the cases cited in the treatise. Maitland's hypothesis of the existence of lost additional 'Note Books' which would have contained the missing cases requires us to posit that there once existed two or more Note Books covering exactly the same terms as each other, with no obvious division of subject matter allocating what went into one Note Book rather than another. This seems rather unlikely.

[90] *BNB*, pl. 1409.

[91] *BNB*, pl. 196: 'Nota quod si quis terram dederit per cartam et quod warantizabit versus omnes preterquam versus tales, si contra tales vocetur non warantizabit. Idem videtur si capiatur homagium salvo jure cujuslibet vel si expresse ne teneatur ad warantiam, secundum W. Briwerr'. cf. Maitland's discussion (*BNB*, i pp. 85–6) which notes that the treatise puts Briwerre's involvement in a slightly different context, that of the maker of many charters which such specific exclusions of warranty against particular individuals.

Thorne may not, however, be right in concluding that the 'Note Book' as we now have it was never intended to play any part in the composition of the treatise. The fact that so few of its cases are cited does not in itself present an insuperable difficulty. It is possible that in the process of revision and copying other citations which may once have been in the text were lost. It is also possible that the collection was put together after part or all of a first version of the treatise was written and with a view to its future revision, a revision which Henry of Bracton never completed. Thorne's point about the author not needing full transcripts of the cases concerned is certainly a good one. It is, however, possible that they were made with a rather different purpose in mind, that of serving as *pièces justificatives* to go with the revised treatise. If the treatise was intended for a wider audience than those immediately involved with the running of the Westminster courts who had access to the plea rolls (and we cannot assume that even they would have had access to the older rolls of Pateshull and Raleigh which seem to have been in Bracton's own custody) but was intended to be supported with the evidence of decided cases some such companion volume of copies of enrolments would surely have been needed for this purpose.

Bracton and English Law in Henry III's reign

Maitland thought that *Bracton* could for the most part be treated as a reliable guide to the law of the royal courts during Henry III's reign. The general idea of a law book and the way it should be organized Bracton had indeed borrowed from the traditions of the learned law. He had also borrowed some general maxims, a few specific rules on matters of rare occurrence and some technical terms which he used on occasion in place of those normally used by common lawyers. However, 'the main matter of his treatise is genuine English law laboriously collected out of the plea rolls of the king's court' and 'whenever we compare his treatise with the records — and this can now be done at innumerable points — he seems to be fairly stating the practice of the king's courts.'[92] Bracton had, it was true, been highly selective in his choice of authorities, for he cites in the main only the decisions of Martin of Pateshull and William Raleigh. This was, however, simply because his purpose had been 'to state the practice, the best and most

---

[92] Pollock and Maitland, i 207–9.

approved practice, of the king's court.'[93] Maitland's picture of English law in the reign of Henry III seems then to have been a relatively static one. He does indeed note that one of the reasons that the treatise cannot have been substantially revised after 1259 is that it takes no account of the Provisions of Westminster. He also notes that the passage on the essoin *de malo lecti* and the computation of the year and a day allowed to a successful essoinee in leap years has not been revised in the light of the 1256 Leap Year ordinance.[94] Yet he seems to accept at face value the implicit assertion that a treatise full of the legal doctrine of the time of Pateshull and Raleigh and which is buttressed by the citation of the decisions of the courts over which they presided represents what is still 'the best and most approved practice of the king's court' in the 1250s.[95]

Although Thorne believed that most of the treatise had been written as much as two decades earlier than Maitland, he too considered that the treatise presented a reliable picture of the actual practice of the king's court. His picture of that practice is, however, a much more dynamic one and takes full account of the fact that the custom of the king's court changed materially over time. Indeed, Thorne argued that much of the textual confusion of the treatise was to be accounted for by imperfect attempts at revision of the text which were intended to take account of changes in the law resulting both from statutory enactments and from doctrinal changes in the Common Law itself.[96]

Barton, by contrast, is sceptical about the degree to which *Bracton* can be seen as being a straight reflexion of the practice of the royal courts, whether in the 1230s or in the 1250s, as 'one reason for which the doctrine of the treatise is frequently difficult to date is that it is the doctrine of the author rather than of the judges.'[97] He makes a good case for that part of the treatise which deals with the trial of issues of bastardy (and more particularly issues of special bastardy) being seen as a polemic, whose author 'must have been well aware that the practice which he was describing was not followed at the date when he was writing, and had not been followed at any time within the memory of the profession'.[98] He also suggests the need for a similar scepticism on other matters as well: as to whether the Bractonian doctrine that *indicavit* did not lie for tithes amounting to less than one

---

[93] Pollock and Maitland, i 209, cf. *BNB*, i pp. 45–52.
[94] *BNB*, i pp. 41–3.
[95] *BNB*, i pp. 50–1.
[96] *Bracton*, iii pp. xiii–xxviii.
[97] Barton, 'Mystery of Bracton', 5 (and cf. 104).
[98] Barton, 'Mystery of Bracton', 18–19.

sixth of the value of a church had ever been adopted or applied as a rule by the courts and whether there ever was a writ allowing a devisee of land to sue for that land in the king's court or a rule allowing a devisee to sue for land in a church court.[99]

Certain parts of the treatise clearly purport to describe current practice or currently existing institutions. The author is not attempting to describe the 'best practice' of the king's courts, but actual existing practice and more work on matching the law and practice of the treatise with the changing law of Henry III's reign would produce further evidence of when the different parts of the treatise were composed. But Barton is also clearly right in supposing that several passages in *Bracton* do not describe the legal doctrine or practice of the king's courts at any specific date, whether in the 1220s, the 1230s or 1250s. Another example is provided by the passage in the tractate on novel disseisin in which the author seems to be arguing for treating certain kinds of unjustified distraint (where there is no pretext for the distraint or where the distresses taken are excessive or where the order of distraints is not observed) as disseisins. Here the very language of the passage indicates that the author is arguing a case rather than stating current or past legal practice.[100] A less obvious example is provided by a preceding passage where the author purports to be giving rules about the order in which distresses should be taken.[101] This has been accepted by at least one distinguished modern legal historian as a valid statement of thirteenth-century English legal rules governing the making of distraints.[102] Some of the preferences can indeed be verified as rules observed and enforced, though generally only by much later evidence. The rule requiring the distraint of a tenant's chattels before those of his sub-tenants was clearly no longer applicable by the early 1250s but may conceivably have been the earlier rule. There is, however, no evidence, of any rule requiring the distraint of the chattels of villein sub-tenants before those of the lord. Indeed, we know that in the case of distraints for the king's debts (admittedly a special case) the contrary rule was applied in Henry II's reign and that the same rule was still valid in 1250 when Henry III reminded the assembled

---

[99] Barton, 'Mystery of Bracton', 24, 45–7.

[100] *Bracton*, f. 217b, Thorne, iii 155: 'Sed cum fieri possit disseisina si cultura per districcionem depereat quare non fit disseisina eodem modo si depereat melioracio? Quia ubi deficit melioracio, perit cultura in parte vel toto. Videtur igitur quod sit disseisina si quis per capcionem averiorum meorum cum non subsit causa distringendi, vel cum sit, modum excedat, vel per excogitatam maliciam ordinem non observaverit. . . . Non video quare non.'

[101] *Bracton*, f. 217, Thorne, iii 154.

[102] D. W. Sutherland, *The Assize of Novel Disseisin* (Oxford, 1973), p. 83.

sheriffs in the Exchequer of its existence.[103] Nor can we see the enforcement of any general rule requiring other *animalia otiosa* to be taken in distraint before sheep prior to legislation of 1275 (*Districciones Scaccarii*) and the fact that certain religious houses obtained royal charters which gave their sheep such a privilege provides strong negative evidence against its existence prior to that date.[104] While it is possible that the author is stating some variety of local customary rule (perhaps the rules which applied in a particular county) he is clearly not stating the regular practice of the king's court.

It also seems clear that the section of the treatise which deals with the action of replevin is not in fact describing the way in which the action was pleaded at any date in the king's court.[105] Here the problem is not that *Bracton* is providing a contentious picture of what English legal custom is or ought to be, but rather that what he is doing (and all, if one reads him carefully, that he is claiming to be doing) is describing the workings of the action in the county court, perhaps even in one particular county court, and the rules and customs described are apparently those of this one particular, albeit unspecified, county court. He also seems to be describing the mechanics of the action at a relatively early period when, even when the plea was initiated by royal writ, jury trial was not available to decide issues of fact arising in pleading, but only the production and examination of suit and wager of law. The few references to replevin litigation in the king's court are clearly all later additions.

Bracton does provide us with a valuable insight into the English Common Law of the late 1220s and 1230s, though we need to be wary of using it as a reliable guide even to the law of that period except where we can check what the treatise says against the evidence of the plea rolls. There is no reason to suppose that it is a reliable guide to the law of any later period. The Common Law was constantly developing and the nature and content of English legal custom during the second half of the reign of Henry III needs to be established from the evidence of the surviving plea rolls and the relatively few minor treatises which were written in that period. Henry III's reign might easily have been the 'Age of Bracton' in yet another sense. The 'Bractonian' synthesis and statement of English law might have helped to crystallize and stabilise English legal custom along the lines established

---

[103] *Dialogus*, pp. 111–12; 'quod nullus rusticus distringatur pro debito domini sui quamdiu dominus suus habuerit per quod poterit distringi . . .' as quoted in M. T. Clanchy, 'Did Henry III have a policy?', *History*, 53 (1968), at p. 216.

[104] *Stat. Realm*, i 197b.

[105] *Bracton*, ff. 156b–59b, Thorne, ii 439–49.

or stated by the treatise. It was not and the reasons are not hard to find. No one apart from Henry of Bracton appears to have had access to the treatise prior to his death. It was therefore impossible during his lifetime for *Bracton* to exercise any influence over the development of English law. By the time Henry of Bracton had died it was perhaps too late for *Bracton* to enjoy the kind of success and influence it might have had if it had gone into circulation at a date closer to the time of its original composition.

Henry of Bracton as a Royal Justice

Henry of Bracton was, for Maitland, one of the major royal justices of the reign of Henry III. This is perhaps no more than implicit in the *History of English Law* where he brackets his name with those of Martin of Pateshull, William Raleigh, Robert of Lexington, and William of York not just as a clerical justice but also as one of the 'great lawyers [who] seem to have earned the respect of all parties in the state'.[106] The introduction to *Bracton's Note Book* makes it plain how Maitland originally formed that opinion. It was not just because Bracton had been the author of a great legal treatise but also because Maitland believed that, after a brief spell as a justice in eyre (in 1245), Bracton had become a justice of the highest regular royal court, the court of King's Bench (by 1248), and had then probably served as a justice of that court continuously down to the time of his death in 1268.[107] By the time he came to write the *History of English Law* Maitland knew that Henry of Bracton had retired or been dismissed from the court of King's Bench in or shortly after 1257. This does not seem, however, to have altered his picture of Henry of Bracton's place in the English judiciary of his period. Maitland also thought that Bracton's training and clerical status made him a typical figure in the royal judiciary of his day. Henry III's judges 'seem for the most part to have worked their way upwards as clerks in the court, in the exchequer, in the chancery'. Many of the royal justices of the reign of Henry III were, like Bracton, ecclesiastics and 'canonries, deaneries and even bishoprics were still to be earned by good service on the bench'. It had only been towards the end of the reign that 'the lay element among the king's judges is beginning to outweigh the ecclesiastical'.[108]

[106] Pollock and Maitland, i 205.
[107] *BNB*, i pp. 18–22.
[108] Pollock and Maitland, i 205.

It now seems clear that Maitland was wrong in supposing that a majority of royal justices of the reign of Henry III were clerks and that it was only in the final years of the reign that a lay element became prominent in the courts. From the very beginning of regular royal courts in England in the reign of Henry II laymen and clerics had been fairly evenly balanced within the ranks of royal justices and this remained true not just during the reign of Henry III but also in the reign of his son, Edward I.[109] It is certainly possible to trace the background of a number of royal justices of Henry's reign in service as clerks in the courts, though recruitment from clerks with experience solely in other branches of the royal administration was perhaps rather less common than Maitland suggests and prior clerical service does not seem to have been the background of a majority of royal justices of the period.[110] Maitland's picture of Bracton as one of the major judicial figures of the reign of Henry III seems even more dubious. Bracton never served as a justice of the main royal court for the hearing of civil litigation (the Common Bench) and only ever sat as a junior eyre justice in three consecutive eyres all held in a single year (1245). Even his service as a justice of the court of King's Bench ran only from 1247 to 1251 and again from 1253 to 1257, no more than ten years in all.[111] His judicial career thus hardly bears comparison with the over thirty years as a Common Bench and eyre justice of Gilbert of Preston or the twenty and more years of judicial service of three other royal justices (Robert of Lexington, Roger of Thirkleby, and Henry of Bath) or even the judicial service of the eight other justices who had careers of between ten and twenty years.[112] Henry of Bracton was thus a comparatively minor judicial figure in the overall context of the English judiciary during Henry III's reign. This is a matter of some importance because it may have been precisely because Henry of Bracton's judicial experience was so limited that he was forced to give up any attempt to bring the treatise itself up to date. *Bracton* had been written by someone with direct experience of the Common Bench and of the eyre both as a clerk and as a justice and this experience was put to good

[109] R. V. Turner, *The English Judiciary in the Age of Glanvill and Bracton* (Cambridge, 1985), p. 291; Paul Brand, *The Making of the Common Law* (London, 1992), pp. 158–65, 196–9.
[110] Paul Brand, *The Origins of the English Legal Profession* (Oxford, 1992), pp. 28–9. The only example Maitland cites of a chancery clerk is William of York but it is now clear that he had served in a position equivalent to that of the later keeper of rolls and writs of the Common Bench for almost a decade prior to his appointment as a royal justice: *Ibid.*, p. 28. A better example would have been Robert Fulks who had served as a chancery clerk for about twenty years prior to his appointment as a Common Bench justice in 1271 but was without any substantial prior court experience.
[111] *Bracton*, iii p. xxxiii.
[112] Brand, *Origins of the English Legal Profession*, pp. 27–8.

use in the writing of the treatise. It needed someone with similar experience to bring or keep it up to date. Henry of Bracton was not that man. He was therefore reduced to claiming that it was deliberate choice on his part only to cite the 'ancient judgments of just men' in the treatise. In reality, he did so because he had no alternative.

Proceedings of the British Academy, **89**, 91–113

Maitland on Family and Kinship

STEPHEN D. WHITE

'Individuals do not cease to be individuals when there are many of them.'[1]

ALTHOUGH FREDERIC WILLIAM MAITLAND DISCUSSED the medieval family in the *History of English Law* and produced some brilliantly polemical passages about it, he should not be mistaken for an historian of the family. He did not perpetuate the earlier form of family history that other lawyers had invented, according to Engels, at the beginning of the 1860s.[2] Nor does Maitland's work in legal history clearly fore-shadow the newer kinds of family history that have been created since the 1960s.[3] On the one hand, he discussed few of the topics that later assumed canonical status in the field of family history, where, in an era of self-consciously interdisciplinary research and *histoire totale*, legal historians of family institutions were joined by historical demographers, economic and social historians, analysts and psycholanalysts of familiar *mentalités*, historical geographers of the body, and historians of gender, aging, childhood, sex, and family violence; and although he was much

---

© The British Academy 1996

[1] Pollock and Maitland, ii 247.

[2] Frederick Engels, *The Origin of the Family, Private Property and the State* (New York, 1942), Preface to the 4th ed. (1891), p. 7. For the reference and for insights into old and new forms of family history, I am indebted to Cynthia Patterson, *The Family in Greek History* (Cambridge, Mass., forthcoming). Beginning in 1861 with the publication of Maine's *Ancient Law* and Johannes Bachofen's *Das Mutterrecht*, ' "sociological" monographs' forming a 'branch of legal studies' and positing 'a direct progression from primitive society through various intermediate stages to modern society' treated the history of the family (Adam Kuper, *The Invention of Primitive Society: Transformations and Illusions* [London, 1988], pp. 2–3).

[3] On work of this kind, see e.g. Lawrence Stone, 'Family history in the 1980s: past achieve-ments and future trends', *Journal of Interdisciplinary History*, 12 (1981), 51–87; and Robert Wheaton, 'Introduction: recent trends in the historical study of the French family', in Robert Wheaton and Tamara K. Hareven, eds., *Family and Sexuality in French History* (Philadelphia, 1980), pp. 3–25; and Louise Tilly and Miriam Cohen, 'Does the family have a history? A review of theory and practice in family history', *Social Science History*, 6 (1982), 131–80. The history of medieval English peasant families is explored from many different perspectives in Barbara A. Hannawalt, *The Ties that Bound: Peasant Families in Medieval England* (New York, 1986).

better positioned, in terms of knowledge and interest, to anticipate modern studies on such topic as 'feudal society and the family in early medieval England', he never addressed this topic directly.[4] On the other hand, writing shortly after the deaths of old-style historians of the family, such as Morgan (d. 1881), Bachofen (d. 1887), Maine (d. 1888), and Fustel de Coulanges (d. 1889), Maitland did not directly engage in what he called 'those interesting controversies about primitive tribes and savage families', which had arisen out of his predecessors' efforts to chart the family's evolution over the prehistoric or barely historic *longue durée*.[5] Instead of either contributing to an old history of the family or helping to construct a new one, Maitland deployed a distinctive style of legal analysis to contest and undermine what he considered to be dogmas, theories, and common-places about the early history of the family. As a legal historian who was sceptical about whether the medieval English family really had much of a legal history, he was interested less in what medieval kinship groups were, what they did, or what their members thought they should be and do than he was in what they were not, what they did not do, and what the law did not allow them to be or do.

In discussing the family in the *History of English Law*, Maitland had one overriding polemical purpose, which was to contest the

[4] See J. C. Holt. 'Feudal society and the family in early medieval England: I. The revolution of 1066', *TRHS*, 5th ser. 32 (1982), 193–212; id., 'Feudal society and the family in early medieval England: II. Notions of patrimony', *TRHS*, 5th ser. 33 (1983), 193–220; id., 'Feudal society and the family in early medieval England: III. Patronage and politics', *TRHS*, 5th ser. 34 (1984), 1–25. See also id., 'What's in a name: Family nomenclature and the Norman conquest', The Stenton Lecture 1981 (University of Reading, 1982); and id., 'Politics and property in early medieval England', *PP*, 57 (1972), 3–52. On the same topic, see Sidney Painter, 'The family and the feudal system in twelfth-century England', *Speculum*, 35 (1960), 1–16, reprinted in id., *Feudalism and Liberty: Articles and Addresses of Sidney Painter*, ed. Fred A. Cazel, Jr. (Baltimore, 1961), pp. 195–219. The last decade has seen the publication of numerous studies linking English family history and legal history.

[5] Pollock and Maitland, ii 240. Discussions of Maine include: R. C. J. Cocks, *Sir Henry Maine: A Study in Victorian Jurisprudence* (Cambridge, 1988); Stefan Collini, Donald Winch and John Burrow, *That Noble Science of Politics: A Study of Nineteenth-Century Intellectual History* (Cambridge, 1983), esp. ch. 7; Stefan Collini, *Public Moralists: Political Thought and Intellectual Life in Britain, 1850–1930* (Oxford, 1991), esp. ch. 7; John Burrow, *Evolution and Society: A Study in Victorian Social Theory* (Cambridge, 1966); id., ' "The Village Community" and the uses of history in late nineteenth-century England', in Neil McKendrick, ed., *Historical Perspectives: Studies in English Thought and Society in Honour of J. H. Plumb* (London, 1974), pp. 255–84; Peter Stein, *Legal Evolution: The Story of an Idea* (Cambridge, 1980), esp. pp. 86–98; G. Feaver, *From Status to Contract* (London, 1969); Kuper, *Invention of Primitive Society*, esp. chs 1–2. On Morgan, see T. R. Trautman, *Lewis Henry Morgan and the Invention of Kinship* (Berkeley, 1987); Kuper, *Invention of Primitive Society*, ch. 3. On Fustel de Coulanges, see François Hartog, *Le XIXe siècle et l'histoire: le cas Fustel de Coulanges* (Paris, 1988); and Fustel de Coulanges, *The Origin of Property in Land*, trans Margaret Ashley (2nd ed., London, 1927).

'common-place among English writers', notably Maine, that 'the family rather than the individual was the "unit" of ancient law.'[6] 'There are some', Maitland later wrote in *Township and Borough*,

> who would have us believe that groups, families, clans, rather than individual men, were the oldest 'units' of law: that there was law for groups long before there was law for individuals. In the earliest stage, we are told, all is 'collective.' Neither crime nor debt, neither property nor marriage nor paternity can be ascribed to the individual. Far [sic] rather the group itself, the clan or family, is the one and only subject of rights and duties.[7]

Although Maitland saw in this argument 'a laudable reaction against the individualism of Natural Law',[8] he also called the thesis 'extravagant', treating it as dogma to be aggressively refuted and totally reversed.[9] In the *History of English Law*, he wrote, 'The student of the middle ages will at first sight see communalism everywhere. It seems to be an all pervading principle . . . A little experience will make him distrust this communalism; he will begin to regard it as the thin cloak of a rough and rude individualism.'[10] Determined to find a single 'all-pervading principle' of early English law and denying that role to communalism, Maitland chose what Vinogradoff later called 'antiquarian individualism'.[11] Just as in *Domesday Book and Beyond* he contested earlier theories about the village community by arguing that 'so far back as we can see, the German village had a solid core of individualism,'[12] he tried in the *History of English Law* to refute

[6] Pollock and Maitland, ii 240.
[7] F. W. Maitland, *Township and Borough* (1894; reprinted Cambridge, 1964), pp. 20–1. On Maitland's criticisms of Maine, see H. E. Bell, *Maitland: A Critical Examination and Assessment* (Cambridge, Mass., 1965), pp. 75–7; Stein, *Legal Evolution*, pp. 106–10; Cocks, *Maine*, pp. 142–5 and 145 n. 1; Burrow, 'Village Community', pp. 275–83; and id., *Whigs and Liberals: Continuity and Change in English Political Thought* (Oxford, 1988), pp. 135–45. According to Stein, 'Vinogradoff accepted Maitland's general criticism of Maine, but believed that Maine's comparative historical method was still valid' (*Legal Evolution*, p. 116).
[8] *Township and Borough*, p. 21. According to Burrow, 'Maine was concerned at various points in his writings to refute the notion, which he associated primarily with Rousseau, and seems to have seen as dangerously democratic, of an original state of nature and individual natural rights' ('Village Community', p. 271). See also Kuper, *Invention of Primitive Society*, pp. 17, 25, 231, 241.
[9] 'It is quite possible that . . .' (Pollock and Maitland, ii 243); 'That there is truth in this saying we are very far from denying' (ibid., ii 240).
[10] Ibid., i 616.
[11] 'Maitland's antiquarian individualism brought him into collision with the teaching about tribal as well as about agrarian communities' (Paul Vinogradoff, 'Frederic William Maitland', in *The Collected Papers of Paul Vinogradoff*, 2 vols. [London, 1928], i 259.)
[12] *Domesday Book and Beyond*, p. 348. For a lucid, contextualized account of Maitland's views on this subject, see Burrow, 'Village Community', esp. pp. 275–83. See also Reba N. Soffer, *Discipline and Power: The University, History, and the Making of an English Elite, 1870–1930* (Stanford, CA, 1994), ch. 3.

Maine's teachings by finding 'rough and rude individualism' in the family, which was not, he insisted, a 'group-unit' — that is a corporate group.[13] Maitland's 'antiquarian individualism' also supported an even broader argument, in which, as Professor Burrow has shown, Maitland reversed 'a famous judgment' of Maine's by proposing that 'while the individual is the unit of ancient, the corporation is the unit of modern law.'[14] This polemical agenda deeply coloured Maitland's arguments about the medieval family, which were constructed less for the purpose of creating a comprehensive legal ethnography of the medieval family than they were for the purpose of refuting Maine's dogmas.

Although Maitland attacked those teachings as the products of dogmatic, undocumentable speculation and searched diligently for texts that would document his own conclusions about early English family law,[15] his own readings of texts were mediated by several interrelated interpretive strategies or schemas that helped him to argue that the English family was not a 'group-unit', could never have been the unit of early English law, and, instead, occupied a marginal position in medieval English society. Maitland achieved his polemical goal by abandoning the comparative method that Maine had used in melding evidence about many 'Indo-European societies' into a single evolutionary schema and by constructing, instead, a court-centred, judge-centred, state-centred national legal history in which kinship groups were almost invisible as active forces capable of shaping their own legal history and appeared, instead, as the passive subjects of external regulation by the state and its judges. 'At the touch of jurisprudence', as he put it in a different context, a group could become 'a mere group of individuals, each with his separate rights'.[16] Because, in the *History of English Law*, Maitland evidently concurred with Pollock in sharply distinguishing 'rules of law' from 'common rules of morals and manners'[17] and in equating 'law', for the purposes of historical inquiry, with 'the sum of the rules administered by courts of justice',[18] and not

---

[13] *Gierke*, p. ix.

[14] *Township and Borough*, p. 15; discussed in Burrow, 'Village Community', p. 283. The most famous form of Maine's judgment was that 'the movement of the progressive societies has hitherto been a movement *from Status to Contract*': Sir Henry Maine, *Ancient Law*, Everyman's Library (London, 1965), p. 100.

[15] Maitland wrote to Pollock: 'I always talk of [Maine] with reluctance, for on the few occasions on which I sought to verify his statements of fact I came to the conclusion that he trusted much to a memory that played him tricks and rarely looked at a book that he had once read': *Letters*, i no. 279.

[16] *Domesday Book and Beyond*, p. 150; paraphrased by Vinogradoff as, 'communalism evaporates at the touch of legal doctrine': 'Maitland', p. 259.

[17] Pollock and Maitland, i p. xciv.

[18] Ibid., i p. xcv.

with custom, he found no place in the legal history of the family, as later historians sometimes have, for the study of how people other than judges thought about kinship and used it in practice to legitimate claims on others.[19] Moreover, because the region he studied was exceptionally well-endowed with legal records he was not obliged — as historians of continental family law have been — to rely heavily on evidence about familial practices, which, in any case, were controlled, he thought, by rules enforced from outside the family.[20] Though keenly aware of 'the hundred forces which play upon our legal history',[21] he excluded many of them from his own writings about the family, which never treated 'family concerns' as 'a driving force for [legal] change'[22] and which represented medieval families as collectivities only to the extent that judges and legislators did so — which, in his opinion, wasn't often. His discussions of family law centred on the analysis of the legal rights accorded to individual family members by English judges, who, he believed, had the power to shape the family because, by Angevin times if not earlier, they were sitting on 'a bold high-handed court which wields the might of a strong kingship'.[23]

Associated with this way of writing legal history were several other interpretive strategies or schemas that largely determined how the family would appear or not appear in Maitland's work. In the *History of English Law*, kinship appears as an unusually weak force partly because he found ways of dissolving families into the individuals composing them, partly because he dispensed with any notion of family solidarity, group personality, or kinship ideology to represent and explain relations among kin, and partly because his penchant for deconstructing family communities contrasted sharply with what Burrow calls 'his readiness to endorse group personalities' under modern law[24] and with his readiness to treat state, church, and feudalism as unified,

---

[19] William Ian Miller, *Bloodtaking and Peacemaking: Feud, Law, and Society in Saga Iceland* (Chicago, 1990), p. 141.

[20] For a different approach to the same problem, see John Hudson, *Land, Law, and Lordship in Anglo-Norman England* (Oxford, 1984), esp. p. 181; and White, *Custom*, esp. chs. 1, 2, and 5. On rules see Pierre Bourdieu, *Outline of a Theory of Practice*, trans. Richard Nice (1977; reprinted Cambridge, 1982), ch. 1; id., *The Logic of Practice*, trans. Richard Nice (Stanford, 1990), Book I, esp. pp. 37–41.

[21] Pollock and Maitland, i 80.

[22] Eileen Spring, *Law, Land & Family: Aristocratic Inheritance in England, 1300 to 1800* (Chapel Hill, NC, 1993), p. 181.

[23] Pollock and Maitland, ii 447.

[24] 'Village Community', p. 279. According to Burrow, Maitland learned 'to see in the organized social group "no fiction, no symbol, no collective name for individuals, but a living organism and a real person"' (ibid., p. 277; citing *Gierke*, p. xxvi). Although Maitland imagined a book on 'the structure of the groups in which men of English race have stood from the days when

collective forces that powerfully shaped the law, even though they, too, could have been deconstructed into their individual elements.[25] Maitland, moreover, saw an inevitable conflict between the needs of the medieval state and the 'archaic habits and claims' of the family[26] and found signs of it in judicial and legislative decisions that he could interpret as subordinating the family's interests to the state's. Further- more, by dividing his discussion of family law into so many different legal subtopics (e.g. inheritance, wills, intestacy, marriage, husband and wife, infancy and guardianship), Maitland ruled out the possibility of addressing practical questions about how people used kinship as an idiom for giving their claims normative force and how family members used the law; and he never really asked how the law did or did not facilitate the efforts of aristocratic kinship groups, whether or not they had true corporate identities, to maintain wealth, power, and enduring social identities.[27] Finally, although Maitland queried 'hasty talk about national character',[28] ridiculed 'ethnical theory' as an explanation for national difference,[29] and emphasised 'the French influence' on English law,[30] his comparisons of English and French family law were still constructed to emphasise English individualism, English 'precocity' in

the revengeful kindred was pursuing the blood-feud to the days when the one-man company is issuing debentures', the family, not being an organized social group, did not figure promi- nently in his efforts to determine 'how Englishmen have conceived their groups' and, more specifically, 'by what thoughts [Englishmen] have striven to distinguish and to reconcile the manyness of the members and the oneness of the body' (ibid., p. xxvii). On 'family solidarity' as an important concept in French discussions of kinship, see e.g. White, *Custom*, pp. 6–11 *passim*. According to Pierre Bourdieu, kinship groups 'continue to exist' partly because 'they rest on a community of dispositions (habitus) and interests which is also the basis of undivided ownership of the material and symbolic patrimony': *Outline*, p. 35.

[25] Positing the existence of a 'feudal force', which was backed by strong 'moral sentiments', Maitland thought that the 'real importance' of homage and fealty lay 'but partly within the field of law': Pollock and Maitland, i 300, 297.

[26] Ibid., i 31. Although the phrase is presumably Pollock's, it would not have troubled Maitland, who wrote that the law of the state was prepared to crush the family 'into atoms': ibid., ii 243.

[27] Ibid., ii 240–447. For discussion of many of the same issues from perspectives very different from Maitland's, see, e.g., Spring *Law, Land, and Family* and Jack Goody, Joan Thirsk and E. P. Thompson, eds., *Family and Inheritance: Rural Society in Western Europe, 1200–1800* (Cambridge, 1976).

[28] Pollock and Maitland, i p. cvi.

[29] Ibid., ii 402.

[30] Ibid., i 81. He also noted 'how exceedingly like our common law once was to a French *coutume*' (ibid., i p. cvi; see also i 87; ii 445) and how many 'invaluable hint[s] for the solution of specifically English problems' could be found in the writings of continental medievalists' (ibid., p. cvi).

suppressing archaisms in family law,[31] and 'a premature simplicity imposed [in England] from above'.[32]

All the interpretive strategies that facilitated Maitland's attack on Maine's teachings about the family were at work in two important sections on the family in the *History of English Law*: first, the brief discussion of feuding that prefaced his entire discussion of the family; and, second, the analysis of the consent of heirs to the alienation of land — a topic to which he returned so often in his *History* as to suggest that he found it particularly important and troubling.[33] In order to incorporate analyses of these two topics into his polemic against Maine, Maitland was obliged to make numerous choices about how to read sparse, difficult evidence; he also had to rely on many different assumptions about matters on which the evidence was largely or completely silent. The choices and assumptions he made may have been sounder than Maine's; but when they are read in the light of the ones subsequently made by writers on the same topics in both England and France, we can see that although Maitland's readings of texts were relatively plausible and harmonized well with his polemic against Maine, they were not the only plausible readings available. Seeing how Maitland bridged the gaps between his attack on Maine and the texts on which he grounded it helps to bridge the gap between the two sides of Maitland identified by Professor Burrow. On the one hand, we have the historian revered for 'the political chastity of his historical writing' and admired for making the *History of English Law* 'the paradigm of a new historical objectivity'. On the other hand, we have Maine's polemical adversary and the author of work on corporations that 'became', as Burrow puts it, 'a political inspiration to social pluralists'.[34] In the middle we have an historian whose 'habits of mind' (as he called them) enabled him to interpret texts in such a way as to create a *History* that was meant to be objective and politically chaste and that included a polemically charged refutation of Maine.[35]

Immediately preceding a longer critique of 'the popular theory that land was owned by families or households before it was owned by individuals',[36] Maitland's brief analysis of blood-feuds set both the

---

[31] Ibid., i 224; see ii 313, 402, 445–7.

[32] Ibid., ii 447.

[33] Ibid., ii 13, 15, 17, 20, 213, 248, 251, 254, 255, 308–13.

[34] See Burrow, 'Village Community'. p. 276.

[35] Letter to Paul Vinogradoff, *Letters*, i no. 59. On the letter and on Maitland's politics generally, see Burrow, 'Village Community'; and id., *Whigs and Politics*, pp. 135–45. On Maine's 'political agenda' in *Ancient Law*, see Kuper, *Invention of Primitive Society*, p. 23.

[36] Pollock and Maitland, ii 245; see also 'the common saying that the land-owning unit was not an individual but a *maegð*, a clan, or *gens*': ii 244.

analytical agenda and the polemical tone of his entire argument on the family by justifying 'warnings' against the 'temptation' of believing 'the common-place ... that the family rather than the individual was the "unit" of ancient law'.[37] Rhetorically, the warnings were effective partly because of Maitland's ironically judicious concessions to dogma and mainly because of his ability to contrast 'theories', 'dogmas', and 'guesses'[38] with statements of what is 'clear' and 'plain' because it is 'what we see'.[39] Before — or after — rejecting a theory, he liked to note that it might be true.[40] But dogmas about the family, it turned out, might be true only of societies about which nothing was or could be known. What Maitland 'saw' he saw clearly revealed in what he saw as perfectly transparent texts.

To attack the dogma that families were the units of early law, Maitland invoked 'rules about ... blood-feud' in Anglo-Saxon codes and the *Leges Henrici Primi*,[41] which he interpreted in such a way as to represent families as fleeting associations of individuals. Several rules stipulated that compensation for homicide was due from the slayer's maternal and paternal kin and was payable to the victim's maternal and paternal kin; other rules provided that a married woman's blood-kinsmen were entitled to her *wer* and that they, rather than her husband and his kin, were liable for vengeance for her misdeeds. What Maitland saw in these 'rules of blood-feud' was 'a practical denial of [the family's] existence' as a legally recognised unit.[42] Unable to resist the temptation of twice proposing extravagantly that under these rules 'there were as many "blood-feud groups" as there were living persons', he withdrew judiciously to the more defensible position that 'at all events each set of brothers and sisters was the centre of a different group.'[43] If so, then 'the blood-feud group' could not have been 'a permanently organized unit':

> If there is a feud to be borne or *wer* to be paid or received, [the group] may organize itself *ad hoc*; but the organization will be of a fleeting kind. The very next deed of violence that is done will call some other blood-feud group

[37] Pollock and Maitland, ii 244.

[38] Also: what 'may be', what 'some will surmise', what 'others will argue' and what 'others, again, may think' (ibid., ii 240–44).

[39] Ibid., ii 242, 243.

[40] 'It may be that in the history of every nation' (ibid., ii 241); 'It is quite possible that' (ii 243).

[41] Ibid., ii 241.

[42] Ibid., ii 243–4.

[43] Ibid., ii 242. He implied, for a second time, that every individual must have had a different family, when he wrote that 'We must resist the temptation to speak of "the *maegð*" as if it were a kind of corporation, otherwise we have as many corporations as there are men and women': ibid., ii 244.

into existence. Along with his brothers and paternal uncles a man goes out to avenge his father's death and is slain. His maternal uncles and cousins, who stood outside the old feud, will claim a share in his *wer*.

This is what we *see* as soon as we see our ancestors.[44]

Although members of a vengeance group would presumably 'meet together and take counsel over a plan of campaign,' they could have no collective legal identity under 'a system which divides the *wergild* among *individual men*'.[45] Could they have any collective identity at all? Finally, after baldly asserting that 'if the law were to treat the clan as an unit for any purpose whatever, this would surely be the purpose of *wer* and blood-feud,'[46] he extended his conclusions about 'blood-feud groups' to the family generally. Since 'the blood-feud group' was a cognatic kindred, not a patrilineal or matrilineal descent group, 'the exclusive domination of either "father-right" or "mother-right" . . . should be placed for our race beyond the extreme limit of history.'[47] For the same reason, 'a system of mutually exclusive clans is imposs-ible,'[48] and 'we ought not to talk of clans at all.'[49] The conclusion that any organization of the 'blood-feud group' will be of 'a fleeting kind'[50] pointed toward a similar conclusion about the family, which could never have played the role in early law that Maine had assigned to it.

Polemically effective as this attack on Maine was, Maitland's read-ing of rules about wergeld took him far beyond what was immediately visible in the texts he read. What he said we saw when he first saw his ancestors he had artfully and imaginatively constructed from texts he read in the light of various unsubstantiated, unstated assumptions, including these: that rules about paying compensation in Anglo-Saxon codes actually regulated this practice and corresponded closely to pre-vailing kinship ideology about paying compensation; that the compo-sition of actual vengeance groups and support groups closely resembled the composition of the groups that can be reconstructed by identify-ing the categories of people who, according to legislators, were either

[44] Ibid., ii 243; italics added. See also ibid., i 32: 'We need not, however, regard the kindred as a defined body like a tribe or clan, indeed this would not stand with the fact that the burden of making and the duty of exacting compensation ran on the mother's side as well as the father's. A father and son, or two half-brothers, would . . . have some of the same kindred in common, but by no means all.'
[45] Ibid., ii 244; italics added.
[46] Ibid., ii 242.
[47] Ibid., ii 243.
[48] Ibid., ii 241.
[49] Ibid., ii 242.
[50] Ibid., ii 242.

legally obligated to pay *wer* or legally entitled to claim it;[51] that cognatic
kindreds can have no enduring group identity; that the existence of
lineages is incompatible with recognition of close ties to kin outside
the lineage; and, finally, that the feuding groups that he thought he
saw and that he pictured for his readers can be taken as a model for
all other significant kinship groups — in short, for the family.[52] An
associated assumption is that externally enforced legal rules formulated
by rulers not only constrain familial practices but virtually constitute
them.

Only by making such assumptions could Maitland have moved from
rules about paying compensation to end blood-feuds, to the practice
of paying compensation to end blood-feuds, to feuds themselves, to
the recruitment of kin into 'blood-feud groups', to the 'fleeting' character of blood-feud groups, and, finally, to the absence of permanently
organized families of any kind. By making these leaps across the gaps
in his evidence, Maitland did more than attack Maine's ideas about
the early legal history of the family; he also represented groups of kin
as being associations so individualistic and ephemeral that their ability
to act collectively for any purpose, however fleeting, was in doubt.
Instead of trying to determine how feuds worked and what they
revealed about kinship,[53] Maitland studied feuding in order to determine why feuding could *not* have worked — or, at least, why the family
could not have been a 'permanent and mutually exclusive [unit]'.[54] He
conceded that 'strong family groups' may well have 'formed themselves

---

[51] 'Liability to a public fine or, in grave cases, corporal or capital punishment, may concur
with liability to make redress to a person wronged or slain, or to his kindred, *or incur his
feud in default*': Pollock and Maitland, i 38; italics added.

[52] For discussions of medieval kinship that query some of these assumptions see, for example,
T. M. Charles-Edwards, 'Kinship, status and the origins of the hide', *PP*, 56 (1972), 21–5, esp.
21 n. 35; Jack Goody, *The Development of the Family and Marriage in Europe* (Cambridge,
1983), p. 226; David Herlihy, *Medieval Households* (Cambridge, Mass., 1985), pp. 82–103;
Miller, *Bloodtaking and Peacemaking*, ch. 5; and White, *Custom*, ch. 4.

[53] On 'permitted or justified private war, of which we do find considerable traces in England',
see Pollock and Maitland, i 39; see also i 46–8, 53, 58, 75. For a recent effort to show that
'feud does not cease to be a topic for study after 1066', see Paul R. Hyams, 'Feud in medieval
England', *Haskins Society Journal*, 3 (1991), 1–21. On French feuds in roughly the same
period, see Stephen D. White, 'Feuding and peace-making in the Touraine around the year
1100', *Traditio*, 42 (1986), 195–263. Theoretical problems involved in the study of medieval
feuds are explored in Miller, *Bloodtaking and Peacemaking*, ch. 6; and Stephen D. White,
'Clotild's Revenge: Politics, Kinship, and Ideology in the Merovingian Bloodfeud', in *Portraits
of Medieval and Renaissance Living: Essays in Memory of David Herlihy* (Ann Arbor, Mich.,
forthcoming). On feuding, see also Patrick Wormald, 'The Age of Bede and Aethelbald', in
James Campbell, Eric John, Patrick Wormald, *The Anglo-Saxons* (Oxford, 1982), p. 98.

[54] Pollock and Maitland, ii 241. English people, he asserted, could not have been 'grouped
together into mutually exclusive clans': ibid., ii 240.

and that the law had to reckon with them'.[55] 'It is quite possible', he wrote, that:

> in England men *as a matter of fact* dwelt together in large groups tilling the land by cooperation, that the members of each group were, or deemed themselves to be, kinsmen in blood, and that as a force for keeping them in these local groups spear-sibship was stronger than spindle-sibship . . . We get a hint of such permanent cohesive groups when we find King Aethelstan legislating against the *maegð* that is so strong . . . that it denies the king's rights and harbours thieves.[56]

Maitland insisted, however, that such groups were doomed; they led the precarious life of outlaws. In a society where the state and the family were enemies, strong family groups formed themselves in opposition to 'a principle which . . . seems to be incompatible with the existence of mutually exclusive gentes as legal entities';[57] such families lived in opposition to the law of the state, which 'will, if possible, treat the *maegð* as an "unit" by crushing it into atoms.'[58]

Just as Maitland cited the 'fleeting' organization of 'blood-feud groups', the law's individualistic *wergild* system, and the state's hostility to powerful kindreds to show that families could not have been permanently organized group-units, he used a similar but more complicated strategy to contest 'the common saying that the [early] land-owning unit was not an individual but a *maegð*, a clan, or a *gens*.'[59] Although his attack on 'the popular theory that land was owned by families or households before it was owned by individuals'[60] relied on the argument that medieval families were not corporate groups, his discussion of land law down to the early thirteenth century also attacked other dogmas. In addition to denying that true 'family ownership' had ever

[55] Ibid., ii 245.
[56] Ibid., ii 243; italics added.
[57] Ibid., ii 245.
[58] Ibid., ii 243.
[59] Ibid., ii 244. According to Vinogradoff, Maitland was 'opposed to the idea of a primitive collectivism shaping the early land law of Indo-European nations, and of England in particular' ('Maitland', p. 259). According to Burrow, *Whigs and Liberals*, p. 142, 'Maitland constantly challenged Maine's version of the history of property relations'.
[60] Pollock and Maitland, ii 245. In *Domesday Book and Beyond* Maitland referred to the same 'theory' (p. 340) and, before moving on to argue that land was not owned by village communities (pp. 346–56), recapitulated arguments previously used in the *History* (pp. 340–6). In 1874 Maine had written: 'The collective ownership of the soil by groups of men either in fact united by blood-relationship, or believing or assuming that they are so united, is now entitled to rank as an ascertained primitive phenomenon, once universally characterizing those communities of mankind between whose civilization and our own there is any distinct connection or analogy': Sir Henry Sumner Maine, *Lectures on the Early History of Institutions* (1875; reprinted London, 1966), pp. 1–2.

'prevailed among the English in England,'[61] Maitland denied that
before the thirteenth century, when the 'common law of inheritance',
he thought, 'was rapidly assuming its final form,'[62] there had been 'a
steady movement' in England towards more individualistic forms of
property ownership.[63] He also denied that in England and France the
history of property law and family law had followed the same paths.[64]
To sustain these attacks on Maine's teachings, Maitland had to reinter-
pret practices 'commonly regarded as the relics of family ownership',[65]
notably the widespread practice — French as well as English — of
giving land with the consent of one or more of the donor's kin.[66] For
the English variant of this practice, Maitland proposed an ingenious
but contestable interpretation that was designed to undermine the
theory that the family had ever owned land.[67]

[61] Pollock and Maitland, ii 255.

[62] Ibid., ii 260.

[63] Ibid., ii 250. On Maitland's 'contemptuous attitude towards historical laws' and on one of
his protests 'against the generalizations of anthropology, comparative jurisprudence, and
inductive politics on laws and stages of development', see Vinogradoff, 'Maitland', p. 269.

[64] Pollock and Maitland, ii 255.

[65] Ibid., ii 251. On 'the inalienability of the family lands' see H. Cabot Lodge, 'Anglo-Saxon
land law', in Essays in Anglo-Saxon Law (1876; reprinted Boston, 1905) p. 75. Arguing more
cautiously than Maine had, Lodge wrote: 'It is of course purely matter of conjecture that
the family as such ever held land. It is, however, a fair inference that in pre-historic times the
Germanic family was regarded more as a legal entity than as an aggregation of individuals.
The course of historical development took the form of the disintegration of the family, and
the further back we go the closer the bond of family becomes, and the stronger the probability
that it held land in its collective capacity'; ibid, p. 74 n. 3.

[66] On approval of French sales by infant expectant heirs, see Pollock and Maitland, ii 213.

[67] As Maitland noted (ibid., ii 251 n. 3), his own reading of Anglo-Saxon charters differed
from the one proposed by Lodge in 'Anglo-Saxon land law', pp. 74–7. More recent discussion
of the consent of heirs to alienations of land in England include: S. E. Thorne, 'English
feudalism and estates in land', CLJ, ns 6 (1959), 193–209, reprinted in id., Essays in
English Legal History (London, 1985), pp. 31–50; Milsom, Legal Framework, esp. pp. 121–4;
and Hudson, Land, Law, and Lordship, ch. 6. On the French laudatio parentum and on
previous discussions of it, see White, Custom, which should be reexamined in the light of:
reviews by Anita Guerreau-Jalabert in Annales E.S.C., 45 (1990), 101–5 and by Gérard
Giordanengo in Revue historique, 574 (1990), 349–51; Barbara H. Rosenwein, To be a
Neighbor of Saint Peter: The Social Meaning of Cluny's Property, 900–1049 (Ithaca, NY,
1989); Constance Brittain Bouchard, Sword, Miter, and Cloister: Nobility and the Church in
Burgundy, 980–1198 (Ithaca, NY, 1987); Emily Zack Tabuteau, Transfers of Property
in Eleventh-Century Norman Law (Chapel Hill, NC, 1988); and Dominique Barthélemy, La
société dans le comté de Vendôme de l'an mil au XIVe siècle (Paris, 1993), Earlier discussions
of the French laudatio include: Louis Falletti, Le retrait lignager en droit coutumier français
(Paris, 1923); J. de Laplanche, La réserve coutumière dans l'ancien droit français (Paris, 1925);
F. Olivier-Martin, Historie du droit français des origines à la révolution (1948; reprinted Paris,
1984); Georges Duby, La société au XIe et XIIe siècles dans la région mâconnaise (1953;
reprinted Paris, 1971); id., 'Lineage, nobility, and knighthood', in idem, The Chivalrous
Society, trans. Cynthia Postan (1977; reprinted Berkeley, 1980), pp. 59–80; id., 'The structure
of kinship and nobility', in Chivalrous Society, pp. 134–48; Robert Fossier, La terre et les
hommes en Picardie jusqu'à la fin du XIIIe siècle (2 vols, Paris, 1968); Paul Ourliac and J. de

Maitland's argument on ownership fell into three main parts. *First,* he construed 'family ownership' as an archaic system in which 'a child . . . acquires [birth-rights] in ancestral land, and this not by gift, bequest, inheritance or any title known to our modern law.'[68] *Next,* having thus transformed the study of family ownership and collective rights in land into the study of the individual birth-rights of children, Maitland then argued that birth-rights could take three different forms — ranging from strong to weaker to very weak — and explained the differences among them by positing a fundamental conflict of interest between the owner and his heir over the question of whether land should be alienated. With 'a strong form of "birthright" ',[69] 'the child was born a landowner' and could block alienations made without his consent. A weaker form of birth-right 'only allows [the child] to recall the alienated land after his father's death'. The weakest form of birth-right is 'a mere *droit de retrait,* a right to redeem the alienated land at the price that has been given for it'.[70]

Third, having reduced family ownership to a system of progressively weaker individual birth-rights defined in ways that presupposed intrafamilial conflict between an individual landholder and his individual heir and that rendered all other family members virtually invisible, Maitland traced the history of birth-rights down to the time of their disappearance in the early thirteenth century, at which time French birth-rights still survived in the very weak form of a *droit de retrait.* Writing of ancestors and heirs generally, he usually limited himself to discussing alienations by upper-class people.[71] Although he rejected 'the theory that among [the Anglo-Saxons] there prevailed anything that ought to be called "family ownership" ',[72] he found two points when the birth-rights of heirs were 'not waning in strength but waxing'.[73] First, 'the

Malafosse, *Histoire du droit privé* (3 vols., Paris, 1968–71); Robert Haidu, 'Family and feudal ties in Poitou, 1100–1300', *Journal of Interdisciplinary History,* 8 (1977), 117–28; Penny Schine Gold, *The Lady and the Virgin: Image, Attitude, and Experience in Twelfth-Century France* (Chicago, Ill., 1985), ch. 4; Jean-Pierre Poly and Eric Bournazel, *La mutation féodale, Xe–XIIe siècle* (2nd ed., Paris, 1991), pp. 185–93.

[68] Pollock and Maitland, ii 248. He reached this position by reducing corporate family ownership to various forms of co-ownership; ibid., ii 245–8.

[69] Ibid., ii 255.

[70] Ibid., ii 248–9.

[71] On whether Maitland's writing on land law is or is not 'directly relevant to all groups in medieval society', see Alan Macfarlane, *The Culture of Capitalism* (Oxford, 1987), p. 195, responding to a review of id., *The Origins of English Individualism: The Family, Property and Social Transition* (Oxford, 1978) by Rodney Hilton ('Individualism and the English peasantry', *New Left Review,* 120 [1980], pp. 109–11).

[72] Pollock and Maitland, ii 251.

[73] Ibid., ii 255.

current of legislation' moved 'in favour of the expectant heirs' in around 900, when the alienation of book-land outside the kindred was forbidden.[74] Doubting that this effort to strengthen birth-rights had had a lasting effect, at least on upper-class practice,[75] Maitland also identified a second period following the conquest when 'the rights of the expectant heir' were strengthened in ways revealed by a comparison of late Anglo-Saxon and Anglo-Norman charters. Whereas 'the Anglo-Saxon thegn who holds book-land does not profess to have his heir's consent when he gives part of that land to a church,' Maitland wrote, 'his successor, the Norman baron, will rarely execute a charter of feoffment which does not express the consent of one heir or many heirs.'[76] To explain the difference between pre-and post-Conquest charters, Maitland asserted that, soon after 1066, when fiefs were heritable and impartible but not yet governed, he thought, by strict primogeniture, a legal rule barring tenants from alienating fiefs without the consent of heirs came into being and was enforced for over a century before it 'silently disappeared' in the early 1200s,[77] 'when the tenant . . . has a perfect right to disappoint his expectant heirs by conveying away the whole of his land by act *inter vivos*'.[78]

Maitland's history of birth-rights was designed to challenge several dogmas about the history of family law. *First*, because even after reducing family ownership to 'a strong form of "birth-right" ' he found no evidence that it had ever 'prevailed among the English in England,'[79] he could reject both the theory that land was owned by families before it was owned by individuals and the theory that the family was the basic unit of early English law. *Second*, the finding that after 1200 birth-rights totally disappeared in England but survived in France in the form of the *retrait lignager*[80] not only demonstrated England's precociousness in legal development;[81] it also undermined the 'unwarrantable hypothesis' that 'the family law of every nation must needs

---

[74] Ibid., ii 253. For a recent discussion of bookland with references to other recent work on it, see Susan Reynolds, *Fiefs and Vassals: The Medieval Evidence Reinterpreted* (Oxford, 1994), pp. 324–42 *passim*.

[75] He thought it 'very likely' that 'among those men who had no books', 'a restraint in favour of the expectant heirs was established': Pollock and Maitland, ii 243.

[76] Ibid., ii 255; see also ii 251.

[77] Ibid., ii 13.

[78] Ibid., ii 308.

[79] Ibid., ii 255.

[80] See ibid., i 344, 647; ii, 249, 311, 313, 330, 446.

[81] Ibid., i 224.

traverse the same route'.[82] *Third*, without denying that English land law became more individualistic when the modern right of inheritance replaced the archaic birth-right, Maitland contested the 'belief' that the history of family law and land law revealed 'steady movement in one direction', as 'birth-rights' and other 'relics' of family ownership slowly, steadily, and inexorably disappeared.[83] Rejecting the 'natural' assumption that 'those forms of birth-right which are least in accord with our own ideas are also the most archaic [and] that the weaker forms are degenerate forms of the stronger',[84] he argued that 'restraints' on a landholder's power of alienation were not 'relics of family ownership',[85] but rather products of judicial compromises between two 'conflicting forces': the interests of landholders, on the one hand, and the interests of heirs, on the other.[86] Maitland also went out of his way to deny that this conflict had changed significantly between the Anglo-Saxon era and his own day:

> In the days before the Conquest a dead man's heirs sometimes attempted to recover land which he had given away. They often did so in the thirteenth century; they sometimes do so at the present day. At the present day a man's expectant heirs do not attempt to interfere with his gifts so long as he is alive; this was not done in the thirteenth century; we have no proof that it was done before the Conquest.[87]

In this way Maitland replaced a theory of natural, steady, inexorable evolution from family ownership of land to individual ownership with a model representing change in land law as 'a series of compromises'[88] that the law had periodically imposed to adjudicate 'a struggle' between owner and heir. The struggle, which continued to the present day, had begun at some ill-defined moment with the appearance of 'purchasers for land' and of 'bishops and priests desirous of acquiring land by gift and willing to offer spiritual benefits in return'.[89]

Like other arguments of Maitland's, this revisionist history of land law depended on textual interpretations that were shaped by his own

---

[82] Ibid., ii 255. Maitland also queried the distinction associated with this hypothesis between 'successful races', whose family laws had all allegedly traversed one route, and 'backward peoples', whose family laws had allegedly 'wandered from the right road'; ibid., ii 255. If every nation's family law had had a different history, how clear was Maine's distinction between 'progressive' and 'non-progressive' peoples (on which see Burrow, 'Village Community', p. 271).

[83] Pollock and Maitland, ii 250.

[84] Ibid., ii 248.

[85] See Lodge, 'Anglo-Saxon land law'.

[86] Pollock and Maitland, ii 250.

[87] Ibid., ii 252.

[88] Ibid., ii 250.

[89] Ibid., ii 249.

way of seeing and not seeing the family. Treating Anglo-Norman and Angevin charters as evidence of restraints on alienation but not 'family ownership',[90] Maitland followed his usual strategies of privileging, when he could, the legal rights of individuals and assuming that the practices of kinship groups were determined by externally enforced legal rules. These interpretive strategies were at work not just when he analysed the consent of heirs to gifts but even when he described this practice. Although he acknowledged that many gifts were made for religious motives,[91] he understood them as alienations similar to sales, not as exchanges of land for prayers for living and/or dead kin.[92] This way of reading gifts had significant implications for Maitland's interpretation of the heir's consent because, in draining gifts of religious meanings, it trivialised the roles of the donor's dead and living kin as beneficiaries of his gifts[93] and limited discussion of questions about why such gifts were made to issues of proprietary right.

In a similar way, Maitland did not see what others have seen as the collective familial dimension of gifts when he represented as the consent of 'heirs'[94] a practice that French historians have long known as 'the consent of kin' (*laudatio parentum*). This choice of descriptive terminology was significant because it prefigured his entire interpretation of the heir's consent. Certain gifts, he found, were made with the consent of kin groups that included wives, sons, daughters, brothers, nephews or grandchildren; other gifts, he indicated, were approved by 'all [the donor's] kinsfolk' or by 'as many of [his] near kinsfolk as can be induced to approve the gift'.[95] Nevertheless, he saw no significance in the exact composition of these groups, which historians of the French *laudatio parentum* have since treated as important evidence about the

[90] See ibid., ii 245–55 *passim*.

[91] He noted that twelfth-century charters often mentioned 'the good of the donor's soul and the souls of his kinsfolk . . . as the motive for the gift' and that 'the prayers of the donees' were sometimes treated as 'services done in return for the land': ibid., ii 243.

[92] 'Every alienation of land, a sale, an onerous lease in fee farm, is a "gift" but no "gift" of land is gratuitous; the donee will always be liable to render service, though it be but the service of prayers': ibid., ii 213.

[93] On this issue, see, e.g., Patrick J. Geary, 'Exchange and interaction between the living and the dead in early medieval society', in id., *Living with the Dead in the Middle Ages* (Ithaca, NY, 1994), pp. 77–92. For theoretical discussions of alienation, see C. A. Gregory, *Gifts and Commodities* (London, 1982); and Annette B. Weiner, *Inalienable Possessions: The Paradox of Keeping-While-Giving* (Cambridge, 1992). On medieval practice and ideology, see Rosenwein, *To be a Neighbor*; and White, *Custom*.

[94] Maitland referred to those who consented to a tenant's gifts as 'apparent or presumptive heirs' (Pollock and Maitland, ii 13), 'expectant heirs' (ii 15), 'apparent or presumptive heirs' (ii 17), 'expectant heirs' (ii 251), 'one heir or many heirs' (ii 255), and 'expectant heirs' (ii 309).

[95] Ibid., ii 310; on the consent of wives, see ii 411, 424.

history of the medieval family.[96] Instead, by describing the groups as groups of heirs or potential heirs — that is, kin who might have inherited the land alienated with their consent[97] — he simply excluded the possibility of interpreting consent to gifts as a collective familial act of a group with present, not future, interests in the property being given and as a transaction in which living members of a family returned land to the dead kin from whom they had received it.[98] To be sure, Maitland acknowledged that the gifts of donors with more than one son were to be approved by several heirs because he believed that a 'stringent' form of primogeniture was not observed in England until around 1200.[99] He also noted cases where gifts were made jointly by tenants and heirs[100] or were approved by as many as nine different kin.[101] But as he described it, consent of a donor's kin to his gift could be understood only as a set of individual acts performed by heirs who were waiving individual rights.

Maitland's preference for individualistic readings of the consent of kin became even clearer when he turned to consider why gifts were made with consent and why this practice eventually disappeared. Without noting that numerous post-Conquest gifts were made without consent[102] and without asking why consenting heirs might have wished to approve gifts,[103] Maitland assumed that donors and donees extracted the consent of heirs in accordance with a binding legal rule. He reached this conclusion after first finding 'numerous examples' of gifts made with the consent of heirs;[104] then by inflating a practice that would 'probably' be found in charters[105] into a practice without which charters were 'rarely executed';[106] and finally by concluding that donors 'had

---

[96] See White, *Custom*, esp. pp. 13–4 and ch. 4. Unlike Maitland, writers on the French *laudatio parentum* (e.g. Fossier, *Picardie*) have studied the consent of heirs, other kin, and wives concurrently.

[97] See Pollock and Maitland, ii 310.

[98] See White, *Custom*, ch. 5.

[99] Ibid., ii 312; see generally ii 260–313. 'That absolute and uncompromising form of primogeniture which prevails in England belongs, not to feudalism in general but to a highly centralized feudalism, in which the king has not much to fear from the power of his mightiest vassals, and is strong enough to impose a law that in his eyes has many merits, above all the great merit of simplicity': ibid., ii 265.

[100] Ibid., ii 311.

[101] Ibid., ii 309–10.

[102] Hudson finds that 'the inclusion of consent clauses is not standard practice even in the charters of lesser laymen' (*Land, Law, and Lordship*, p. 188) and is rare in royal charters and in great laymen's charters (pp. 184, 185).

[103] See ibid., pp. 188–97; see also White, *Custom*, ch. 5.

[104] Pollock and Maitland, ii 309.

[105] Ibid., ii 251.

[106] Ibid., ii 255.

very commonly to seek [it]'.[107] He then asked why the law sanctioned this 'restraint' on a landowner's power of alienation.

He answered his question in two ways, focusing first on how the heir acquired the right to restrain alienations and then on why the judges enforced the right. Instead of seeing the heir's right as a 'relic of family ownership' or at least as an adjunct of the heir's weak birth-right to his ancestor's land, Maitland saw it as originating either in a 'common-law rule forbidding disherison or in the form of a [lord's] gift [to the tenant and his heirs,] which seemed to declare that after the donee's death the land was to be enjoyed by his heir and by none other.'[108] In either case, the heir did not acquire the power to restrain alienations by virtue of his genealogical position in a family.[109] Whether the power came from the state or whether it came from the ancestor's lord and was then enforced by the state, the power was no longer based, as it once had been, according to Maitland, on birth into a family. Preparing the way for the power's silent disappearance in around 1200, Maitland was silently transforming the archaic birth-right into something that looked more like a title recognized by modern law.

As to why judges, as a matter of policy, enforced the rule against alienating land without the heir's consent, Maitland, with no evidence to guide him, was free to speculate and did so in a revealing passage. Convinced that common law judges barely recognized, much less protected, the family's interests in land, he insisted that 'the object of the restraint' [was not] solely, perhaps not mainly, the retention of land *"in a family"*.'[110] Its main purpose, before the establishment of strict primogeniture, was to '[secure] an equal division of land among sons.'[111] The rule achieved this goal by empowering the tenant's sons to restrain him from alienating too much of the fief that they would divide on his death and from making gifts to one or more sons that could undermine the principle of equal division among sons. Constructing a choice for himself between a very late date for the advent of strict primogeniture and a rule designed to keep land 'in a family', Maitland took the first option, which harmonized better with his polemic against Maine. Although he noted that a donor's kin sometimes tried to block his gifts or to recover them[112] and although he could have used such cases as evidence about the primary social function of consent,[113] he slighted

[107] Ibid., ii 13.
[108] Ibid., ii 13.
[109] As it was in French models of the *laudatio parentum*.
[110] Pollock and Maitland, ii 312.
[111] Ibid., ii 312.
[112] Ibid., ii 310, 311 n.3.
[113] For discussions of such cases see White, *Custom*, esp. chs. 2–5.

this evidence on the grounds that in *any* age 'expectant heirs do not like to see property given away'.[114]

Maitland's assumption that kinship groups were strictly controlled by law resurfaced even when he described the disappearance of the practice of making gifts with the consent of heirs. 'The change', he wrote, 'if we consider its great importance, seems to have been effected rapidly, even suddenly.'[115] But how sudden was the change? Just as Maitland exaggerated the frequency with which Anglo-Norman gifts were made with the consent of heirs because he saw donors and their kin as following a legal rule that he had largely invented for them to obey,[116] he exaggerated the suddenness with which the practice disappeared probably because he assumed that the judges could simply abolish it and did so. In fact, the practice of making gifts with the consent of heirs probably did *not* disappear rapidly or suddenly. Instead, the percentage of gifts made with the consent of kin — which, in a Yorkshire sample, reached a peak of only 55 per cent in the 1150s — dropped steadily during the second half of the century, until, in Yorkshire, it stood at 15 per cent in the 1190s.[117] A similar decline in the *laudatio parentum* occurred in various regions of thirteenth-century France.[118] Evidence of this kind from both France and England would have been difficult to fit into a model in which judges determined the history of family law.

Maitland invoked this model once more when he attributed the disappearance of the heir's consent to a judicial act. He saw this 'sudden' change as 'the complement of that new stringent primogeniture which the king's court had begun to enforce'.[119] Once it became clear, he thought, that a tenancy would not be divided among the tenant's sons and that the eldest son would have it all, then a practice that had previously served the benevolent purpose of preventing the tenant from unduly privileging one son over the others by barring him from alienating land without their consent became 'useless, inappropriate, unbearable' — unbearable because the eldest son, the only heir, would now use it to prevent the tenant from providing for his younger sons.[120] Why the disinheritance of younger sons, though unbearable for

---

[114] Pollock and Maitland, ii 252. Maitland was here writing of wills but the remark applies perfectly well to other alienations.

[115] Ibid., ii 311.

[116] Practice was Maitland's only evidence for the existence of the rule before the time of *Glanvill*: Pollock and Maitland, ii 208–11.

[117] These rough statistics are based on charters in *EYC*, vols. 1–11.

[118] Fossier, *Picardie*, i 265–6.

[119] Pollock and Maitland, ii 312.

[120] Ibid., ii 312.

judges, was promoted by fathers was a question that Maitland could have answered only by shifting the focus of his entire discussion from courts to families. But instead of seeing either primogeniture or changes in the roles that kin played — or didn't play in gifts — as long-term processes associated with long-term changes in family organization, Maitland attributed both developments to judicial acts. As he saw it, these changes in family law were largely determined by the fact that 'above our law at a critical moment stood a high-handed court of professional justices who were all for simplicity and could abolish a whole chapter of ancient jurisprudence by two or three bold decisions.'[121]

When Maitland interpreted documents very similar to ones later analysed by other historians in France as well as in England, the logic of his polemic against Maine, his decision to write a certain kind of legal history, and other interpretive choices he made often led him to see kinship groups as associations of individuals. Later, many of his successors, especially in France, preferred the opposite interpretive strategy of privileging familial collectivism. Whether or not Maitland chose the right strategy or the wrong one and whether he fully appreciated the force of arguments for alternative ways of writing family history, his own ways of looking at kinship groups, interpreting texts, and evaluating earlier historical work left marks on the way in which he wrote the legal history of the family. Yet Maitland's own work on this subject was far from being a dated exercise in polemics, ideological projection, and tendentious readings of evidence. As a lens through which to examine the history of the family, his legal individualism, combined with his scepticism about evolutionary thought, had strengths, enabling him to see enough to contest the theories of Maine and other 'speculative lawyers'[122] and to grasp important issues in the history of medieval kinship.

First, Maitland's scepticism about theories of unilinear evolution made him quick to spot evidence indicating that the history of English family law did not move steadily and inexorably from archaic collectivism to modern individualism. Whether or not he always interpreted the evidence correctly, he used it effectively in the 1890s to anticipate campaigns that historians of the medieval family were waging in the 1960s against the view, still espoused by Marc Bloch and others, that

---

[121] Ibid., ii 313.
[122] Kuper, *Invention of Primitive Society*, p. 8.

family ties grew steadily weaker over the course of the middle ages. When Georges Duby, Robert Fossier, and David Herlihy contested the theory, each, in his own way, followed Maitland in citing changes in the roles that kin played in alienating land.[123] Moreover, in arguing that there were significant discrepancies between medieval English and medieval French family law and in associating them with the relative freedom of English, as compared with French, landholders to alienate land away from their kin, Maitland not only foreshadowed Alan Macfarlane's bold argument of the late 1970s for England's precocious, individualistic exceptionalism;[124] Maitland also drew attention to significant differences, after 1200, between the two regions with respect to the participation of kin in the alienation of land. In fact, the differences are evident even earlier than he thought they were. Comparisons of English and Northwestern French charters indicate, first, that throughout the twelfth century, English gifts were less likely to be made with the consent of kin than French gifts were and, second, that English kin groups participating in gifts to churches were smaller in size, simpler in structure, and less likely to include collateral kin or non-co-residential kin than their counterparts in France were.[125] Although these findings do not necessarily confirm Maitland's belief

[123] According to David Herlihy, 'Perhaps the most evident weakness with the concept of progressive nuclearization is the assumption that this movement toward nuclear families was, or had to be, progressive': 'Family solidarity in medieval Italian history', reprinted in id., *The Social History of Italy* (London, 1978), pp. 174–5. Fossier cited both Duby's work and data from Picardy to justify 'l'opinion nuancée qui refuse de voir dans l'histoire familiale une courbe continue, évolution régulière': *Picardie*, i 266. See also id., 'Les structures de la famille en occident au moyen âge', in *XVe Congrès international des sciences historiques* (2 vols., Bucarest, 1980), ii 225–35; idem, *Enfance de l'Europe, Xe–XIIe siècles: aspects économiques et sociaux* (2 vols., Paris, 1982), ii 905–27; and White, *Custom*, ch. 3.

[124] *Origins of English Individualism*. According to Elton, *Maitland*, pp. 100–1 Macfarlane found in Maitland's work 'the guidance he needed to break out of the traditional opinions concerning the "peasantry" of England and to fight his way to an interpretation so shocking to convention that the conventional have ganged up to drown him'. In addition to the critiques of this book that Macfarlane cites in *Culture of Capitalism* at pp. 240–41 and discusses at pp. 191–222, see Stephen D. White and Richard T. Vann, 'The invention of English individualism: Alan Macfarlane and the modernization of pre-modern England', *Social History*, 8 (1983), 345–63.

[125] These conclusions are supported both by soundings of English and French twelfth-century charters and by a detailed statistical analysis of the participation of kin in twelfth-century gifts to religious houses in Yorkshire and the regions around Chartres. The Yorkshire charters surveyed are in *EYC*, vols. 1–11. The French documents studied are in: *Cartulaire de la Sainte-Trinité de Tiron*, ed. L. Merlet (2 vols., Chartres, 1883); *Cartulaire de Saint-Jean-en-Vallée de Chartres*, ed. R. Merlet, Collection de cartulaires chartrains, vol. 1 (Chartres, 1906); *Cartulaire du Grand-Beaulieu-lès-Chartres et du prieuré de Notre-Dame de la Bourdinière*, ed. R. Merlet and M. Jusselin, Collection de cartulaires chartrains, vol. 2, part 1 (Chartres, 1909); *Cartulaire de Notre-Dame de Josaphat*, ed. Charles Métais (2 vols., Chartres, 1909). I am indebted to the late David Herlihy for help in compiling the statistics.

in the 'precocity' of English legal development in the sphere of family law and although they are hard to reconcile with his belief that the relative simplicity of English family was imposed from above, they are at least consistent with his underlying idea that kinship somehow counted for less in twelfth-century England than it did in twelfth-century France.

Finally, when considering how Maitland's antiquarian individualism sometimes facilitated understanding of medieval kinship, it is worth noting that although he exaggerated the ephemerality of medieval kinship groups,[126] the power and will of medieval states to control them, and the freedom of medieval people to act independently of them, he raised a critical question about medieval families that subsequent writers on the medieval family have frequently overlooked by reflexively reifying family cohesion, lineage solidarity, kinship structure, and familial collectivism: How were kinship groups actually formed and re-formed for such purposes as feuding or approving gifts of land? Maitland was surely right in seeing this as a problem[127] and in thinking that people had to be actively recruited into larger kin groups by members of smaller ones or by individuals.[128] From there, it is not a long step to anthropological 'action theories' about how individual entrepreneurs recruit people into non-groups or quasi-groups[129] and to the position of one recent writer on medieval feuds that 'it always fell to someone' — that is, to some individual — 'to recruit his or her kin for the particular enterprise at hand.'[130] Whatever the theoretical merits of the individualistic 'action theories' that Maitland's antiquarian indi-

---

[126] See Miller, *Bloodtaking and Peacemaking*, p. 155.

[127] The problem would have worried him even more if he had had access to evidence indicating that in both England and France different alienations by a single donor were approved by kin groups so different in composition that the differences cannot be explained either by assuming that the gifts concerned different inheritances or by relying on the usual expedients of killing off some relatives, bringing others into the world at the proper moment, and sending others still on crusade or on other journeys from which they can be recalled when needed to approve a gift. See White, *Custom*, ch. 3.

[128] Pollock and Maitland, ii 242. Maitland's observation that consent to alienations is procured from 'as many of the donor's near kinsfolk as can be induced to approve [it]' (ibid., ii 310) helps us to see the kin groups that participated in such gifts, not, as some historians have suggested, as enduring 'families', but rather as groups that were recruited for specific purposes. See White, *Custom*, ch. 3. For English evidence indicating how much variation there could be in the composition of the groups that approved different gifts by a single donor, see the gifts by Adam son of Peter de Birkin: *EYC*, iii nos. 1722, 1725–35, 1737–43, 1745, 1747, 1871, 1872; vi no. 67; *The Chartulary of Rievaulx* (Surtees Society, 83, 1887), nos. 92, 97, 100, 356.

[129] See Joan Vincent, *Anthropology and Politics: Visions, Traditions, and Trends* (Tucson, 1990), pp. 341–53; and Ted C. Lewellen, *Political Anthropology: An Introduction* (2nd ed., Westport, CT, 1992), chs. 6–7.

[130] Miller, *Bloodtaking and Peacemaking*, p. 155.

vidualism foreshadows, his belief that medieval communalism was 'a thin cloak for a rough and rude individualism' is still an effective antidote, at times, to 'easy talk', as Maitland would have called it, about family cohesion or lineage solidarity and to the tendency to confuse the family, understood as a cultural category, with actual groups of kin and to conflate kinship ideology with kinship practice.[131] As a weapon against the dogma that 'the family was the unit of ancient law' and against other kinds of easy talk about the early history of family, Maitland provided a counter-maxim that has remained thought-pro-vokingly effective. Although he never said that there was no such thing as the medieval family, there were only individuals, he did say: 'Individuals do not cease to be individuals when there are many of them.'[132]

---

[131] As formulated in Roger M. Keesing, *Kin Groups and Social Structure* (New York, 1975), pp. 9–11, the distinction is used in White, *Custom*, pp. 127–9.
[132] Pollock and Maitland, ii 247.

Proceedings of the British Academy, **89**, 115–143

Maitland and the Criminal Law in the Age of *Bracton*

HENRY SUMMERSON

In discussing Maitland's analysis of the criminal law and the administration of justice in thirteenth-century England, it is usually easier to
say where he was mistaken or misguided than it is to suggest how, in
the circumstances of the years around 1900, he could have done any
better. To criticize errors perceived as originating in his personal temperament or outlook, or as resulting from the *mores* of his age and
class, is in effect to criticize him for not having been somebody else.
Maitland did not breathe late twentieth-century air, though we treat
him as if he did. His achievement is all the more remarkable when one
considers the inadequacy of the textual armoury put at his disposal by
the scholarship of his age. The bibliography prefacing the *History of
English Law* refers to the 1569 edition of *Bracton* (though in his
footnotes Maitland preferred to give manuscript citations), to *Glanvill*
in an edition of 1604 and to *Fleta* in an edition of 1685. Only F. M.
Nichols's edition of *Britton*, published in 1865, could be regarded as
satisfactory by present-day standards, or even by Victorian ones — Sir
Travers Twiss's edition of *Bracton*, published by the Rolls Series
between 1878 and 1883, was so ineptly produced that Maitland ignored
it.[1] As far as the unpublished resources of the Public Record Office
were concerned, Maitland urged their exploitation by others and set
an admirable example himself, but although his footnotes to the *History
of English Law* occasionally show him using unprinted sources,[2] for
the elucidation of criminal law in the age of *Bracton* he relied more
on records in print — the publications of the Rolls Series and Record
Commission, Selden Society volumes (several of them his own work),
a few county record society publications, and ultimately anything he
could find. As far as the first half of the thirteenth century was con-

---

[1] Fifoot, *Life*, pp. 61–2, 132.
[2] E.g. Pollock and Maitland, ii 535 n. 2, 565–7, 623 n. 1, 629 n. 4, 647 n. 2, 648 n. 1, 649 n. 2.

cerned, there were no pipe rolls, no Curia Regis rolls, and no close or patent rolls after 1227 available to him in print.

For the administration of the criminal law, Maitland relied basically on *Bracton*, supplemented or corrected where possible by other sources. Well aware of the quantity of potentially relevant material which remained unknown to him, he was often guarded in his conclusions. Nevertheless, considering how handicapped he was by an insufficiency of basic sources, it is astonishing how much Maitland got right. For instance, he noticed a change in the treatment of clerics charged with felony, who were thereafter given jury trial before being handed over to the ecclesiastical courts, and correctly associated it with the year 1247.[3] He saw that rape was less severely treated by the courts than the textbooks prescribed.[4] He anticipated present-day perceptions when he wrote that lords valued possession of a view of frankpledge most of all for 'the power that was thus secured them. Twice a year the villagers, bond and free, had to report themselves and tell tales of one another. . .'. [5]

Even when caution led Maitland to qualify his arguments, subsequent research has often either confirmed them, or shown that they err only in their cautiousness. Thus he mentioned in passing the degree to which women were regarded as being under the control of their husbands, and in a footnote drew attention to the implications of this for their position under the criminal law, in that a wife could be cleared of a felony in which she had participated with her husband, on the grounds that she was obliged to act as he demanded.[6] *Bracton* was imprecise on this issue, declaring that wives should try to keep their husbands from crime, and that, where they participated in evildoing with their husbands, as 'partners in crime they will be partners in punishment.'[7] In 1220 a woman was condemned to be burnt after confessing 'that she was present along with her husband at the slaying of three men and one woman at Barnet.'[8] But attitudes seem to have been changing — *Fleta* was firmly exculpatory towards wives who stole in their husbands' company,[9] while several cases bear out the extent to which court procedure, on this point at least, came to operate to

[3] Ibid., i 442 and n. 2.
[4] Ibid., ii 490–1.
[5] Ibid., i 581; cf. R. H. Hilton, *A Medieval Society: the West Midlands at the end of the thirteenth century* (London, 1966), pp. 25, 235.
[6] Pollock and Maitland, ii 406. See also Hyams, below, pp. 228–31.
[7] *Bracton*, f. 151b, Thorne, ii 428.
[8] F. W. Maitland, ed., *Select Pleas of the Crown Vol. I: A.D. 1200–1225* (Selden Soc., 1, 1887), no. 191.
[9] H. G. Richardson and G. O. Sayles, eds, *Fleta Vol. II* (Selden Soc., 72, 1953), p. 92.

the advantage of wives. When a man and his wife were charged with theft at the 1250/1 Norfolk eyre, the husband went to the gallows, but, the record continues, 'Agnes was Gilbert's wife, and did what she did on her lord's orders. It is testified by the jurors that she did no crime without an order from her lord. So let her go quit . . .'.[10] At the 1257 Yorkshire eyre a woman was found to have been present at the bedside of a woman murdered by her husband when he did the deed, but 'as she was his married wife, and could not contradict her husband's wish, and the jurors testify to this on oath, she is quit.'[11] Even when the husband was an outlaw, his wife seems to have remained under his orders. At the 1255 Surrey eyre Alice, wife of William le Sleghe, was charged with harbouring her husband, an outlaw. It may have helped her that she could claim that since William had been outlawed in Hampshire, Alice did not know of his criminal status. But the court's judgment did not mention this, declaring only that 'since Alice was married to the said William her husband and could not refuse him, it is decided that she is quit.'[12] Nor did the responsibility of husbands for their wives stop there. Cases from Devon show one man being imprisoned when his wife's appeal failed, and another being taken into custody when his wife was convicted of assault.[13] Women were not in frankpledge, and producing them in court was their husbands' responsibility. As Maitland observed, when Milisent, wife of Ivo de Clifford, fled after committing arson, the justices at Gloucester in 1221 were emphatic that Ivo should bring her before the eyre.[14] He drew the appropriate conclusions as to the inferior status of women under the law, but, probably for lack of supporting evidence, did not develop them as far as he might have done.

At other points Maitland stopped well short of positions taken by later scholars, though he helped to clear the ground for them. It is now apparent that the process whereby homicide ceased to be regarded as an emendable offence, for which the killer could hope to make or buy his peace with the kinsfolk of his victim, and became a felony which should normally place the slayer's life and members at the disposal of the king, had begun long before the twelfth century, where Maitland placed it.[15] But Maitland was nevertheless correct to indicate that older

[10] PRO, JUST/1/564, m. 3.
[11] PRO, JUST/1/1109, m. 3.
[12] PRO, JUST/1/872, m. 33d.
[13] H. Summerson, ed., *Crown Pleas of the Devon Eyre of 1238* (Devon and Cornwall Record Society, ns 28, 1985), no. 524 and note.
[14] F. W. Maitland, ed., *Pleas of the Crown for the County of Gloucester 1221* (London, 1884), no. 244, and note on p. 147.
[15] See the discussion in Pollock and Maitland, ii 483–6; also Wormald, above, pp. 13–14.

attitudes persisted, manifesting themselves in attempts at out-of-court settlements which bypassed the processes of royal justice. And in support of this observation he cited the Gloucestershire case of Robert Basset, hanged in 1221 for killing Geoffrey of Sutton, notwithstanding an out-of-court settlement which involved the marriage of his son to Geoffrey's daughter and the conveyance to the couple of a virgate of land.[16] In his note on this case in his edition of the 1221 Gloucestershire crown pleas, Maitland commented that 'it is too late in the day for this sort of thing . . .'. But his examination of this issue extended only to its legal implications, and it has been left to Professor T. A. Green to show how these were circumvented by jury verdicts which took the edge of felony off homicide charges, by presenting killings committed in brawls and temporary flare-ups as done in self-defence, and so deserving a royal pardon.[17] Green based his findings on extensive research on several classes of document in the Public Record Office. Maitland, working at high speed and with many other claims on his energies, had no time for the sort of detailed scrutiny of records which yielded such dividends for Green, though he would certainly have applauded it.

Similarly it may be confidently assumed that Maitland would have approved the work of C. A. F. Meekings, the scholar who in the twentieth century has done more than anyone else to elucidate the workings of the general eyre and its place in the judicial administration of thirteenth-century England.[18] Employed in the Public Record Office itself, Meekings devoted most of his career to the study of medieval legal records. He acknowledged the value of Maitland's insights, for instance on the problem of juries which apparently contradicted themselves by acquitting suspects they had themselves indicted — 'Maitland, by posing the question correctly, showed that there was really no problem . . .'.[19] But a comparison of Meekings's editions of Wiltshire and Surrey eyre records with Maitland's edition of the 1221 Gloucestershire crown pleas shows in the former a command of the relevant sources which neither Maitland nor anyone else could match, together with a skilful placing of the institutions recorded in them in a wider context, both of governmental activity and of the

---

[16] *Gloucestershire Crown Pleas*, no. 101 and note on p. 143.

[17] T. A. Green, *Verdict According to Conscience* (Chicago, 1985).

[18] C. A. F. Meekings, ed., *Crown Pleas of the Wiltshire Eyre 1249* (Wiltshire Archaeological and Natural History Society, Records Branch, 16, 1960); *The 1235 Surrey Eyre* (Surrey Record Society, 31, 32, 1979, 1983); (with R. E. Latham) 'Veredictum of Chippenham hundred, 1281', in N. J. Williams, ed., *Collectanea* (Wiltshire Archaeological and Natural History Society, Records Branch, 12, 1956).

[19] *Wiltshire Crown Pleas 1249*, pp. 95–6.

society of the counties involved, beside which Maitland's work is bound to appear lacking in focus and density. This was inevitable in the circumstances. Maitland was a pioneer of genius, but in modern parlance he had an inadequate data-base, and parts of his work — essentially those least well covered by the legal texts upon which he depended heavily — were bound to become obsolete once the available documents came to be methodically examined.

Thus he followed *Bracton* in the heavy stress he placed upon the importance of the appeal of felony as a means of prosecuting serious crime — 'The ancient and still the normal mode of bringing a criminal to justice', was how he described it in the introduction to his own edition of the Gloucestershire crown pleas of 1221.[20] The claim is surprising in the circumstances, since those same crown pleas do not show the appeal to have been particularly important, with only twenty-two appeals of homicide recorded, and just eight killers said to have been outlawed by appeals since the previous eyre, compared with 129 put in exigent at the eyre itself, to be outlawed at the king's suit. At the next recorded Gloucestershire eyre, that of 1248, the pattern was the same, with a mere nine outlawries to set beside 102 exigents for homicide. In other counties, too, the appeal, though in some cases more often employed and for longer than in Gloucestershire, tended to lose ground steadily, especially as a means of prosecuting suspected killers.[21] In Essex, for instance, outlawries still outnumbered exigents in 1227, with fourteen to set against nine, but in 1248 there were only two outlawries for homicide recorded, but fifty-five exigents.[22] Maitland was misled largely by the date he (in common with all other historians of his time) attributed to *Bracton*, some thirty years later than that normally ascribed to it following Professor Thorne's work. He believed it described the practice of the 1250s, and since the appeal bulks very large in *Bracton*'s pages (indictment, by contrast, is briefly covered by an awkward later insertion), he assumed it did so also in the practice of the king's courts at that time.[23] His mistake proved irreparable because he had relatively little opportunity to compare what *Bracton* wrote with court records from the 1250s, which might have persuaded him to reconsider his views on the prominence of the appeal. Some of the other shortcomings we can now detect in Maitland's work on the

---

[20] *Gloucestershire Crown Pleas 1221*, p. xxxvi.

[21] Figures from PRO, JUST/1/274.

[22] Essex figures from PRO, JUST/1/227 and H. R. T. Summerson, *The Maintenance of Law and Order in England, 1227–1263, Ph.D. thesis* (Cambridge, 1976), pp. 80–1.

[23] For the appeal see particularly *Bracton*, ff. 137–43b, Thorne, ii 385–406; indictment is discussed at ff. 142b–3, ii 402–3.

pleas of the crown can be assumed to have had similar origins — his failure to take account of the plaint as a means of initiating proceedings, for instance, or his underestimation of the importance of gaol deliveries in law enforcement. But it should be acknowledged that these gaps were only filled after years of detailed research, undertaken by H. G. Richardson and G. O. Sayles, and by R. B. Pugh, respectively.[24]

However, in considering Maitland's work on criminal law, it is also necessary to take into account aspects of his personality and background which, though necessarily inseparable from his achievement, would nevertheless appear to have had important effects upon it, effects which, a century later, do not always appear to have been entirely beneficial. In the first place, Maitland was in politics a convinced Liberal. To be a Liberal in the years round 1900 was no longer to be an advocate of a Gladstonian minimum state; on the contrary, early in 1906, the year Maitland died, a Liberal government was returned which would, with the introduction of the old age pension, lay the first foundations of a British welfare state. For the direction of affairs Maitland and those who thought like him looked for decisive action by a centralized and centralizing government — *mutatis mutandis*, one remarkably like that of Henry II and his ministers which Maitland so admired. Along with this, as he showed in his review of Gomme, Maitland exhibited a marked lack of sympathy for what he there called 'communalism', for the idea of village communities as embodiments of bucolic wisdom, autonomously conducting their affairs according to the dictates of age-old custom.[25] Finally, it is probably significant that Maitland's first professional training was as a lawyer, for he had something of the tendency, often observed in lawyers, to measure people and events in terms of clearcut differences — good and evil, guilt and innocence. When he wrote to P. E. Dove, advocating a volume of selected crown pleas as the first publication of the Selden Society, among the reasons he gave was that such criminal cases 'bring one at once to the great rules of right and wrong'.[26]

The result was an attitude towards medieval law enforcement of linear directness. Law, made by kings and enforced by judges, was imposed from above. The processes whereby order was maintained and crime prevented were ones in which local communities — shires,

---

[24] H. G. Richardson and G. O. Sayles, eds, *Select Cases of Procedure without Writ under Henry III* (Selden Soc., 60, 1941); R. B. Pugh, *Imprisonment in Medieval England* (Cambridge, 1968).

[25] F. W. Maitland, 'The survival of archaic communities', in *Collected Papers*, ii 313–65; see also White, above.

[26] *Letters*, i no. 26 (p. 28).

boroughs, hundreds and vills — had parts to play, but they acted them under firm central direction, and with little freedom of movement, still less power to improvise. And the success or failure of those processes was easily gaged — in the last resort, by the number of criminals hanged. Maitland was a humane man, but he had no qualms about the gallows, at any rate for medieval felons (perhaps another consequence of his lawyer's training). Of the case of John the miller, convicted at Gloucester in 1221 of killing a fellow-servant of Petronilla of Stanway, but licensed to abjure when Petronilla offered 40s. for his life, Maitland notes that 'unfortunately his mistress, Petronilla, interferes and buys him permission to abjure the realm'.[27] Such a remission is clearly something to be regretted. On the hanging of eleven thieves his comment is no less blunt: 'this is the only satisfactory bit of hanging that is recorded.'[28] When he summed up his opinions on the standard of medieval law enforcement, his position is equally clear, recording 'our belief that crimes of violence were common and that the criminal law was exceedingly inefficient . . . even in quiet times few out of many criminals came to their appointed ends . . .'.[29]

If the only proper end for a killer or a thief was the gallows, and if the efficiency of criminal law enforcement was measured solely in terms of the numbers hanged, Maitland's conclusions would be justified. But the circumstances of medieval English life were such as to make it unlikely that success and failure were in fact perceived in terms so straightforward. In the first place, the number of acquittals of suspects, and the way in which juries circumvented the rigidity of the law of homicide by presenting as self-defence killings committed in hot blood, not to mention the occasions on which even convicted felons might be rescued on their way to the gallows,[30] or their executions so bungled that they escaped death,[31] make it clear that there were occasions on which the ostensibly law abiding simply did not want to take the lives of men and women who had committed felony. But much more important in this context is the fact that although Maitland was able to provide a most lucid account of the institutions of local government responsible for the maintenance of law and order, his over-centralized perspective, perhaps reinforced by suspicion of anything smacking of communal initiatives, led him to overlook the basic principles which directed their operation.

[27] *Gloucestershire Crown Pleas 1221*, no. 330 and note on p. 149.
[28] Ibid., no. 472, and note on p. 154.
[29] Pollock and Maitland, ii 557.
[30] E.g. PRO, JUST/1/701, m. 19; JUST/1/361, m. 57d.
[31] E.g. PRO, JUST/1/700, m. 12d.

Those principles may be defined as publicity and exclusion.[32] All deeds of violence or theft, indeed all suspicious actions which led to the raising of the hue, were to be successively presented by the vills where they occurred to the three-weekly hundred court, to the six-monthly sheriff's tourn, to the monthly county court, and quite possibly to the eyre as well. Homicides would also be subjects of coroners' inquests, attended by men from the four nearest vills. The hue, raised by shouting and blowing horns, was itself a means of publicity, which could also be used to give legitimacy to actions otherwise suspicious. It was an essential component of an appeal of felony, which might otherwise appear malicious, and it gave authority to acts of summary justice — a Yorkshireman who beheaded the two killers of his brother was himself sentenced to outlawry because 'it is testified that the hue was not raised before Richard took vengeance on them'.[33] Its raising was the first step in the process of ensuring that everyone in a county knew who was suspected of law-breaking, a process continued by repeated presentments in local courts. Within vills all unfree men over the age of twelve were to be inhibited from crime by their being formed into tithings (in many parts these were groups of ten, but in some regions, especially the south-west, a whole vill might constitute a tithing), whose members were not only sworn to keep the peace themselves, but were also made responsible for the good behaviour of their fellows. Anyone coming into a vill from the outside world except for temporary purposes should be enrolled in a tithing — if he was not, a vill would be penalized. Outsiders should be excluded, not only by the suspicions of the villagers themselves, but also by the watch, an institution only regularized in 1233,[34] but clearly in existence before then; by 1221 there seems to have been a system of watches at Worcester, in which the tenants of the Hospitallers refused to participate,[35] while at the 1227 Buckinghamshire eyre a man and woman charged with homicide were said to have been questioned at their going out, and again at their return, by the watchmen of Aylesbury.[36] The plea rolls record many strangers as suspected of crime. Some came from far away, while others, on the evidence of their names, were outsiders in their counties of origin. What they all had in common was their being perceived as having no fixed abode, and as therefore being

[32] The discussion which follows is based on H. R. T. Summerson, 'The structure of law enforcement in thirteenth-century England', in *American Journal of Legal History*, 23 (1979), 313–27.
[33] PRO, JUST/1/1043, m. 12d.
[34] *Close Rolls, 1231–1234*, pp. 309–10.
[35] *Select Pleas of the Crown I*, no. 149.
[36] PRO, JUST/1/54, m. 16d.

dangerous. Those with a place in rural communities were to be controlled and supervised, those with no such place were to be kept outside.

In the circumstances of thirteenth-century rural life, when most of those who had any stable habitation lived in villages and hamlets surrounded by expanses of wood, heath and other open country, arrests were always going to be hard to make, because in such conditions it was so easy for suspects both to get away and to stay out of reach of pursuers. But publicity and exclusion could then be used against them. All should know who they were and what they had done, so that they could be arrested if they attempted to return to the company of the law-abiding. And if they escaped arrest, exclusion could be given legal form by the processes of outlawry, processes which extended the business of publicizing suspicion. Either through a personal accusation — the appeal of felony — or through the public accusation embodied in the process of exigent after an eyre, a suspect's attendance would be publicly demanded at four successive sessions of the county court. If he failed to appear, he would be declared an outlaw at the next session. Maitland observed signs of change in the status of outlawry in the thirteenth century, that 'instead of being a substantive punishment, it becomes mere "criminal process", a means of compelling accused persons to stand their trial'.[37] But the change is not one visible in the judicial records of the age of *Bracton*, and it seems hard to see how a condition which reduced a killer or thief to the condition of hunted vermin, liable to be arrested on sight, and to be killed if he resisted arrest or fled, can be described as other than punitive.

The effectiveness of outlawry as a penalty is impossible to estimate in exact terms, but there were certainly numerous occasions when outlaws reappeared among the law-abiding and paid the penalty. At the 1257 Norfolk eyre, for instance, it was presented that one Roger le Vacher, outlawed in the county court 'a long time ago', had turned up in Happisburgh, only to be beheaded by the prior of Wymondham's bailiff.[38] To move from one county to another was no guarantee of safety, since officials exchanged information about criminals.[39] John le Mazun, outlawed in Northamptonshire, was arrested as an outlaw in Buckinghamshire, and only escaped the rope by fleeing to a church

---

[37] Pollock and Maitland, i 476.
[38] PRO, JUST/1/568, m. 32.
[39] *Surrey Eyre of 1235*, ii no. 361 and note on pp. 519–20; *Crown Pleas of the Devon Eyre of 1238*, no. 189 and note.

and abjuring the realm.[40] Such cases argue that outlawry was considerably more than a sign of weakness in the law. No doubt there were many killers and thieves whom villagers would gladly have hanged, but given the conditions which so often placed such men out of reach, the use of the courts and other processes of law to make them known, and then to exclude them from the society of the law-abiding, on pain of death if they returned, was a far from ineffective substitute for the gallows.

In the introduction to his edition of the 1221 Gloucestershire crown pleas, Maitland wrote that: 'If we were to regard an eyre merely as a mode of bringing accused persons to trial, then we should have to regard this eyre as a very wretched failure. Murders and robberies there have been in plenty; indeed this roll bears witness to an enormous mass of violent crime: but in far the greater number of cases either no one is suspected of the crime, or the suspected person has escaped, and no more can be done than to outlaw him . . .'.[41] Maitland thus put failure to name a suspect on the same level as outlawry. It is argued here that this was a mistake, that a relatively low number of arrests and convictions in court was inevitable in the prevailing conditions, and that outlawry should be regarded as at least a qualified success for those responsible for law and order — a culprit had been identified with a fair measure of confidence (it was by no means unknown for those named as responsible for homicide or theft to appear in court later in an eyre and be acquitted), his identity was made public, any chattels were forfeited, and, once the process of outlawry was complete, he was liable to arrest and execution if he showed his face among the law-abiding. An abjuration should probably be seen in the same light. It represented a near miss, a killer or thief obliged under pressure of imminent arrest to take sanctuary in a church, and there either to surrender to the king's peace, or to make a formal confession of his misdeeds to a coroner, after which he swore to leave the country and never return. An abjuration was given publicity by being conducted in the presence of the men of, usually, four neighbouring vills, and it was also presented to the local courts, as well as to the next eyre. As with outlaws, some abjurors failed to complete their journeys out of the realm and returned to, or stayed in, their counties of origin, but if they were detected they suffered the same penalty as returning outlaws. One example among many is that of Adam Roules, recorded in 1248 as having abjured the realm at Ludlow, but as later making his way

---

[40] PRO, JUST/1/614B, m. 48d.
[41] *Gloucestershire Crown Pleas 1221*, pp. xxxiii–xxxiv.

back to Shropshire; the hue was raised upon him and he was arrested and beheaded.[42]

Maitland's criteria for judging the effectiveness of law enforcement in thirteenth-century England, effectively confined to the number of reported hangings, were too restricted. Outlawries and abjurations also need to be taken into account, and only felonies attributed solely to unknown criminals should be construed as unequivocal signs of failure. It may be instructive, therefore, to reconsider the 1221 Gloucestershire crown pleas in the light of these considerations. This means dealing almost entirely with cases of homicide — for whatever reason, thieves and robbers are only occasionally recorded. For the number of people killed Maitland provided two different figures: in 1884 he wrote that 'some 250 persons have met their deaths by what would now be called murder', while in 1895 he referred to what he called 'an appalling tale of crime which comprised some 330 acts of homicide'.[43] He was certainly aware in 1884 of the possibility of distinguishing between what modern parlance defines as murder and manslaughter, observing, prior to a discussion of the murder fine, that 'the word *murder* is never used to differentiate two degrees of homicidal guilt . . .',[44] but he did not qualify his statistics to suggest that he had made that distinction here, so we must suppose that he was using the word 'murder' in a loose and general — and also anachronistic — sense, for statistics which also seem to have been rather carelessly compiled. The plea roll is indeed sometimes ambiguous as to how many people died in particular cases, but the total number of deaths inflicted by violence appears to have been about 363. In describing his total of 1895 as 'appalling' Maitland was handicapped not only by a lack of figures from other eyres with which to compare it, but also by his inability to discover how long a period the Gloucestershire eyre covered. In fact the previous eyre in the county had taken place as long ago as November 1203,[45] so that of 1221 covered very nearly eighteen years, with an average homicide rate of about twenty per annum.

This was certainly a very high rate — eyres of the early and mid-1230s in Buckinghamshire, Essex and Surrey record an average rate of nine or ten homicides per annum.[46] But since the 1248 eyre recorded

---

[42] PRO, JUST/1/733B, m. 3.
[43] *Gloucestershire Crown Pleas 1221*, p. xxxv; Pollock and Maitland, ii 557.
[44] *Gloucestershire Crown Pleas 1221*, p. xxix.
[45] D. Crook, *Records of the General Eyre* (London, 1984), p. 68.
[46] See Summerson, 'Maintenance of law and order', 71–80.

148 killings in the previous seven years,[47] an average of twenty-one per annum, it would appear that Gloucestershire was a county unusually liable to suffer from criminal activity. The civil war of 1215–17 doubtless contributed to the crime rate recorded in 1221, and is in fact referred to in a number of cases,[48] though the county was not directly involved in the war, which helps to explain the choice of Gloucester as an appropriately safe place for the coronation of the young Henry III. As a basis for Angevin power it is likely to have seen much military activity, and to have served as a haven for people fleeing from more troubled parts. But as a large and prosperous county, with a good road system to facilitate movement, with the second-largest town in England at Bristol to attract the footloose, the needy, and the ambitious, and with a good deal of woodland to afford protection to wanderers and evildoers — not least the Forest of Dean, with its population of unruly and independent miners and charcoal-burners — Gloucestershire was likely to be attractive to vagrants anyway. Felons named in 1221 included people from Warwickshire, Herefordshire, Worcestershire, Wiltshire, Bedfordshire, Wales and Ireland. How great a threat such people posed can be seen in the number of killings attributed to unknown criminals, 184 in all, almost exactly half the total. Many of these will have been the work of criminal bands, of the sort that J. B. Given, using Bedfordshire coroners' rolls of the late 1260s, has shown descending on vills and attacking several houses in succession.[49] In Gloucestershire such malefactors were responsible for the slaughter of whole households, often containing between six and eight people, including women and children. For instance, the Whitstone jurors told how criminals came by night to the house of Robert Kari, killed Robert, his wife, and the child at his wife's breast (*quendam puerum lactantem*), and then to the house of Adam son of Andrew, where they killed Adam, his wife, a little old woman and two children, 'that is, all who were in those houses'.[50]

Some of these raids seem to have resulted from problems with the control of Gloucestershire's county boundaries, which were exacerbated by the existence of a substantial ring of woods which ran round

---

[47] Figures from PRO, JUST/1/274. The total number of homicides for 1248 would certainly have been higher, but for the previous year's grant by Henry III to Fecamp Abbey of the hundreds of Cheltenham and Slaughter, and the vills of Slaughter and Stow on the Wold, on terms which removed them from the jurisdiction of the eyre.

[48] *Gloucestershire Crown Pleas 1221*, nos. 15, 35, 147, 161, 178, 181, 200, 254, 264, 393, 419, 431, 466.

[49] J. B. Given, *Society and Homicide in Thirteenth-century England* (Stanford, California, 1977), pp. 119–21.

[50] *Gloucestershire Crown Pleas 1221*, no. 437.

much of the county's eastern and southern borders, and doubtless gave cover to such brigands.[51] In the small southern hundred of Pucklechurch, for instance, twelve out of thirteen killings, in just two attacks which claimed six lives each, were attributed to unknown criminals.[52] But whatever the reason, the fact remains that communities were found in 1221 to have been repeatedly unable to keep such marauders out, and in that respect Maitland was correct to argue that the law had been badly, or at any rate unsuccessfully, enforced in Gloucestershire. The qualificatory clause seems advisable, for not all the evidence is so negative. A total of 137 suspects had either been already outlawed or were put in exigent at the eyre, their identities known and made public, their chattels forfeited, their futures heavily circumscribed; and another twenty-five killers were recorded as having abjured the realm, by procedures which condemned them to much the same fate as that of an outlaw, and also attest at least some communal vigilance on the part of vills which detected and pursued them. Another twenty-seven killers were either hanged at the eyre or were reported to have been hanged in the years prior to it, at gaol deliveries or elsewhere. And these figures do not include the killer who confessed his crime and died in prison, two other suspects who died in prison untried, two clerics convicted and saved from the gallows by their clergy, another cleric previously handed over to his bishop and declared suspected at the eyre, and five people whose guilt or innocence could not be satisfactorily decided because they refused a jury's verdict (two other men who refused a jury were nonetheless convicted, one being hanged and the other permitted to abjure the realm).

No doubt some killings attributed to unknown criminals were the result of enmities between villagers, while the fact that eighteen named suspects were described as strangers shows that some wanderers stayed long enough for their identities to become known. These, with another twenty described as harboured outside frankpledge, show that not only had vills been unable to keep strangers away, but they had also been unable entirely to absorb outsiders who gained admission to them. It should be said that not all those labelled strangers in a plea roll were necessarily bandits in disguise. There were those whose livelihoods made them largely rootless; tinkers and pedlars, for instance, whose skills and whose wares small communities would probably have found it hard to do without, and men like Roger the shepherd, described by

[51] See C. R. Young, *The Royal Forests of Medieval England* (Leicester, 1979), pp. 62–3; *VCH Gloucestershire* vol. II (1907), pp. 128, 263–4; H. C. Darby and I. B. Terrett, eds, *The Domesday Geography of Midland England* (2nd ed., Cambridge, 1971), pp. 28–9.
[52] *Gloucestershire Crown Pleas 1221*, nos. 278–9.

Corse vill in 1221 as 'not residing in his vill but itinerant from place to place'.[53] Sheep-farming, especially on the Cotswold plateau, was an essential component of the rural economy of Gloucestershire, which must have contained many men like Roger, required by their work to keep moving. Bringing such people into the respectable stability represented by membership of a tithing was never going to be easy. Even so, Gloucestershire in 1221 may have been finding it hard to operate a system of frankpledge. In about forty cases the statuses of fugitive and suspected killers went unrecorded, and only fifty-six were categorically said to have belonged to tithings. Another twenty-five were recorded as having belonged to mainpasts, that is, to the households of lords, secular and ecclesiastical, who were held responsible for the good conduct of the dependents who, as the word 'mainpast' itself indicates, ate their bread. When felons were convicted, it was irrelevant, and was not recorded, whether they had belonged to tithings or mainpasts. But of the 162 outlaws, exigents and abjurors, only eighty-one, exactly half, had been within the network of collective responsibility designed to control the behaviour of the inhabitants of vills, while thirty-eight, nearly a quarter, had managed to slip through that network.

It would appear that law and order were indeed being ill-served in Gloucestershire in the years before 1221. The grounds Maitland gave for believing this to be the case were inadequate, but when inquiry is broadened to take into account the thirteenth century's own criteria for assessing the extent to which the law was being enforced, it becomes apparent that his judgment was still broadly correct. It does not follow, however, that the criminal law was always inefficient. This is one of the points on which Maitland was handicapped by a lack of source material as well as by his own preconceptions; his own edition of the Gloucestershire crown pleas was one of the few easily accessible sources of statistical evidence at his disposal, and for the *History of English Law* it, and William Page's edition of plea rolls from Northumberland in 1256 and 1279, were the only ones he used for this purpose. The Northumberland figures suggest a much lower level of criminal activity in that county than in Gloucestershire, and reasons connected with its geographical position and economic make-up have been offered for believing that the latter county was always likely to suffer from a high rate of crime. But a closer inspection of the records may still suggest that, though they show a system functioning under

---

[53] Ibid., no. 86.

considerable strain, it was not a system incapable of better performance.

Further comparisons between Gloucestershire in 1221 and in 1248 may be illuminating here. Although there was no difference between the homicide rates recorded at the two eyres, in 1248 only thirty-eight out of 148 killings were attributed to unknown criminals, a ratio of one in four, compared with one in two in 1221. It was probably important that the keeping of watches had been set on a regular footing in 1233, leading to greater success in keeping brigands out of the vills. There also seems to have been a tightening up of frankpledge, doubtless at the behest of the county's officials. In 1221 some tithings had consisted of whole vills, while others had consisted of groups, each recorded under the name of the tithingman at its head. By 1248 all the recorded Gloucestershire tithings were of the latter kind. The growth of population — the thirteenth century saw much assarting in the county[54] — probably accounts for the change; the vills were coming to contain too many men, who could no longer all be expected to keep an eye on one another, and had to be divided into smaller groups. The homicide rate did not fall as a result — frictions within an expanding population may well have seen to that — but nevertheless there is one piece of negative evidence to suggest that this change did have some effect. One hundred, that of Berkeley, was said in 1248 to contain no tithings at all, of any kind.[55] With twenty-three killings, it had the highest homicide rate in the county, nearly twice that of the second most afflicted hundred. Without a reorganization of frankpledge, matters might have been even worse than they were.

Similarly with the 1221 eyre, the failures to arrest, to pursue, to present suspicious and criminous acts to local courts and officials, to ensure that those who should be were enrolled in tithings — all these numerous shortcomings should not be permitted to conceal the occasions on which vills fulfilled their obligations, sometimes in desperate circumstances. Although many more suspects were found to have evaded a place within frankpledge than should have done, it is still noteworthy that within this system were many from the very lowest levels of settled village society. Nineteen fugitives who were recorded as belonging to tithings were said to have had no chattels at all, many more to have had goods worth only a few shillings or even pence. Yet humble though they were, they had a place within the national system of law enforcement, and had been registered as such. All too often the

[54] H. E. Hallam, *Rural England 1066–1348* (London, 1981), pp. 147–50.
[55] PRO, JUST/1/274, m. 8d.

man who killed another in a brawl was able to make an immediate get-away, but not always. The justices at Gloucester heard Richard the forester, a royal bailiff, describe how John Spirewin had killed Peter son of Walter in St Briavels during a quarrel over a game of dice, and how 'he with many others followed him and arrested him fleeing with the bloody knife in his hand with the hue raised, defending himself with the same knife . . .'.[56] John was hanged at the eyre, and so was William son of Matilda, likewise seized immediately after killing a man, the stick which had struck the fatal blow still in his hand.[57] Not every pursuit ended so successfully. The Westbury jurors told how one night bandits attacked the house of Basilia, the wife of Robert the smith, when Robert was away in Worcester. The hue was raised and the neighbourhood came, but the attackers killed one villager and wounded another before making themselves scarce.[58]

Answering the hue could thus be a dangerous business, and the significance of all these episodes, in the present context, lies in the fact that people were prepared to take the risks involved in the pursuit of armed and dangerous men. The hanging in an unidentified court of eleven criminals who had just killed three women in one house appears to show a willingness to tackle a whole gang.[59] There are also cases which show an impressive degree of communal vigilance and alertness. William de Fonte and his son Alexander were suspected of the death of a merchant, in the first instance because 'he stayed in William's house, and was seen to stay there, and he never left it except as a dead man', and though they denied the death, further details emerged, that Alexander and his mother Agnes had killed him, with William's connivance, and had carried his body away, after taking from it £10 and a belt.[60] When Matilda, widow of Richard le Butiller of Acton, came under suspicion of her husband's death, the jurors were able to report on the quarrels between Richard and Matilda, on the way he often beat her, alleging unfaithfulness on her part, and how she would often return to her father's house, 'and to the house of Robert Waifer who had married a friend of Matilda's', and how Robert and others had often come with Matilda to Richard's house, and had threatened Richard.[61] We can surely see in such a case both the continuing operation of the system of multiple presentment, whereby represen-

[56] *Gloucestershire Crown Pleas 1221*, no. 189.
[57] Ibid., no. 394.
[58] Ibid., no. 336.
[59] Ibid., no. 472.
[60] Ibid., no. 213.
[61] Ibid., no. 111.

tatives of vills drew on local knowledge to inform the countryside of brawls and disturbances, and also the rumours and tale-bearing which must often have fed that system, in the rather sordid details which the Deerhurst jurors were able to supply about this case.

It was certainly a system which, if not closely scrutinized, could provide scope for malice and vindictiveness. *Bracton*, as Meekings showed, declared that the justices should be ready to probe juries' indictments to get at the truth.[62] Maitland's vivid representation of justices presiding at an eyre is made in a different spirit — 'We are reminded of a schoolmaster before whom stands a class of boys saying their lesson. He knows when they go wrong, for he has the book.'[63] The justices did indeed have access to coroners' and sheriffs' records, and could use them to monitor what the jurors said. But they also used them, and all the other sources of information available to them, in efforts to get at the facts of the cases presented before them. An eyre was a dynamic affair, and the justices presided over proceedings much more like a forum than a catechism. Testimony could be given by the whole county, or by the sheriff and a range of lesser officials. Great men like the earl of Gloucester, the earl Marshal and the abbot of Cirencester might appear at the eyre to speak up on behalf of their interests.[64] At a much humbler level, after the Dudstone jurors presented details of the killing of Roger le Frankelein, Roger's widow Gunilda, who had been beaten up in the course of the attack, came into court to tell how 'there was ancient hatred between Roger and Henry le Cupere over Henry's beasts which Roger had often impounded, and so she thinks he was killed by him'. It was then found that Henry had already been arrested for theft, and when he came into court, the coroners, jurors and four nearest vills declared 'with one voice' that he was guilty of both homicide and theft.[65] When a jury made a presentment or indictment, it might be prepared to speak up again in defence of it. After John the miller had not only denied killing Henry, servant of Petronilla of Stoneway, but also said he never knew him, the Westbury jurors gave as one reason for believing him to be guilty the fact that 'he denies being in Henry's company and that he did not know him, and this they know to be false . . .'.[66]

An important part was played by the representatives of vills, in the form of four men and the reeve from each community. These men may

[62] *Wiltshire Crown Pleas 1249*, pp. 95–6.
[63] Pollock and Maitland, ii 646.
[64] *Gloucestershire Crown Pleas 1221*, nos. 234, 254, 268.
[65] Ibid., no. 414.
[66] Ibid., no. 330.

well have cooperated with juries in the presentment of offences, which often seems to have been made in geographical sequence, vill by vill, rather than in some other pre-arranged order. And they could also be questioned by the justices. Hence a case like that of Roger of Meon and his brother Ranulf Eynolk, presented by the Kiftsgate jurors as having killed William son of Henry and fled, so that they were put in exigent. But it was later testified — and the phrase *postea testatum est* often appears to indicate further inquiry — that Roger was not guilty, and that his only fault lay in his having been present at the killing. Along with this discovery went amercements imposed on Meon and Admington vills. Meon had not wanted to say anything about Roger, while Admington had not only been likewise silent, but had also falsely presented the death of William's wife Hawise, who had appealed the two fugitives of her husband's death; she was in fact still alive.[67] The jurors would appear to have believed at first that Roger was guilty, the two vills to have believed in his innocence, to the extent that they tried to protect him by concealing and misrepresenting facts. Paradoxically, it looks as it was the discovery of their efforts, perhaps by reference to the county court rolls, which should have recorded Hawise's appeal, that led to the re-examination of the case and Roger's eventual acquittal. The Deerhurst jurors presented that a thief who broke into the house of a widow called Elvina and carried off her goods had been pursued and killed by two neighbours. The two men came before the justices, and the jurors upheld their statement that they had killed the man as he fled. Finally Elvina came into court, to claim the stolen goods, 'and nothing else was testified except that he was a thief and was killed in flight' — a choice of words which suggests strongly that there had been a last cross-questioning by the justices of the jurors and others, to ensure that the thief's death, though violent, had nevertheless been lawful.[68]

The records of cases from the 1221 Gloucestershire eyre are seldom very full, and generally contain less detail than those of later eyres — hence the frequent omission of information about tithings. As the plea rolls become more communicative, it is possible to see more of the same sorts of processes as those employed in Gloucestershire, and to get a clearer picture of the justices at work, and of their methods of getting at the facts behind cases. It should be said that by comparison with later gaol deliveries, where trials appear to have taken only a few minutes, eyres were relatively leisurely affairs. A rudimentary timetable

---

[67] Ibid., no. 11.
[68] Ibid., no. 89.

survives from the 1238 Devon eyre, which suggests that the justices got through about thirty cases a day,[69] and these would have included presentments of accidental deaths, royal rights, infringements of the assizes of cloth and wine, and other matters which would usually have required little examination or discussion. Where justices itinerant wanted to go into a case in detail, they are unlikely to have felt constrained by lack of time. A good example of the way they might take time and trouble is provided by the 1248 Sussex eyre, where the Eastbourne jurors presented that Remigius de Esthalle had been found dead on the seashore; he had, they said, drowned himself. But a check against his roll showed that the coroner had seen nothing to suggest suicide. The justices clearly then decided to look more deeply into this case, because further testimony was produced to show that 'the men of Eastbourne hated Remigius greatly, and hardly let him be buried in the cemetery'. Armed with this evidence for misrepresentation, they then turned to the first finder of the corpse, and he must have broken down under questioning, it being recorded that 'he vacillates in his presentment'. Finally it was admitted that Remigius died by misadventure, falling from his horse into the sea, but so determined had the men of Eastbourne been to ruin him posthumously that they had presented this case falsely to the county court as well as to the eyre. Only the determination of the king's justices to uncover it had brought the truth about his death to light.[70]

Nor was it only the first finder of a corpse who might be required to testify in court. Other witnesses, or presumed witnesses, might also give evidence, and be examined. At the 1235 Essex eyre the Lexden jurors presented details of the killing of Adam le Franceys of Tolleshunt, who had stayed in the house of Stephen le Macecre on the night before his death. Before the sheriff and coroners Stephen had told how Adam arrived and left in daylight, and had departed carrying 6s.4d. of Stephen's to pay to a Tolleshunt man, money subsequently found tied in his shirt. And he produced two witnesses to corroborate his testimony. But at the eyre not only did Stephen tell a different story, but his witnesses also let him down. At first one of them denied ever setting eyes on the dead man, and then they both denied seeing anything, presumably under questioning in court. Stephen was hanged.[71] Jurors might themselves be questioned. At the 1262 Buckinghamshire eyre the Bunstey jury gave particulars of the death of an unknown woman, arrested at Beachampton on suspicion of theft

[69] *Crown Pleas of the Devon Eyre of 1238*, pp. xii–xiii.
[70] PRO, JUST/1/909A, m. 28d.
[71] PRO, JUST/1/230, m. 2d.

by two men who went on to beat her up so brutally that she died. Her body was then buried in the church cemetery without a coroner's view, and the justices clearly suspected that this was not the limit of attempts at concealment, because they questioned five members of other juries singly, both about the circumstances of the woman's death and about the efforts to conceal it. No more suspects came to light, but two local worthies made fine for twenty marks each, and several other men paid smaller sums.[72]

Maitland could hardly have known about such cases without a much more extensive scrutiny of unpublished records than he ever had time for. He saw how the financial penalties imposed by eyres served to impress on communities and individuals their responsibilities in the work of keeping the king's peace — 'a just and regular infliction of pecuniary penalties was the only means of bringing the unprofessional policeman (and every man ought to be a policeman) to a sense of his duties . . .'.[73] But although he showed by this comment that he was perfectly aware that law enforcement was a process which went on between eyres, he gave remarkably little attention to those agents who above all others represented continuity in that process, namely the sheriff and all the other officials who proliferated in thirteenth-century England. He described the sheriff's tourn, bringing out its resemblances to the eyre, in the use of written articles to which jurors must give answers,[74] but of officialdom as a whole he declared that 'we need say but little since constitutional history has taken them under her protection'.[75] The attention which officials received from constitutional history was one which placed them in the background to important developments like the issue of Magna Carta, the struggles between Henry III and Simon de Montfort, and the beginnings of parliament, and not for another thirty-five years were they spotlighted as playing a significant part in the day-by-day administration of the country. 1995 was also the sixty-fifth anniversary of the publication of Helen Cam's *The Hundred and the Hundred Rolls*, a book which has arguably still not received its due — a consequence perhaps of its first appearing in a series not usually regarded as part of the academic publishing mainstream, and possibly also of a graceful and often humorous style which softened the impact of Cam's message.

For where Maitland and his successors looked down at medieval administration from the perspective of a royal government which

---

[72] PRO, JUST/1/58, mm. 26, 27.
[73] *Gloucestershire Crown Pleas 1221*, pp. xxxiii–xxxiv.
[74] Pollock and Maitland, i 558–60.
[75] Ibid., i 533.

enacted legislation and gave orders in the expectation that they would be obeyed, Cam observed it from a very different perspective, that of those who distributed those orders locally and of those who finally received them. Far from giving rise to grateful reflections upon the 'tremendous empire of kingly majesty',[76] Cam, using the *Rotuli Hundredorum* of the early years of Edward I's reign, portrayed a society in the grip of whole regiments of petty tyrants, uncertainly and distantly presided over by a king whose intervention, even when well-intentioned, was liable to seem capricious, and was more likely to appear either expensive or extortionate, and quite possibly both. Maitland made use of the *Rotuli Hundredorum*, but primarily for information about units of local government — the distribution of suits to courts, the places where courts met, the shortcomings and transgressions of village communities, and the like — and his terms of reference prevented his examining the activities of sheriffs and their underlings, and of their equivalents in private jurisdictions, for the light these might shed upon the enforcement of the criminal law. Of course, many of the allegations recorded in the *Rotuli* will have been exaggerations, if not pure fiction, but even so, they, and similar accusations made at cyres, show something of the range of activities undertaken by the men so accused.

In Gloucestershire, for instance, officials are shown holding courts, sometimes more often than they should have done — the undersheriff of the county was holding four tourns a year, instead of the two prescribed by custom. They received indictments, and arrested those indicted, though they might then take bribes for releasing them again. The earl of Warwick's steward arrested Robert le Holdere, described as 'a faithful man', imprisoned him, and then made him abjure Wickwan vill, without a coroner or royal bailiff being present. They might hold inquests into deaths, or at least give orders that inquests be held. When a woman's body was found in the Severn, the bailiff of Henbury hundred sent the tithingman of Aust and others to inquire, and when they could not identify her, threatened to accuse one of the men who made the inquest. They might come to terms with one another to ensure that suspects were, in their own eyes, duly punished. A thief arrested at Sodbury fled to Bristol; the bailiffs of Sodbury followed him there, and paid John de Mucegros's bailiff one mark to allow him to flee thence, but the flight was a stage-managed one, for as soon as the thief was outside Bristol he found his pursuers waiting for him, and they arrested him, took him back to Sodbury, and hanged

[76] Ibid., i 107.

him there.[77] The exact particulars of these allegations are not at issue here; the officials involved may have been maligned, or they may have been genuinely brutal and corrupt. What is significant in this context is that in these presentments they can be seen holding courts and inquests, making arrests, even taking steps to have a suspect hanged — all processes without which the criminal law could not be enforced.

Similar activities, often associated with abuses of power, but also demonstrating how power was exercised, are recorded in many crown plea rolls from eyres. Like justices itinerant, officials reviewed the workings of local courts and other instruments of law enforcement. Thus in 1255 the bailiffs of Faversham hundred in Kent were reported as having taken money from vills and individuals for not attending inquests into homicides and the raising of the hue, for raising the hue but not following it, and for acting as host to unknown criminals.[78] Officials are frequently recorded as arresting suspects, and as taking bribes for releasing those arrested, and they also exploited their control of prisons, several times being said to have refused to accept prisoners from their captors. The Buckinghamshire vill of Edlesborough sent three times to the sheriff asking that he receive Adam Spregy, arrested in the act of burglary, into the county gaol, and each time the sheriff refused, so that in the end Adam escaped.[79] In such a case the sheriff was probably holding out for a bribe, or at any rate some informal *douceur* for the trouble he would be put to in sending men to take Adam to prison, though it is possible that officials sometimes refused to accept prisoners because they doubted their guilt.

Sheriffs and bailiffs certainly needed to be alert and well-informed, and to keep their ears to the ground for reports of ill-doing and dubious behaviour. When Algar of Charton departed on pilgrimage, the bailiff of the Devon hundred of Axminster came and took Algar's chattels precisely because he had been away for a long time; he had not been indicted, but his prolonged absence clearly seemed suspicious.[80] They could also hear petitions for redress, as when Henry de la Gare complained to the sheriff of Kent that Adam son of Hugh had maimed him; since at the 1241 Kent eyre it was found that there was no record of an appeal, this must have been an essentially informal representation, though it led to Adam being arrested.[81] To the same end officials

[77] Cases from W. Illingworth, ed., *Rotuli Hundredorum* i (Record Commission, 1812), pp. 166–83.
[78] PRO, JUST/1/361, m. 50d.
[79] PRO, JUST/1/58, m. 25.
[80] PRO, JUST/1/176, m. 28.
[81] PRO, JUST/1/359, m. 31d.

seem to have held numerous inquests, whose findings they might direct; when Nicholas de Wauncy, sheriff of Surrey, held an inquest into the killing of Robert le Bost, he 'threatened to penalize the vills concerned' if they did not indict Ralph of Anjou, as they then did, though Ralph was acquitted at the 1241 eyre.[82] But on other occasions they might hold inquests and then allow themselves to be bribed to ignore their findings. In 1262 the Kineton jurors told how William Mansel, then sheriff of Warwickshire, had held an inquest on Alcester bridge 'into criminals in those parts', at which the gentleman-gangster Robert de Castello and several of his followers were indicted, but for a bribe of 100s. he agreed to leave them alone, thereby enabling them to commit many more crimes.[83] Mansel was sheriff of Warwickshire and Leicester-shire for three and a half years in the 1250s, having previously been undersheriff to Philip Marmion. A local man, he may have had tenurial links with Robert de Castello. His record illustrates the danger that officials would become over-sensitive to local interests, and unmindful of the king's. The risk was increased by the very long terms that some of them served in the mid-thirteenth century, for instance the twelve years of William Heron in Northumberland (1246–58) and the fifteen years of Walter of Bath in Devon (1236–51). In 1258 the baronial reformers called for sheriffs to be replaced annually,[84] but neither then nor later did this prove practicable. Lesser officials, who might have bought their offices, could prove equally long-lasting, their local knowledge making them well-nigh indispensable even when they proved incorrigibly corrupt.[85] As far as law enforcement was concerned, there were obvious advantages in having an official who knew his 'patch', including its shadier inhabitants.

It sometimes happened that an official would use his position to bestow respectability on a man who did not deserve it. At the 1250/1 Norfolk eyre the Freebridge jurors presented that Peter of Pinchbeck, outlawed in Lincolnshire, had paid one mark to the sheriff of Norfolk 'for allowing him to stay and announcing that he was faithful'.[86] In fact the sheriff quite possibly did not know of Peter's outlawry, and the significance of this case lies as much in the fact that the truth of his status had nevertheless been revealed, as in the light it sheds on the

---

[82] PRO, JUST/1/869, m. 2.

[83] PRO, JUST/1/954, m. 48; see also Summerson, 'The maintenance of law and order', 169–71.

[84] R. F. Treharne and I. J. Saunders, eds, *Documents of the Baronial Movement of Reform and Rebellion, 1258–1267* (Oxford, 1973), pp. 108–9.

[85] Discussed by H. M. Cam, *The Hundred and the Hundred Rolls* (London 1930), pp. 145–53; see also R. C. Palmer, *The County Courts of Medieval England, 1150–1350* (Princeton, New Jersey, 1982), pp. 28–55.

[86] PRO, JUST/1/564, m. 25.

power which his office gave the sheriff to confer acceptability on a dubious character. How the facts about Peter's outlawry became known is not recorded, and it is clear that there were many ways for such disclosures to be made, not all of them overtly formal. The whole structure of thirteenth-century law enforcement, with its elaborate system of continuous presentments at inquests and courts, was itself the product of a rural society in which everybody was expected to be perpetually alert and suspicious, their ears and eyes open for evidence of violent or dishonest behaviour, ready to raise or follow the hue, to pick up and to circulate rumour, both to one another and to officials. An Essex woman who found a cowl belonging to the prior of Blackmore informed the parish priest, who in his turn told her to report her find to the bailiff of Writtle.[87] A presentment of treasure trove at the 1232 Warwickshire eyre was specifically said to have originated in women's gossip — 'ex confabulationibus mulierum.'[88] At the same eyre a presentment concerning a man who died in St John's hospital in Coventry was found to have originated with the woman who had laid out his corpse.[89] Petty thieves were often punished by the loss of an ear, and to be detected with such a mutilation was to risk instant arrest. Hence enrolments on the patent rolls like that which proclaimed that 'Walter son of Roger de Sumery lost his left ear by some evildoers in the forest of Clarendon and not on account of any felony'.[90] Otherwise Walter stood in danger of the fate of the woman with only one ear, and the man with a thumb cut off, who were arrested on suspicion in Berkshire.[91] Vagrants could expect to be stopped for questioning, like the Buckinghamshire man who claimed to be a servant of Gilbert of Seagrave but 'varied in what he said, and was therefore arrested and imprisoned at Aylesbury', though in the end no charge was brought against him.[92]

Not surprisingly, the use of written instruments, attesting the honesty and good repute of those who carried them, began to proliferate. William of Badgeworth, accused of theft in Sussex, returned home to Gloucestershire, where the Badgeworth manor court provided him with 'litteras testimoniales de fidelitate' under the seals of the bailiff and suitors, which he then carried back to Bramber.[93] Equally unsurprisingly, in such conditions malevolent rumour also circulated freely.

[87] PRO, JUST/1/1189, m. 6d.
[88] PRO, JUST/1/951A, m. 4.
[89] Ibid., m. 7d.
[90] *Calendar of Patent Rolls, 1247–1258*, p. 167.
[91] PRO, JUST/1/36, m. 5d.
[92] PRO, JUST/1/62, m. 4.
[93] PRO, JUST/1/911, m. 8.

At the 1262/3 Kent eyre Hamo Petch complained that, following the discovery of a stranger's corpse in Ash wood, Isobel, widow of Nicholas Denne, and her son Richard had put it about that the body was that of Isobel's son John, and that Hamo had killed him, 'with the result that Hamo was held in such suspicion for the death that he barely escaped hanging', a complaint which the Hildenborough jury confirmed 'in every detail'.[94] The fact that so much information was so regularly called for from communities increased the chances that dishonesty, malice or straightforward error would eventually be winnowed out and the truth emerge. In the case of Hamo Petch that is indeed what happened, though apparently not until the eyre. The eyre was the apex of the whole system, but it remained a part of that system. Much of what was said and done at an eyre derived from what had already been presented to inferior courts, and it was by drawing on these earlier proceedings, and on the communicative capacity of rural society as a whole, that eyre juries were sometimes able to testify with an impressive precision and weight of detail.

At the Hertfordshire eyre of the late spring of 1248 John of Standon and Alice, daughter of Hugh le Seler, suspected of the death of Alexander the mason, paid one mark for a special verdict. In due course the jurors of three hundreds came into court, and stated that:

> On the Wednesday before Michaelmas in the twenty-ninth year [27 September 1245] Alexander ate at the home of Henry of Buckland in Buckland, and immediately after dinner Alexander set out from there in good health, saying he would go to Royston. And while on the journey to Royston he spoke to Lawrence of Therfield. From there he went on towards Royston and crossed onto Ermine street, and there Alice saw him, wearing a blue gown and black surcoat, and from there he crossed to Royston and entered the house of Hugh le Seler, dressed in a blue gown and blue surcoat, and Alexander Nictegale saw him in that house. And from there he went to the house of Mabbe Veiri in Royston, where there were John of Standon and a certain Leonard who was later arrested, but he was never afterwards seen alive in that house, and they say that a quarrel arose between Alexander and John of Standon, so that Alexander suddenly struck him, and John was much threatened. And next day he was found dead in Read field.[95]

How this case ended is unknown, and it looks possible that John of Standon, at least, was convicted. But even if the charge against John was not made to stick, the system which could produce so much circumstantial information about an event of over two and a half years earlier should hardly be dismissed as 'exceedingly inefficient'.

It was, however, a system highly exacting for everybody involved

---

[94] PRO, JUST/1/1582, m. 5d.
[95] PRO, JUST/1/318, m. 20.

in its operation, in terms of the labour involved, and also in that its workings took precedence over all the claims of family or neighbourhood. Every suspect had to be arrested or pursued, every suspicion reported, regardless of who might be involved. The Gloucestershire man reported in 1221 to have driven away his own son after he came under suspicion of theft was doing what every law-abiding man and woman should do,[96] but it is not surprising that there were many who did not imitate him, in spite of the danger of financial penalties or even of a charge of harbouring or abetting a felon, which was itself a felony.[97] Every possible pressure had to be exerted in order to instil a proper sense of the heinousness of crime and the need to remain vigilant against those who perpetrated it — the communal pressure embodied in frankpledge, the supervisory pressure represented by courts and officials, and the moral pressure embodied above all in the sanctions of the church. This last was an aspect of medieval life with which Maitland, described by his daughter as 'a very Protestant agnostic',[98] did not show a great deal of sympathy. He appreciated the importance of church courts, and devoted a good deal of space to their workings, but does not seem to have concerned himself much with the social effects of religious doctrine. Yet felonies like homicide, theft, rape and arson were not just breaches of the king's peace, they were also offences against God, and homicide, in particular, was a mortal sin, which Bishop Richard Poore of Salisbury, in his early thirteenth-century synodal statutes, decreed could only be absolved by the pope or the pope's legate. Poore reissued his statutes when he became bishop of Durham; they included a clause directing confessors not to absolve and enjoin penance to thieves until they had restored what they had stolen.[99] Since it was presented at the 1242/3 Durham eyre that one Robert son of John of Sleekburn, suspected of stealing cattle, had given satisfaction to his victims on the recommendation of the chaplain to whom he had made confession, it would appear that such injunctions could be effective.[100] One of the canons of the council which the papal legate Otto held in 1237 was directed 'against the scourge of thieves, in whom the realm of England abounds to excess', and forbade anyone to harbour or protect them, on pain of excommunication.[101] The effects

---

[96] *Gloucestershire Crown Pleas 1221*, no. 228.
[97] E.g. *Crown Pleas of the Devon Eyre of 1238* no. 267.
[98] Fifoot, *Life*, p. 180.
[99] F. M. Powicke and C. R. Cheney, eds, *Councils and Synods 1204–1313*, vol ii part i (Oxford, 1964), pp. 73–4.
[100] K. E. Bayley, ed., 'Two thirteenth-century assize rolls for the County of Durham', in *Miscellanea Vol. II* (Surtees Society, 127, 1916), no. 357.
[101] *Councils and Synods*, ii part i, p. 253.

of such an order cannot be known, but that it was given at all may serve to draw attention to the fact that there was a spiritual dimension to medieval law enforcement, which should not be overlooked.

Between his edition of the *Pleas of the Crown for the County of Gloucester, 1221*, in 1884, and the *History of English Law* in 1895, Maitland published in 1888 a volume of *Select Pleas of the Crown 1200–1225* for the Selden Society. On the workings of the criminal law his opinion in the last was much the same as in the other two — it was 'extremely ineffectual; the punishment of a criminal was a rare event . . .'. In making his selection of pleas, he stated his aim to be 'the thorough illustration of the normal course of criminal justice'.[102] His choice of cases certainly conveys a distinct impression of ineffectiveness on the part of the criminal law. This must in part be attributable to the fact that many appeals, in particular, had no recorded conclusion, and that the fate of most of those defendants who went to the ordeal was likewise unreported. But the editor's decision to illustrate the workings of the criminal law by way of numerous illustrations of its failings and shortcomings is also in part responsible. The reader who encounters misrepresentations by juries, failures to hold inquests or make presentments to local courts, extortionate or dishonest officials, failures to arrest, appeals found to be malicious, or simply quashed on every possible ground, and such individual cases as a wager of a duel annulled when it was found that the proper processes of arrest had not been gone through, a man tonsured while awaiting proceedings in court, a killer removed from the church where he had taken sanctuary in order to become a monk, and the obstruction offered to those attempting to follow the trail of stolen cattle through the streets of Bridgnorth, can hardly fail to regard the entire system as characterized by confusion and futility.[103]

Yet the cases which Maitland chose are not entirely without evidence for a better state of affairs. Not only do they record a fair number of hangings, but there are also occasions when criminals are pursued and arrested, returning abjurors are caught, a thief is killed in flight by the hue, a suspect is arrested by a hundred serjeant's men, and a man imprisoned in another man's house sends to the sheriff for help, which is forthcoming in the form of one of the sheriff's serjeants and others. There are also several glimpses of local courts going about their business. And when some of the cases which Maitland did *not* include are taken into consideration, here too are indications that

---

[102] *Select Pleas of the Crown*, p. xxiv.
[103] These last three examples are ibid., nos. 43, 135, 173.

not all was chaos and incompetence. Maitland selected twenty cases from the 1201 Cornwall eyre.[104] They include five homicides, three burglaries, an appeal of rape, seven appeals alleging robbery, wounding and assault in various combinations, a charge of harbouring an outlaw, and a silly presentment by the jury. Nobody was hanged, though an entire vill was outlawed for one killing. Two suspects succeeded at the ordeal. The rape was settled by marriage. Some appeals got as far as ordeals, others were quashed; one proved to have originated in a quarrel over a villein, another to have been made by a harlot whose cloak two boys had pawned for two gallons of wine. Yet these unimpressive proceedings also record an inquest held on the sheriff's orders, the tracing of goods stolen in a burglary to the suspect's house, and an investigation of the circumstances of a killing which disclosed, of the suspect and his victim, that 'the day before he had threatened her body and goods'. And cases which Maitland omitted show a wood where malefactors were known to lurk being searched by men of the neighbourhood, led by the hundred serjeant, with the result that two criminals were killed, and a man coming under suspicion because his tunic was found and recognized in a burgled house.[105]

In these last two cases arrests were made. But equally significant are cases where nobody was captured, but in which the processes of law enforcement can be seen as having been so mobilized as to minimize, as far as possible, the consequences of material conditions which were bound to make arrests very hard to effect. For instance, the Eastwivelshire jurors presented the death of a hospitaller named Hugh. Two men were suspected, both of them being identified. One had fled. He had been a member of a tithing, and he had left chattels worth 10s., which had been valued in advance of the eyre — brother Robert of the hospital was to answer for them. The other suspect came to the eyre, and as he was a clerk, he was handed over to Court Christian. Four men and a woman were suspected of harbouring the suspects. The woman had been arrested and imprisoned, though she was apparently released to pledges through the agency of the bishop of Exeter. Two of the other suspects were cleared, but still had to find pledges for their good behaviour, while the other two were taken into custody as suspected. Nobody was hanged, but it is difficult to see what else could have been done by way of either precaution or punishment. The fugitive suspect, who had been placed under as much restraint as possible through his belonging to a tithing, had been identified, his

---

[104] Ibid., nos. 1–20.
[105] Additional cases from the 1201 Cornwall eyre discussed here are printed as *PKJ*, ii nos. 312, 322, 332.

chattels forfeited, his status would doubtless be advertized by his being outlawed, which would itself reduce him to the condition of a wild beast. Other suspects had been produced in court. In thirteenth-century terms such an outcome could hardly be termed a complete failure.

Maitland was aware of the problems involved in making a selection of case material, and although in his letter to Dove, quoted above, he observed that 'many of these criminal cases are very interesting and even entertaining . . .', he guarded against producing an anthology made up of lurid and picturesque incidents and anecdotes, by including 'many entries which may fairly be styled "common form entries" '. But given that Maitland regarded the characteristics of medieval criminal law as including a basic ineffectiveness, it may still be surmised that he omitted a case like that of Hugh the hospitaller because he saw medieval law enforcement in a perspective which, though not without its own validity, was nevertheless flawed by its incompleteness. His strong centralizing viewpoint was one which could yield notable rewards, as it did with his work on parliament, but was inadequate for the processes of law enforcement, which only intermittently came within the purviews of the king's government. There was a world elsewhere. What Maitland saw and analysed, he often described with admirable lucidity and thoroughness, but too often he failed to appreciate the extent to which it had a life of its own, and operated according to principles which were only partly imposed from above. Above all, he missed the way in which local courts and other processes of law enforcement functioned together as a *system*, one able to interlock with the agencies of central government, and above all with the eyre, but also able, and indeed required, to operate in their absence. Whereas the strongest impression one takes away from Maitland's accounts of all the various courts is of their separateness, they were in fact intended to work together, and to ends which were only incidentally identical with those of Victorian criminal law. It amounts to rather more than a cavil to argue that Maitland's view of medieval law enforcement was fundamentally flawed. Yet even if the arguments proposed here be accepted, much of abiding value remains. In the last resort, it hardly seems to matter whether, in the perspective of a century's additional scholarship, Maitland was right or wrong. Even where he has come to be perceived as mistaken, Maitland's writings will continue to be worth reading, for the pleasures and benefits to be gained from following a great historian as he engages with issues of continuing interest and importance.

Proceedings of the British Academy, **89**, 145–169

The Learned Laws in 'Pollock and Maitland'

R. H. HELMHOLZ

THIS ESSAY IS MEANT TO DESCRIBE the place of the Roman and Canon Laws in Pollock and Maitland's *History of English Law.* The assignment given to me also calls for some discussion of the several ways the subject of the role of the European *ius commune* in the development of English law looks different (and the same) one hundred years later. The essay's purpose is thus to examine the role which the book's authors themselves regarded the learned laws as having played in the development of English law and also to review briefly the progress in scholarship, the changes in attitude, and the stability in viewpoint that have occurred during the intervening years. It will also say a word, or perhaps two words, about Maitland's overall approach to the *ius commune.* At the end of the paper, there is a hesitant comment about the future of this subject. But my principal goal has not been prediction. Still less has it been providing direction for others. It has been description — and I hope accurate description — of what has already happened. No speaker should imagine that his hearers have their pencils at the ready in hopes of being assigned a research topic. To approach the task of description, it seems appropriate first to set out the assumptions and definitions upon which the description will be based.

Definitions

The term 'learned laws' refers to the Roman and Canon Laws, known together as the *ius commune,* and more specifically it means these two laws as they existed from the revival of legal science in the twelfth century to the end of the nineteenth century.[1] The definition encompasses the contents of the *Corpus iuris civilis* and the *Corpus iuris canonici*, together with the medieval glosses and the other early commentaries written upon them. One might also include the *Libri feudorum*, because this compilation was regularly printed in medieval and early modern copies of the *Corpus iuris civilis* and because it played a larger role in the development of Western law than is allowed in most of our textbooks.[2] But this is a small matter, particularly since 'Pollock and Maitland' refers to it only exceptionally.

This definition excludes several sources of law that could be called 'learned' without doing violence to the term. It excludes what Continental scholars call the *ius proprium*, that is the laws of particular regions or cities. It excludes maritime and urban law and the so-called *lex mercatoria*. And of course it excludes the English common law, although I would not wish to be thought to hold the view that the adjective 'learned' would be wholly inappropriate in describing it. But the Roman and Canon Laws were what was taught in the Universities, in England as on the Continent, and this fact must fix the definition of 'learned' for purposes of this contribution, as it did for Pollock and Maitland themselves.

The temporal limitations imposed on this definition should also be stated at the outset. By 'Roman Law' is not meant the law of antiquity, the law of classical Rome. The term refers to the Roman Law as understood and interpreted by the medieval jurists. Maitland was quick to point out the significance of the gap on this score between the ancient and the medieval. Sparked by the rediscovery of the *Digest* during the eleventh century, the revival of the scientific study and exposition of the civil law led to very different conclusions and assumptions from those that had governed the world in which the texts of the Digest were formulated. The discussion of the Italian developments in the fifth chapter of Volume One is particularly worth reading on this score. The medieval law of civil and criminal procedure, for example, turned out to be very different from that which prevailed during the

---

[1] Fuller treatments of the subject are: James A. Brundage, *Medieval Canon Law* (London, 1995); Péter Erdö, *Introductio in historiam scientiae canonicae* (Rome, 1990); Jean Gaudemet, *Les sources du droit canonique VIIIe–XXe siècle* (Paris, 1993); id., *Église et Cité: histoire du droit canonique* (Paris, 1994); E. J. H. Schrage & H. Dondrop, *Utrumque ius, eine Einführung in das Studium der Quellen des mittelalterlichen gelehrten Rechts* (Berlin, 1992). All contain abundant references to prior and more specialized scholarly work. For treatments putting the canon law into contemporary context, see Manlio Bellomo, *The Common Legal Past of Europe 1000–1800* (Washington, D.C., 1995); Ennio Cortese, *Il Rinascimento giuridico medievale* (Rome, 1992), pp. 48–61: Harold J. Berman, *Law and Revolution* (Cambridge, Mass., 1983, pp. 199–254.
[2] See Walter Ullmann, *Law and Politics in the Middle Ages* (Ithaca, N.Y.), 1975, p. 217.

Roman Republic or Empire.[3] Equally, the *litis contestatio* turned out
to be something different in the thirteenth century than it had been in
the second.[4] The term was retained in the *ius commune;* its significance
in practice changed. Thus, the 'learned laws' of this contribution's title
were themselves in the flux, even of formulation, during the period
covered by the *History of English Law*. And it was this living law upon
which one must focus in studying the question of its impact in England
during the twelfth and thirteenth centuries.[5]

The quality of 'coming into being' was particularly true for the
Canon Law. Beginning with Gratian's *Concordance of Discordant
Canons*, the *Decretum* compiled in 1140, the Canon Law had itself
entered a new era of development that would separate it decisively
from the Church's law of the previous thousand years. What had gone
before would come to look incomplete, incoherent, and unworthy of
citation, when it was set beside the Canon Law in the form it assumed
in the thirteenth century and thereafter. The first volume of 'Pollock
and Maitland' sketches this feature admirably. Indeed its pages on the
subject read better and contain more information than many such
descriptions written more recently.[6] They contain some gems, as for
example a wonderful and (to me) quite unexpected comparison of
Gratian's *Decretum* to Coke upon Littleton.[7] It is a comparison that
illumines with a deft stroke the regard in which the work of the Father
of the Canon Law was held by the medieval canonists.

Temporal limitations exist at the other end as well. In dealing with
the Common Law, Maitland trespassed with some frequency on the
limit set by the reign of Edward I, but even so his primary focus
remained fixed on the period before the fourteenth century. That limit
excludes much development in the learned laws as well, principally
what used to be called the era of the 'post-glossators'. Bartolus and
Panormitanus, the most complete expositors of the medieval Roman
and Canon Laws, lie on the other side of the line. So does much,
though not quite all, of the encyclopedic literature of the *ius commune*.
The *glossa ordinaria* to the texts of the laws, together with the works
of some of the first commentators, Hostiensis and Azo for example,

---

[3] Knut Wolfgang Nörr, 'Päpstliche Dekretalen und römish-kanonischer Zivilprozeß', in Walter
Wilhelm, ed., *Studien zur europäischen Rechtsgeschichte* (Frankfurt, 1972), pp. 53–65.

[4] See Allesandro Giuliani, 'Dalla "litis contestatio" al "Pleading system", Riflessioni sui
fondamenti del processo comune europeo', *Index: Quaderni camerti di studi romanistici*, 22
(1994), 433–45.

[5] See for instance the example of this found at Pollock and Maitland, ii 89, dealing with the
importance of *traditio* in Roman law.

[6] Pollock and Maitland, i 111–35.

[7] Pollock and Maitland, i 113.

must therefore hold the attention of the student of Maitland's approach to the learned laws.

The Importance of the Learned Laws

Turning now to an assessment of the place of the Roman and Canon Laws in 'Pollock and Maitland', I may say that my first review inclined me to an affirmative answer. The two laws seemed to have played an important role in the account of English law's growth. However, more fully considered, my conclusion turned out to be the opposite. They turned out to have exerted no more than a superficial influence on the content of the Common Law, although they did exert a strong impulse in forcing English lawyers to formulate their own law. I have followed my own experience in what follows, and I hope that this is something more than a modern parody of Abelard's *Sic et Non*. In fact, I believe both views are contained in 'Pollock and Maitland', and that they are not in the end mutually contradictory.

The argument for the importance of the Roman and Canon Laws in 'Pollock and Maitland' rests ultimately on three things: first, the relative frequency with which they are mentioned in the work; second, the authors' acknowledgement of the significance in English history of the jurisdiction of the courts (principally those of the Church) where the two laws held sway; and third, the serious consideration they give to the possibility that the Canon and Roman Laws exerted more than a fleeting influence on the contents and development of the English Common Law.

The Frequency of Mention

Both Pollock and Maitland were conscious of the existence of the learned laws and of the foundational place they have occupied in the Western legal tradition. Pollock was perhaps the more learned of the two in the Roman Law, but Maitland was certainly no amateur. It must have been natural, second nature one might almost say, for them to have had recourse to the Roman and Canon Laws in thinking about English developments. So one finds. Discussion of the early years of the English law of contract in 'Pollock and Maitland', for instance, is filled with citation to Roman Law and civilian terminology. The *stipulatio*, the *commodatum*, the *nudum pactum* all figure in its pages.[8]

---

[8] Pollock and Maitland, ii 194–5.

PLATE 1

Sir FREDERICK POLLOCK, Bart., 1845–1937
Photograph by J. Caswall Smith

PLATE 2

A poster attacking Maitland for his views on women students
Reproduced by permission of the Syndics of Cambridge University Library
(CUL, UA, CUR 61, no. 154)

PLATE 3

Address of Condolence on the Death of the late Professor Maitland

GONVILLE AND CAIUS COLLEGE LODGE.   4 *February* 1907.

The Vice-Chancellor publishes to the Senate the following Address of Condolence to the University on the death of the late Professor MAITLAND which he has received from the University of Oxford :

TO THE CHANCELLOR, MASTERS AND SCHOLARS OF THE UNIVERSITY
OF CAMBRIDGE.

We, the Chancellor, Masters and Scholars of the University of Oxford, desire to express to you our profound regret at the heavy loss sustained by your University through the lamented death of the distinguished Professor of the Laws of England, FREDERIC WILLIAM MAITLAND.

We feel that we are privileged to claim some part in so gifted a man, who honoured us by receiving at our Encaenia in 1899 the Hon. degree of D.C.L., and who had already given us proof of his genius in the Ford Lectures delivered by him two years previously.

It is seldom that the great qualities of a student and writer in the wide field of Law and History have won such universal appreciation. But no one could fail to be attracted by Professor Maitland's singular patience in research, combined with that rich faculty of imagination, which gave life and light to the most severe dissertations.

It would be impossible to overrate the loss of one who has thus passed away in the full maturity of his powers; diligent beyond the limitations of feeble health ; eager, strenuous, and sympathetic; beloved by friends and disciples; respected and admired by the University of which he was so brilliant an ornament; and approved by the universal verdict of all serious students. We ask you to accept our respectful homage to the Professor's memory, and we assure you of our most heartfelt sympathy with you in your loss.

Given in our House of Convocation on the Twenty-ninth day of
January One thousand nine hundred and seven.

The Oxford message of condolence on Maitland's death
Reproduced by permission of the Syndics of Cambridge University Library
(CUL, UA, CUR 39 (21); *Cambridge University Reporter*, 37 (1906–7), 526)

PLATE 4

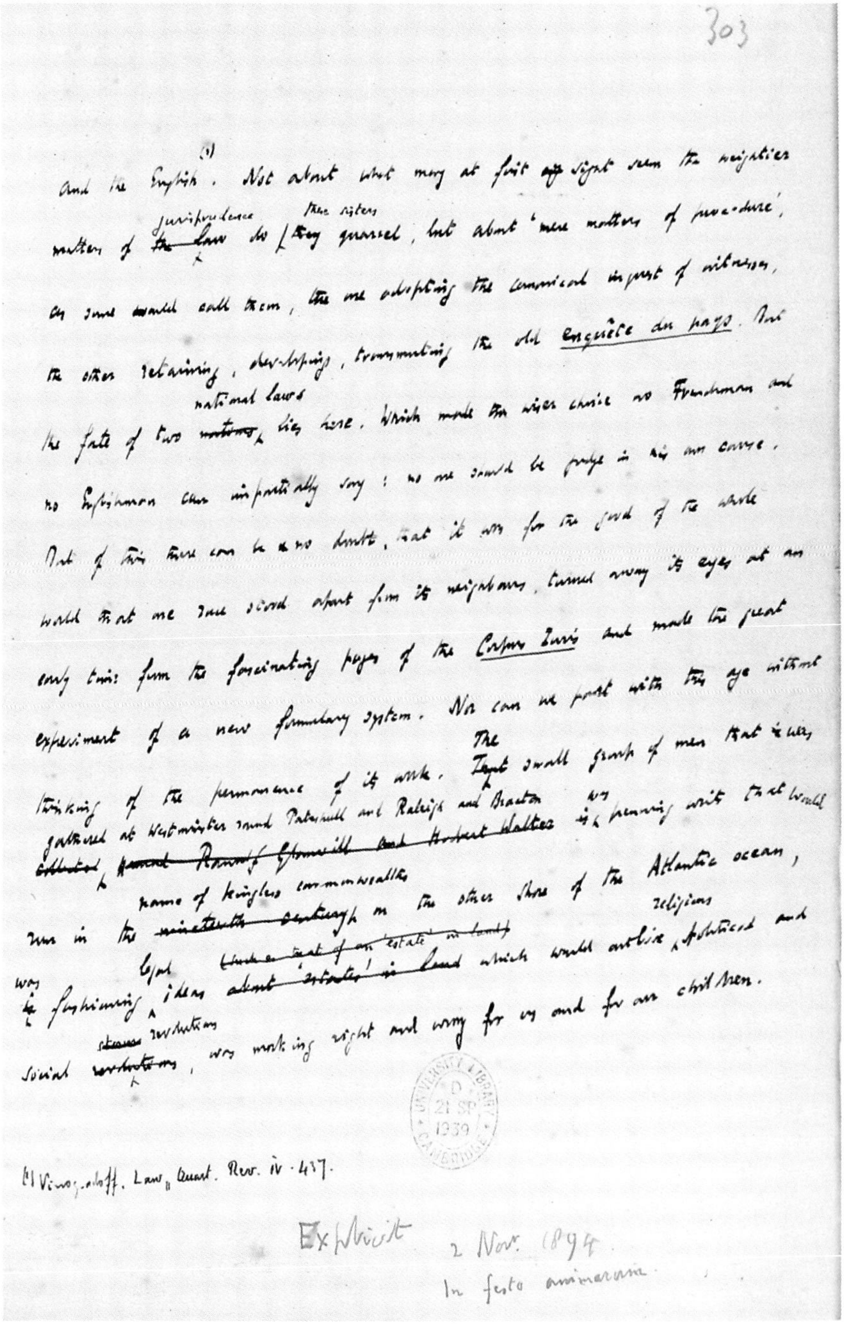
303

And the English.[1] Not about what may at first sight seem the weightier matters of jurisprudence do the sisters quarrel, but about 'mere matters of procedure', as some would call them, the one adopting the canonical inquest of witnesses, the other retaining, developing, transmuting the old enquête du pays. But the fate of two national laws lies here. Which made the wiser choice no Frenchman and no Englishman can impartially say: no one should be judge in his own cause. But of this there can be no doubt, that it was for the good of the whole world that one race stood apart from its neighbours, turned away its eyes at an early time from the fascinating pages of the Corpus Iuris and made the great experiment of a new formulary system. Nor can we part with this age without thinking of the permanence of its work. The small group of men that is always gathered at Westminster round Pateshull and Raleigh and Bracton was penning writs that would run in the name of kingless commonwealths on the other shore of the Atlantic ocean, was fashioning legal ideas which would outlive religious, political and social revolutions, was making right and wrong for us and for our children.

(1) Vinogradoff. Law Quart. Rev. iv. 437.

Explicit 2 Nov. 1894
In festo animarum

The page of the manuscript of *The History of English Law* in which Maitland celebrates finishing
Reproduced by permission of the Syndics of Cambridge University Library
(CUL, Add MS 6994, p. 303).

Nor did Pollock ignore the Canon Law in his account of the subject. The canonists' affirmation of the principle that actions could arise from promises and the central place of the pledge of faith in the canonists' scheme of obligations are both brought to the fore.[9]

It might be said that this was inevitable, given the rudimentary state of the early common law of contract. This would be the truth, but it would not be the whole truth. Maitland often referred to the institutions of Roman and Canon Law even where there was no such obvious stimulation. The parallel between the formulary system of the Romans and the development of the writ system in the Common Law is given full play. It is a parallel 'so patent that it has naturally aroused the suggestion that the one must have been the model for the other.'[10] Maitland is prompt to discredit this opinion, but the habit of comparison remains strong in his subsequent treatment. And it is easy to find other instances, some of them quite surprising. Roman Law's *lex talionis* and the English practice of amercing an unsuccessful plaintiff *pro falso clamore suo* is one.[11] The canonical institution of synodal witnesses, recorded in the *Libri duo de synodalibus causis* of Regino of Prüm (d. 915), and the early English presentment juries is another.[12] Roman criminal law and the English treatment of the 'crime against nature' is a third.[13] None of these subjects cried out for mention of the Roman and Canon Laws. But mention there is all the same.

The explanation for this habit must be, in part, that it grew from the assumptions we associate with comparative law. The idea is that the comparative method will illuminate what is special, and what is common, about almost any legal system. Certainly this was second-nature to Pollock, and Maitland seems to have shared the impulse. One sees its impact not only with respect to Romanist institutions. When he discussed the institution of marital property, Maitland looked naturally enough at the customs of France and Germany for illumination of the English situation.[14] For him, the contrast revealed something useful, and also otherwise in danger of being overlooked, even if there was no direct tie. But there is more than this. Not all references to Roman and Canon Laws in the work can be explained this way. References to the learned laws crop up so regularly in 'Pollock and Maitland' that one is bound to ascribe a special character to them.

[9] Pollock and Maitland, ii 197–9.
[10] Pollock and Maitland, ii 559.
[11] Pollock and Maitland, ii 539. See also ii 560, on the chancellor and the praetor, ii 597, on the development of the law of costs: ii 636, on the use of 'decisory oaths'.
[12] Pollock and Maitland, i 152.
[13] Pollock and Maitland, ii 556.
[14] Pollock and Maitland, ii 402.

This was not the habit of simple 'comparativism'. It was comparative law with an aim.

The Role of the Spiritual Courts

It bears repeating that 'Pollock and Maitland' was not meant to be simply the history of English Common Law. It is the history of English law, and English law embraced courts where the *ius commune* was regularly applied. The tribunals of the king were courts of limited jurisdiction, and the regulation of much of human life occurred outside them. Foremost among these other institutions were the courts of the Church, although there were others where the learned laws came to be applied in some measure. The courts of the ancient universities are of course a prominent example. At least from what we know so far, it appears that they were governed by the *ius commune*, although it is hard to speak with assurance about these courts since their records, though not untouched, still await their historian.

Maitland certainly appreciated the role played by the spiritual tribunals in the development of English law. He devoted a not inconsiderable number of his pages to the law of marriage and divorce, to probate jurisdiction, to the 'criminal' jurisdiction of the ecclesiastical courts, and even to the Church's contentious claim to enforce contractual obligations under the rubric of breach of faith. Not only does 'Pollock and Maitland' contain explicit treatment of the sources and nature of both the civil and Canon Laws, it carries them into English legal practice, looking with care at the courts where they were put into effect.

This did not mean that these courts, or the law they enforced, earned uniformly high marks from Maitland. It would be more accurate to say the reverse. They earned low marks. If it is a common failing among historians to admire the things about which they write, or else to write about things they admire, it is a temptation Maitland successfully resisted. The Church's marriage law Maitland described as 'no masterpiece of human wisdom',[15] going on to speak with apparent feeling about the 'incalculable harm done by a marriage law which was a maze of flighty fancies and misapplied logic.'[16] Maitland regarded the separation of chattels from realty that provided the basis for the English Church's jurisdiction over testaments as the product of an 'evil

---

[15] Pollock and Maitland, ii 368.
[16] Pollock and Maitland, ii 389. See also i 447, speaking of the 'enormous harm' done by the exercise of matrimonial jurisdiction by the Church.

hour'.[17] 'The consequences', he wrote, 'have been evil. We rue them at the present day'.[18] He regarded canonical compurgation, the principal means of proof used within the criminal jurisdiction of the Church as 'little better than a farce' already in the thirteenth century,[19] and he treated the Church's pious request for mercy in the cases of men and women found guilty of heresy and handed over to the secular power for burning with the contempt it so fully deserves.[20] Maitland had little instinctive sympathy towards modern apologies for medieval religion, at least in its legal side. Admiration for the law of the Church did not come easily to him.

Still, if there was little in the way of sympathy or admiration, Maitland had an appreciation of the historical importance of the ecclesiastical courts and the *ius commune* administered within them. He did not ignore the significance of the Church as an influential twelfth-century landholder. Nor should it be forgotten that it was the authority and significance of the Roman Canon Law in England that he vindicated in the celebrated dispute with Bishop Stubbs. The conclusions he drew from that controversy found their way into 'Pollock and Maitland', and as he himself put it, they 'compelled [him] to make some inquiry about the rules that were enforced by the ecclesiastical tribunals in this country.'[21]

The Influence of Roman and Canon Laws on the Common Law

I have now reached the question of the extent to which the Roman and Canon Laws exerted any significant influence upon the course of the English Common Law. It was a contentious question one hundred years ago, and it remains so today. Every serious student admits that there was *some* influence. Maitland wrote, for example, 'The history of law in England, and even the history of English law, could not but be influenced by them.'[22] He ascribed the very name of the English Common Law to the inspiration of the canonists.[23] But that tepid acknowledgement cannot be the end of the matter. The question is

---

[17] Pollock and Maitland, ii 114–15.
[18] Pollock and Maitland, ii 363. See also i 480, speaking of the inconveniences caused by the ability 'to postpone to an indefinite date' the sentence, this by means of the system of canonical appeals.
[19] Pollock and Maitland, i 443. See also i 447, speaking of the 'invidious and mischievous immunity' of the clerical order.
[20] Pollock and Maitland, ii 545.
[21] *Roman Canon Law in the Church of England* (London, 1898), p. 1.
[22] Pollock and Maitland, i 117.,
[23] Pollock and Maitland, i 176–7.

when and in what areas influence occurred, and how pervasive it proved to be.[24] Particularly troublesome is the need to arrive at a satisfactory evaluation of the use of civilian terminology by English lawyers. This sort of usage is not infrequent in the historical record. But did making use of the words and phrases of the learned laws mean that there was real influence, or simply that the common lawyers were placing a pretty civilian window dressing on law that was *au fond* purely English?

One finds this question oft raised in the literature, and a confident answer one way or the other sometimes given. Going further with what is a difficult problem remains one of the tasks for legal historians of our generation and the future. I myself think it would be well if we were to admit frankly the difficulty of the inquiry, perhaps even of giving up the search for a general conclusion for the moment. Here I speak as one more likely to exaggerate than to ignore the influence of the learned laws. This admission will not resolve the ultimate question; indeed it could retard attempts to answer it. However, it may help us get further into the heads of the lawyers whose habits we are describing and it will help us to understand the various possibilities inherent in the process of transmission of legal ideas from one legal culture to another if we do not reach for an all-or-nothing conclusion. We may better understand the lawyers, better understand the meaning of borrowing vocabulary without necessarily taking over underlying principles of substantive law, if we do not jump quickly for a satisfying conclusion one way or the other.

When one turns back to 'Pollock and Maitland' itself, there are more than a few examples where borrowing from the learned laws is said to have occurred. These instances are noted, perhaps not infrequently, but certainly with regularity. The idea that law could be a true science Maitland attributed to the attractive force of Roman and Canon Laws.[25] The importance of the *exceptio spolii* in the formulation of the assize of novel disseisin is acknowledged, if it is not given great prominence.[26] The influence of Roman legal theory on the English

---

[24] See Andrew Lewis, 'What Marcellus says is against you: Roman Law and Common Law', in A. D. E. Lewis and D. J. Ibbetson, eds, *The Roman Legal Tradition* (Cambridge, 1994), pp. 199–208.

[25] Pollock and Maitland, i 131–5.

[26] Pollock and Maitland, i 146, ii 48. This connection now seems established; see Mary Cheney, 'Possessio/proprietas in ecclesiastical courts in mid-twelfth-century England', in Garnett and Hudson, *Law and Government*, pp. 245–54; Paul Brand, ' "Multis vigiliis excogitatam et inventam"; Henry II and the creation of the English Common Law', *Haskins Society Journal*, 2 (1990), 196–222; Donald W. Sutherland, *The Assize of Novel Disseisin* (Oxford, 1973), pp. 20–1.

law's grant of rights to the holder of land for a term of years is stated.[27] And the notion that theories drawn from the learned laws or from the Franciscan experience with the Canon Law were influential in the development of the English feoffment to uses is described as 'very possible'.[28] These are but examples, and when one totes them up, it might well be concluded that 'Pollock and Maitland' takes the position that the Roman and Canon Laws had more than a marginal force in the history of English law. All in all, it starts out by looking as though the Roman and Canon Laws must have played a creative part in the law of England.

The Unimportance of the Learned Laws

A more leisurely consideration of the contents of 'Pollock and Maitland', however, shows that this view requires considerable modification. The role of the Roman and Canon Laws in shaping English law turns out to have been less than the accumulation of the evidence so far presented suggests, and what substantial influence there was turns out also to have been as much by repulsion as by attraction.[29] In other words, as often as not, the Roman and Canon Laws stimulated the English lawyers to develop their own law, but it happened as if from fear or revulsion against the *ius commune*. They wished to ensure that there would be an alternative. It is a little like Maitland's own view of the law administered in the ecclesiastical courts described above. He admitted the possibility of following it, but in the end he found the effect of doing so to have been either repellent or unfortunate. More often than not, he lamented the consequences of following the *ius commune*, where it had been followed. He stressed the necessity felt by the English lawyers for quick reaction to ward off its possible influence, where room for manoeuvre had remained.

[27] Pollock and Maitland, ii 114. See also i 353: borrowing of the action *cessavit per biennium*. He adds, however, 'It is one of the very few English actions that we can trace directly to a foreign model.'

[28] Pollock and Maitland, ii 238. See also ii 171, dealing with the law of bailments.

[29] E.g. Pollock and Maitland, ii 355, where the establishment of freedom of testation is ascribed in part to the attitude that if the opposite rule were upheld in the ecclesiastical courts, this 'was sufficient to convince royal justices and lay lords that something wrong was being done'.

The Limited Interest in Roman and Canon Laws

The attitude that Maitland brought to the task of coming to grips with medieval *ius commune* is stated with disarming frankness in the Preface to his *Roman Canon Law in the Church of England*. Speaking about the *History of English Law*, he wrote, 'On pain of leaving the book shamefully incomplete, I was compelled to make an incursion into a region that was unfamiliar to me, namely, that of ecclesiastical jurisprudence.'[30] In my opinion, this statement is becomingly modest and not entirely inaccurate. Maitland was certainly capable of looking at and making use of the texts, the glosses, and the distinctions characteristic of the *ius commune*. He made the incursion. 'Pollock and Maitland' shows this, for example, in its extensive and sophisticated coverage of the Becket controversy, and of course it is what underlay the controversy between Maitland and Bishop Stubbs over the place of the Canon Law in the medieval English Church. At the same time, when Maitland undertook these incursions, he did so not by inclination. He entered most of them either by force of necessity, or else by way of applying the methods of comparative law, which need ascribe no particular importance to the system to which one's own is being compared, other than revealing more about the 'home legal system' than would otherwise be possible.

Maitland himself cannot have been particularly *interested* by the intricacies of the medieval *ius commune*. He took it up, as he said himself, by compulsion, often looking no further than the decretal or *lex* that stated the basic rule. But it was not his favorite reading. He preferred *Bracton* or the Yearbooks. And where overlap in coverage gave him a choice — as in dealing with the legal capacity of monks, the effects of excommunication, or the character of an ecclesiastical pension — he very often eschewed any exploration of the Canon Law in favour of the English Common Law on the subject.[31]

Moreover, when he was obliged to deal with areas outside the purview of the Common Law, Maitland customarily referred to a secondary source wherever there was an adequate treatment in existence. He used these almost (but not quite) to the exclusion of working through the learned laws themselves. Thus the general treatment of Roman and Canon Law in Volume I is drawn almost entirely from J. F. von Schulte's *Die Geschichte der Quellen und Literatur des canonischen Rechts* and some of the English chronicles.[32] The treatment of 'Cor-

---

[30] *Roman Canon Law in the Church of England*, p. v.
[31] Pollock and Maitland, i 437, 480–1; ii 134–5.
[32] See Pollock and Maitland, i 112 n.3 and pages immediately following.

porations and Churches' relies heavily — perhaps a little too heavily —
on Otto von Gierke's *Das deutsche Genossenschaftsrecht*.[33] Except for
special situations, 'Pollock and Maitland' rarely takes its readers into
the pages of Hostiensis, William Durantis, or even the *glossa ordinaria*.[34]

For the most part, reliance on secondary sources caused no harm.
Von Schulte's work is reliable. And who could write anything if he did
not make use of the work of others? But there are places in 'Pollock
and Maitland' where a more first-hand exploration of the *ius commune*
would have been useful. Maitland's treatment of the law of last wills
and testaments relied very heavily on what he termed 'an intense and
holy horror of intestacy'.[35] The evidence adduced to show that horror
comes from a few monastic chronicles, rather than from the Canon or
Roman Law on the point, and this limitation gives a one-sidedness to
the book's presentation of the jurisdictional boundaries reached in
England. A more balanced view of the subject of intestacy, one that
comes easily from examining the learned laws themselves, would, I
think, have improved the pages in 'Pollock and Maitland' on the subject. The same can be said of the treatment of ecclesiastical offenses.
Little is said in it about any offense save heresy. No reference at all is
made to the abundant literature of the *ius commune* that deals with
crime and criminal procedure.[36]

The Absence of Significant Influence

I noted a minute ago that 'Pollock and Maitland' makes room for the
possibility of influence running from the learned laws to the English
Common Law. This was but half of an adequate description, and
perhaps it was the lesser half. When one examines the characterization
of that influence most often found in 'Pollock and Maitland', one
quickly sees that it did not amount to much at bottom. Thus the
influence of the *ius commune* on the English law of contract is
described as 'but superficial and transient'.[37] Importation of law from

[33] Pollock and Maitland, i 486 n. 1 and pages immediately following. I say too heavily because
some of the legal principles of the learned laws were actually less mysterious than an English
speaking reader gathers from reading Gierke's text. See also i 124, on the law of jurisdiction,
citing Paul Hinschius, *Die Kirchenrecht der Katholiken und Protestanten in Deutschland*
(1896–97); ii 67, 137, on the canon law of possession, citing Carl Bruns, *Das Recht des Bisitzes
im Mittelalter und in der Gegenwart* (1848); the work was reprinted in 1965.
[34] Special situations: Pollock and Maitland, ii 195 n. 2 (Hostiensis on contract); ii 336 n. 2
(Durantis on executors).
[35] Pollock and Maitland, ii 356, 326.
[36] Pollock and Maitland, ii 543–57.
[37] Pollock and Maitland, ii 193.

without is described as 'rare'.[38] Already in the time of *Bracton*, any Romanist influence there may once have been in England was already 'on the wane',[39] and where (as in the case of the possessory assizes) there is acknowledged influence, English law has acted on the remedy 'very speedily [to make] it her own'.[40] Between the English and the Continental laws, there had come to be what Maitland called 'an unfathomable gulf' by the time that Bracton's treatise had assumed its final form.[41]

Above all, except as a stimulus to formulation of the Common Law, there was an abiding lack of interest in Roman and Canon Laws among English lawyers. Their habitual lack of training in University law faculties is crucial. Their education in the Inns of Courts marks them off irretrievably from their Continental brethren. Even when the English common lawyer quoted a canonical maxim, in Maitland's view, more likely than not the English lawyer was 'profoundly ignorant' of its source.[42] What is added to this statement by the word 'profoundly', I cannot say. But I am sure that the lawyer who emerges from the pages of 'Pollock and Maitland' is a man not much interested in legal theory, and particularly uninterested in any theory drawn from the learned laws. By the reign of Edward I, it could be said that the common lawyers — at least most of them — 'know nothing of any system but their own'.[43]

The Language of Contest

A striking impression in re-reading the pages of 'Pollock and Maitland', at least for me, has been the prevalence of images of conflict in the descriptions of the relationship between the learned laws and the English Common Law. The smell of something very like a battle rises from the pages. Or perhaps it is a quasi-Darwinian struggle for survival. It is at any rate a contest for mastery within the law of England, and it was being fought between the English law and the massed forces of the *ius commune*. The conflict was all the sharper for the attractiveness

---

[38] Pollock and Maitland, i 134.

[39] Pollock and Maitland, i 218.

[40] Pollock and Maitland, ii 48. See also ii 571: 'After a brief attempt to be Roman our law falls back into old Germanic habits'.

[41] Pollock and Maitland, ii 561, speaking of procedure and the forms of action. See also ii 6 n. 1: Roman terminology related to land 'quite alien to the spirit of English law'; ii 197: 'But, before the thirteenth century was out, both Roman and canon law had lost their power to control the development of English temporal law'.

[42] Pollock and Maitland, i 218. See also ii 297.

[43] Pollock and Maitland, i 225.

of the Roman Law half of the *ius commune*. Like the Lorelei, Romanism had the power to enchant. But its siren song led in the end to the rocks.[44]

The example of Germany stood behind this view of the relationship between the law of England and that of Rome. The possibility of a wholesale 'Reception' of Roman Law, displacing native law with something more sophisticated and worse, was a very real one for Maitland. It had happened elsewhere. He had it very much in his mind in the Rede Lectures of 1901,[45] and it served as something like a leitmotiv in the *History of English Law* itself. The same thing could have happened in England. In the twelfth and thirteenth centuries, the *ius commune* was at the gate. There was a real possibility that it would be allowed to win its way inside.

The picture is that of a continuing struggle. The relationship between the courts where the *ius commune* held sway, the courts of the Church, is customarily put in terms of a contest between two rival powers.[46] After the dispute between Becket and Henry II over the treatment of criminous clerks, the king is said to be still 'in possession of the greater part of the field of battle'.[47] Where there is agreement, it is the result of 'a concordat' between rival combatants.[48] Where there is no agreement, there always remains a 'border-land that might be more or less plausibly fought for'.[49] The Romano-canonical procedure is the 'one great rival' to that of trial by jury,[50] and engagement with it had led to 'a perilous moment' for English forces.[51]

At the end of the day, the 'peril' was averted and the enemy kept outside the gates. Although, as Maitland put it, 'the escape was narrow',

[44] Maitland was not alone in this view; see James Q. Whitman, 'The disease of Roman Law: a century later', in *Syracuse Journal of International Law and Commerce*, 20 (1994), 227–34. See also the description in Kenneth Pennington, 'Learned Law, Droit Savant, Gelehrtes Recht: the tyranny of a concept', *Rivista internazionale di diritto commune*, 5 (1995), 199–200.

[45] 'English Law and the Renaissance', reprinted in *Select Essays in Anglo-American Legal History* (Boston, 1907), i 168–207, and also, without most of the footnotes, in Helen M. Cam, ed., *Selected Historical Essays of F. W. Maitland* (Cambridge, 1957), 135–51.

[46] E.g. Pollock and Maitland, i 132: 'opposition' between the two systems; i 241: 'severe struggle' over land held by spiritual tenure; ii 198: 'Struggle between ecclesiastical and temporal justice' in law of contracts; ii 333: 'Victory of the Church courts' in questions of testamentary succession; ii 429: 'struggle' between temporal and spiritual courts over married women's power of testation.

[47] Pollock and Maitland, i 125. See also ii 200, speaking of ecclesiastical 'retaliation' for use of writs of prohibition.

[48] Pollock and Maitland, ii 333. See also ii 201: 'Both parties were in their turn aggressors.'

[49] . Pollock and Maitland, ii 198. See also i 127: 'border warfare' over tithes; i 479: 'always a brisk border warfare simmering'.

[50] Pollock and Maitland, ii 656. See also ii 639, where it is said that the *ius commune* 'for the moment . . . gains a foothold'.

[51] Pollock and Maitland, ii 673.

escape there was.[52] And it had happened by the reign of Edward I. This was one reason Maitland felt secure in covering only the history of English law up to that date. He regarded the period between *Glanvill* and *Bracton* as the critical moment in English legal history. It was during this time that the common lawyers developed the law of their country sufficiently so that it could withstand, both then and afterwards, any threat of a reception of the *ius commune*. The presence of the Canon and Roman Laws, menacing and seductive in turn, and the struggle for mastery over English legal institutions, had led the English lawyers to formulate their own law. They did so well enough that their law would withstand all assaults from without. 'It is,' Maitland wrote, 'in opposition to "the canons and Roman laws" that English law "becomes conscious of its own existence".'[53]

Repulsion is (or at least may be) as fruitful as adulation, and the contest between systems, the younger taking only enough from the elder to make its own position impregnable, decided the fate of English law. This is the reason that, when the question is fully considered, there is no real contradiction between the importance and the unimportance of the *ius commune* in 'Pollock and Maitland'. The learned laws played a significant role, but there was more stimulation than imitation in it. With English law, there was not to be 'dictation from without.'[54]

Maitland and the *ius commune*

This has been a summary of the role of the *ius commune* found in 'Pollock and Maitland'. I turn now to the subject of how it all looks in hindsight, and in particular to the question of how Maitland's understanding of the *ius commune* stands up in light of what has been learned in the one hundred years since he wrote. In most of its particulars, my conclusion is that it stands up very well. As a guide to the nature of the *ius commune* itself, however, I think it has proved less trustworthy.

Advances and Alterations in Scholarship

It would be surprising, indeed it would be astounding, if there had been no advances in our knowledge about the subjects covered in 'Pollock and Maitland' and if these advances had not overthrown some of the conclusions in it. After reviewing them, however, one must be

---

[52] Pollock and Maitland, ii 658.
[53] Pollock and Maitland, i 131.
[54] Pollock and Maitland, i 135.

struck by how few there turn out to have been. One is surprised, moreover, by how often it has happened that what can have been no more than guesses on Maitland's part have turned out to be right, now that we know more.

For example, thanks to the labours of Professor Stein, Sir Richard Southern and others, we are now better informed about Vacarius and the *Liber pauperum* than Maitland was.[55] It seems that Vacarius did not actually teach in Oxford, for no law school existed there at the time, and that he was as concerned with the jurisdiction exercised in the ecclesiastical courts as with the academic side of Roman Law. When one looks at the treatment in 'Pollock and Maitland', however, it is notable how cautious Maitland was on these points.[56] There is very little to fault in his words. We now also know, thanks to the efforts of Dr Duggan, Professor Kuttner and others, that the high percentage of English decretals found in the *Decretales Gregorii IX* had nothing to do with papal policy or the need to bring England into obedience to the papacy, but rather with the prominence of English canonists among those who did the work of collecting papal decretals.[57] Again, however, Maitland expressed his conclusions on this score with caution, and in neither case was he relying on his own research.

In at least one instance where Maitland had himself looked into the details of the *ius commune*, that of Henry II's position under the Canon Law in his dispute with Thomas Becket over the trial of criminous clerks, the conclusions to which Maitland was drawn looked a few years ago to have been entirely overthrown.[58] Today, however, in light of further research, it appears that Maitland was pretty much correct after all.[59] Henry II seems to have

[55] See R. W. Southern, 'Master Vacarius and the beginning of an English academic tradition', in J. Alexander and M. Gibson, eds, *Medieval Learning and Literature: Essays for R. W. Hunt*, (Oxford, 1976), pp. 257–86; Francis de Zulueta and Peter Stein, *The Teaching of Roman Law in England around 1200* (Selden Soc. Supplementary Series, 8, 1990).

[56] Pollock and Maitland, i 118–19.

[57] Pollock and Maitland, i 115. Compare Charles Duggan, *Twelfth-century Decretal Collections and their Importance in English History* (London, 1963); and see also Stephan Kuttner and Eleanor Rathbone, 'Anglo-Norman Canonists of the twelfth century', *Traditio*, 7 (1951), 279–358; Peter Landau, 'Die Entstehung der systematischen Dekretalensammllungen und die europäische Kanonstik des 12. Jahrhunderts', *Zeitschrift der Savigny-Stiftung für Rechtsgeschichte*, kan. Abt. 65 (1979), 127–32; Mary G. Cheney, *Roger, Bishop of Worcester 1164–1179: an English Bishop in the Age of Becket* (Oxford, 1980), pp. 197–208.

[58] Charles Duggan, 'The Becket dispute and the criminous clerks', *BIHR*, 35 (1962), 1–28, reprinted in *Canon Law in Medieval England* (London, 1982), No. X.

[59] Richard Fraher, 'The Becket dispute and two decretist traditions', *JMH*, 4 (1978), 347–68; Dr Duggan's rejoinder (*Canon Law*, cited in previous note, Addenda, p. 6), to the effect that 'Fraher attaches insufficient importance to the Church's discretionary rights in applying or denying permissible procedures', unfortunately does nothing to restore his side of the argument.

had the better of the canonical argument, just as Maitland had originally concluded.[60]

Probably the greatest advances that have taken place since 1895 in
the study of the place of the learned laws in England have come
from the exploration of the records of the ecclesiastical courts. Maitland knew of the existence of these records. He urged that they be
explored.[61] He made surmises about what they might contain. He
expressed conclusions with the express proviso that they might be
proved wrong by such future exploration. As it turned out, most of his
surmises have not in fact been proved wrong by examination of the
records. They have been proved right. He supposed, for example, that
uses might first have been enforced in the ecclesiastical courts. The
records show that they were so enforced,[62] at least in some dioceses,
though for reasons that seem quite incoherent to me the most recent
book that deals with the subject has seen fit to treat that enforcement
as inconsequential.[63] Similarly, Maitland guessed that 'probably the
ecclesiastical courts did something' to provide guardianship protection
for children,[64] and indeed that guess proves to have been the fact.[65]
His surmise about the absence of causes involving *miserables personae*
from the English ecclesiastical court records has also proved correct.[66]
It is true that Maitland underestimated the staying power of ecclesiasti-

[60] The argument is found in 'Henry II and the criminous clerks', in his *Roman Canon Law in the Church of England*, pp. 132–47.
[61] E.g. Pollock and Maitland, ii 352, relating to the children's right to legitim.
[62] See my 'The early enforcement of uses', in *Canon Law and the Law of England* (London, 1987), 341–53.
[63] Robert C. Palmer, *English Law in the Age of the Black Death: a Transformation of Governance and Law* (Chapel Hill, N. C., 1993), pp. 111–16. The enforcment of uses is found only in the ecclesiastical records for the dioceses of Canterbury and Rochester. The question of what this means is raised because no regular runs of act books survive from other dioceses during the fourteenth century. Palmer maintains that 'uses were not usually frequent in Kent', and that it follows that the article's conclusion that ecclesiastical courts enforced feoffments to uses before the Chancery began to do so must be rejected. It is difficult to follow the argument. As a matter of logic, the exact opposite conclusion seems to follow from his premise. If uses were infrequent in one area and if records mentioning them survived in that area but not elsewhere, this would suggest that there were probably more cases of enforcement where uses were more frequent, but that we cannot discover them because of the failure of records to survive from those areas. I would not myself put great faith in deductive reasoning in an area like this, but the logic of the argument that the appearance of uses in ecclesiastical records from dioceses in counties where uses were not frequent means that we can disregard the evidence of their enforcement in the ecclesiastical forum altogether eludes me.
[64] Pollock and Maitland, ii 444.
[65] I have tried to present this evidence in 'The Roman Law of guardianship in England, 1300–1600', in my *Canon Law and the Law of England*, pp. 211–45.
[66] Pollock and Maitland, i 131.

cal jurisdiction in dealing with sworn contracts and testamentary debts.[67] In fact, the records show that these sources of ecclesiastical jurisdiction flourished well into the fifteenth century.[68] Overall, however, it is remarkable how few such factual corrections there are to be made in the account found in 'Pollock and Maitland'. Most of his surmises have been confirmed by the records.

It should also be said that there has since been scholarly opinion opposed to some of Maitland's conclusions, particularly about the law of the Church. Maitland saved some of his harshest judgments for the laws of marriage, testamentary succession, and criminal procedure administered by the Church. In each case, the medieval Church has found its modern defenders. Some of this seems a little extreme, even to one of those defenders. It is being asserted today, for instance, that in developing legal protection of the rights of criminal defendants, the courts of the Roman Inquisition were in the van.[69] Most of the disagreements, however, seem to me to come down to questions of personal opinion rather than provable facts, or even reasonably clear inference. My own views do differ from those of Maitland in some particulars, but I could not with any confidence charge him with error on that account. Why should anyone prefer my prejudices to his? Besides, his opinions have stimulated work on many occasions, and not for me alone. They make for good reading, and they are a spur to research. I shall omit discussion of my own opinions.

The Question of Influence from the ius commune

It is difficult to say a great deal about developments related to the question of the extent to which Roman and Canon Laws influenced the English Common Law. In some ways the question stands today only slightly removed from where it stood one hundred years ago. On the one side, some scholars treat the notion that English law developed largely in isolation from Continental law as 'a myth'.[70] Others see structural differences so fundamental that it remains right to speak of a fundamental and continuing division of European law into two camps,

[67] Pollock and Maitland, ii 343, 346.
[68] Brian Woodcock, *Medieval Ecclesiastical Courts in the Diocese of Canterbury* (Oxford, 1952), p. 84.
[69] See e.g. John Tedeschi, 'Introduction', *The Prosecution of Heresy: Collected Studies of the Inquisition in Early Modern Italy* (Binghamton, N. Y., 1991).
[70] E.g. Reinhard Zimmermann, 'Civil Code or Civil Law? — Towards a new European private law', in *Syracuse Journal of International Law and Commerce*, 20 (1994), 220.

and that the English camp was isolated from the Continental.[71] Now, as at the time Maitland wrote, all serious scholars admit that influence occurred, but they are not agreed about how extensive it was, at what periods it was at its strongest, and at what levels it operated. About recent developments, two observations having to do with changes in the scholarly position over the past hundred years seem worth making. They work in opposite directions.

First, as pointed out by a perceptive young Spaniard, the view that there were continuing connections between English and European laws is more likely to be held by Continental scholars and by North Americans than by English historians.[72] There are exceptions to this statement, as he himself admits, but it seems to be as sound as most such generalizations. The result is that today there is more scholarship devoted to showing the connections, simply because more European scholars are interesting themselves in the law of England. To this extent there has been movement towards ascribing a greater fundamental importance to the *ius commune* than was true for Pollock and Maitland.

However, there is also a 'counter-trend'. Seeing legal development as a product of small, and often unintended, changes resulting from choices made by lawyers in the immediate interests of their clients, a view most persuasively expressed by Professor Milsom, has pushed historiography on this subject in the opposite direction. If legal change is driven chiefly by practitioners, not by treatise writers or large thinkers, and if Bracton's treatise is the learned exception rather than the faithful depiction of English medieval law, then it must seem less likely that the Roman and Canon Laws have influenced the course of the Common Law. It is hard to envision the humble drafter of pleadings with Accursius at his elbow. To this extent, there is less room in the historiography of English law today for the *ius commune* than there was at the time of 'Pollock and Maitland' itself.

Maitland's View of the ius commune

If these questions have not reached a satisfactory conclusion and can only be mentioned on that account, there is nonetheless good reason to dwell upon developments relating to Maitland's more general depiction

---

[71] See e.g. R. C. van Caenegem, *The Birth of the English Common Law* (Cambridge, 1973), p. 105, arguing that: 'England became an island in the Romanist sea', and that its law was 'a freak in the history of western civilization'.

[72] Javier Martínez-Torrón, *Derecho Angloamericano y derecho canónico. Las raíces canónicas de la 'common law'* (Madrid, 1991), p. 37. See e.g. Michele Graziadei, 'Il patto e il dolo', in *Scritti in onore de Rodolfo Sacco*, Paolo Cendon ed. vol. 1 (Milan, 1994), pp. 589–612.

of the nature of the Canon Law. It is here that his work on the learned laws is commonly cited today. The fullest expression of his views on this subject is found in *Roman Canon Law in the Church of England*, rather than in *The History of English Law* itself, but the subject is taken up in both. It calls for remark and somewhat more detailed exploration.

It has just been noted that Maitland's personal excursions into the learned laws were occasional and not prolonged. He was capable of working through the *ius commune*, but he himself claimed no more than to having put his toe into the vast ocean of Continental legal learning. This is true, but coming from a self-professed wader, some of his comments seem remarkably shrewd a hundred years on. For instance, the seemingly off-hand remark that 'to the canonist there was nothing so sacred that it might not be expressed in definite rules', pithily describes one of the Canon Law's most salient features.[73] The canonists did enter into the most detailed, and private areas of human life, attempting to guide the users of the law if they could not coerce them. Similar is Maitland's remark about the canonical impediments to marriage — that they were the work of men who were 'reckless of mundane consequences'.[74] This captures an important truth about the canonists. They began not with practical consequence, but with divine law and established texts. They did not adopt a utilitarian, still less a 'person-centred' view of the law. It was men's responsibility to adjust their behaviour to fit legal norms, not the legislator's responsibility to adjust the law to promote human happiness.[75]

Having said this, however, one must also say that his overall view of the subject suffers from his not having gone deeper and that this omission affected his side in the famous, and sometimes exaggerated, dispute with Bishop Stubbs about the nature of legal relations between England and the Papacy during the period. The question was whether the English Church enforced papal decretals as 'binding statute law' during the middle ages. Stubbs had written that although the decretals were regarded 'as of great authority in England', they were 'not held to be binding on the courts'.[76]

In Maitland's opinion this was flat wrong. The papal law books were treated as 'binding statute law' by the spiritual courts in medieval England. He made appropriate reservations for simple ignorance at the lowest levels of ecclesiastical administration, but otherwise he held

---

[73] Pollock and Maitland, ii 436.
[74] Pollock and Maitland, ii 385.
[75] Georg May and Anna Egler, *Einführung in die kirchenrechtliche Methode* (Regensburg, 1986), pp. 14–15.
[76] *Report of the Ecclesiastical Courts Commission* (London, 1883), p. xviii.

that the only situations in which the spiritual tribunals in England ignored the papal law-books were cases where the 'strong hand of the king' prevented them from doing so. The law of advowsons, the canonical *ius patronatus*, and the rules about bastardy after the Council of Merton were typical examples where this had happened, but apart from these instances, the ecclesiastical courts followed the law of the papal decretals as a modern court follows a statute enacted by king and Parliament.

In my view, Maitland's treatment gives a misleading impression of the nature of the *ius commune*. The papal decretals were not then treated as 'binding statutes' — not by the popes who promulgated them, not by the medieval canonists, and even less so in the working world of the spiritual courts.[77] *The stylus curiae* had a place in canonical practice that must be reckoned with in any full description of the law. And familiarity with the work of the canonists dispels the clarity of Maitland's depiction of an ordered statutory regime.

To take only the clearest example from England, a papal decretal required the presence of two witnesses and the parish priest to sustain the validity of a last will and testament.[78] English practice, however, routinely sanctioned wills proved by two witnesses, and often even less.[79] Similarly, papal decretals relating to minor excommunication,[80] the specific enforcement of espousals by *verba de futuro*,[81] and the availability of a canonical *restitutio in integrum*,[82] seem not to have

[77] See Charles Donahue, Jr., 'Roman Canon Law in the medieval English Church: Stubbs vs. Maitland re-examined after 75 years in the light of some records from the Church courts', *Michigan L. Rev.*, 72 (1972), 647–716.

[78] X 3.26.10, 11.

[79] Probate 'in common form' required no witnesses at all, and if this be regarded as resting simply on the absence of contest, the movement was clearly away from requiring the presence of a priest. See also in my 'The origin of holographic wills in English law', *Journal of Legal History*, 15 (1994), 97–108.

[80] Only major excommunication and suspension *ab ingressu ecclesie*, a form of personal interdict, seem to have been applied in medieval practice. It is not yet clear whether this was an English peculiarity; see also the comment to this effect by Panormitanus, *Commentaria in Decretalium libros* (Venice, 1617), ad X 5.39. pr. no. 3.

[81] X 4.1.10; contrast X 4.1.17. Practice in the ecclesiastical courts seems also to have varied. See Rudolf Weigand, 'Die Rechtsprechung des Regensburger Gerichts in Ehesachen', in *Leibe und Ehe im Mittelalter* (Goldbach, 1993), p. 286; such sentences cannot be found in the English records.

[82] X 1.41.1, allowing a church to invoke the privilege of restitution. The remedy was apparently restricted to English practice to permitting the introduction of evidence or legal argument after the proper term of introduction has passed. E.g. Snow c. Wood (Lichfield, 1465), Jt. Rec. Office, Lichfield, Act book B/C/1/1, f.9, in which the judge 'restituit dictum Thomam ad terminum tercii productionis'. See also a fifteenth-century English formulary, British Library MS. Harl. 3378, fols. 92v–94, the only relevant form included being a 'Petitio in integrum restitutionis per quam pars possit producere testes postquam conclusum fuerit in causa'.

been put into use in medieval England. In these matters, there was no impediment placed in the way of the ecclesiastical courts by the 'strong hand' of the king. No writ of prohibition lay. But the records of the ecclesiastical courts show that these decretals were not applied in practice.

It is unfortunate in this regard that Maitland devoted such a large portion of his investigation to William Lyndwood's *Provinciale*.[83] It must have seemed a reasonable enough choice — Lyndwood's subject was the law of the English provincial constitutions. However, in fact, it turns out that it was not the best choice. As a remarkable article by Brian Ferme has recently shown in dealing with the law of testaments and probate administration, Lyndwood's *thèse de prédilection* was the harmonization of English practice with the *ius commune*.[84] To have laid any weight upon the places where there was divergence between papal law and local custom would have subverted this theme, and Lyndwood did not do it.

I do not mean to suggest that there was anything anti-papal in the habits of the medieval English Church. There was not. Canonists were able to assert in one breath that the pope's legal opinion was superior to that of all bishops together, then in the next, that papal decretals might give way to contrary, legitimate usages.[85] Nor was there anything unique about the English position. Churches in other parts of Europe stood in a similar position. A recent study of the church of Toulouse, for instance, speaks similarly of 'une certaine originalité' in its legal practice when compared with the texts of the Canon Law.[86] The reality is that the medieval *ius commune* admitted a greater latitude of interpretation by the jurists and a greater role for customary practice by the courts than is compatible with the regime of papal legislative sovereignty that Maitland carried into his famous dispute with Stubbs.

Further examples from the Canon Law itself are not hard to find. A papal decretal specifically reserved to the Roman church all interpretations of papal privileges. However, by the time the canonists were finished glossing this decretal, the rule it stated had been so limited as

---

[83] See *Letters*, i nos. 168, 179.
[84] 'The testamentary executor in Lyndwood's *Provinciale*', *The Jurist*, 49 (1989), 677.
[85] See *gl. ord.* ad *Decretum Gratiani*, Dist. 4, c. 3 and d.p. id.
[86] E.g. Jean-Louis Gazzaniga, 'Droit et pratique: notes sur les décisions de la Chapelle toulousaine', in *L'Église et le droit dans le Midi (XIIIe–XIVe siècle)* (Cahiers de Fanjeaux 29) (Fanjeaux 1994), p. 332; and p. 325, where the author discusses and gives further examples of 'le particularisme toulousain'. See also Anne Lefebvre-Teillard, *Les officialités à la veille du Concile de Trente* (Paris, 1973), pp. 87–9.

to make its application in practice an extraordinary situation.[87] To have read the decretal as a 'binding statute' would have hindered the doing of justice in hundreds of quite ordinary disputes, and the canonists recognized the possibility. They also met it, exercising a freedom in treating the decretal which allowed them to avoid this unfortunate, though apparently statutorily required, result. It is thus not startling to find the frank comment of a canonist beside a papal decretal: 'Sed hoc non servatur'.[88]

This feature is observable with particular clarity in the Canon Law relating to custom. The validity of a custom contrary to the *ius commune* of the Church was measured not by whether it contradicted a statute or a papal decretal.[89] It was measured instead by two tests: first, by whether or not it conformed to reason and natural law; and second, by whether it met the tests of valid prescription, principally long usage and acceptance by the people affected by it. Thus the Canon Law left room for a *consuetudo praeter ius* and even for a *consuetudo contra ius*. Panormitanus commented, for example, 'Note that the constitution of a Pope does not extend to those who have a contrary custom.'[90] He meant, of course, a valid custom, and one not specifically condemned by the papal constitution. The Canon Law was concerned principally with ensuring that customs did not sanction wrongful conduct, interfere with the Church's system of government, or induce *periculum animae* among those subject to the law. In other words, the test of validity was not whether or not the custom was consistent with an existing statute or papal decretal, but whether it conformed to tests of reason and legitimacy that had little to do with the tenets of legislative sovereignty.[91]

There were seeds of a more rigorous and hierarchical attitude towards custom contained in some of the texts of the classical Canon

---

[87] This was true from an early date: see e.g. Hostiensis, *Lectura in libros Decretalium* ad X 2.1.12, nos. 4–7. See also Kenneth Pennington, *Pope and Bishops: the Papal Monarchy in the Twelfth and Thirteenth Centuries* (Philadelphia, Pa., 1984), pp. 154–89.

[88] *Gl. ord.* ad X 2.7.1., s.v. *inconsulto*. The decretal required a bishop to have recourse to the supreme pontiff before swearing the oath *de calumnia*.

[89] See DD ad X 1.4.11; see Alain Sériaux, 'Réflexions sur le pouvoir normatif de la coutume en droit canonique', *Droits: Revue française de théorie juridique*, 3 (1986), 63–7; Udo Wolter, 'Die "consuetudo" im kanonischen Recht bis zum Ende des 13. Jahrhunderts', in Gerhard Dilcher et al., eds, *Gewohnheitsrecht und Rechtsgewohnheiten im Mittelalter* (Berlin, 1992), pp. 104–14.

[90] *Commentaria ad libros Decretalium* (Venice, 1617), ad X 3.42.1, no. 7: 'Et sic bene et singulariter nota quod constitutio papae non extenditur ad alios habentes consuetudinem contrariam'. The text involved had to do with baptismal customs.

[91] See Peter Leisching, 'Prolegomena zum Begriff der ratio in der Kanonistik', *Zeitschrift der Savigny-Stiftung für Rechtsgeschichte (kan. Abt.)*, 72 (1986), 329–37.

Law.[92] In the sixteenth century, attempts were made to bring the wide scope that had long been afforded to customary practices within such a regime of legislative supremacy, by asserting that the custom obtained its *vis legis* by virtue of the consent, or at least the acquiescence, of the legislator. In these terms the formal *causa* of the custom's force could be said to be the will of the papal legislator. But the fit was never perfect, opinion was never unanimous, and it reads the medieval evidence anachronistically to suppose that this way of looking at things had been the point of departure for the medieval law.[93]

The situation in later canonistic thought was in fact something like the mirror image of the argument that the Canon Law was received in England only because it had the sanction of the king. The argument may be said to contain a good deal of truth in the climate of the late sixteenth century, but it is not an accurate portrayal of the medieval law. The disagreement between Stubbs and Maitland, as it seems to me, was carried on without recognizing this characteristic of the medieval Canon Law. It was conducted with the anachronistic assumption that the medieval *ius commune* fit the juristic tenets of legal positivism, or at any rate those of the Council of Trent. On this account it continues to mislead, and Maitland's clear victory in the dispute with Stubbs has hindered us from seeing the *ius commune* as it actually was.

To repeat, it is widely assumed today that Maitland had much the better of the argument, and that his refutation of the claims of the Church of England showed him at his best as an historian.[94] The first half of this statement is correct, although it is wrong to dismiss Stubbs' views as harshly as is sometimes done.[95] However, the second half is not. The relations between the papal lawgiver and his subjects, clerical or lay, did not fit the system of legislative sovereignty that

[92] E.g. *gl. ord.* ad Dist. 4 c. 3: 'Dicas quod sententia Papae praevalet ut [C. 35 q. 9 c. 5], nam etiam error principis legem facit.' And see *gl. ord.* ad. d. p. c. 3 s.v. *abrogatae:* 'Sed credo quod consuetudo rationabilis et praescripta tollat leges, ut [X 1.4.11] etiam sine scientia principis; difficile enim esset eum omnes consuetudines quae servantur scire.' See also *gl. ord.* ad Dist. 12 d. a. c. 1 s. v. *et minores.*

[93] Perhaps the best example would be in the law of tithes, where in order to fit ecclesiastical court practice to the strict model of the Canon Law, it would have to be said that the popes had tacitly approved a great many customs contrary to the law, when in fact the medieval popes had condemned most of them. See e.g. Gene A. Brucker, 'Ecclesiastical courts in fifteenth-century Florence and Fiesole', *Mediaeval Studies*, 53 (1991), 248–9; A. G. Little, 'Personal tithes', *EHR*, 60 (1945), 67–88.

[94] Elton, *Maitland*, pp. 69–79.

[95] For recognition of the merits of his side, see Dorothy M. Owen, *The Medieval Canon Law: Teaching, Literature and Transmission* (Cambridge, 1990), p. 64; E. W. Kemp, *An Introduction to Canon Law in the Church of England*, (London, 1957), pp. 30–2; J. W. Gray, 'Canon Law in England: some reflections on the Stubbs-Maitland controversy', *Studies in Church History*, 3 (1966), 48–68.

Maitland assumed.[96] Some decretals were treated that way. Some were not. The *ius commune* permitted a degree of uncertainty, of 'flexibility' if you like, about the law that ill accords with a regime of 'binding statute law'.[97] In a real sense the question put at issue in the Stubbs-Maitland dispute seems to me to have been a *question mal posée.*

In this assertion I am very conscious of being out of step with a strong and learned tradition in English historiography. It is revealing, for example, that the Festschrift published by the Cambridge University Press in honour of the teacher who has done most to interest English scholars in the canon law was called *Authority and Power.*[98] The title was well chosen. The law of the Church is described in Walter Ullmann's work as the exercise of sovereign power. That was his theme. And it certainly is part of the story. But it is not the whole story. And overall, it seems to me misleading to treat the law and literature of the *ius commune* in terms primarily of the exercise of power. The 'descending theory of government' is incompatible with a system of law that allowed so much authority to the opinions of jurists and such a large role to customary rights of jurisdiction. The exercise of authority there was, but laying single-minded stress upon it may easily obscure the character of the learned laws.

The Future

It is time to conclude. I do so with a word about the future, and it will be brief. The question is whether 'Pollock and Maitland' after one hundred years has retained the ability to inspire, and by now it must be clear that I believe it does. Although amended in details, augmented in parts, and replaced in spots, and although deficient (at least by my lights) in its understanding of the inner nature of the *ius commune,* 'Pollock and Maitland' remains the best overall treatment of the place of the learned laws in medieval England. It is the volume scholars still turn to for guidance and inspiration. My prediction is that it will continue to do so for the immediate future, and that research will continue along present lines — that is, by beginning with 'Pollock and

---

[96] The canonistic developments are well summarized in Peter Landau, 'Neuere Forschungen zu Quellen und Institutionem des klassischen kanonischen Rechts bis zum Liber Sextus: Ergebnisse and Zukuntsperspektiven', *Proceedings of the Seventh International Congress of Medieval Canon Law,* (1988), 36–47.

[97] See the pertinent remarks, with supporting references, by Laurent Mayali, in *Rechtshistorisches Journal,* 10 (1991), 81–3.

[98] Brian Tierney and Peter Linehan, eds., *Authority and Power: Studies on Medieval Law and Government presented to Walter Ullmann on his Seventieth Birthday* (Cambridge, 1980).

Maitland' and seeking to assess its conclusions in light of further exploration of court records and the learned laws.

In my own view, the second of these is actually more urgent than the first. We have made good progress in the archives. However, on the ecclesiastical side of the fence at least, legal and administrative history is very often being written from the records alone. I do not mean to disparage the fruits of that research. I have presented some of it myself. However, treatment of many subjects — benefit of clergy for example — would be improved by examination of the formal Canon Law of these subjects.[99]

A German writer has said that, in comparison with the study of the academic law, in Continental scholarship, investigation of ecclesiastical court records is something of a 'step-child'.[100] Legal doctrine absorbs the bulk of the Germans' attention. In the field of English history, something like the reverse has been true. The history of the Church's institutions is often described without any reference to the Canon and Roman Laws. The balance needs to be redressed, in my view, and for this the example of Maitland's work provides a spur. Maitland made the excursion into the law of the Church, even if it was one he made grudgingly. He regarded it as alien territory for an English lawyer, and perhaps it was. But he surveyed it in a way that still impresses. Over the years, 'Pollock and Maitland' has proved to have a great power — both a staying power and an inspiring power. On this view of things, it still has some inspiration left to impart.

---

[99] Several of J. H. Baker's additions and improvements to Laura Gabel's classic account of the institution, *Benefit of Clergy in England*, (Northampton, Mass., 1928), come from taking a look at the Canon Law on the subject. See his 'Some early Newgate reports (1315–28)', in Chantal Stebbings, ed., *Law Reporting in England* (London, 1995), pp. 46–53.

[100] Rudolf Weigand, 'Zur mittelalterlichen kirchlichen Ehegerischtsbarkeit', in *Liebe und Ehe im Mittelalter*, (Goldbach, 1993), p. 307: 'ein Stiefkind der historischen Forschung'.

Proceedings of the British Academy, **89**, 171–214

The Origins of the Crown

GEORGE GARNETT

SECRETED AWAY IN THE MIDST OF his posthumously published lectures on English constitutional history is one of those thought-provoking observations by Maitland which have lain largely undisturbed for ninety years:

> There is one term against which I wish to warn you, and that term is 'the crown'. You will certainly read that the crown does this and the crown does that. As a matter of fact we know that the crown does nothing but lie in the Tower of London to be gazed at by sight-seers. No, the crown is a convenient cover for ignorance: it saves us from asking difficult questions. . . . [1]

Partly under the influence of his reading of German scholars, most notably Gierke, Maitland had begun to address questions of this nature in a series of essays on corporate personality, and in a few luminous, tantalizing pages in the *History of English Law*.[2] Plucknett conceded that the issues raised by these questions, which he characterized as metaphysical, formed the foundations of legal history, but added, severely, that 'prolonged contemplation of them may warp the judgement.' Not, of course, that Maitland had been found wanting: Plucknett thought him acutely aware of the potential dangers of abstraction. But less well-seasoned timbers would scarcely bear up under the strain.[3]

Plucknett need not have worried. The judgements of English his-

---

© The British Academy 1996

[1] Maitland, *Constitutional History*, p. 418; cf. Pollock and Maitland, i 525: 'that "metaphor kept in the Tower," as Tom Paine called it'; F. W. Maitland, 'The Crown as corporation', reprinted in his *Collected Papers*, iii 244–70 at 257: 'a chattel now lying in the Tower and partaking (so it is said [by Coke]) of the nature of an heirloom'; *Gierke*, p. xxxvi: '. . . the "Subject" (or subjectified object) that lies in the Jewel House of the Tower'.

[2] See esp. 'The corporation sole', 'The Crown as corporation', 'The unicorporate body', 'Trust and corporation', reprinted in *Collected Papers*, iii 210–43, 244–70, 271–84, 321–404; Pollock and Maitland, i 511–26 (which appealed to Heinrich Brunner: see his review in *Political Science Quarterly*, 11 (1896), 534–44 at 539); and his introduction to *Gierke*. Maitland's 'repeated perusal' of Gierke after the publication of the first edition of 'Pollock and Maitland' prompted some of the most substantial changes in the second edition; but these were concerned with ecclesiastical corporations: Pollock and Maitland, i 486 n. 1.

[3] T. F. T. Plucknett, *Early English Legal Literature* (Cambridge, 1958), p. 16.

torians have, in this regard, never been put to the test. For both the essays, which concentrated on the later middle ages and the sixteenth and seventeenth centuries, and the section in the *History of English Law*, which focused on the thirteenth century, have been largely ignored since they were written.[4] Although Maitland gave plenty of pregnant hints about the implications for the period prior to the thirteenth century, particularly in the *History of English Law*, they have not been pursued either. Yet for precisely these reasons the crown, usually appearing in the guise of the Crown, or 'The Crown', has continued its unthinking career in the historiography of medieval England, from the Anglo-Saxon period on. It is one of those 'foundations' of legal history which are assumed rather than contemplated. We still do read, in the work of the most distinguished authorities, that the Crown does this and the Crown does that. But as Maitland pointed out, the term tends to be used as a synonym for king.[5] Elegance of expression is thereby sought at the cost of historical accuracy, for nothing in the sources justifies this usage. Moreover, in almost every instance where 'Crown' cannot simply be replaced by 'king', the sloppiness of thought detected by Maitland is still more apparent. For what is usually meant by 'The Crown' in these cases is something vaguely akin to 'state' or 'sovereignty' — certainly something distinct from the person of the king. But finding nothing corresponding to these anachronistic terms in the sources, historians turn instead to the more traditional-sounding 'Crown', in an undefined abstract sense. The Crown sounds traditional because, as Maitland himself demonstrated, it had become an important, if ill-defined, term in English constitutional debate from the later middle ages on. The imprecision of the term when used by historians is therefore, according to Maitland, no more than a reflection of its imprecision in the sources.

Although 'crown' is not used as a synonym for 'king' in the sources for the period on which I wish to concentrate — that prior to the thirteenth century, where Maitland effectively began his story — I was careful to qualify my comments about its use in other senses by historians. For

[4] E. H. Kantorowicz, *The King's Two Bodies. A Study in Medieval Political Theology* (Princeton, 1957) is the notable — and, of course, unEnglish — exception. It is only too easy to infer what Plucknett's opinion of this book would have been. F. Hartung, 'Die Krone als Symbol der monarchischen Herrschaft im ausgehenden Mittelalter', *Abhandlungen der Preussischen Akademie der Wissenschaften*, phil.-hist. Kl., 13 (1941), 3–46 at 6–19, does little more than summarize Maitland's analysis.

[5] Pollock and Maitland, i 525; 'Crown as corporation', 257.

there is some warrant for such usages in the sources. This does not apply to Anglo-Saxon England, where I have found no reference to *cynehelm* or *corona* as anything other than a physical object.[6] But within twenty or thirty years of the Conquest *corona* begins to appear in contexts where it cannot refer simply to the physical object. I shall try to argue that there were in fact two apparently unrelated shifts in the meaning of the term; and that they represent distinct attempts to wrestle with the problems created for ecclesiastical tenure by a new system, consequent on the Conquest, in which all tenure depended upon the king.

The first instance I have traced is in the *De Iniusta Vexacione Willelmi Episcopi*, most of which consists of the *libellus* recording the proceedings taken by William Rufus against William of St Calais, bishop of Durham, in 1088. Professor Offler's case for its being a later (though still undated) forgery has recently sustained further, probably fatal, damage,[7] and even he conceded that the author must have used material compiled in 1088.[8] But if doubts linger about its authenticity, the emergence of the usage cannot be pushed much more than twenty years further forward, for in the *Historia Novorum* Eadmer uses *corona* and *corona regni* in what I take to be a closely related sense. What is this sense?

William of St Calais was suspected by William Rufus of being a party to the treasonable conspiracy against him on the part of the Anglo-Norman magnates in 1088 who 'regnum suum pariter sibi et coronam auferre volebant.'[9] A down-to-earth reading of this would see it as a straightforward reference to the crown as physical object, albeit the distinctive symbol of the king's status. If so, there would be no reason, in this regard, to differentiate the *De Iniusta Vexacione* from, say, William of Poitiers, who emphasizes Duke William's transform-

[6] J. L. Nelson, 'The earliest surviving royal *ordo*', in B. Tierney and P. A. Linehan, eds, *Authority and Power: Studies on Medieval Law and Government presented to Walter Ullmann on his seventieth birthday* (Cambridge, 1980), pp. 29–48 at 45; J. Kirschner, *Die Bezeichnungen fur Kranz und Krone im Altenglischen* (Munich, 1975). Note the shift into Latin to describe the *corona* which Archbishop Ealdred placed on William the Conqueror's head in *ASC* (D) *s.a.* 1066.

[7] M. Philpott, 'The *De Iniusta Vexacione Willelmi Episcopi Primi* and Canon Law in Anglo-Norman Durham', in D. Rollason, M. Harvey and M. Prestwich, eds, *Anglo-Norman Durham* (Woodbridge, 1995), pp. 125–37.

[8] H. S. Offler, 'The tractate De Iniusta Vexacione Willelmi Episcopi Primi', *EHR*, 66 (1951), 321–41 at 341; H. S. Offler, unpublished typescript edition of *De Iniusta Vexacione Willelmi Episcopi Primi per Willelmum Regem Fil<l>ium Willelmi Magni Regis*, p. 7. I am indebted to Mrs Offler for permission to use this edition, which will supersede all existing editions. For convenience sake, I shall give references also to the version in *English Lawsuits*, no. 134.

[9] 'Who wanted to take from him at the same time his kingdom and his crown': *DIV*, ed. Offler, p. 38; *English Lawsuits*, i p. 97.

ation into a king in terms of his assumption of a *corona*.[10] That *corona* here begins to mean something more than, and something more specific than, simply a physical symbol of regality is indicated both by the context in which it is found, and by Eadmer's use of the term.

It first appears in the *Historia Novorum* in Eadmer's account of Anselm's confrontation with William Rufus at Gillingham at the beginning of 1095. At the king's urgent instigation Anselm had, in 1093, been brought over from Normandy in order to become archbishop of Canterbury. In his previous capacity as abbot of Bec Anselm had, long before, recognized Urban II as pope.[11] But Rufus, like his father before him, had studiously avoided recognizing either of the competing claimants for the see of Rome. At Gillingham Anselm sought the king's permission to petition Urban II for his archiepiscopal *pallium*, without which he would not be able to exercise many of the functions of his office.[12] Eadmer reports the king's outraged response:

> the king said that he had not yet recognized Urban as pope, and that it had not been customary under him or his father for anyone to nominate a pope in the kingdom of England except by the king's *licentia* and *electio*, and that anyone who wished to snatch from him the power of this dignity, would be at one with someone trying to remove his *corona* from him.[13]

Close to the beginning of his book Eadmer had listed the 'new usages' which William the Conqueror had introduced into England, and, bearing out the claim put into Rufus's mouth, this *consuetudo* is one of them.[14]

When, shortly afterwards, Anselm was put on trial at the council

---

[10] Guillaume de Poitiers, *Histoire de Guillaume le Conquérant*, ed. and trans. R. Foreville (Paris, 1952), pp. 216 ('Orant post haec [the submission of London] ut coronam sumat una pontifices atque caeteri summates, se quidem solitos esse regi servire, regem dominum habere vellere'; William was more anxious to have a peaceful kingdom than the *corona*), 220 (at his coronation the English are asked 'an consentirent eum sibi dominum coronari'; Ealdred, archbishop of York 'imposuit ei regium diadema'), 230 ('coronatus est'), 260 (Mathilda is commonly given the title of queen 'etsi nondum coronata'); cf. pp. 1 (on Cnut's death his son Harold Harefoot 'coronam eandem cum throno . . . obtinuit'), 30 (Edward the Confessor's acquiring the *corona* through Duke William's support), 146 (the English land had lost King Edward 'et ejus corona Heraldum ornatum'), 206 (the *corona* which Harold had perfidiously usurped). Note that the Bayeux Tapestry shows, and says it shows, Harold being offered a 'CORONAM REGIS' immediately before his coronation (although the crown depicted in the coronation scene is different, and resembles the one which Edward is shown wearing): *The Bayeux Tapestry*, ed. D. M. Wilson (London, 1985), pl. 31.

[11] *S. Anselmi Cantuariensis Archiepiscopi Opera Omnia*, ed. F. S. Schmitt (6 vols, Edinburgh and London, 1940–61), iii *ep*. 124.

[12] R. W. Southern, *St Anselm: A Portrait in a Landscape* (Cambridge, 1990), pp. 268–70.

[13] Eadmer, *Historia Novorum in Anglia*, ed. M. Rule (London, 1884), p. 53.

[14] *Historia Novorum*, pp. 9–10; there are similarities between the contents, if not the phrasing, of Eadmer's list and a letter of Anselm's of 1099–1100: *Opera Omnia*, iii *ep*. 210.

of Rockingham, Eadmer records the archbishop's report of the king's words to him. We can have some confidence in accepting Eadmer's account as roughly accurate, not only because we know he was in close attendance on Anselm at this time,[15] but also because it has been shown that he used the notes he had taken of Anselm's public statements and private conversation as the basis for the words he placed in the archbishop's mouth. They were not rhetorical compositions in the classical mode, of the type found in more conventional historians.[16] The king's alleged words explain more clearly what attempting to remove his *corona* might mean: ' "If in my kingdom you recognize this Urban or anyone else as pope without my *electio* and authority, or having already recognized him, you hold to him, you act contrary to the *fides* which you owe to me, and in doing so you offend me no less than if you sought to remove my crown." '[17] In other words, according to Eadmer's account of Anselm's account of the king's words, breaking *fides* with the king was tantamount to trying to remove his crown, and recognition of a pope without royal approval, or refusal to renounce a recognition already given long before the pledging of *fides* to the king, amounted to such a breach of *fides*. The point is underlined by the bishops, accompanied by a few of the *principes*, in a time-serving reprimand to the trouble-maker:

> 'The question is clear enough and needs no elaboration. For you should know that the whole kingdom is complaining against you that you are trying to remove from our common lord the crown and ornament of his rule [*quod nostro communi domino conaris decus imperii sui coronam auferre*]. Whoever takes from him the customs of the royal dignity takes from him at the same instant the crown and the kingdom. For we are convinced that one cannot be held properly [*decenter*] without the other.'[18]

The bishops' words are an almost exact echo of the charge levelled against William of St Calais in 1088: obstinate refusal to renounce allegiance to a pope and rebellion are both characterized as trying to snatch simultaneously the king's crown and kingdom. In the view of the bishops, and that of the king, the crown and kingdom could not be

---

[15] Southern, *St Anselm*, pp. 247–8, 411.
[16] Southern, *St Anselm*, pp. 423–6.
[17] *Historia Novorum*, p. 54. The same point is made, although the term *corona* is not used, in Eadmer's parallel account of the council in *Vita Anselmi*, ed. and trans. R. W. Southern (Oxford, 1972), pp. 85–6. William of Malmesbury, who used Eadmer as his principal source for these events, summarized the king's reasoning thus: 'Consuetudo regni mei est a patre meo instituta, ut nullus praeter licentiam regis appeletur papa. Qui consuetudines regni tollit, potestatem quoque et coronam regni violat. Qui coronam mihi aufert, inimicitiis et infidelitate in me agit.' (*De Gestis Pontificum*, ed. N.E.S.A. Hamilton (London, 1870), p. 87).
[18] *Historia Novorum*, p. 58.

held *decenter* without the customs introduced, according to Eadmer, by William the Conqueror. Whether or not Eadmer was in this instance repeating the terminology used in the debates at Rockingham, for him the term *corona* clearly encapsulated the innovations in royal power introduced at the Conquest. After all, the title of his book might be translated as 'A History of the Novelties'. What were these novelties?

Some of them are set out in the list near the beginning, and from them Eadmer invites his readers to infer the rest. All of those mentioned are concerned with the claims to control which William the Conqueror and his sons enforced over clerics and the church in England. But Eadmer adds that although he has omitted whatever William might have promulgated 'in saecularibus' because it was none of his business, as an ecclesiastical historian, to discuss such matters, it would be easy enough to infer these other innovations from what he had to say about 'divine matters'.[19] In other words, what was shown to be the case with the church was also true in the lay sphere. He listed these innovations because, he said, knowledge of them was essential to an understanding of the principal point of his book, its *causa*. Once this *causa* has been grasped, it becomes easy to see how and why he wrought his *corona*.

The *germen* of this *causa* is identified in his preface: 'From the time that William, *comes* of Normandy subdued this land to himself by warfare, no-one, prior to Anselm, was made a bishop or abbot in it who had not first been made the king's man [*homo*], and had received investiture of his bishopric or abbacy from the king's hand by the tradition of a pastoral staff.' The only exceptions to this, Eadmer scrupulously points out, are bishops of Rochester.[20] Like most prefaces, this was written after the rest of the book, when these issues of clerical homage and lay investiture had become the nub of the dispute between Anselm and William Rufus, and, more particularly, Henry I.[21] We know that Eadmer must have written extremely detailed notes, or even some kind of draft, prior to the outbreak of the investiture contest in England,[22] which was occasioned by Anselm's attendance (accompanied by Eadmer) at the Easter Council in St Peter's in Rome in 1099, where they both heard for the first time the papal prohibitions

---

[19] *Historia Novorum*, p. 10.

[20] *Historia Novorum*, pp. 1–2.

[21] Southern, *St Anselm*, p. 415.

[22] R. W. Southern, *St Anselm and his Biographer* (Cambridge, 1963), pp. 299–300, shows that whereas the text of the first four books as it survives includes several references to a time after Anselm's death in 1109 (one of which (p. 211) implies that Archbishop Thomas of York, who died in 1114, is also dead), it must be based on notes made at the time of many of the events described.

against lay investiture and clerical homage.[23] For Eadmer in the course of his narrative says that Anselm, on his accession to the archbishopric in 1093, did homage to Rufus 'pro usu terrae'.[24] So while it might casuistically be true that Anselm had not received investiture at the king's hands — Rufus being so ill that the clerics around his sickbed had had to act in his stead[25] — with respect to homage Eadmer himself gives the lie to the claim he makes in his preface that Anselm had acted differently from earlier bishops and abbots. Eadmer's detailed account of Anselm's elevation to the see of Canterbury demonstrates that what made Anselm archbishop was not election or consecration; nor was it investiture. It was by Rufus's receipt of his homage, thereby seising him with the lands of the see, that Anselm became archbishop.[26] This was because, at Lanfranc's death, the church of Canterbury had escheated to the king.[27] Hence the pernicious powers of kings to exploit vacant churches.

By force of the Conquest bishoprics and many abbacies had become tenancies held by bishops and abbots directly of the king, that is, tenancies-in-chief. Not only do we have Eadmer's word for it that all new bishops (with the exception of bishops of Rochester) did homage to the king; some existing English bishops and abbots are elsewhere reported to have submitted to the Conqueror, and in the Norman sources the submission took the form of homage.[28] The same must have been true of other English bishops and abbots. That Eadmer was right to think that homage had transformed the tenure of bishops and abbots into a tenure dependent in most instances directly on the king, and that this must have applied to surviving English clerics too, is suggested by the fact that Æthelwig, abbot of Evesham, owed five

[23] Southern, *St Anselm*, pp. 280–4; cf. 191 for Anselm's ignorance of the decree prohibiting lay investiture issued at the Lateran synod of 1078.
[24] *Historia Novorum*, p. 41; for other evidence of Anselm's homage, see *RRAN*, i nos. 336, 337; for the significance of Eadmer's slip see Southern, *St Anselm and his Biographer*, p. 310.
[25] *Historia Novorum*, p. 35.
[26] *Historia Novorum*, p. 41: 'more et exemplo praedecessoris sui inductus, pro usu terrae homo regis factus est, et, sicut Lanfrancus suo tempore fuerat, de toto archiepiscopatu saisisi jussus.' This was immediately followed by Anselm's ceremonial reception and enthronement in Canterbury on 25 September. The election — or what passed for the election — had happened on 6 March: p. 35. He is described as being 'in pontificatu' prior to his consecration on 4 December: p. 42. See further Southern, *St Anselm*, pp. 189–91.
[27] *Historia Novorum*, p. 26. Eadmer uses the loaded verb *invadere* — usurp — to describe the manner in which the church of Canterbury came into the king's hands.
[28] *ASC* (D) s.a. 1066 (Ealdred, archbishop of York); *The Chronicle of John of Worcester*, ed. R. R. Darlington and P. McGurk (3 vols, Oxford, 1995–), s.a. 1066, ii 606 (Ealdred; Wulfstan, bishop of Worcester; Walter, bishop of Hereford); Guillaume de Poitiers, p. 216 (Stigand 'manibus ei sese dedit, fidem sacramento confirmavit'; it is implied that other unspecified *pontifices* submit).

knights 'de abb[at]ia tua' to the king by 1073 at the latest.[29] As Professor Holt has reconfirmed, the *servitia debita* are a post-Conquest phenomenon;[30] Æthelwig's case indicates that they were imposed on ecclesiastical tenants-in-chief at a very early stage. They are a mark of the new dependency, Rochester being the exception which proves the rule. For as Eadmer himself pointed out, a bishop-elect of Rochester did homage and swore fealty to the archbishop of Canterbury, not to the king, and the archbishop gave him his *episcopatus*;[31] a bishop of Rochester owed military service to the archbishop, not to the king.[32] Eadmer perceived the implications of this strict dependency more articulately than any other contemporary.

Its effect was to blur the distinction between the possessions held by a bishop or abbot and their respective offices, as is suggested by the use of the terms *(archi)episcopatus* or *abbatia* to mean either and both. According to the *De Iniusta Vexacione*, William of St Calais attempted to turn this to his own advantage. He argued that being disseised even of some of the lands of his see by the king's agents meant being disseised of his *episcopatus*, and he demanded its restoration to him before he would stand trial.[33] Although he accepted that the lands of the see — if not the *pecunia* and his *homines* — were held of the king,[34] by treating his *episcopatus* as an indivisible entity he sought to

---

[29] *RRAN*, i no. 63, which survives in a thirteenth-century cartulary copy; on the date, see R. R. Darlington, 'Æthelwig, abbot of Evesham', *EHR*, 48 (1933), 1–22, 177–98 at 17 n. 4. David Bates argues, *Regesta Regum Anglo-Normannorum: The Acta of William I, 1066–1087* (Oxford, forthcoming), no. 131, that it is probably (but not certainly) a forgery, dating either from early in Henry II's reign or from the thirteenth century. His main reason for doing so is that the writ is in some respects unusual, in terms of both diplomatic form and vocabulary, in comparison with other eleventh-century writs. But since there is no other surviving writ of summons from this period, the uniqueness of the writ cannot in itself count either in favour of or against its authenticity. He concedes that it is much simpler than the thirteenth-century writs of summons with which he compares it, but suggests that this may be because the forger lacked precise information. A more straightforward explanation would be that it is simpler because it is more primitive, representing the earliest stage in a new diplomatic form. If it is a forgery, then Bates — as he himself concedes — gives no entirely convincing answer to the question *cui bono*? For these reasons, I am inclined to support his alternative, traditional assessment: that it is a unique survival. I should like to thank David Bates for generously supplying me with print outs of this and a large number of other documents.

[30] J. C. Holt, 'The introduction of knight service in England', *ANS*, 6 (1984), 89–106.

[31] *Historia Novorum*, pp. 196–7; further, R. A. L. Smith, 'The place of Gundulf in the Anglo-Norman Church', *EHR*, 58 (1943), 257–72 at 261–2; F. Barlow, *The English Church: 1066–1154* (London, 1979), p. 47.

[32] *The Domesday Monachorum of Christ Church Canterbury*, ed. D. C. Douglas (London, 1944), pp. 70, 105, 106–7; J. H. Round, *Feudal England: Historical Studies of the XIth and XIIth Centuries* (London, 1909), p. 250.

[33] *DIV*, ed. Offler, p. 35; *English Lawsuits*, i p. 96.

[34] *DIV*, ed. Offler, p. 32; *English Lawsuits*, i p. 94; *DIV*, ed. Offler, pp. 27, 29, *English Lawsuits*, i pp. 91, 92, for *pecunia* and *homines*.

establish that he was justiciable as its holder only by other prelates — not lay and ecclesiastical barons sitting together in the king's court — and only in accordance with Canon Law.[35] He might be a *homo* and *fidelis* of the king,[36] of whom he held his lands,[37] but he was unwilling to concede that his *episcopatus* was a fief.[38] Ironically, Lanfranc was forced to respond that the king's concern was with William's fief, not his *episcopatus*, and that he would be tried solely with respect to the former before the undifferentiated king's court of lay and ecclesiastical tenants-in-chief.[39] In other words, he found himself arguing that a bishopric and the lands held by the bishop were in some sense distinct, and, by implication, that the former was not justiciable before the king's court according to secular law. Yet this was quite at odds with the system which Eadmer depicted and which William of St Calais sought to twist against the king: that *episcopatus* and *abbatia* were held by bishops and abbots of the king as a function of the *fides* they owed him, arising from the homage they had done. When the relationship between king and prelate ceased, either because of the death of the prelate or for some other reason — like Anselm's exiles[40] — the lands (and therefore the revenues) reverted to the king as lord. Although it is never suggested that stripping a bishop of his estates deposed him from his office, there was, therefore, a sacrilegious legal logic to Rufus's defiant boast, reported by Eadmer, that, after the death of Lanfranc, no-one would be archbishop of Canterbury 'except me'.[41] The lands of the see had come into his hands by a process which Eadmer character-

---

[35] *DIV*, ed. Offler, pp. 31, 33, 37, 39; *English Lawsuits*, i pp. 93, 94, 97, 98. William appears to distinguish his *sedes* from his *episcopatus* — *DIV*, ed. Offler, pp. 36, 43, 45, 50; *English Lawsuits* i pp. 96, 100, 101, 104 — but it is clear from the context that by the former he means Durham itself, as the physical seat of his bishopric.

[36] *DIV*, ed. Offler, pp. 27, 29, 32, *English Lawsuits*, pp. 91, 92, 94.

[37] *DIV*, ed. Offler, p. 32, *English Lawsuits*, i p. 94.

[38] *DIV*, ed. Offler, pp. 39, 41; *English Lawsuits*, i pp. 98, 99.

[39] *DIV*, ed. Offler, pp. 35, 39, 41; *English Lawsuits*, i pp. 96, 98, 99. At one point Lanfranc inadvertently adopts William of St Calais' usage, when he promises that if the bishop dropped his threatened appeal to Rome, the king would restore to him his *episcopatus* (except the city of Durham): *DIV*, ed. Offler, p. 45; *English Lawsuits*, i p. 101. The treatment of Odo of Bayeux in 1082 which Lanfranc is said to have invoked as a precedent is misleading, perhaps deliberately so. Odo's fief in England had nothing to do with his office as bishop of Bayeux. Other treatments of the case focus on Odo's status as an earl in England, rather than on the nature of his tenure: William of Malmesbury, *De Gestis Regum*, ed. W. Stubbs (2 vols, London, 1887–9), ii 360–1; cf. Orderic, iv 40–2; cf. Orderic, iv pp. xxvii–xxx. In the *DIV*, ed. Offler, p. 41, the two issues are blurred in Lanfranc's speech.

[40] First exile: *Historia Novorum*, pp. 88–9, repeated verbatim in *Vita Anselmi*, p. 100; *ep.* no 210. Second exile: *Historia Novorum*, p. 159; *Vita Anselmi*, p. 132: 'Rex ... Heinricus ... mox archiepiscopatum in dominium suum *re*degit, et Anselmum suis omnibus spoliavit.' (My italics.)

[41] *Historia Novorum*, p. 30.

izes as usurpation;[42] they had reverted to him. So, in a crucial sense, had the office been 'usurped' by the king. This might, even in the king's view, merit the damnation of his soul;[43] but it followed inexorably from the way in which the king had become the source of all tenure, both lay and ecclesiastical, at the Conquest. Hence Eadmer's invitation to his reader to infer the nature of the Conqueror's innovations in secular law from what he had to say about 'divine matters';[44] and hence his leitmotiv, adapting a classical commonplace, that 'all things, spiritual and temporal alike, waited on the nod of the king.'[45]

This explains why Anselm's insistence on maintaining his previous recognition of Urban II was viewed as a breach of *fides* with the king: it meant that Anselm's links with the papacy were not strictly subject to royal sanction; that, in other words, they did not wait upon the king's nod. Rufus did not consider himself 'to be possessed of his royal dignity intact [*integrum*] so long as anyone anywhere throughout his whole land had or could be said to have anything other than through him, even if it were according to the will of God.'[46] Eadmer's strikingly tactile language shows why even something as untenurial as recognition of a pope without royal sanction was deemed to be an affront to the king's position as the lord on whom all tenures depended. The other bishops at Rockingham made the same point to Anselm: he was blaspheming against the king 'simply because in his kingdom and without his concession [Anselm] had dared to ascribe anything even to God.'[47] In post-Conquest England deference to God without royal sanction was, according to Eadmer, treated as no less an attack upon the king's possession of his dignity than the open rebellion with which William of St Calais was said to have colluded.[48] William of St Calais' subsequent request for the king's *licencia* to appeal to the papal *curia*,[49] and his attempt to make such an appeal even when permission had been refused,[50] amounted to a more nuanced, two-pronged attack on the king's position. Threatening to mount an appeal in the absence of a royal *licencia* contravened the royal control over communications between English clerics and the papacy which was one of the main

---

[42] See above, n. 27.
[43] *Historia Novorum*, pp. 33–4.
[44] *Historia Novorum*, p. 10.
[45] *Historia Novorum*, p. 9; cf. pp. 32, 237.
[46] *Historia Novorum*, p. 60.
[47] *Vita Anselmi*, p. 86.
[48] Above, n. 9.
[49] *DIV*, ed. Offler, p. 41; *English Lawsuits*, i p. 99.
[50] *DIV*, ed. Offler, p. 45; *English Lawsuits*, i p. 101.

concerns of those of the Conqueror's innovations listed by Eadmer;[51] and in any event Rufus had no more accepted one of the competing candidates for the Roman see in 1088 than he had done by 1093. Any appeal to the *curia* in 1088 would therefore have amounted to a recognition by William of St Calais of (in this case) Urban II, the very action which Eadmer said the king had characterized at Rockingham as trying to remove his crown.[52]

For Eadmer, and just conceivably for William Rufus himself,[53] *corona* was therefore a shorthand term for the rights which the king possessed as a result of his unique tenurial position in post-Conquest England. It was a far more pointed metonym than the classical *nutum*. It evoked images of the ceremonies developed by the Norman kings to display with some regularity their newly won status in terms of this most distinctive item of regalia.[54] But the metonym was deeply ironic. Writing at Canterbury, Eadmer is likely to have been aware that the *laudes* sung at these crown-wearings conventionally opened with an acclamation of the pope as the pinnacle of the earthly hierarchy, followed by one of the king as *a Deo coronato*.[55] He is even more likely to have known that the traditional English prayer in the coronation *ordo* which accompanied the king's inaugural crowning opened with the words 'Coronet te deus corona glorie atque iusticie . . .'.[56] The

---

[51] *Historia Novorum*, p. 10.

[52] *Historia Novorum*, p. 54; this, of course, assumes that the *DIV* is a genuine record of proceedings in 1088. We know that William of St Calais appealed to Urban because a letter of Urban's, preserved in the *Collectio Britannica*, reprimanded Rufus and ordered the matter to be brought to judgement at the *curia*: *Epistolae Pontificum Romanorum Ineditae*, ed. S. Loewenfeld (Leipzig, 1885), no. 129.

[53] Above, p. 175.

[54] Above, n. 10; the impression of regularity given by *ASC* (E) *s.a.* 1086 (*recte* 1087) is to some extent belied by the details of the Conqueror's actual itinerary: D. Bates, 'The Conqueror's charters', in C. Hicks, ed., *England in the Eleventh Century* (Stamford, 1992), pp. 1–16 at 5–9. At Christmas 1070 he had a *corona* and other royal insignia brought to him in York: Orderic, ii 232. M. Hare, *The Two Anglo-Saxon Minsters of Gloucester* (Deerhurst Lecture, 1992), pp. 17–23, cautiously constructs an intriguing case for the introduction of ritual crown-wearing into England in the late 1050s, but there is no direct evidence.

[55] H. E. J. Cowdrey, 'The Anglo-Norman Laudes Regiae', *Viator*, 12 (1981), 37–78 at 70 for the *laudes* of 1068 (found in a section of BL, MS Cotton Vitellius E. XII which is to be associated with York rather than Canterbury: M. Lapidge, 'Ealdred of York and MS Cotton Vitellius E. xii', *The Yorkshire Archaeological Journal*, 55 (1983), 11–25); 72 for a late eleventh-century Canterbury text. Cowdrey argues, 65, that the absence of a pope's name from the latter makes it likely that these *laudes* were devised between 1084 and 1095, when no pope was recognized in England. His argument, 53, that the former carefully qualifies the subordination of king to pope has been questioned by J. L. Nelson, 'The rites of the Conqueror', *ANS*, 4 (1982), 117–32, 210–21 at 129.

[56] This prayer, found in Anglo-Saxon copies of the second recension of the *ordo* — for instance Cambridge, Corpus Christi College MS 44, a Canterbury pontifical of the second half of the eleventh century, printed in *Three Coronation Orders*, ed. J. Wickham Legg

Norman Anonymous explained the point with uncharacteristic conven-
tionality (and terseness) in his commentary on the *ordo*.[57] Yet Eadmer's
incorporeal *corona* was the antithesis of the physical crown worn by
the king at his coronation and at crown wearings: it embraced the
king's denial of due respect to the pope, and more generally his blas-
phemous refusal to allow anyone in his kingdom to ascribe anything
to God other than by his leave. Whereas the crowning prayer presented
the divinely bestowed *corona glorie atque iusticie* as the means by
which, with right faith and good works, the king would eventually
accede to the *corona* of the 'everlasting kingdom', according to Eadmer
even William Rufus recognized that by exercising the rights encapsulated by the term *corona* he would bring upon himself everlasting
damnation.[58] The crown thus defined in this world debarred the king
from a crown in the next. It was a symbol of shame and injustice: the
royal rights which it embodied contravened not only, in a peculiarly
sacrilegious way, the papal prohibitions against clerical homage, but
also, as both the *De Iniusta Vexacione* and Eadmer stress, the canonical
requirement to place no bar on appeals to Rome. And the latter was
not a recent papal ruling. It was laid down in Lanfranc's version of the
Pseudo-Isidorian decretals, and marked for ease of reference, just in
case William of St Calais' legendary memory should fail him, in the
Durham copy of the collection to which the bishop referred during
the hearing.[59] The injustice which took sacrilegious form when royal

(Henry Bradshaw Society, 19, 1900), p. 57 — is one of the few traditional forms preserved
in the third recension: *The Pontifical of Magdalen College*, ed. H. A. Wilson (Henry Bradshaw
Society, 39, 1910), p. 93. The earliest surviving pontifical (also from Canterbury) which
contains the third recension of the *ordo* — Dublin, Trinity College MS 98 — has been
attributed to Christ Church by Tessa Webber and dated to the very end of the eleventh
century or the first years of the twelfth. The hands are, she informs me, typical of those in
which the few surviving *acta* of Anselm are written; see further G. S. Garnett, 'The third
recension of the English coronation *ordo*: the manuscripts', *Journal of Ecclesiastical History*,
(forthcoming), esp. n. 60.

[57] *Die Texte des Normannischen Anonymus*, ed. K. Pellens (3 vols, Wiesbaden, 1966), i 159.
This is his only discussion of the crown.

[58] *Historia Novorum*, pp. 33–4, discussed above, p. 180.

[59] *Decretales Pseudo-Isidoriane et Capitula Angilramni*, ed. P. Hinschius (Leipzig, 1879),
'Decreta Felicis II. papae, confirmatio', cap. xiv, p. 489; Cambridge, Trinity College MS B.
16. 44, fo. 38v, cap. xviiii (Lanfranc's personal copy, as demonstrated by Z. N. Brooke, *The
English Church and the Papacy from the Conquest to the Reign of King John* (Cambridge,
1931), pp. 57–83); Cambridge, Peterhouse MS 74, fo. 46v, cap. xviiii (William of St Calais'
personal copy, as demonstrated by Philpott, '*De Iniusta Vexacione*', pp. 131–2. The marginal
marks match the canonical citations and allusions in the *DIV*). The manuscript references
for this canon are given in M. Philpott, *Archbishop Lanfranc and Canon Law*, D. Phil. thesis
(Oxford, 1993), p. 123. The bishop explicitly mentions the book of Canon Law which he has
before him: *DIV*, ed. Offler, p. 45, *English Lawsuits*, i p. 101. For details of other canons
reserving a right of appeal to the apostolic see, see H. E. J. Cowdrey, 'The enigma of
Archbishop Lanfranc', *Haskins Society Journal*, 6 (1994), 129–52 at 145 n. 79 (I am grateful

rights were asserted over clerics and the church was also inflicted on laymen, as Eadmer had hinted.[60] This was what *corona* meant, and why Eadmer considered it was created by the Conquest.

An irony — very possibly a deliberate irony — [61] which emerges from juxtaposing the *De Iniusta Vexacione* with the *Historia Novorum* is that William of St Calais, presented as the nimble-witted victim in 1088, was Anselm's chief prosecutor at Rockingham in 1095. He accused Anselm of trying to take from Rufus, contrary to his *fides*, 'what your lord and ours held of chief importance [*praecipuum*] in all his lordship [*dominatio*], and in which he certainly excelled all other kings . . .'[62] — in other words, his *corona*.[63] So the author of *Quadripartitus* was not simply gushing sycophantically when he defined the 'unique majesty' of the king's lordship over his kingdom in similar terms.[64] He was also the author of the *Leges Henrici Primi*,[65] and therefore knew a thing or two about the king's power. But William of St Calais was probably even better qualified to comment on the uniqueness of Norman kings in England: not only had William in 1088 been in a position in many ways analogous to that in which Anselm found himself in 1095; it has also recently been shown that the 'very difficult affairs' in which William had revealed his *industria* in William the Conqueror's service[66] probably included the compilation of Domesday Book, for he has been convincingly identified as 'the man behind the Survey'.[67] Domesday Book can be used to confirm that William of St Calais, or Eadmer, was right; that the meaning of what the king held *praecipuum* in all his lordship, or his *corona*, was originally unique. As a metonym for royal powers over tenure derived from the Conquest

---

to John Cowdrey for supplying me with a copy of his essay in advance of publication). On William's memory, see Symeon of Durham, *Opera Omnia*, ed. T. Arnold (2 vols, London, 1882–5), i 120.

[60] *Historia Novorum*, p. 10.

[61] For some striking parallels between the *DIV* and the *Historia Novorum*, see Offler, 'Tractate', 328 n. 2, 340 and n. 2.

[62] *Historia Novorum*, pp. 60–1.

[63] *Historia Novorum*, pp. 53, 54, 58, discussed above, pp. 174–6.

[64] *Quadripartitus*, II, *praefatio*, 1–2, edited in *Gesetze*, i 542; for a translation, see R. Sharpe, 'The prefaces of *Quadripartitus*', in Garnett and Hudson, *Law and Government*, pp. 148–72 at 169.

[65] See Downer, *LHP*, pp. 12–28, and P. Wormald, '*Quadripartitus*', in *Law and Government*, pp. 111–47 at 135–9.

[66] *DIV*, ed. Offler, p. 26; *English Lawsuits*, i p. 91; cf. Florence of Worcester, *Chronicon ex Chronicis*, ed. B. Thorpe (2 vols, London, 1848–9), ii 22 for his role early in Rufus's reign: 'eiusque consiliis totius Anglie tractabatur respublica'.

[67] P. Chaplais, 'William of St Calais and the Domesday Survey', in J. C. Holt, ed., *Domesday Studies* (Woodbridge, 1987), pp. 65–77. The epithet was coined by V. H. Galbraith, *Domesday Book: Its Place in Administrative History* (Oxford, 1974), p. 50.

it will already be apparent that this incorporeal *corona* bears almost no relation to that more familiar abstraction, 'The Crown'.

It is a fundamental, and often observed, characteristic of Domesday Book that its layout demonstrates that the king is the ultimate source of all tenure. He is so because he is presented as the successor to his *antecessor*, Edward the Confessor;[68] the kingdom, the whole land, is his.[69] As Maitland put it, 'the king's land is the king's land and there is no more to be said about it.'[70] If the kingdom is his, the *terra regis* within it may be negatively defined as what William the Conqueror had not granted to his tenants-in-chief to be held of him.[71] Entries describing land which the king has *in dominio*[72] or *dominica terra regis*[73] may either, as in the former cases, be simply a synonym for *terra regis* thus defined, or, as in the latter case, may refer to the manorial demesne of a king's manor — that part of the manor not occupied by peasant tenants, but exploited directly by the king's agents.[74] Use of the term *in dominio* in either sense does not, therefore,

---

[68] Just as Domesday Book does not state explicitly that the king is the source of all tenure, so it never states explicitly that Edward is William's *antecessor*, although reference is made to Edward's *antecessores* as king: *DB*, i 137c, 142a. Both assumptions are connected, and are intrinsic to the framework of the survey. For writs referring to Edward as the Conqueror's *antecessor* or *praedecessor*, see *RRAN*, i nos. 22, 26, 53.

[69] *LHP*, 10. 1, Downer, p. 108: 'Hec sunt iura que rex Anglie solus et super omnes homines habet in terra sua . . .'; cf. *RRAN*, ii no. 531 (1101) which required the taking of an oath to Henry I 'terram meam Anglie ad tenendam & ad defendendam'; edited by W. H. Stevenson, 'An inedited charter of King Henry I, June-July 1101', *EHR*, 21 (1906), 505–9.

[70] Pollock and Maitland, i 520.

[71] The boroughs require some qualification of this simple distinction, although they show no consistent pattern. Thus the city of Hereford is held by the king 'in dominio', but is outside the Herefordshire *terra regis* (*DB*, i 179a), whereas Bath is within the *terra regis* in Somerset (*DB*, i 87b): B. P. Wolffe, *The Royal Demesne in English History: The Crown Estate in the Governance of the Realm from the Conquest to 1509* (London, 1971), p. 19. It has been suggested that the information on boroughs was derived from sources other than, and probably earlier than, the survey: S. P. J. Harvey, 'Domesday Book and Anglo-Norman governance', *TRHS*, 5th ser. 25 (1975), 175–93 at 178. There are no questions about boroughs or towns in the terms of reference preserved in the *Inquisitio Eliensis: Inquisitio Comitatus Cantabrigiensis subjicitur Eliensis*, ed. N. E. S. A. Hamilton (London, 1886), p. 97.

[72] *DB*, i 16a, 30a–d, 38a–d, 56d–57a, etc.

[73] *DB*, i 57d.

[74] That Domesday uses the phrase *in dominio* or the like in these two quite different senses is established by R. S. Hoyt, *The Royal Demesne in English Constitutional History, 1066–1272* (Cornell, 1950), pp. 27–9. He shows that it was the manorial demesne which was regularly exempt from geld, like the manorial demesne of tenants-in-chief. On the generally low level of demesne agriculture in the *terra regis*, see S. P. J. Harvey, 'Domesday England', in H. E. Hallam, ed., *The Agrarian History of England and Wales*, vol. ii (1042–1350), (Cambridge, 1988), pp. 88–91.

complicate the distinction between *terra regis* and tenures dependent on the king; and it does not justify drawing distinctions between different categories of *terra regis* on anything other than a tenurial basis.

Indeed, 'the man behind the Survey' seems to have felt ill at ease with the categorisation of royal land in terms of anything other than its tenurial history. Thus the mysterious heading 'Dominicatus regis ad regnum pertinens in Devenescira' in Exon Domesday[75] was excised when the provincial draft was rearranged in the process of compiling Great Domesday. The lands included in this category in Exon are recorded as having been held by King Edward — or by a tenant 'under' him — TRE.[76] Although the main scribe of Great Domesday kept them together as a discrete section within the *terra regis*, he rearranged them[77] and labelled them differently: 'Haec XIX maneria fuerunt in dominio regis Edwardi et pertinent ad regem.'[78] In other words the scribe decided to categorise them explicitly in terms of the *antecessor*, rather than attributing them 'ad regnum'. Exon Domesday's second category of *terra regis* in Devon, grouped under the heading 'Dominicatus regis in Devenesira',[79] and comprising lands held TRE almost exclusively by members of the Godwine family, is rearranged by the Great Domesday scribe, and subdivided and labelled in terms of the individual *antecessores*. The final Exon category, 'Terra Mahillis reginae in Devenesira',[80] was also rearranged and preserved by the Great Domesday scribe, but again he felt it necessary to specify in his heading who had been the *antecessor*.[81] Unlike Exon, in Great Domesday the newly labelled antecessorial categories are brought under the overall heading 'Terra regis'.[82] Although the details differ, the general pattern is repeated in several of the other counties covered by Exon

[75] *DB*, iv 83a.

[76] *DB*, iv 83a–88a; *DB*, i 100b–c. The one exception is the city of Exeter, which comes under this heading in Exon, but which precedes the list of landholders and the *terra regis* in Great Domesday: *DB*, i 100a.

[77] For details, see the Phillimore edn: *Domesday Book*, vol. ix, *Devon*, ed. C. and F. Thorn (2 vols, Chichester, 1985), i. general notes, ch. 1. It has been shown that Great Domesday is probably the work of one main scribe and a corrector: M. Gullick and C. Thorn, 'The scribes of Great Domesday Book: a preliminary account', *Journal of the Society of Archivists*, 8 (1986), 78–80.

[78] *DB*, i 100c; the contraction could stand for 'pertinuerunt' rather than 'pertinent'.

[79] *DB*, iv 93a.

[80] *DB*, iv 108a.

[81] *DB*, i 101b.

[82] *DB*, i 100b.

Domesday: categories within what Great Domesday termed *terra regis* were relabelled by reference to *antecessores*.[83]

Whatever the Exon scribes may have meant by distinguishing between *dominicatus regis ad regnum pertinens* and *dominicatus regis*,[84] it is clear that the Great Domesday scribe felt uncomfortable with such distinctions. Had he had the chance to revise that other provincial draft, covering the East Anglian shires and now known as Little Domesday, doubtless he would also have excised its few references to 'Terrae regis de regno' and the like.[85] In the same way the categorisation of royal manors as *de regione* in Little Domesday[86] or *de comitatu* in Exon[87] — which are probably equivalents, meaning lands traditionally assigned to the local earl — would be of no interest to whoever devised the final format of Great Domesday.[88] Thus the heading *mansiones de comitatu* does not survive in Great Domesday for Somerset. At these lingering traces of Anglo-Saxon distinctions between different categories of royal land[89] 'the man behind the Survey' snapped his mind

[83] For instance, the category labelled 'Dominicatus regis in Dorseta' in Exon — *DB*, iv 25a — is subdivided into lands which Edward had held (not distinguished by a specific heading) — *DB*, i 75a — and manors which Earl Harold had held TRE — *DB*, i 75b; for further discussion, R. W. Finn, *Domesday Studies: The Liber Exoniensis* (London, 1964), pp. 137–9. The appended list of the contents of about half the surviving sections of Exon, in a quite different order from that in which they are found in the manuscript, begins with 'Dominicatus Regis', with a half-formed letter 'S' between the two words: *DB*, iv 532a. A. R. Rumble, 'The palaeography of the Domesday manuscripts', in P. H. Sawyer ed., *Domesday Book: A Reassessment* (London, 1985), pp. 28–49 at 31, suggests that the scribe had originally intended to write 'Suus', but changed his mind and failed to delete the error.

[84] Some of the scribes who wrote entries for the *terra regis*, though not whoever wrote these two headings, are identified by T. Webber, 'Salisbury and the Exon Domesday: some observations concerning the origin of Exeter Cathedral MS 3500', *English Manuscript Studies*, 1 (1989), 1–18 at 12–13.

[85] *DB*, ii 289b, 119b.

[86] *DB*, ii 144a, 281b, 408b; cf. *DB*, i 298b.

[87] *DB*, iv 106b.

[88] Hoyt, *Royal Demesne*, p. 17. As V. H. Galbraith points out in his review of Hoyt, *EHR*, 67 (1952), 259–63 at 262 n. 1, Round's argument, *Feudal England*, p. 140, to the effect that *regio* in Little Domesday is a scribal blunder for *regno* may be rejected because each of five entries seems to be in the hand of a different scribe, and because in two of the entries (281b, 408b) the manor of Thorney is referred to consistently as *de regione*. For a breakdown of hands in Little Domesday, see A. R. Rumble, 'The Domesday manuscripts: scribes and scriptoria', in *Domesday Studies*, pp. 79–99 at 98–9. He appears to differ from Galbraith about the number of scribes involved in these entries, identifying three, but he agrees that the two Thorney entries are in different hands. Maitland, *Domesday Book and Beyond*, p. 167 n. 2, did not pursue his suggestion that *regio* meant kingship, as opposed to kingdom (*regnum*).

[89] A detailed examination of Alfred's will and Anglo-Saxon charters would begin to shade in the different ways in which an Anglo-Saxon king might exploit his estates, and demonstrate that reference to 'royal demesne' in the Anglo-Saxon period is a crude oversimplification. But such a study must be deferred until another occasion. In any case the present argument seeks to establish that the subtleties of Anglo-Saxon royal tenure are almost entirely irrelevant to 'The Crown'.

sharply shut. They were irrelevant to his purpose. Indeed, the form in which he attempted to establish continuity with the Anglo-Saxon past rendered such distinctions meaningless. That form, intrinsic to the framework of the survey, was the *antecessor*.

There may turn out to be some truth in Maitland's carefully hedged hunch that, in the Anglo-Saxon period, it would be on the death of a king that the necessity would first arise of drawing some distinction between what belonged to the king as king and 'what belonged to him — if we may use so modern a phrase — in his private capacity'.[90] But from the vantage point of 1086 such a view with regard to the death of Edward the Confessor would be erroneous in a twofold sense. First, there was no indication that such a distinction had been drawn on or after the 'day on which King Edward was alive and dead'.[91] Far from Edward's estates being divided, they must have undergone massive accretion as lands Harold already held — many of them comital manors — were added to them; there is no indication that Edgar aetheling had been given, either by Edward or Harold, any of the estates which had been used for the maintenance of aethelings in the tenth century.[92] Second, the lands which Harold, members of his family, and many other tenants had held prior to Edward's death were consolidated into Domesday's *terra regis*. There is no indication that these manors constituted a category or categories of *terra regis* in which the Conqueror enjoyed rights different from those he had in the lands the Confessor had held, simply *because* someone other than the king was recorded as having held them TRE. For instance, as Hoyt established, there is no strict congruence between (partial or total) geld exemption for certain royal manors and the manors Edward had held, although a majority of exempt royal lands are recorded as having been Edward's.[93] In Great Domesday even the grouping of royal estates

---

[90] *Domesday Book and Beyond*, p. 253.

[91] For the formula, see V. H. Galbraith, *The Making of Domesday Book* (Oxford, 1961), p. 109; Galbraith, *Domesday Book in Administrative History*, p. 69. The fact that lands are recorded as having been held by Queen Edith TRE means that she was thought to have held them in some way distinct from her husband *prior* to his death.

[92] S no. 937 (990–1006, probably 999). In view of its chronological framework, Domesday Book cannot prove that Edgar aetheling held no land under Harold. But it does show that he had held none by the time of Edward's death, and it seems unlikely that Harold remedied the omission. For Edgar's two manors in 1086, one of which was held of him, see *DB*, i 142a. There is no indication that either had ever been a royal estate of any description.

[93] Hoyt, *Royal Demesne*, pp. 18–21, esp. 19–20 nn. 30–32. Hoyt concedes, pp. 21–3, that the manors which Domesday records as owing the special payment of 'the farm of one [or more, or a fraction thereof] night[s or days]' come closest to justifying a theory of 'ancient demesne'. But there are examples of manors of this type which were no longer in King William's hands in 1086: Eastbourne, Beddingham (*DB*, i 20c); Beeding (*DB*, i 28a), etc. Conversely, where this custom applied to manors within the *terra regis* in 1086, they are not invariably said to

in terms of *antecessores* is scarcely found outside the south-western counties.[94] The king may have enjoyed different customs in his different estates, but the effect of the Conquest was to homogenize them all within the one overarching category.

The reason is simple. Although many different TRE tenants were identified for individual manors within the *terra regis* in 1086, and the king therefore appeared to have many *antecessores*, in fact the notion of the *antecessor* was modelled on the king's claim to be the legitimate, direct successor of Edward the Confessor.[95] In a crucial sense the king's own claim to the kingdom provided the template for determining the rights of every Domesday tenant. But each Domesday tenant succeeded his Edwardian *antecessor(es)* by force, either direct or mediated, of a royal grant or grants: this is rarely articulated, yet is implicit in the layout of Domesday Book. Indeed, the very concept of the *antecessor* — the person who was established to have held the land on the day of Edward the Confessor's death[96] — read back into the Anglo-Saxon past a strict tenurial dependency which was quite foreign to it. For there is no hint in Anglo-Saxon history that legitimate rights to land were to be defined by reference to the legitimate tenure of the throne, or that all land was held immediately or mediately of the king. So in their attempt to establish continuity with the Anglo-

have been held by King Edward: Brightlingsea (*DB*, ii 6a) is recorded as having been Harold's TRE, as are Writtle (*DB*, ii 5b), Lawford (*DB*, ii 6a) and Newport (*DB*, ii 7a); moreover, Great Baddow, which had been Earl Ælfgar's TRE, was held by St-Etienne, Caen in 1086 (*DB*, ii 21b). Because no *terra regis* is recorded as having been held by Edward, Round suggested, *VCH, Essex*, i 336, that manors were attributed to Harold which he had acquired only on becoming king. But this assumes that the explicit statements to the contrary are simply wrong; and it also ignores the parallel example of Great Baddow, held by Harold's successor as earl of East Anglia (Harold having ceased to be earl in 1053). Perhaps confusion arose because the nature of Harold's (and Ælfgar's) tenure of these manors puzzled the commissioners; as Round points out, one hide at Writtle held in 1086 by the bishop of Hereford is entered twice: in the *terra regis* as having been 'in feudo regis' TRE (*DB*, i 5b), and in the *terra episcopi Herefordensis* as having been in 'feudo haroldi' (*DB*, i 26a). For the complexities and regional variations of the system as it applied to many — but by no means all — of Edward the Confessor's Domesday manors, see P. A. Stafford, 'The "Farm of One Night" and the organization of King Edward's estates in Domesday', *Economic History Review*, 2nd ser. 33 (1980), 491–502; for more general discussion, R. V. Lennard, *Rural England: 1066–1135* (Oxford, 1959), pp. 128–30. Hoyt demonstrates that there is no correlation between liability to render such a farm and geld exemption.
[94] Finn, *Liber Exoniensis*, p. 138.
[95] G. S. Garnett, 'Coronation and propaganda: some implications of the Norman claim to the throne of England in 1066', *TRHS*, 5th ser. 36 (1986), 91–116 at 105–7.
[96] This precision is not recognized by R. Fleming, *Kings and Lords in Conquest England* (Cambridge, 1991), p. 110 n. 8, in her only attempt to define the term. What 'held' meant in any specific context was often open to dispute and misunderstanding. With overlapping Anglo-Saxon rights of tenure, commendation, and soke it is a wonder that Domesday does not record more unresolved *clamores* and *invasiones*.

Saxon past, the Domesday commissioners unwittingly showed how all continuity had been severed. And the fact that *antecessores* other than King Edward are identified for King William in many of the manors subsumed within the *terra regis* does not derogate from Edward's role as William's *antecessor* in the whole kingdom; each of those lesser *antecessores* was such, by definition, in relation to Edward. The difference between the king and other Domesday tenants lay in the fact that William had not succeeded to these *antecessores* by royal grant; on the contrary, it was because he had not granted out these manors that someone else had not become *successor*. Many manors which had been King Edward's were held of the king by 1086. Thus does Domesday underline the nature of the distinction between the *terra regis* and the rest of the kingdom, and the king's role as the source of all tenure. Drawing a distinction in the Anglo-Saxon period between what belonged to the king as king and what belonged to him 'in his private capacity' left Maitland feeling uncomfortably anachronistic; Domesday Book shows that the effect of the Conquest was to render it nonsensical, indeed inconceivable. If William of St Calais was 'the man behind the Survey', he knew this better than anyone.

Domesday Book therefore corroborates much of Eadmer's analysis of post-Conquest kingship, and illustrates one of the few features of the new system which Eadmer did not perceive: that the rights of every tenant were defined by terms of reference modelled on the king's own. If, unlike 'the man behind the Survey', he failed to see this, he did appreciate its crucial corollary: that the king, as the source of all tenure, differed from other tenants in the sense that he was the only lord who was not a tenant; he was the only lord whose *dominium* was not in turn part of his own lord's subinfeudated land, for he had no lord. It was this unarticulated distinction between the *dominus rex* — a neologism where England was concerned, adopted by Eadmer[97] — and

---

[97] *Historia Novorum*, pp. 35, 48, 54, 55, 56, 57, 58, 66, 70, etc.; *Vita Anselmi*, p. 130. The term is more appropriately used by someone for whom the king was *dominus*, rather than by the king of himself: *RRAN*, i no. 101 (= Bates, *Regesta*, no. 71), a writ of Odo of Bayeux (1070–82/3); Bates, *Regesta*, no. 74, a writ of Odo of Bayeux (1070–82/3); *RRAN*, i no. 173 (= Bates, *Regesta*, no. 282), a grant by Herbert, son of Geoffrey, to the abbey of Troarn, confirmed by the king (1079–82); Bates, *Regesta*, no. 246, a grant to St.-Ouen of Rouen by Ingelrann fitz Ilbert, confirmed by the king (1080); *RRAN*, i no. 192 (= Bates, *Regesta*, no. 101), grant of St Pancras, Lewes to Cluny by William de Warenne and his wife, attested by the king (1078–80/1); etc, etc. It is noticeable that all these *acta* are either recording grants to Norman donees, or (as in the case of *RRAN*, i. no. 192) are written in the style of a continental diploma, or are issued by Odo of Bayeux. *Dominus dux/comes/princeps* was

every other *dominus* that Eadmer attempted to encapsulate in his definition of *corona* or royal dignity. While Domesday shows why the king's position as lord was necessarily anomalous,[98] it also reveals why it was so difficult to conceive of the rights arising from this position in terms of an abstraction. For what Domesday Book describes is a society consisting in personal — and therefore in this context tenurial — bonds between individuals. As I have tried to show, the king was the nexus of all those bonds and his right to succeed Edward the Confessor provided the template for what might be termed that society's legal framework. It is very difficult indeed to make the mental leap from viewing the king's rights as inseparable from his person, to characterizing them as in some sense distinct from him — hence Great Domesday's redefinition of Exon Domesday's *dominicatus regis ad regnum pertinens* as belonging *ad regem*.[99] Paradoxically, Eadmer was forced into doing so by the king's anomalous position as lord. He was doomed to failure, but the reasons for his failure are illuminating.

In the *De Iniusta Vexacione* William of St Calais is shown to have been adept at wielding the canon law of *exceptio spolii*, whereby a cleric — usually a bishop — had to be in control of, or, if already dispossessed, restored to his church and its appurtenances before he could be tried. Indeed it could be said that the whole hearing turns on this issue.[100] Time and again he confounds the king's advisers — including Lanfranc, who was no mean lawyer himself — by demanding the restoration of his lands, money, and vassals,[101] otherwise termed his *episcopatus*[102] or *episcopium*,[103] of which he had been 'disseised

---

a term in Norman diplomatic before 1066: Fauroux, *Recueil*, nos. 107 (1046–7 or 1048); 135 (1037–55); 167 (1035–66); 169 (1035–66); 191 (1050–66); 211 (1055–66); 223 (1063–6); 225 (1063–6). It usually appears in documents recording grants by others which the duke confirms. The term is not found in genuine Anglo-Saxon royal charters. I am grateful to David Bates for help with this note.

[98] This is a major theme of my *Royal Succession in England: 1066–1154*, Ph.D. thesis (Cambridge, 1987), ch. 2.

[99] See above, pp. 185–6.

[100] Offler, 'Tractate', 332–3; Philpott, '*De Iniusta Vexacione*', pp. 131–2, 134; Philpott, *Archbishop Lanfranc and Canon Law*, pp. 169–71; Cowdrey, 'Enigma', 143–5, 148–51.

[101] *DIV*, ed. Offler, pp. 27, 29; *English Lawsuits*, i pp. 9, 92. Interestingly, the term 'investiture' is used as a synonym for restoring or reseising the bishop with his *episcopatus*: *DIV*, ed. Offler, pp. 37, 38, 39; *English Lawsuits*, i pp. 97, 98. It is clearly not being used in its technical, canonical sense, which is surprising in a work which shows such sensitivity to Canon Law. Given that the distinction between clerical homage and lay investiture was clarified by the settlement of the investiture contest in England, this usage is another indication that the *DIV* is early in date.

[102] *DIV*, ed. Offler, pp. 35, 36, 37, 38, 39; *English Lawsuits*, i pp. 96, 97, 98; for the equation, see above, p. 178.

[103] *DIV*, ed. Offler, p. 40; *English Lawsuits*, i p. 99.

unjustly'[104] and 'without judgement'.[105] Canons affirming this rule are marked for ease of reference in the manuscript of Lanfranc's version of the Pseudo-Isidorian decretals which William of St Calais almost certainly used at the hearing.[106] At Rockingham the poacher of 1088 found it very easy to turn gamekeeper: Eadmer reports that he told Anselm that he, Anselm, would have to restore to the king the *debita imperii sui dignitas* of which he had deprived Rufus[107] — what Eadmer elsewhere terms his *corona*[108] — before the adjournment in proceedings which Anselm sought could be granted. Eadmer thought William of St Calais had twisted the concept of *exceptio spolii* and applied it to the king, with the accused archbishop in the role of despoiler. Whereas the *res litigiosa* in 1088 had been William's *episcopatus*, that in 1095 was Rufus's *corona* or *dignitas*. What for Eadmer had been an incorporeal metonym for the king's rights derived from the Conquest, had begun to shade into an abstraction which was in some sense distinguishable from the king, for it could be taken away from him (not unlike a bishop's *episcopatus*). It might therefore be concluded that Eadmer's *corona* or 'royal dignity' was an adaptation of a canonical concept, developed on the basis of an analogy between the position of a bishop and that of a king. Drawing this analogy would be facilitated by the fact that the original model for the Domesday *antecessor* was the canonical *antecessor* — a previous holder of ecclesiastical office — and that Lanfranc, working from his Pseudo-Isidorian collection, is probably the author of the concept.[109] But such a conclusion would be erroneous, or at least it would demonstrate a revealing double-think on Eadmer's part.

For there was a sophisticated body of Canon Law relating to clerical office which could not, by definition, be applied to the king in post-Conquest England. He held no office, with rights and duties defined and delimited by a body of written — or any other form of — law. A successful claimant was not appointed to the equivalent of an *episopatus* or *abbatia*. *Regnum* was not analogous to them, for in this period it lacked their particular ambiguity; while it had meanings other than the territorial entity — for instance, in regnal dates — it did not signify

---

[104] *DIV*, ed. Offler, p. 27; *English Lawsuits*, i p. 91.

[105] *DIV*, ed. Offler, p. 35; *English Lawsuits*, i p. 96.

[106] Above, p. 182. Philpott, *Archbishop Lanfranc and Canon Law*, p. 163; '*De Iniusta Vexacione*', p. 131, identifies Peterhouse MS 74, fo. 45v, ch. viii (Hinschius, p. 486, ch. ix); fo. 46, ch. xviii (Hinschius, p. 489, ch. xiv) as marked in this way. For other passages, see Cowdrey, 'Enigma', 144 n. 76.

[107] *Historia Novorum*, p. 60.

[108] *Historia Novorum*, pp. 53, 54, 58.

[109] Garnett, 'Coronation and propaganda', 106–9.

an office. The claimant became king when he was anointed as such
and received his crown. As Maitland might put it, there was no more
to be said. This inapplicability of Canon Law models may be demonstrated in two ways, from the records of royal government rather than
canonical compilations.

First, a grant to a church was made sometimes to God and the saint
to whom the church was dedicated, sometimes to the saint alone,
sometimes to the church, sometimes to the abbot and monks or bishop
and canons or other cleric(s), and to any combination of these.[110] A
gift made to God and a saint, or to the saint alone, was by definition
made to an undying recipient. Maitland detected a tendency for the
saint gradually to retire 'behind his churches; the church rather than
the saint is thought of as the holder of the lands and chattels.'[111] In the
process the saint's immortal personality rubbed off on the church: it
became the undying subject of the tenurial rights which had been
conferred upon it, or, in Maitland's rather Germanic phrase, 'an ideal,
juristic person.' Little Domesday in particular is packed with entries
recording the landed endowments of parish churches.[112] They might be
located in manors held by tenants, and in some instances the priest is
recorded as holding the church of the tenant of the manor,[113] but the
lands were appurtenances specifically of the churches. They were said
to 'lie in the church', however far they might be physically from the
building.[114] Indeed, it was an exception deserving of special note when
a church did not have lands attached to it.[115] The interchangeability
between church and saint is illustrated by those cases in which churches
other than parish ones are recorded as dependent tenants holding
manors, but Domesday's rubrics attribute tenancy to the saint,[116] and
vice versa.[117] The land might be described as that of the saint, but the
church held it of the king; or the land was the church's, held by
the saint.[118] In the cases of abbeys, bishoprics and some secular min-

---

[110] Pollock and Maitland, i 243–4, 499–501; F. W. Maitland, 'Frankalmoign in the twelfth and
thirteenth centuries', *Collected Papers*, ii 205–22 at 210.

[111] Pollock and Maitland, i 500.

[112] To take a few random examples from Suffolk: *DB*, ii 281b (Thorney, Bramford); 282a
(Blythburgh); 298b (Framsden); 303a (Ousden); 304a (Edwardstone); 330b (Kelsale); 331a
(Denham).

[113] *DB*, i 60b.

[114] For example, *DB*, i 91c, 210d, both cited by Pollock and Maitland, i 499 n. 4.

[115] *DB*, ii 286b (Cornard); 355a (Worlington); 382a (Undley), and the other examples cited
by Lennard, *Rural England*, p. 306 n. 4.

[116] *DB*, i 165d (St Mary's, Evesham); 166a (St Mary's, Abingdon; St Mary's, Pershore).

[117] *DB*, i 165b (Lands of church of Bath; Lands of church of Glastonbury; Lands of church
of Malmesbury).

[118] *DB*, i 104b; 165b, both examples cited by Pollock and Maitland, i 500–1.

sters the sempiternal nature of the church did not arise simply from its personification in a saint: it was a corporational structure, defined in Canon Law. A church of this type remained the same even though the abbot and monks, or bishop and monks or canons, changed. There was, therefore, an articulated specificity about how the continuous life of such a church manifested itself, unlike the unalloyed mysticism of the parish church's saint. The Normans were already used to making perpetual grants to such churches by the time of the Conquest, long before the development of a fully-fledged formula of perpetual alms.[119] A grant in perpetuity could only be made to a perpetual recipient.

Traces of legal precision in the corporate structure of such churches have been left in Domesday Book, where the lands of a bishop or abbot are sometimes distinguished from those of the canons or monks.[120] The division of revenues occasionally manifests itself in recorded tenurial distinctions: the canons of Chichester are said to hold sixteen hides 'communiter' within the land of the bishop of Chichester.[121] The canons of St Paul's appear to be treated as a (collective) tenant-in-chief, distinct from the bishop of London; and the lands they held are some-

---

[119] For the significance of grants *in perpetua hereditate* and *in perpetuam hereditatem* to churches in Normandy before 1066, see J. C. Holt, 'Feudal society and the family in early medieval England. II. Notions of patrimony', *TRHS*, 5th ser. 33 (1983), 193–220 at 199–204; for examples, see Fauroux, *Recueil*, nos. 43 (1015–26), 71 (1034), 83 (1030–5), 84 (1030–5), 93 (1035–c. 1040), 101 (1043), 123 (1051), 201 (1051–66), 202 (1051–66), 233 (1066). On alms and alms tenure in Normandy, see J. Yver, 'Une boutade de Guillaume le Conquérant. Note sur le genèse de la tenure en aumône', *Etudes d'histoire du droit canonique dédiées à Gabriel Le Bras* (2 vols, Paris, 1965), i 783–96; E. Z. Tabuteau, *Transfers of Property in Eleventh-Century Norman Law* (Chapel Hill, N.C., 1988), pp. 36–41. On the reasons for the replacement of the language of inheritance, which was becoming lay, with that of alms, see J. G. H. Hudson, *Land, Law, and Lordship in Anglo-Norman England* (Oxford, 1994), pp. 90–1.

[120] In Kent the lands of the church of Canterbury are divided into three sections: 'Terra Archiepiscopi Cantuariensis' (*DB*, i 3a–4a); 'Terra Militum Ejus' (4b–c); 'Terra Monachorum Archiepiscopi' (4d–5b). But each entry for the manors in the third section begins 'Ipse Archiepiscopus tenuit . . .', showing that manors which were in some respect specifically devoted to the maintenance of the monks were still formally held by the archbishop of the king. (Sandwich is the one apparent exception to this, being said to belong 'ad dominium monachorum' (5b); but it is also entered in the first section where it is said to be for 'the clothing of the monks' (3a); cf. *Domesday Monachorum*, p. 89). The division of revenues is shown to be pre-Conquest by B. W. Kissan, 'Lanfranc's alleged division of lands between archbishop and community', *EHR*, 54 (1939), 285–93. There is a parallel in the nine manors devoted to the sustenance of the monks of Sherborne, one of which is said to be held by the monks, and the other eight by the bishop of Salisbury, within whose land they are all listed: *DB*, i 77a–b. For a manor which had been part of the 'dominica firma monachorum' within the land of [the abbey of] St Peter, Cerne Abbas, *DB*, i 78a; for several examples within the manors listed under the rubric 'Terra Abbatie de Elyg', *DB*, i. 191b. For further Domesday and other evidence, see Hudson, *Land, Law, and Lordship*, p. 235; M. Howell, 'Abbatial vacancies and the divided *mensa* in medieval England', *Journal of Ecclesiastical History*, 33 (1982), 173–92 at 173–7.

[121] *DB*, i 17a.

times said to have been given to St Paul or to 'lie in St Paul's church'.[122] Most of the lands of the church of Hereford, including those held variously by the bishop, the canons, the nuns, and some constituent churches, are detailed under the sub-rubric: 'Hae terrae subter scriptae pertinent ad canonicos de Hereford'.[123] But as even these exceptional examples indicate, in the case of episcopal and abbatial churches Domesday Book tended to identify a cleric or clerics of the church as tenant just where the church's corporate status was easiest to define, and where, therefore, one might more readily conceive of the church, rather than its cleric (or clerics), as the holder of its land and chattels.

This is only a tendency, with many exceptions where the *ecclesia* or saint is recorded as holding.[124] But the point may be highlighted by the infrequency of two other terms. On those few occasions where *episcopatus* appears in Domesday as a subject of tenurial rights, it is usually mentioned in passing, in the middle of the entry.[125] A rubric of the type 'Terra Episcopi Tedfordensis ad epipscopatum pertinens TRE', found in the provincial draft which is Little Domesday,[126] is even rarer than one attributing the king's lands 'ad regnum' or 'ad regionem'.[127] Appearances of *abbatia* in anything like this sense are almost non-existent.[128] The reason for Domesday's tendency in the cases of bishoprics and abbeys to attribute tenurial rights to the clerics, rather than to the church, is that the bishops and many abbots held directly of the king. To attribute tenure in these cases to the church, or *episcopatus*, or *abbatia*, or even to the saint, was to cut against the grain of Domesday Book. Such a church's status as an abstract subject of tenurial rights fitted ill with the precarious tenurial dependence of

---

[122] *DB*, i 34a, 136b, 211a; ii 12b; *Early Charters of the Cathedral Church of St Paul, London*, ed. M. Gibbs (Camden Third Series, 58, 1939), pp. xviii n. 2, xxii–xxiii; cf. *DB*, i 127b–128b, 'Terra Episcopi Lundoniensis', which rubric includes manors held collectively by the canons, and by individual canons holding of the canons as a collectivity.

[123] *DB*, i 181c.

[124] See the entry for the bishopric of Worcester in the Gloucestershire survey, where 'Æcclesia de Wirecestre' and 'Sancta Maria de Wirecestre' are recorded as holding, but note that subtenants hold of the bishop, not of the church or saint: *DB*, i 164b–165a; cf. *DB*, i 103c–d for the 'Æcclesia de Tavestoch' holding, but the tenants holding of the abbot. Both examples cited by Pollock and Maitland, i 501.

[125] For instance, *DB*, i 43a, 58b, 77a, 89b, 127b; ii 117b, 194a, 195a.

[126] *DB*, ii 191a.

[127] Above, pp. 185–6.

[128] *DB*, i 78b, 104a (both entries recording that a manor is *caput abbatiae*, and therefore only questionably using the term in this sense), 252a, 252c; ii 218b (*sedes abbatiae*, also questionable), 381b (for the *abbatia* being in the king's hand). In *Domesday Book*, ix, *Devon*, ii ch. 5.2, the editors point out that the contraction in one of the entries for Tavistock Abbey (cf. above, n. 109) may mean that the abbey, rather than the abbot, holds the manor of Milton. The fact that the contraction *abb'* may stand for either does not affect my point, because its appearance in Domesday is rare.

its bishop or abbot on what Eadmer termed the king's nod. It was precisely in the case of tenancy-in-chief that the structuring of post-Conquest society on the basis of personal — and therefore in this context tenurial — bonds between individuals was most evident. Indeed, it was the unresolved tension between the king's rights as lord within this structure and the existence of episcopal and abbatial churches as corporate entities which gave rise to Eadmer's incorporeal *corona*.

As Eadmer appreciated, this tension was most evident when the *dominus rex* resumed immediate lordship over an ecclesiastical barony, usually on the death of the ecclesiastical baron. But the escheat of a bishopric or abbey did not mean that it ceased to exist. The lands and chattels were administered on the king's behalf as a discrete entity, sometimes (but by no means always) by a member of the cathedral chapter or monk of the house: thus on William of St Calais' death a certain 'G. Dunelmensis' was charged with this task by Rufus.[129] Not only did the *episcopatus* or *abbatia* remain in being in its material aspect, although in the king's hand, it did so in its spiritual aspect too. The church did not cease to function because its lands had reverted; indeed revenues accruing from its spiritual functions would form an element in the receipts which the king, or those to whom he had sold his rights, now enjoyed. In some cases the amount of material support allowed by royal agents to the chapter or monks from the escheated lands became a cause of resentment;[130] but, whatever the amount, the king thereby recognized the continuing life of the church during a vacancy.[131] The existence of a church of this type as an abstract entity, and the discrete nature of its endowment in terms of lands, chattels, and men, was therefore acknowledged at the very point at which the royal lordship, decried by Eadmer as tyranny,[132] was at its most intense.

---

[129] T. A. M. Bishop and P. Chaplais, eds, *Facsimiles of English Royal Writs to A.D. 1100 presented to V. H. Galbraith* (Oxford, 1957), pl. x (1096–7); 'G.' has been plausibly identified with the monk Geoffrey, who seems to have been the bishop's administrative deputy: Offler, *DIV*, pp. 81–2. But custodians were by no means always members of the chapter or monks of the house: for examples of royal officials performing the role, see M. Howell, *Regalian Right in Medieval England* (London, 1962), p. 7. Rufus auctioned the custody of Canterbury to the highest bidder: Eadmer, *Historia Novorum*, pp. 26–7.

[130] The evidence is surveyed by Howell, *Regalian Right*, pp. 14–17.

[131] Bury St Edmunds, where royal custodians during an abbatial vacancy later had no claims over lands specifically assigned to the monks, seems to have been unique: see *Feudal Documents from the Abbey of Bury St Edmunds*, ed. D. C. Douglas (London, 1932), no. 35; Jocelin of Brakelond, *Cronica de Rebus Gestis Samsonis Abbatis Monasterii Sancti Edmundi*, ed. and trans. H. E. Butler (Edinburgh, 1949), pp. 8, 72–3, 81; discussed by Howell, 'Abbatial vacancies', 177–8.

[132] *Historia Novorum*, p. 61.

Where the dividing line lay between the spiritual functions of the church and the king's lordship was by no means clear; but the continuing existence of the church made it necessary to draw a dividing line somewhere.

The example of ecclesiastical vacancy leads me to the second way in which governmental records show that the canonical definitions at the back of Eadmer's mind were inapplicable to the case of the king. Henry I's first undertaking in his coronation charter was to 'make the church of God free', in the sense that he would not sell it or put it out to farm 'nec, mortuo archiepiscopo sive episcopo sive abbate, aliquid accipiam de dominio aecclesiae vel de hominibus eius donec successor in eam ingrediatur.'[133] In other words the draftsman of the charter recognized that the church had and continued to have *dominium* while it was in the king's hand following the death of the bishop or abbot. The church, not the dead bishop or abbot, also continued to have vassals, for the possessive adjective 'eius' can only refer to it; the king is, temporarily, their direct lord, but they remain the church's. The church, the undying subject of rights, is what the *successor* will enter into when the king accepts his homage, thereby seising him.

In this crucial respect the charter shows that escheat during an ecclesiastical vacancy differed from escheat on the death of a lay tenant-in-chief. For in the latter case the land was attributed to no abstract entity, but rather to the 'heir'. Henry undertook that an heir 'shall not redeem *his* land as he did in the time of my brother, but shall relieve it by a just and lawful relief.' 'Likewise' the vassals of his barons 'shall relieve *their* lands from *their* lords.'[134] A daughter left as 'heir' shall be given in marriage 'cum terra *sua*', only with the counsel of Henry's barons.[135] In each case the land is described as the 'heir's' prior to his (or her husband's) being seised with it. The draftsman thereby demonstrated both the extent to which the Normans were accustomed to heirs inheriting, and the fact that post-Conquest dependency sliced through such Norman conventions, for the heir's land could not be held by the heir (or the heir's husband) until the lord had decided to accede to the heir's claim, and had seised him (or her husband) with it. Henry's promise that the widow or the most suitable relative should be *custos* of the land and children of a dead tenant-in-

---

[133] *Cap.* 1.1; *Gesetze*, i 521–3: '. . . nor, on the death of an archbishop or bishop or abbot, will I take anything from the demesne of a church or from its men until a successor has entered into it.' I am grateful to Martin Brett for allowing me to use the typescript of his edition, which supersedes Liebermann's; his edition of this clause is in *Councils & Synods*, I, ii 652–5.
[134] *Cap.* 2, 2.1.
[135] *Cap.* 3.2; on which see Holt, 'Notions of patrimony', 218.

chief, and his order to his barons to treat the sons and daughters or the wives of their vassals 'likewise', may well have been another concession to those conventions, effectively recognizing in advance the claim(s) of the infant(s), and renouncing lordly control of land and heir.[136] But these clauses show that in the case of a (lay) heir there was nothing to correspond to the undying church into which a (clerical) successor entered. As Domesday Book also reveals, in the case of the church it was impossible to maintain a purely personal interpretation of lordship and tenure.

The charter reveals that, conceptually speaking, the king fell closer to the lay side of this divide. I have tried to show elsewhere that there is a partial analogy between the charter's precise delineation of the three day period of interregnum following Rufus's death and prior to Henry's coronation, and its treatment of escheat during an ecclesiastical vacancy.[137] But the analogy is only partial, in two linked respects. First, by definition the kingdom could not escheat to any lord, as the churches previously held by clerical tenants-in-chief did to the king (or, indeed, as the lands held by a lay baron did). There was, therefore, no way in which the draftsman could conceive of how the fines, pleas, and debts which had been owed to Rufus had not lapsed with his death, but had somehow bridged the gap and started to be due to Henry at his coronation. Nevertheless, this is how he presents them.[138] Second, the charter's opening clause demonstrates that in the king's case there could be nothing analogous to a church, or saint, or cathedral chapter, or convent of monks. It states: 'Sciatis me Dei misericordia et communi consilio baronum regni Angliae eiusdem regni regem coronatum esse.' (Note, by the way, the stress on crowning, echoed elsewhere in the charter, rather than anointing.[139]) The charter is full of references to Henry's *barones* and *homines*.[140] They are assumed to be *his* from the point at which he became king, before most of them could have done homage to him. It seems that homage, like fines, pleas, and debts, was understood to have been somehow carried over the interregnum. But the draftsman of the charter clearly did not feel that the barons, who, like a conventional honorial court, are presented as offering their 'common counsel' that Henry should be crowned, could be described as Henry's, for he was not yet king. Since a baron was a tenant-in-

---

[136] *Cap.* 4.1, 2; for this interpretation, see S. F. C. Milsom, 'The origin of prerogative wardship', in Garnett and Hudson, *Law and Government*, pp. 223–44 at 234–7.

[137] Garnett, 'Coronation and propaganda', 114–15. As should be clear from the above, I now think my use of the term royal office anachronistic.

[138] *Caps.* 9, 6.

[139] *Cap.* 1; for coronation, see also *cap.* 9.

[140] Address clause; *caps.* 2, 3, 4, 7, 8, 10; for the Conqueror's barons, *cap.* 13.

chief, a status which depended on a personal relationship with a king, they could not be described as Rufus's either, for Rufus was dead. Hence the nonsensical neologism *barones regni Angliae*. It was a nonsense because homage could only be owed to a person, not to an abstraction. If the draftsman had in mind a parallel with his attribution of vassals (*homines*) to churches during a vacancy, he was anxious to drop it at the earliest possible juncture. As soon as Henry has been crowned he started to term the barons 'mine'. The kingdom could not have barons in the same way that a church had vassals or *dominium*, because it was not a well-defined abstract entity. As a figment to stop a gap,[141] the draftsman's *regnum* left a lot to be desired. It could not act as a bearer of rights previously exercised by Rufus, in the interim before Henry acceded to it and began to exercise them anew.

Moreover, the seemingly closer parallel with lay escheat turns out to be largely illusory. There was, for instance, no parallel between Henry and a lay heir attempting to recover land described as 'his' from a lord who (in the case of an aspiring subtenant, but apparently not in that of an aspiring tenant-in-chief) might also be described as 'his'. This was because the king was the only lord who was not a tenant, holding of a lord. Seigneurial conventions of escheat therefore could not fit the case of an interregnum: it remained an inexplicable void, when the king's rights were in temporary abeyance, and when the king's peace had ceased to exist.[142] The king was the necessary contradiction of the terms of the system which depended upon him.

Henry I's coronation charter, like Domesday Book, therefore shows why Eadmer's *corona* was not evidence of some precocious notion of the king's two bodies — that 'marvellous . . . display of metaphysical — or we might say metaphysiological — nonsense'.[143] Indeed, insofar as Eadmer's notion is an abstract one, the main focus of his book demonstrates that he would have seen his *corona* as the virtual antithesis of the undying royal dignity, which is what is usually understood by the term 'Crown'. His account of William of St Calais' invocation of *exceptio spolii* at the council of Rockingham may have led him to explore the partial analogy with ecclesiastical office, much like the draftsman of Henry I's coronation charter. If so, he had far too sharp a legal mind, and had thought too deeply about the position of bishops and abbots following the Conquest, to conclude that the analogy was a perfect one. For he realized that Norman kingship in England was, of necessity, more anomalous than analogous, and this is what he

---

[141] 'Corporation sole', 242.

[142] *Caps.* 12, 14, discussed by Garnett, 'Coronation and propaganda', 114–15.

[143] 'Crown as corporation', 249.

attempted to encapsulate in his *corona*. As William of Malmesbury —
no indulgent critic — wrote, 'He expounds it all so clearly that in some
sense it seems to happen before our very eyes.'[144] Towards the end of
his essay on the corporation sole Maitland uttered one of his lapidary
epigrams: 'English law has liked its persons to be real.'[145] Writing
long before the emergence of the Common Law which Maitland was
considering, Eadmer, who was no mean aphorist himself, could only
have nodded in wry agreement.

In its origins, therefore, a fitting description for this incorporeal, post-
Conquest *corona* might be 'juristic abortion', which was one of Maitland's two suggested characterizations of the (much later) corporations
sole of Crown and parson (his alternative — 'a natural man' — is
clearly inapplicable in this case).[146] But despite this unpromising first
appearance, during the first half of the twelfth century *corona* emerged
as part of the official language of royal government, rather than a term
of reproach from its critics. The chronological coincidence between the
emergence of these two usages appears to be just that: I have been
unable to establish any link between them, and, as should become
clear, the quite different official sense of the term makes the existence
of any such link highly unlikely. The fragile nature of the early evidence
for the official *corona* will support no more than a few suggestions
about the reasons for its apparently independent emergence.

The first instances I have identified date from early in the reign of
Henry I. In the writ he issued in June-July 1101 to strengthen support
for himself in the face of his brother's invasion, he referred, in a
straightforwardly physical way, to his first reception of a *corona*.[147] But
two other writs issued at much the same time use the word quite
differently. The king ordered that the soke of eight and a half hundreds
should continue to be fully attached to the 'monastery' of Bury St
Edmund's 'forever (*omnibus diebus*) with all liberties and dignities and
penalties (*forisfacturae*) belonging to the king's crown (*ad coronam
regis pertinentibus*).' This soke had been given to 'St Edmund' by
Edward the Confessor 'in alms (*in elemosinam*) in all things as fully
as he himself held it in his hand and confirmed by his charter, which I

[144] *Gesta Pontificum*, p. 74.
[145] 'Corporation sole', 242.
[146] 'Corporation sole', 243; cf. 'Crown as corporation', 251.
[147] *RRAN*, ii no. 531, printed by Stevenson, 'Inedited charter', 506.

have seen.'[148] The phrase does not appear in earlier royal confirmations to the abbey, or in Edward's original grant.[149] It seems to be a synonym for the 'regales consuetudines' of Abbot Baldwin's *Feudal Book*.[150] The second example is also a grant of jurisdictional rights, to 'God and the church of St Martin of Battle'. Anyone seeking to implead one of the abbot's men had to do so in the abbot's court: this privilege is characterized as *regia dignitas*, and the abbot, or any of the monks who happened to preside in the court, was to do 'full justice with royal dignity'. If the suit could not there be brought to a conclusion, it was at the abbot's summons to be transferred to the king's court, so that 'salvo jure et dignitate signi regiae coronae, id est ecclesiae sancti Martini de Bello' it might be finally settled in the presence of the abbot.[151] Provided this document is the original it seems to be, this phrase, coined in a royal charter, looks like the source of the usage which may be traced through the Battle forgeries and the *Battle Chronicle*: the abbey is 'signum corone regie Anglie', a symbol of what the Conqueror had won on the battlefield where he founded it.[152] It is equated with 'that which gave me my crown'.[153]

These two usages of *corona* appear to be different. In the case of Bury St Edmunds, the soke rights which were confirmed were defined in terms of the 'liberties, dignities and penalties *(forisfacturae)*' belonging to the 'king's crown'; in the case of Battle, the abbey's jurisdictional rights were defined in terms of 'royal dignity', but this 'right and

[148] *RRAN*, ii no. 644, edited by Douglas, *Feudal Documents*, no. 21 (Sept. 1102–Easter 1103); for Edward the Confessor's grant, see F. E. Harmer, *Anglo-Saxon Writs* (Manchester, 1952), no. 9, and for the circumstances, pp. 145–8.

[149] Douglas, *Feudal Documents*, nos. 3 (1066–70), 4 (1066–70), 6 (1066–87, probably early in the reign), 12 (probably 1087), 15 (1087–1100), 16 (1087–98), 18 (1087–1100), 19 (1093–1100).

[150] *Feudal Documents*, p. 9; also clv–clvi.

[151] *RRAN*, ii no. 529 (1101, *c.* June 24); discussed by E. Searle, *Lordship and Community: Battle Abbey and its Banlieu 1066–1538* (Toronto, 1974), p. 212. N. Hurnard, 'The Anglo-Norman franchises', *EHR*, 64 (1949), 289–327, 433–60 at 436 argues that no forger would have invented a provision for dealing with the incompetence of the abbot's court to settle a case.

[152] *RRAN*, i no. 113, a charter attributed to William I, which David Bates, *Regesta*, no. 17, argues was forged in the late twelfth or early thirteenth century; see also no. 262, also attributed to William I, discussed in following note; *The Chronicle of Battle Abbey*, ed. and trans. E. Searle (Oxford, 1980), pp. 108, 160, 170, 178, 182 ('signum triumphi').

[153] *RRAN*, i no. 262: 'sicut illa que mihi coronam tribuit, et per quam viget decus nostri regiminis'. This charter survives in two versions; the first was shown by E. Searle, 'Battle Abbey and exemption: the forged charters', *EHR*, 83 (1968), 449–80 at 458–9, to have been forged between Henry II's first hearing, in Lent 1155, of the dispute between the abbot of Battle and the bishop of Chichester, and 28 May 1157, when it was presented to the king at Colchester. Bates, *Regesta*, no. 23, further narrows the date to 1156–7. It is notable that the forged charter of William I which Searle, 'Battle Abbey and exemption', 454–5, argues was produced before the king in 1155 does not contain this particular phrase: *RRAN*, i no 62 (= Bates, *Regesta*, no. 22).

dignity' was what the king conferred on the abbey as 'the emblem of the royal crown'. For Bury, the crown was an abstract subject of rights; for Battle, it is not clear that the crown, although abstract, was a subject of rights at all. Battle's exceptional status, arising from the Conqueror's motives in founding it, is reflected in its unique characterization as the symbol of an abstraction. But the charters of Henry I provide several parallels with the confirmation to Bury.

Thus between 1107 and 1111 Henry granted 'in perpetuum' to God, St Benedict and Aldwin, abbot of Ramsey, sake and soke, tol and team, infangenetheof, forestal, blodwite, murdrum, treasure trove, 'and all other liberties belonging to my crown (*libertates coronae meae pertinentes*) in the land they hold within one league (*leugata*) around the church of St Benedict, and all other pleas belonging to my crown (*placita coronae meae pertinentia*) as I myself hold best and most fully in my kingdom.'[154] So although the use of *corona* with respect to Battle appears different, there are obvious similarities between the liberties — characterized as 'royal dignity' — conferred upon it, and the liberties belonging to the king's crown which were confirmed on Bury and conferred on Ramsey. It seems that the abstraction of *corona* was in some way originally connected with the grant by the king of special jurisdictional liberties or immunities to churches. Why did it begin to be conceived of as an abstract subject of rights in this context?

Paradoxically, the charters later forged in favour of Westminster and Battle, largely for the benefit of royal and papal audiences, explain the meaning of the term with an elaborated precision not found in the terse formulae of genuine royal documents. Kings had donated physical crowns to churches prior to the Conquest.[155] William the Conqueror and Queen Mathilda bequeathed crowns to their respective pre-Conquest penitential foundations in Normandy. In contrast, the king's penitential foundation in England symbolized the immaterial crown; it

---

[154] *RRAN*, ii no. 999; cf. nos. 1134 (1107–16), 1301 (1121, after August 5; there is some doubt about its authenticity), 1325 (1122, May 17–20).

[155] In a charter of dubious authenticity in favour of Christ Church, Canterbury — S 959 (1023) — Cnut is said to have laid his crown on the altar when he gave Sandwich; two centuries later Gervase of Canterbury, ii 56, states that the crown was given together with Sandwich. According to Henry of Huntingdon, *Historia Anglorum*, p. 189, after his celebrated experience of the incoming tide Cnut refused ever again to wear a crown, and placed his on a crucifix. For these and other examples, including a possible gift to the church of Winchester by Cnut, and a gift to the college at Waltham by a noblewoman, see M. K. Lawson, *Cnut. The Danes in England in the Early Eleventh Century* (London, 1993), pp. 134–7.

did not receive a material one.[156] The case of Westminster exemplifies the transition between these two usages: we can, as it were, watch the physical crown begin to dematerialize.

For Westminster allegedly possessed Edward the Confessor's crown and other regalia. If Prior Osbert of Clare, writing in or not long after 1138, is to be believed, a crown, ring, and sceptre had been found when Edward's tomb was opened in 1102.[157] If so, they were not initially treated by everyone at the abbey with the reverence which Osbert thought they deserved: the abbot and some of the monks seem still to have been ready to sell off Edward's regalia in 1138.[158] It was at this time that Osbert probably set about forging the charters which, amongst other things, justified the abbey's claim to be the repository of the regalia.[159] The key document in this regard is the so-called third charter of Edward, which recites a spurious bull of Pope Nicholas II to this effect.[160] But, like the other Anglo-Saxon charter forged by Osbert to justify Westminter's role as the *locus consecrationis* or *sedes regia* of the kingdom, it makes no specific mention of a crown.[161] The term does appear in the so-called first charter of the Conqueror, also the work of Osbert.[162] This records that Edward the Confessor had left

---

[156] L. Musset, ed., *Les Actes de Guillaume le Conquérant et de la reine Mathilde pour les abbayes caennaises*, (Mémoires de la société des antiquaires de Normandie, 37, Caen, 1967), no. 24 (1096–8) (= *RRAN*, i no. 397), a notice recalling the Conqueror's gift, on his deathbed, to St-Etienne of a crown used at crown-wearings together with other items of regalia, some of which are said to belong to the crown. They were all redeemed by William Rufus in return for the gift of a manor. Cf. *RRAN*, ii nos. 601 (1101–2), 1575 (1129). Musset, *Abbayes caennaises*, no. 16 (probably 1083) (= Bates, *Regesta*, no. 63), a notice of Mathilda's gift to La-Trinité.

[157] M. Bloch, 'La vie de S. Edouard le Confesseur par Osbert de Clare', *Analecta Bollandiana*, 41 (1923), 5–131 at 121. Osbert was almost certainly not an eye witness: *The Life of King Edward Who Rests at Westminster*, ed. and trans. F. Barlow, 2nd edn. (Oxford, 1992), p. 151.

[158] What purports to be a letter of Pope Innocent II rebuking the abbot and convent of Westminster: *Papsturkunden*, i no. 24. B. F. Harvey, 'Abbot Gervase de Blois and the fee-farms of Westminster Abbey', *BIHR*, 40 (1967), 127–42 at 128–9, shows that the letter is likely to have been the work of Osbert.

[159] P. Chaplais, 'The original charters of Herbert and Gervase, abbots of Westminster (1121–1157)', in P. M. Barnes and C. F. Slade, eds, *A Medieval Miscellany for Doris Mary Stenton*, (PRS, ns 36, 1962), pp. 89–110.

[160] S 1041 (1065, December 28).

[161] Both phrases are found in the so-called first charter of King Edgar, discussed by Chaplais, 'Original charters', p. 94: S 774 (969). The phrase *sedes regia* is found also in the third charter of the Confessor, and in a letter sent by King Stephen to Innocent II and drafted by Osbert: *The Letters of Osbert of Clare, Prior of Westminster*, ed. E. W. Williamson (Oxford, 1929), no. 17.

[162] *RRAN*, i no. 11 (1067) (= Bates, *Regesta*, no. 290); cf. the so-called *Telligraphus regis Willelmi primi videlicet Conquestoris*, *RRAN*, i no. 251 (= Bates, *Regesta*, no. 323), in the early sections of which there are extensive verbal parallels with William's 'first' charter. But note that the *Telligraphus* includes no reference to *corona*. The documents diverge when the

a crown and other (unspecified) regalia to Westminster, that William had there been solemnly crowned with the *corona regni* in the year of his victory, and refers twice to the regular thrice-yearly crown-wearings which took place there (and at Winchester and Gloucester). William had, allegedly, granted Battersea, with its berewick of Wandsworth, to the abbey, in order to redeem 'the crown of the aforementioned king and the other royal insignia'. There is no reason to believe that this had been the king's motive when he had given the manor,[163] but the practice is attested elsewhere in the notices recording grants and confirmations of lands in England by William Rufus and Henry I to St-Etienne, Caen in order to 'redeem' the crown which the Conqueror had bequeathed to it (which is also said to have been used at crown-wearings).[164] The practice was not, therefore, simply a pious invention on Osbert's part; and thus far *corona* in his forgeries seems to be conventionally physical.

That its physicality may begin to be qualified in this charter is indicated by the record of the king's confirmation 'ob reverentiam et coronae meae dignitatem' to the churches of Westminster, Winchester and Gloucester of certain customs 'which the wise men attest they had of old' — in other words, in the time of King Edward.[165] The Conqueror is presented as doing so in recognition of the *dignity* of his crown (formerly Edward's), which he wore at the regular, formal crown-wear-ings staged in these churches. Indeed, it might be argued that Osbert considered this was implicitly true of the other grants to Westminster catalogued in this quasi *pancarte*:[166] all of them sprang from the fact — elaborated in the preamble — that William had received the *corona regni*, along with royal anointing, in the abbey; and Battersea was explicitly said to have been given to redeem this crown. A crown the dignity of which the king recognized in making a grant to the church

---

'first' charter goes on to detail grants made to Westminster by the citizens of London, and the *Telligraphus* describes grants made by the barons. Chaplais, 'Original charters', pp. 92–5, shows that Osbert is the author of the 'first' charter. Westminster is there described as 'prima sedes regalis'. Cf. also the so-called 'third' charter, also the work of Osbert: *RRAN*, i no. 90 (= Bates, *Regesta*, no. 305).

[163] *RRAN*, i no. 45 (1066–7); *DB*, i 32b records that it was given to St Peter 'in exchange for Windsor'.

[164] Musset, *Abbayes caennaises*, no. 24, *RRAN*, ii nos. 601, 1575; there is no indication that Mathilda's crown was ever redeemed from La-Trinité.

[165] Various liberties are confirmed to the abbey as they were 'tempore regis Eaduuardi'; and other customs 'as I was informed by the English nobles and the wise men'.

[166] David Bates, *Regesta*, no. 290, compares this charter with a Norman *pancarte*, but points out that it is different in two respects: it purports to have been issued on a single occasion, which *pancartes* do not, and its witness list is a complete fabrication, rather than being adapted from a genuine document of the Conqueror's reign.

from which he had redeemed it, and where he regularly wore it, was on the way to becoming something more than a physical object; it was already the subject of a dignity. The gap is not great between this and the characterization of the abbey itself as *corona regni*, the description in Pope Innocent II's supposed mandate of 1133, addressed to Henry I, which exempted the abbey from the authority of the diocesan, made it a 'special daughter' of the Roman church, and committed it to the protection of the king and his successors.

This has hitherto been accepted as genuine by most authorities,[167] but is almost certainly a heavily interpolated version of a genuine document.[168] As Barbara Harvey has explained to me, it is highly unlikely that in this period a pope — even one in Innocent II's weak position — would have labelled a church thus in correspondence with a king. Moreover the neat attempt to explain away the bishop of London's celebration of masses in the abbey as having no bearing on the abbey's claim to immunity from episcopal jurisdiction looks suspiciously like the work of the monks, rather than of a pope.[169] Given the link between custody of the regalia and immunity established in Osbert's forged bull of Paschal II,[170] and his probable forging of the letter of Innocent II (on the basis of a simpler, genuine document entrusted to him in Rome in 1139) which uses the same phrase about the regalia,[171] Innocent's supposed mandate clearly fits into a Westminster tradition, inaugurated by Osbert. The reference to 'regum antiquorum privilegia', the clause of exemption from episcopal jurisdiction, and the clause enjoining Henry I to take the abbey under his special protection, all occur in more general terms in the forged bull of Nicholas II, which is certainly Osbert's work.[172] However, there is no evidence that Osbert ever referred to Westminster as *corona regni*,[173] and Pierre Chaplais thinks it likely that Innocent's mandate was not interpolated

---

[167] *Papsturkunden*, i no. 17; cf. E. Mason and J. Bray, eds, *Westminster Abbey Charters 1066–c. 1214* (London Record Society, 25, 1988), no. 155. It is described as 'dubious' by Searle, 'Battle Abbey and exemption', 458.

[168] Pierre Chaplais points out to me that the mention of the monk Godfrey would be an odd insertion in a complete fabrication.

[169] Personal letter; Pierre Chaplais has kindly told me that he concurs.

[170] *Papsturkunden*, i no. 9; on which see Chaplais, 'Original charters', p. 92.

[171] Above, n. 158.

[172] Pierre Chaplais, personal letter.

[173] There is nothing of this sort in his *Life of Edward the Confessor*. In *Letters of Osbert*, no. 17, p. 86, he refers to the 'ornaments' with which Edward had endowed the abbey, and describes it as 'regia sedes mea et specialis sanctae Romanae ecclesiae filia'. This characterization of the abbey's relationship with the Roman church is, of course, found in Innocent's forged mandate.

until much later in the twelfth century.[174] Whether it was Osbert's own work or a later development of his work is not very important in the present regard: what is important is that there was some sort of association between the abbey's characterization as *corona regni* and claims to immunity from the authority of the diocesan.

This association becomes clearer in the case of Battle Abbey, where there was no question of the presence of a physical crown to act as a spur to abstraction. The description of the abbey as *signum corone regie Anglie*, first coined in an apparently original charter of Henry I,[175] is amplified in the Battle forgeries. Thus in the forged charter of William the Conqueror presented to Henry II at Colchester at Pentecost 1157, William is made to ordain that the church 'together with the *leuga* surrounding it, should be as free from all domination and oppression of bishops as that which gave me my crown, and through which the splendour of our rule is strengthened (*sicut illa quae mihi coronam tribuit, et per quam viget decus nostri regiminis*).'[176] It has been suggested that the equation here is with Westminster.[177] The likelihood that this was what was in the forger's mind is strengthened by the fact that the surviving fragments of a seal have been identified with the forged so-called first seal of the Conqueror, used on Westminster forgeries, including Osbert of Clare's first charter of William.[178] The dispute which this charter was forged to settle was over Battle's claim to immunity from the jurisdiction of the bishop of Chichester.[179] But why, at Westminster and Battle, were claims to immunity from the jurisdiction of the diocesan somehow encapsulated in a description of the church either as an item of regalia or as a symbol of that item?

The Battle forgeries point the way to an answer. In what purports to be the foundation charter, which Searle has shown was read out to

---

[174] Personal letter. He regards the fact that the mandate is not quoted in the forged charters of Stephen and Henry II — *RRAN*, iii nos. 928–9; J. C. Holt and R. Mortimer, eds, *Acta of Henry II and Richard I* (List & Index Society, special ser. 21, 1986), no. H 294 — as an indication that it was concocted late in the twelfth century.

[175] *RRAN*, ii no. 529; see above, n. 151.

[176] *RRAN*, i no. 262 (= Bates, *Regesta*, no. 23).

[177] D. Knowles, 'Essays in monastic history, IV. The growth of exemption', *Downside Review*, ns 31 (1932), 201–31, 396–436 at 222 n. 1. Searle, 'Battle Abbey and exemption', 458 n. 3 asserts that the phrase refers to Battle, and that it is 'merely borrowed from Westminster'; but she thereby ignores the use of 'sicut', and the fact that the phrase is found in no document in favour of Westminster.

[178] Bishop and Chaplais, *Facsimiles*, pp. xxi–xxii; Bates, *Regesta*, nos. 23, 290. The original of the interpolated version of this Battle charter, now lost, still survived in the seventeenth century, when Selden drew the seal: Eadmer, *Historiae Novorum sive Sui Saeculi, Libri VI*, ed. J. Selden (London, 1623), p. 166. Bates comments that this also shows some similarity with the forged seal used at Westminster, although the correspondence is by no means exact.

[179] Searle, 'Battle Abbey and exemption', 458–9 and *passim*.

Henry II for confirmation in Lent 1155, having probably been forged after Stephen's death, William the Conqueror is made to endow the abbey in a single act with what appears to be an accurate list of its possessions as recorded in Domesday Book.[180] Amongst other things, he gives the abbey the *regale manerium* of Wye together 'with all its appendages *ex mea dominica corona*, with all liberties and royal customs, as freely and quit as I held it most freely and quit, or as a king is able to give', followed by a long list of exemptions. Together with its own hundred, Wye had, according to Domesday Book, 'sake and soke and all penalties which justly belonged to the king from twenty-two hundreds.'[181] This is merely an addition to the king's concession of 'the dignity of royal authority', meaning that the abbey has its own court and 'royal liberty and custom' to deal with its affairs and to do justice — in other words, what Henry I had granted in 1101.[182] In exercising this dignity it was to be 'free and quit in perpetuity from all subjection to bishops or domination by other persons'; moreover its *leuga*, within which the church was to enjoy liberties similar to those granted with Wye, was to be 'free from all custom of earthly service and all exactions by bishops.' Holes became apparent in this charter when it was challenged in the royal court at Lent 1155.[183] As we have seen, the charter forged to plug them not only equated Battle, in terms of its immunity from diocesan jurisdiction, with 'that which gave me my crown', it also warned that anyone acting against the liberties and dignities of the church would commit a *forisfactura regiae coronae*.[184] It equated the abbey's freedom from subjection with that of a king's *dominica capella*; in other words, what the forged foundation charter asserted about the grant of Wye was in this sense true of all the lands and jurisdictional rights with which the abbey was endowed.[185] Battle

---

[180] *RRAN*, i no. 62 (= Bates, *Regesta*, no. 22); Searle, 'Battle Abbey and exemption', 454–5; for the uproar in the king's court occasioned by the reading out of the charter, see *Battle Chronicle*, p. 158. For the abbey's endowment as recorded in Domesday Book: *DB*, i 11d, 17d, 34a, 59d–60a, 157a; ii 20b.

[181] *DB*, i 11d; cf. *Battle Chronicle*, pp. 76–8.

[182] *RRAN*, ii no. 529, discussed above, p. 200.

[183] Searle, 'Battle Abbey and exemption', 454–5; *Battle Chronicle*, p. 158.

[184] *RRAN*, i no. 262 (= Bates, *Regesta*, no. 23).

[185] J. H. Denton, *English Royal Free Chapels, 1100–1300. A Constitutional Study* (Manchester, 1970), pp. 82–5, argues that Battle was not a 'royal demesne chapel'. One of his reasons for doing so is that it was 'apparently not founded on royal demesne', by which he can only mean that the site of the abbey was recorded in Domesday Book as having been held by someone other than the king TRE: *DB*, i 17d. But this interpretation misses the point repeatedly emphasized in the *Battle Chronicle*, pp. 36, 148: that the Conqueror gave to God the field on which he had won the battle, as freely as he had won it. Whether or not Edward had held the lands was irrelevant. Denton, pp. 41–4, attributes considerable significance to the case of the 'royal free chapel' of Wolverhampton. In what purports to be a confirmation

was a symbol of the crown not only because it was founded on the spot where William had won his crown, but also because by royal grant it enjoyed throughout its lands liberties so absolute that they could only be defined in terms of the king's own rights. Exemption from episcopal jurisdiction was an important liberty; but it was only one aspect of a much more widely drawn immunity. Such is the refrain of the *Battle Chronicle*, much of which is based on these and other forgeries.[186] This explains the references to the 'dignity of royal authority' and 'royal custom', and the similar concessions of exemption from *regia consuetudo* or 'omnes leges et consuetudines que ad me pertinent' in Osbert's 'first' charter of the Conqueror in favour of Westminster Abbey.[187] But it would not explain the fact that what has been granted is occasionally attributed to the *corona*, rather than to the king. And this usage is not an invention of the Battle forgeries; as we have seen, it is warranted by genuine royal documents from early in Henry I's reign. So why did it arise?

The early examples of Bury St Edmunds and Ramsey show that, except in the unique case of Battle, originally it was royal liberties and *placita* — jurisdictional immunities and rights conceded exclusively by the king — which were conceived of as attributes of the crown.[188] The usage seems sometimes to have been extended to land because lands were also part of the king's *dominium*. That the crown should have been selected as the subject of royal judicial rights may perhaps be explained in the same way as Eadmer's ironic usage: it was the symbol of royal justice in the coronation *ordo*.[189] But that does not in itself explain why the subject came to be an abstraction distinct from the king. In the *Leges Henrici Primi*, composed *c.* 1114–18, the *dominica placita regis* are precisely that[190] — the pleas reserved to the king everywhere, 'whether it be on the king's *terra dominica* and soke, or someone else's'.[191] The list of '*iura* which the king of England has alone

by Robert of Limesey, bishop of Coventry, of the gift of the church of Wolverhampton to the monks of Worcester, Wolverhampton is characterized thus: 'una erat antiquitus de propriis regis capellis que ad coronam spectabant.' It has been dated to 1102–13: *The Cartulary of Worcester Priory (Register I)*, ed. R. R. Darlington (PRS, ns 38, 1968), no. 265. If this were genuine it would be by far the earliest description of a 'royal chapel' in these terms. However Pierre Chaplais has kindly advised me that in his view it is a later forgery.
[186] Searle, 'Battle Abbey and exemption', 449, 454–5, 458–9; *Battle Chronicle*, pp. 8–9.
[187] *RRAN*, i no. 11 (= Bates, *Regesta*, no. 290).
[188] Above, pp. 199–201.
[189] Above, p. 182.
[190] *LHP*, 10.4; cf. 7.3, 52, 60.3, Downer, pp. 108; 100, 168, 192; and Henry I's 'Decree on county and hundred courts', 2.1, where the king's pleas are described as 'mea dominica necessaria': *Gesetze*, i 524.
[191] *LHP*, 19.1, Downer, p. 122.

and over all men in his land, reserved through a proper ordering of peace and security'[192] includes many of the pleas which were specially conceded on occasion to recipients like Bury St Edmunds, or Ramsey, or Battle. But nowhere in the *Leges Henrici Primi* are they termed *placita coronae*, perhaps because the compiler's sources were for the most part Anglo-Saxon law codes, in which this early twelfth-century neologism is not found.[193] Conversely the author of the *Leis Willelme* (1090–1135) departs from his source, Cnut's second code, to label certain pleas as belonging 'a la curune le rei'.[194] The term appears in Henry's surviving pipe roll, which records a render for keeping 'placita que corone regis pertinent';[195] and he conceded that the citizens of London should keep and plead 'placita corone mee'.[196] Although both these instances from the end of the reign relate to lay recipients, it is striking that the term is first used to define what is being granted to churches, and in this lies the key to the invention of an abstract subject for the king's rights, distinct from the king himself.

At an earlier stage of the argument I tried to show that the undying quality of a church fitted uneasily into the personal, dependent system of tenure created in England after the Conquest, and that this incongruity was, of necessity, most striking in the case of bishoprics and abbacies. Bishops and abbots died, but their churches did not. Bishops and abbots, as tenants-in-chief, held lands of the king, but although the lands reverted to the king on their deaths, the lands continued, even while in the king's hands, to be the lands of the churches.[197] Gifts of land were made to churches in perpetuity long before the formula of tenure in 'free, pure and perpetual alms' became fixed in the twelfth century.[198] It was the perpetual nature of the endowment which secured spiritual benefits for the donor.[199] Such gifts were possible for two reasons: because the donees — that is to say, the churches, not individual clerics — were perpetual; and because donors could somehow assert more than a life-interest in the land given. In the latter respect

---

[192] *LHP*, 10.1, Downer, p. 108.
[193] I am indebted to John Hudson for this suggestion.
[194] *Leis Willelme*, 2a, in *Gesetze*, i 492; cf. I Cnut 2.3; II Cnut 12, 14.
[195] *PR 31 Henry I*, p. 91.
[196] C. N. L. Brooke, G. Keir, and S. Reynolds, 'Henry I's charter for the city of London', *Journal of the Society of Archivists*, 4 (1973), 558–78 at 575. They cast some doubt on the charter's authenticity, but even their most sceptical assessment would only push it forward into Stephen's reign. A powerful case for its being genuine after all — a possibility conceded by the editors — is put by C. W. Hollister, 'London's first charter of liberties: is it genuine?', *Journal of Medieval History*, 6 (1980), 289–306.
[197] Above, pp. 195–6.
[198] B. J. Thompson, 'Free alms tenure in the twelfth century', *ANS*, 16 (1994), 221–43 at 235–7.
[199] Thompson, 'Free alms tenure', 229.

it has been suggested that in early Normandy it was the growth of such gifts in perpetuity which strengthened the hereditary right of the donor.[200] In the first forty years after the Conquest no one other than the king appears to have held by hereditary right;[201] but there is no evidence for there being a logical nexus between his assertion of this right and his granting lands and rights to churches in perpetuity.[202] Indeed, the king's rights over ecclesiastical tenants-in-chief appeared to slice through the perpetual implications of the endowments of episcopal and abbatial churches. The implicit contradiction was at its sharpest in a case like Battle, founded by the Conqueror in compliance with the injunction of Ermenfrid of Sion's penitential ordinance that any member of the invading army with sufficient resources should 'redeem [his sin] with perpetual alms, either by founding or enlarging a church.'[203] Yet even perpetually-endowed Battle escheated to the king when its abbot died, however benevolently the royal custodians administered their charge.[204] In post-Conquest England this tension was irresolvable. Two pieces of evidence may suffice to illustrate this point. Henry I's foundation of Reading Abbey, which was almost certainly endowed with jurisdictional rights 'inasmuch as they belonged to the *regia potestas*',[205] enjoyed the special privilege of custody by the prior and monks during an abbatial vacancy.[206] And *Glanvill* later stated that the baronies of ecclesiastical tenants-in-chief were 'of the alms of the lord king'.[207]

It was, I suggest, because the king granted jurisdictional rights in perpetuity to certain churches that draftsmen began in the early twelfth century to attribute them to a subject other than the king. It was the perpetual nature of the gift to a perpetual donee which made draftsmen grope for something other than the mortal donor to which the rights being granted might be attributed. It is striking that all the early writs in which the term *corona* is used in this sense, with the unique exception

---

[200] Holt, 'Notions of patrimony', 199–204.

[201] Holt, 'Notions of patrimony', 214–16.

[202] *RRAN*, i nos. 101 (1070–82/3), 246, (1066–87), 274 (1080–7), 283 (1070–87), *Feudal Documents*, no. 9 (1066–87), for some instances of the Conqueror making grants to churches in perpetuity. I am grateful to John Hudson for supplying me with many of these examples.

[203] *Councils & Synods*, I, ii 583.

[204] For the vacancy of 1102–7, see *Battle Chronicle*, pp. 108–18.

[205] *Reading Cartularies*, i nos. 1, 2, 18, 20, 21, and pp. 18, 20–1. Although many of these charters are regarded by the editor as interpolated or spurious in their present form, the consistency of terminology is striking. It looks as if Reading's *regia potestas* was a synonym for *corona*.

[206] *Reading Cartularies*, i nos. 1, 18, 20, and p. 18.

[207] *Glanvill*, vii 1, Hall, p. 74.

of Battle, record grants which are explicitly said to be perpetual; and in the case of Battle it seems very likely that the gift was intended to be permanent. It is as if the *corona* is in this sense a reflection of the undying church. It is also striking that, with the possible exception of Henry I's charter to Battle Abbey, the first instances look to be in beneficiary-drafted documents. If so, the surviving pipe roll and the charter to the Londoners show that the royal administration was quick to pick up the usage.

Instances under Henry I are few, and the example of Reading indicates that the terminology probably took some time to become formalized. Under Stephen the usage continued in much the same vein. When confirming the gift made to the 'church of St John the Baptist at Colchester and the monks there serving God', Stephen added that the church and monks should hold this land free and quit 'of all secular exaction and service, and especially quit of danegeld and pleas and customs belonging to my crown.'[208] Sometimes 'customs pertaining to the dignity of my crown' were reserved.[209] Much the same is true of *placita coronae*, although in their case reservations are more common.[210] But the unusual circumstances of the reign also led to a new emphasis of the abstraction of the concept.

At Midsummer 1141 Mathilda, styled *regis Henrici filia et Anglorum domina*, made Geoffrey de Mandeville, amongst other things, chief justice in Essex 'hereditabiliter mea et heredum meorum de placitis et forisfactis quae pertinuerint ad coronam meam . . .'.[211] Mathilda may have recovered a crown from the treasury in Winchester where this charter was issued,[212] but she had not yet been crowned, nor was she

---

[208] *RRAN*, iii nos. 235 (1136–52); cf. nos. 658, 659 (1140–54), both grants in perpetuity to Peterborough Abbey.

[209] *RRAN*, iii nos. 34 (1140–52), grant to Barking Abbey 'salvis meis regalibus consuetudinibus que ad coronam meam pertinent'; 846 (1147–8), to 'the soldier-brothers of the Temple'.

[210] *RRAN*, iii nos. 3 (1139–54), warranty that the abbot of Abingdon and his men shall plead pleas of the crown only before the king at Oxford; 36 (1139–52), granting Becontree Hundred to Barking Abbey with all the rights and liberties enjoyed by Bury St Edmunds and Ely in their respective hundreds, 'salvis tantum placitis corone mee que per justitiam meam debent placitari'; 767 (1135–45), grants in Beccles to Bury St Edmunds, the king retaining nothing except 'placita corone mee pertinentia'.

[211] *RRAN*, iii no. 274 (= iv pl. xiv); J. C. Holt, review of *RRAN*, iii, iv in *Economic History Review*, 2nd ser. 24 (1971), 480–3 expresses doubts about the authenticity of this charter, but it is hardly surprising, given the circumstances in which it was issued, that the charter has unusual characteristics.

[212] *Gesta Stephani*, ed K. R. Potter (Oxford, 1976), p. 118; Florence of Worcester, ii p. 130. The crown worn by Mathilda on her authentic seal must have been intended to represent its legend: '+ MATHILDIS DEI GRATIA ROMANORUM REGINA.' See *RRAN*, iv pl. xiii.

queen.[213] Yet the royal pleas she conceded to Geoffrey were labelled as belonging to her (abstract) crown. With the exception of Henry I's charter to the Londoners, this is the first charter record of such a grant to a lay recipient; it is noteworthy that it was made 'hereditarily', with Mathilda attempting to bind her heirs to recognize the gift.

When her heir arrived in England in 1153, the motives for Angevin adaptation of this usage became clearer. Between January and May 1153 — in other words, long before the deal struck with the king at Winchester in November 1153 — Duke Henry conceded and confirmed to St Augustine's, Bristol all the 'lands and revenues belonging to the crown of England, which have been given in alms or shall be given in the future to the said church of St Augustine and the aforesaid canons by me or by another.'[214] Henry as duke had given lands and revenues said to have belonged to the crown, which on this occasion was defined as that of England, rather than the duke's, perhaps because he assumed the right to confirm what had been given 'by another' (it being clear who that other, with the unmentionable name, was). In an original charter confirming the foundation of Biddlesden Abbey, which was certainly issued before April 1154, and probably c. 7 June 1153 — therefore also prior to the 'treaty' of Winchester — he gave it a long list of jurisdictional and financial exemptions, rounded off with the phrase 'and all customs belonging to my crown'.[215] A charter recording grants 'in perpetual alms' by the duke to Bermondsey Priory which cannot be dated more precisely than 1153–April 1154, describes the revenues as belonging 'ad coronam regis': Henry could dispose of these now, but undertook to confirm the gifts 'with royal authority' and to corroborate them 'with the witness of the royal seal' if and when 'with the support of God I shall accede to the kingdom of England.'[216] The explicit contrast drawn in this charter between the duke's ability to grant as duke what belonged to the 'king's crown', and his promise to confirm these grants if and when he became king, makes the point nicely. He claimed to control what belonged to the abstract crown,

---

[213] A seal once attached to the charter may have had the legend 'S. MATILDIS IMPER-ATRIX ROM' ET REGINA ANGLIAE'; for doubts about the accuracy of the seventeenth-century transcriptions, and for a full consideration of the other charters in which Mathilda uses the title *Anglorum regina*, see Holt, review of *RRAN*, iii, iv, 482; J. O. Prestwich, 'The treason of Geoffrey de Mandeville', *EHR*, 103 (1988), 283–312 at 311–12; M. M. Chibnall, 'The charters of the Empress Mathilda', in Garnett and Hudson, *Law and Government*, pp. 276–98 at 279–80.
[214] *RRAN*, iii no. 126 (Jan.–May 1153).
[215] *RRAN*, iii no. 104 (1153–Apr. 1154, probably c. 7 June 1153).
[216] *RRAN*, iii no. 90 (1153–Apr. 1154).

although he had as yet no physical crown,[217] just as he did not yet have the royal seal. For both Mathilda and Henry, claiming to be Henry I's rightful heirs, and on the whole refusing explicitly to recognize Stephen's existence prior to the 'treaty' of Winchester,[218] clutched at the abstract crown with even more urgency than at the physical one. Circumstances forced them — or rather, the draftsmen of their charters — to postulate the existence of an entity distinct from the person of the king to which royal rights might be attributed. And in the charter issued by the king summarizing the agreement reached at Winchester in November 1153, Stephen himself recognized the complete severance of the abstract crown from the physical one: for he ordained that castles belonging 'ad coronam' should be handed over to the duke on his, Stephen's, death, long before Henry would be crowned.[219]

This formulation of an abstract crown as a passive subject of royal rights had a distinguished future, unlike that revealing pair of juristic abortions, Eadmer's *corona* and the *regnum* of Henry I's coronation charter. It may be traced through the administrative, diplomatic, legal and chronicle records of Henry II's reign, to the London version of the *Leges Edwardi Confessoris*, and thence to *Bracton*.[220] But that is another story, and one which others, including Maitland, have already told in part.[221] This attempt to delve into the origins of 'The Crown' should have demonstrated that originally it had nothing to do with the convenience of the royal administration in the absence of the king,

---

[217] *RRAN*, iii no. 725 (*c.* 7 December 1154), in which Henry terminates a dispute immediately prior to crossing the Channel 'ad suscipiendam coronam regni Anglorum'.

[218] Mathilda exceptionally refers to Stephen as king in *RRAN*, iii no. 274 because with him imprisoned, she considered that she had won and was about to be crowned as queen; cf. nos. 368 (Feb.–July 1141), 393 (25 July 1141), 275 (dated by the editors to 25–31 July 1141, but now convincingly redated to the first half of 1142, probably in the spring or early summer, by Prestwich, 'Treason of Geoffrey de Mandeville', esp. 286–94, and 'Geoffrey de Mandeville: a further comment', *EHR*, 103 (1988), 960–6 at 964.

[219] *RRAN*, iii no. 272 (Nov.–Dec. 1153).

[220] The fullest analysis of the period up to Edward I's reign may be garnered from Kantorowicz, *King's Two Bodies*, esp. pp. 149–87 (for *Bracton*), 342–64; cf. E. H. Kantorowicz, 'Inalienability: a note on canonical practice and the English coronation oath in the thirteenth century', *Speculum*, 29 (1954), 488–502; H. Hoffmann, 'Die Unveräusserlichkeit der Kronrechte im Mittelalter', *Deutsches Archiv*, 20 (1964), 389–474 at 420–33.

[221] Hoyt, *Royal Demesne*, pp. 120–4, 140–7, 162–5; Holt, *Magna Carta*, pp. 88, 93–5, 118–19, 286; 'Ricardus rex Anglorum et dux Normannorum', reprinted in his *Magna Carta and Medieval Government* (London, 1985), pp. 67–84 at 67–8; 'Rights and liberties in Magna Carta', reprinted in *Magna Carta and Medieval Government*, pp. 203–16 at 207–9.

one of the reasons sometimes given for its emergence.[222] As Maitland himself pointed out, it was perfectly possible for the royal administration to function in the king's name in his absence,[223] and this is precisely what it can be shown to have done, even during an interregnum.[224] Nor in its origins may 'The Crown' be said to have anything to do with what Maitland was pleased to call 'the continuous life of the State',[225] except in a heavily qualified sense — as a reflection of the undying nature of the churches to which kings made grants, and in the peculiar circumstances of Stephen's reign as an Angevin circumlocution to avoid addressing the issue of how Mathilda and Henry disposed of royal rights. If the argument presented above be valid, it has also shown that the concept of 'The Crown' cannot be attributed to the influence of Suger and the diplomatic practice of St-Denis.[226] Not only does the English usage long predate Suger's coining of the term around about 1150,[227] the circumstances which gave rise to the abstract crown in post-Conquest England were quite different from those in Capetian France, hence the precision of its meanings in the former context and its vagueness in the latter.

Maitland drew attention to 'a certain thoughtlessness or poverty of ideas' which he said the Conquest had 'facilitated',[228] by which I take him to mean the implications of the system of dependent personal tenure discussed earlier in this essay. But the invention of the abstract crown, whether by Eadmer or (with a quite different meaning) by those who drafted royal charters, showed why it rapidly became impossible to

---

[222] Prestwich, 'Treason of Geoffrey de Mandeville', 300.

[223] Pollock and Maitland, i 512.

[224] See, for instance, the essoin roll of the quinzaine of Easter (2 May) 1199, which is entitled 'Anno regni regis Ricardi x'; and the fixing in this roll of a day of appearance in a plea in which one party was said to have proceeded in a suit 'contra preceptum Domini Regis': *RCR*, i 259, 264, discussed at pp. lxxxiv–lxxxv. This record must have been made after Richard's death on 6 April. It shows that the judicial system continued to function, and that the dead king's instruments were regarded as valid. Reference is made to John as *dominus dux* — 266, 274, 288, 290, 324 etc. — and as *dominus Angliae* — 307, 309, 311, 314 etc. — in the period before he became king (at his coronation); but there is no indication that royal authority was considered to be vested in some sort of abstraction during the interregnum. This is a subject to which I hope to return.

[225] *Gierke*, p. xxxvii.

[226] B. W. Scholz, 'Two forged charters from the abbey of Westminster and their relationship with St Denis', *EHR*, 76 (1961), 466–73, shows that some Westminster forgeries were influenced by St-Denis models, possibly — as suggested by Chaplais, 'Original charters', p. 92 — a St-Denis formulary. But there is no evidence that the Westminster usage of *corona* was borrowed from this source.

[227] E. Bournazel, *Le Gouvernment capétien au xiie siècle, 1108–1180* (Limoges, 1975), pp. 171–3, who argues that the formulation of an abstract notion of the crown was due to Louis VII's protracted absence on crusade; cf. Kantorowicz, *King's Two Bodies*, pp. 340–2.

[228] *Gierke*, p. x.

preserve that thoughtlessness unalloyed, at least where the king was concerned. In his eulogy of Maitland, Plucknett quotes with empiricist approval Maitland's aphorism that, where law is concerned, 'logic yields to life, protesting all the while that it is only becoming more logical.'[229] In the unusual case of the crown, however, it would be more true to say that life had to yield to logic.[230]

---

[229] *Year Books of Edward II. 1 & 2 Edward II, A.D. 1307–1309*, ed. F. W. Maitland, (Selden Soc., 17, 1903), p. xix.

[230] I am grateful to John Hudson and Magnus Ryan for discussing this essay with me on a number of occasions, and to David Bates, Pierre Chaplais, Barbara Harvey, Jim Holt and Richard Sharpe for remedying my ignorance on particular points. The medievalists at St Andrews generously invited me to give the first part of the argument a trial outing. I am also grateful to the British Academy for funding a term's special leave, during which I did much of the reading and thinking.

Proceedings of the British Academy, **89**, 215–241

Maitland and the Rest of Us

PAUL R. HYAMS

THE AUTHOR OF the *History of English Law* was self-evidently an insider. He wrote for himself first, then the rest of his peers, the few,[1] each of whom like himself felt heir to the achievements of their legal ancestors and proud to be Englishmen. It was important and self-evidently worthwhile to give such people a clear account of the main lines of development of their Common Law and its role in the maintenance of justice and order in the kingdom of England. The first part of that great story was to reach 1272.

Patently, the failed barrister was nevertheless a fine advocate who could have made a brilliant case for the disempowered had it occurred to him to do so. This self-styled 'dissenter from all churches'[2] sympathised as easily with the oppressed as any Victorian liberal. Sympathy is of course a long way from action or identification. If Maitland identified with any of the excluded groups who are my subject today, it was probably the heretics.

He never attempted the imaginative reconstruction of the feelings of those at the sharp receiving end of the sword of justice. For all his immense technical skills, not least sensitive readings of texts and what they did not say, Maitland was absolutely not a deconstructionist *avant la lettre*. His instinct, when confronted by absences, was to fill them with patterns borrowed from the better documented moments of a later period. This was the well-known and much considered method of *Domesday Book and Beyond*. The critics who place him, inexplicably to my younger self, behind Stubbs as an historian, mainly, as far as I could see, on grounds of moral force and human sympathies, may have a tiny point. A man bereft of a deep spiritual life of his own is

[1] *Letters*, i no. 495. *Letters*, ii no. 116 is a very telling indication that the disempowered were no part of the target audience; writing to Dicey in 1896, he says: 'The only direct utility of legal history . . . lies in its lesson that each generation has an enormous power of shaping its own law.' *Cf. Letters*, ii no. 350, and Pollock and Maitland, ii 205 for an indication of the social level of the audience.

[2] Fifoot, *Life*, pp. 157, 180.

protected, as it were, from judging the past in a fully present-minded fashion, but he is poorly positioned to recreate voices that were never recorded in their own day. That is one reason why history is so often the story of the winners, a sad fact that gave Maitland no pleasure at all.

Texts like the *History of English Law* present today's readers with a huge problem. They demand first a substantial measure of technical competence, and then to be placed in their contemporary context within late Victorian intellectual and cultural history. But even after all that, the 'real' Maitland remains well-guarded by his authorial reticence, his rhetorical skills and his unequalled ability to nuance. The kind father who delighted his daughters with his reading and story-telling, the loyal and amusing friend, the man who froze up before the camera, all seem now long gone and almost beyond recovery.

The task I assign myself here is to seek out aspects of the *History* relating to the excluded and the powerless, in order to move a little forward towards an understanding of the kind of insider Maitland was, to learn something of the emotional associations and bonds that must have influenced his judgements and working methods. I leave judgements to a higher court, and endeavour here more to assemble suitable materials for submission *ad loquendum*. I shall focus on the faces that the good liberal did not normally see, together with one group, women, with whose welfare he was much involved on occasion, and another, heretics, that seems to have attracted the perpetual sceptic in our man. I shall consider them under four heads. First there are those who were not Englishmen, then those who were not male. Third comes the under-class, mostly examining villeinage. And fourth I shall see to what preliminary conclusions about the man and historian a miscellany of odd groups (in various senses), including lepers and lunatics,[3] heretics and homosexuals, can lead us.

The Englishman, the Aliens and the Jews

The chorus constantly repeats how very English Maitland was. The Englishness is easy to see. Maitland constantly refers to 'our' Common

---

[3] Reasons of space rule out lepers and lunatics from consideration here. N. Walker, *Crime and Insanity in England* (2 vols, Edinburgh, 1968), vol. i ch. 1 (based largely on plea-roll materials provided by Mr J. M. Kaye) remains the only attempt at a general account of the insane in medieval law that I know!

Law and 'we' Englishmen, who made it.[4] He seeks in the *History* quite expressly to expound the roots of a system of law that lasted through his own life but quite largely expired around 1925 thanks to F. E. Smith.[5] To chronicle the development of England's national law, he firmly believed, was a job for Englishmen or at worst their common-law cousins from the United States. He was proud that around 1200 the Common Law 'takes for a short while the lead among the states of Europe' (i 167), in much the way that Englishmen felt a few years later about Scott's race for the South Pole. It would be shameful, indeed, to leave the editing of the law's great texts to 'Germans, Frenchmen and Russians' (i xxxv), little less so had the Common Law failed to resist a Roman Law Reception.[6] His trust in that Common Law's professional tradition of its own origins, 'in the main . . . sound and truthful' (i xxxiv) was one source of the *Domesday Book and Beyond* hindsight method, as of most of the errors on which posterity has been able to secure a conviction.[7]

There is a certain irony here, given how much better read he was in the various relevant European learned literatures than most of the later scholars who have followed his trail, present company not excepted.[8] This proud Victorian was a convinced *comparatiste* from the very start of his historial career. His *History* was to disentangle in various 'Germanic strains' the roots of 'institutions which have now-a-days the most homely and English appearance' (i xxxi, xxxiii, xxxv–vi).

[4] E.g. Pollock and Maitland, i 677, 684; ii 344, 413, 543. He had clearly internalised Savigny's view of a people's legal institutions as one more expression of its identity, J. W. Burrow, *A Liberal Descent: Victorian Historians and the English Past* (Cambridge, 1981), p. 123.

[5] The five Property Acts of 1925 form a natural and widely recognized watershed. However, my father was admitted a solicitor in 1929, very much in their aftermath. He used to recount as the view of the established practitioners of his early days in the profession that the Land Transfer Act of 1897 marked the real start of the changes. Professor Milsom suggested to me that the Settled Land Acts earlier still also have a claim.

[6] E.g. Pollock and Maitland, i 79; cf. ii 2 where Roman Law is called 'foreign jurisprudence'. 'The Laws of the Anglo-Saxons', *Collected Papers*, iii 447–73, a review of Liebermann's first volume, is to the point here.

[7] The lawyer in Maitland took much more care to cite and amend the views of Coke, Hale, Blackstone and his legal forebears on medieval developments than any contemporary scholar would.

[8] M. Graziadei, 'Changing images of the law in XIX century English legal thought (The Continental impulse)', in M. Reimann, ed., *The Reception of Continental Ideas in the Common Law World, 1820–1920* (Comp. Studies in Cont. & Anglo-American Legal History, 13, 1993), pp. 115–63 goes far to place Maitland in his intellectual context alongside both American and European scholars. I am not aware of much research on Maitland's reading in specific areas. But De L. J. Guth and M. H. Hoeflich, 'F. W. Maitland and Roman Law: an Uncollected Letter, with Comments and Notes', *U. Illinois L. R.* 2 (1982), 441–8 marks a good starting-point. And cf. *Letters*, i nos. 4, 92; *Letters*, ii nos 37, 174, 237, 285 etc. etc.

He was always alert to acknowledge Continental borrowings,[9] and very much able to show how distinctive some English choices look in a perspective taken from the other side of the English Channel.[10]

This English patriotism, lightly and naturally worn, is evident in his *History's* depiction of foreign bodies within the law. Some treatment of aliens was doubtless called for by his decision (prompted perhaps by the influence of Blackstone and the *Institutes*) to follow the initial historical sketch of his first volume with some account of legal status (i 460–5). Few legal historians have made the effort since, despite some good studies of the export of English law to Wales and Ireland.[11] Maitland's treatment can be applauded for its existence. It is not very profound or interesting. The five pages he allowed himself did not permit mention of the problems raised by Welshmen and Scots, for example, suing in the English royal courts, a matter of some practical significance before the end of his period which he had very likely noticed in the pleas rolls. This might have enticed him into a little more of the potentially very illuminating comparisons between legal systems within the British Isles that his friendship with Neilson and his own interest in Scots law had occasionally suggested to him.[12] But since much of the better evidence for this post-dates his stated terminus of 1272, it is perhaps not surprising that he eschewed the largely manuscript researches that such investigations would have demanded.

For my present purpose, what remains with me from the pages on aliens is their workmanlike approach and tone. All this changes when one reads on a few pages to the section of very similar length on 'the

[9] A good example is his acceptance of a Frankish derivation for the Jury, basically in the wake of Brunner, Pollock and Maitland, i 80–93. This debate burns fiercely on and on without much hope for material to lead to conclusive judgement.

[10] One good illustration is the demonstration that curtesy, 'a peculiar favour shown to the husband', was unknown even in Normandy, Pollock and Maitland, ii 415–20. Compare S. F. C. Milsom, 'Inheritance by women in the 12th and 13th centuries', in his *Studies in the History of the Common Law* (London, 1985), ch. 12, esp. pp. 254 sq. with my own, 'The Common Law and the French Connection', *ANS*, 4 (1982), App. 1, 87–90, esp. at p. 90 commenting on *Glanvill*, vii 18, ed. Hall, pp. 92–3. Other illustrations in Pollock and Maitland, ii 445, 449, 484.

[11] G. J. P. Hand, *English Law in Ireland, 1290–1324* (Cambridge, 1967). Cf. F. H. Newark, 'The bringing of English Law to Ireland', *Northern Ireland Law Quarterly*, 23 (1972), 3–15 and Hand, 'English Law in Ireland, 1172–1351', ibid., 393–422.

[12] For Neilson, see E. L. G. Stones, ed., *F. W. Maitland: Letters to George Neilson* (Glasgow, 1976) and *Letters*, ii s.n. Excellent examples of the 'British' approach with particular reference to Ireland will be found in P. A. Brand, *The Making of the Common Law* (London, 1992), chs 2, 13, 19–20 etc. On Scotland, see H. MacQueen, *Common Law and Feudal Society in Medieval Scotland* (Edinburgh, 1993). Minor efforts of my own in this direction are visible in my *King, Lords and Peasants in Medieval England: the Common Law of Villeinage in the 12th and 13th Centuries* (Oxford, 1980), pp. 229–32 and also in my article 'The Charter as a source for the Common Law', *Journal of Legal History*, 12 (1991), 173–89 at 179.

Jews'.[13] This is slightly curious given that Jews, whether high-profile financiers in society or very foreign-looking paupers in the East End of London, are likely to have been one of the first connotations for anyone hearing the word 'alien' in 1895.[14]

We cannot take such a contrast lightly. Maitland's use of language is frequently revealing, because he patently applied such care to it. His masterly control of his pen reflects both his confidence in his ability to say exactly what he wished and a deep if unschooled interest in language. Something of a 'language maven',[15] he frequently makes perceptive comments on words and language patterns both in the past and in his own day.[16] In his own writings, he generally maintained a proper lawyer's preference for a stable terminology over the greater variation for stylistic variety affected by many of the historians of his day. The very fact of this double degree of attention to language invests breaches of the rule with extra significance. Thus careful study of Maitland's language may yet prove a route into some of the inner life of this private man.

The present occasion being inappropriate for an exercise of that kind, I merely point to a problem posed by his choice of language in this brief section on Jews. He refers to them in three different ways. They are, here and elsewhere (as in his private letters), 'Israelites' and 'Hebrews' as well as 'Jews'. A people (or 'race') rather than a religious group like the Saracens of the crusades, their antonym is the 'gentile' (i 469), a term I cannot find used elsewhere in the *History*. There has to be some significance to all this.[17] Unlike historians, lawyers never vary their terms for purely stylistic reasons in technical writing. What is one to make of a usage so different from his normal practice? Certainly there is no necessary intent to defame. 'Hebrew', for example, had for contemporaries many positive connotations stemming from biblical associations with the Old Testament, and may have evoked

[13] He may have found the Jews a harder task from the start, *Letters*, i no. 87. In contrast A. C. Dicey, *Law and Public Opinion in England* (London, 1948), pp. 344–5 and n. 3 refers to Jewish emancipation in a fully neutral tone.

[14] Maitland must have known something of the East End. A distant cousin had held a parish there rather earlier, Fifoot, *Life*, pp. 28–30. So had J. R. Green, whose occasionally revealing letters Leslie Stephen edited in 1902. Even more to the point, Florence Maitland's first cousin, George Duckworth, was involved with Charles Booth's investigations of the area at much the time of the *History*; his papers survive, D. Feldman, *Englishmen and Jews: Social Relations and Political Culture, 1840–1914* (London, 1994), p. 166n.

[15] See Steven Pinker, *The Language Instinct* (London, 1993), ch. 12.

[16] The grammar of 'Law French' he wrote from scratch in his first Selden Year Book volume is cited in this context with notorious frequency, Fifoot, *Life*, pp. 260–2 and, *Letters*, i nos. 279, 301, 323, 346, 357, 376, 379, 383; *Letters*, ii no. 237. See also any of the many comments on vocabulary scattered through Pollock and Maitland, e.g. i 236 n. 3.

[17] *Letters*, i no 346 shows his sensitivity to the comparably different connotations of 'Yanqui' and 'Americano' in Spanish.

special feelings among nonconformists and their liberal friends.[18] No simple interpretation of this quite common usage suggests itself. Some say that 'Jew' was the shocking word, that everything Jewish shocked conventional people of the kind whom Maitland expected to find among his readers. So he may have been softening his usage in deference to feelings, his own perhaps but more likely those of others.[19]

How then, one may ask, could a student of Maitland's day most usefully approach this minor constituent of the population of England subject to jurisdiction in its courts? It demanded some treatment in the interests of completeness, and might by its very differentness illuminate unexpected aspects of the majority host community.[20] One of the more promising answering strategies to meet the challenge is to situate such a minority by analogy with some other comparable group. The choice of apposite comparison is critical and can be controversial. When well handled, this approach illuminates more than the lawyers' disposal of their difficulty in finding a place for the Jews, say, within their system. It may tell us something about the majority community's response to its minority. This is a route much travelled by recent scholarship.[21]

Maitland saw both the problem and its solution with his habitual clarity. He registered the one absolutely basic fact about the English Jewry, that it was supremely dependent upon the king. For the early middle ages, he translated this as a similarity of legal condition with that of the 'friendly stranger' under the *mund* or protection of some great man (i 460). He was possibly encouraged by this insight to point out that discrimination did not necessarily imply the Jew's disadvantage, that the Jew was 'a highly privileged person' in regard to mortgages, for example (ii 123). He also knew another quite widespread analogy in the high middle ages, that of servility, as in the chamber servitude of Jews in Germany. This is generally and plausibly held to have proved deeply damaging to Jewish condition at the time. Maitland is throughout the *History* and elsewhere so deeply engaged by the concept of seisin that one might almost term it an intellectual

---

[18] Cf. Pollock and Maitland, ii 488–9, incl. n. 2.

[19] But he follows similar usage in his correspondence about the Selden Society volume on the Exchequer of the Jews, *Letters*, i nos. 117, 118, 124, 130, 152, 158–9, 161, 163, 174, 185, 212, 311, 317; he also asks Fisher in 1906: 'How the devil can Belloc know the income of the average English Jew of the thirteenth century?', *Letters*, i no. 469.

[20] This was my goal in writing 'The Jews as an immigrant minority, 1066–1290', *Journal of Jewish Studies*, 25 (1974), 270–93, for a Past & Present Conference on Immigrant Minorities in English history.

[21] See especially G. I. Langmuir, *Toward a Definition of Antisemitism* (Los Angeles, 1990). Also the contributions of Patschowsky and myself to *England and Germany in the High Middle Ages* (Oxford, forthcoming), ed. A. Haverkamp and H. Vollrath.

obsession.[22] He therefore read the notion of Jewish servitude along the lines he so brilliantly recreated for villeinage in the Age of Bracton, that is, in terms of 'relativity', as he called it.[23] All stemmed from the relationship with the king, a kind of seisin over his Jews. But they suffered, he insisted, only a 'relative servility', for they were free as regards everyone except the king (i 468–9, 472). The implication, presumably, is that Jews operated in the courts and elsewhere on the basis of equality with the king's other subjects. It is true that Jews sued and were sued, sometimes, though as time went on exceptionally, in the ordinary royal courts, but it is also true that they suffered a number of legal disabilities.[24] Maitland's dictum is just defensible as a summary of the twelfth-century situation, which also provides our best evidence of Jewish servitude in England.[25] It is certainly not good law after the Jewry legislation of 1269–75 and already extremely doubtful before then. Moreover, where the relativity idea is abundantly justified for villeins, Maitland lacks any Bractonian authority for his application of it to the Jews.

This is not quite what we expect from our Maitland. His account overall shows very little indeed of the evident discomfort with the law's treatment of Jews that he feels about women. Indeed the mild emphasis he gives to the Jews' privileges might suggest that their discriminatory treatment mattered less than one might think. He noted apropos of women in their matrimonial role a special protecting function of the king. When their primary protectors, first the husband, then their blood kinsmen, defaulted on their duty, recourse might be had to the king 'that guardian of all guardians' (ii 413). He shows no similar concern for Jewish well-being, though it might have led him towards a much favoured explanation for the Expulsion in 1290, which he hardly seems to find even problematic, perhaps because it created no obvious legal problems.

The obvious fact is that Maitland had no real interest in the Jews except as a source of minor conceptual difficulties for England's secular but Christian law. Here he is in his element, supremely adept at tracing the logic of the Common-Law system as contemporaries might have

[22] Graziadei, 'Changing images of the law', esp. 139–41, 149 sq. begins to make this comprehensible.

[23] Below at n. 74.

[24] C. Roth, *A History of the Jews in England* (3rd edn, Oxford, 1964) and H. G. Richardson, *The English Jewry under Angevin Kings* (London 1960) are the best starting-points for inquiry.

[25] On the quite unofficial 'Leges Edwardi Confessoris', Patschowsky in *England and Germany in the High Middle Ages* is probably to be preferred to earlier views including my own in the same volume.

meant it to operate. His gift for teasing out the internal logic of institutions and rules that initially seem strange and illogical draws upon the strengths of a powerful and philosophically trained mind.[26]

When one attempts this task, the challenge for the historian, as opposed to the advocate, is to separate his voice from the ones he is recreating. I do not think that Maitland succeeds as well here as he does elsewhere. His fondness for the historic present tense tends to exacerbate the risk, as do, ironically, all the familiar rhetorical skills. The result indisputably contains a far higher proportion of stereotype than is evident elsewhere in the book. And this seems to come from Maitland's own mouth. He is quite peremptory when he comments of Jewish landholding in fee, 'this was not to be borne' (i 473), or clothes a perfectly correct observation about the Jews' role as a social solvent with an emotive phrase on 'the touch of Jewish gold' (i 475).[27] When he has similar remarks to make about women, for example, he distances himself and his own voice with off-setting comment. Here there is none.

It is hard to avoid the suspicion that his presentation may be coloured by some share of the feelings current and respectable at the time. He does little to disguise his distaste for moneylending, no matter who practised it. Having discovered that chancery officials were guilty of its practise — and he should only have known the full extent of the shady business dealings that went on in Edward I's court! — he feels he must expose 'the fact, for fact it is' (ii 204). Because the Jewish gage was 'among Englishmen a novel and an alien institution', he pronounced judgement that 'this moneylending business required some governmental regulation' (i 469).[28] Two further dicta deserve quotation. 'Despised and disliked the once chosen people would always have been in a society of medieval Christians; perhaps they would always have been accused of occasionally massacring children and occasionally massacred; but they would not have been so persistently hated, as they were, had they not been made the engines of royal indigence' (i 470–1).

[26] Mathematical and philosophical studies at Cambridge and the close association with Sidgwick are patently highly formative of Maitland's approach to law reform and history. Now that James Campbell has brought to my notice A. H. Inman, *Domesday and Feudal Statistics* (London, 1900), I see that this is not all cause for congratulation. Maitland's quantitative methods in *Domesday Book and Beyond* come in for brisk criticism here!

[27] The footnote citations are to very partisan statements, on which see perhaps my own 'The Jews as an immigrant minority'. Fifoot, *Life*, p. 3 mentions the 1828 trip of S. R. Maitland to check on the progress of the conversion of the Jews in Central Europe; this hints at a possibly relevant influence.

[28] He is speaking here of the twelfth century. I doubt whether modern scholars would agree on this explanation for royal regulation, or that the novelty was any greater in England than anywhere else north of the Alps.

'The Jew belongs to a despicable race and professed a detestable creed'
(i 472).

Such remarks wrongly dismiss all possibility of toleration for Jews
in the middle ages, against the evidence of his own 'friendly stranger'
analogy. They also betray a confusion of voice which no one writing
in the area today would risk, and they cast in my mind at least a certain
shadow over the great liberal. It is true that Maitland was very fond
of irony, not least when his all-encompassing mind perceived difficulties
in the view it wished to propound. I cannot, however, believe after
careful bouts of rereading, that any of this was intended to be read in
such a manner. And even if others are able to detect irony here, this
would rather underline Maitland's ambivalences.

These are not too hard to guess. Maitland was an undergraduate
during the years immediately following the vast extension to the franchise in 1867, years when Gladstone's Midlothian Campaign demonstrated the prizes to be won by addressing a new mass electorate. The
new less romantic conception of the nation that resulted inevitably
raised the requirements for conformity brought to bear upon anomalous groups like the Jews. Their anomaly status hardened too over the
years. The message of liberal theologians that the Old Testament was
written for a backward people, the Hebrews, incapable of assimilating
the full New Testament message was rapidly coming to represent
received opinion. Observations of endogamy and apartness in contemporary Jewish life promoted the identification of these English Jews
with the ancient Hebrews. Otherwise, they took their public image in
the 1890s still largely from the few very rich financiers increasingly
often depicted in novels of a kind that Maitland had probably read. It
is true that Maitland's own brand of patriotism was restrained and
far from jingoist. He disapproved deeply of Joseph Chamberlain's
imperialist ventures and, for example, of the Boer War in letters
notable for containing some of his few expressions of political views.[29]
But the combination of an opposition to imperialism and finance capital
with coolness towards a Jewish community all too closely associated
with both is pretty characteristic of many liberals of the day.[30]

One should not press the point too far. The real message from
Maitland's treatment of Jewish status is perhaps a general one concerning his model-making method. He has for once constructed his models

[29] *Letters*, i nos. 258, 260–1; *Letters*, ii nos. 198–200. He was much more alert to university
politics, ibid., ii pp. 7–11.
[30] I am in the main following here Feldman, *Englishmen and Jews*, chs 3–4, and am extremely
grateful to the author for some personal guidance. Also Burrow, *A Liberal Descent*, chs
5–6, 11.

from a relative ignorance, so as to permit, perhaps even to require supplementation from those prejudices that we all carry within us. That there should be a degree of Victorian projection here is hardly surprising and not too important when we compare him with certain contemporaries.[31] Feelings of this kind strike me as natural enough in the circumstances and no crime. To levy some unprovable charge of anti-semitism is of no value in this context. It was not Maitland's way to pronounce collective anathemas on any group of people. Always proud to be an Englishman himself, his references to those less fortunate are more often than not somewhat ambivalent and ironical.[32] 'Hebrews', themselves English and representing a 'Jewish Historical Society' expressly called 'of England'[33] must have presented a problem. This is highly relevant to the semantic field within which Maitland, the protestant agnostic, probed the significance of religion and more especially christian orthodoxy, and is worth closer inquiry than I can give it here. In any event, it does no harm to know that our man is human.

The Gentleman and his Women

It is also pleasant to view him in action on the side of the angels. His speech in favour of women's admission to Cambridge, delivered between the two editions of the *History*, is said to have gained numerous votes for the losing side. He approached the issue in his usual whole-hearted manner, while yet conveying the impression that he felt it to be an unfortunate diversion from his real tasks. And like his mentor, Sidgwick, he was very concerned not to trample too heavily on vested interests tending in the other direction.[34] Nonetheless, Maitland had the right to consider himself a feminist.

He starts his account by professing unhappiness that four pages (i 482–5) must suffice for 'half the inhabitants of England'. Yet he must accept that males were, like it or not, the norm for medieval lawyers. 'The lay Englishman, free but not noble, who is of full age and who

---

[31] For E. A. Freeman and Goldwin Smith (like me, of both Oxford and Cornell), see Feldman, *Englishmen and Jews*, pp. 74–5, 90–3, 99–102, 129 and Burrow, *A Liberal Descent*, Part III, esp. p. 204. I am grateful to have seen in draft R. Fleming, 'Henry Adams and the Anglo-Saxons', in P. Szarmach, ed., *The Preservation of Anglo-Saxon Culture* (in press).

[32] Letters from his enforced winter holidays give a number of illustrations. E.g. *Letters*, i nos 236, 370; *Letters* ii nos 185, 199.

[33] The Jewish Historical Society of England was founded in 1893. It is a pity that Feldman did not study the society in his *Englishmen and Jews*.

[34] Fifoot, *Life*, pp. 105–7; *Letters*, ii p. 7. Cf. *Letters*, i nos 188, 193–4, 212. *Letters*, ii no. 152 is intriguing in this connection.

has forfeited none of his rights by crime or sin, is the law's typical *man*, typical person' (i 407, my emphasis). He can set out the principles governing the woman's legal rights and duties with trenchant concision. 'Private law with few exceptions puts women on a par with men; public law gives a woman no rights and exacts from her no duties.' (i 482; cf. i 485) Although he opposes the belief current when he wrote that women's condition improved during the period — it was rather 'waning than waxing' (ii 403, 426) — the general impression these statements give is not too bad. He does not seem particularly critical of woman's situation in the way one might expect.

He is, of course, well aware that full equality of the sexes would have been much better, and applauds any efforts of the Church that seem to move in the right direction. Just like writers of women's history today, he happily collects examples of things women actually could do despite their unequal status, and displays any discomfort he may feel in having such news to report only in the delight with which he clutches the occasional straw of gender equality.[35] Some of these prove rather illusory on closer examination. The husband's constant need for his wife's concurrence to his dispositions and the wife's ability to use fines as 'the married woman's conveyance' by *Bracton*'s day (ii 102, 407) are true facts but not particularly nice ones. We have every reason to believe that these were occasions for the exercise of male dominance not a check upon it. Not infrequently is a wife's concurrence noted as being made 'lacrimabiliter' or accompanied by other signs of duress. These points deserve emphasis, since the ownership and control of land in medieval England must have been quite as much a key to social identity for women as it was for their menfolk. One thinks of the re-emergence of that identity in 'liege' widowhood, when having perhaps provided for her husband's soul out of his inheritance, a woman like Countess Clementia de Fougères was finally free to seek her own salvation by a benefaction from her own inheritance to her birth family's favoured Savigniac monks.[36]

On at least two aspects of women's legal condition, Maitland's words deserve rather more extended commentary. I turn first to marriage and the relations engendered by it between husband and wife. The author of *Canon Law and the Church of England* was far better

---

[35] E.g. Pollock and Maitland, ii 407, 413. They could act as attorney, even for their husband (i 213; ii 408); do homage at least in Bracton's day (i 305); inherit even lands held under military tenure (i 308 and cf. i 280); stand guardian of both land and heir in socage tenure (i 321) etc. etc.

[36] BL, Add. Charters, 39, 998 is a nice illustration, whereby the lady Clemency freed two villeins on terms that required them to contribute to a Savigny priory at Long Bennington in Lincolnshire, for which see *VCH, Lincs.*, ii 242.

read in the *Corpus Iuris Canonici* and its medieval commentaries than virtually any of the English legal historians who have followed him, despite the considerable strides that the history of canonistic legal science has made since his day. He grasped the supreme importance of the twelfth-century construction of a new definition of binding marriage destined to offer the West including England a brand-new paradigm of ideal Christian secular life. He was, however, pretty contemptuous of the results. 'The ecclesiastical court . . . is', for his taste, 'only too ready to regulate the most intimate relations between married people.' (ii 409) He has little patience for the clever, un-English impracticalities that ruled there. This is not the conclusion of recent scholarship,[37] basing itself largely on the case records of church courts whose very existence Maitland came to doubt.[38]

He seems to have been especially intrigued by the conceptual complications thrown up by the biblical principle that marriage made husband and wife 'one flesh'. Since no court system could afford to assimilate into its law all the corollaries, this became just one more tag to be produced with a flourish by needy pleaders. Maitland certainly saw much of the absurdity. He waxed a trifle ironical on the law's refusal to make a husband responsible for felonies committed by his wife. He also knew to report both that the husband who maimed or killed his wife faced the normal penalties on life and limb and that the wife who killed her husband was guilty not merely of homicide but of petty treason, for which the standard penalty was death by burning.[39] But these observations are separated by many pages, and the failure either to juxtapose the facts or to offer comment must seem weak to readers in an age desperately concerned with wife-battering. Patently the balance of power and violence within marriage — and we know from church misericord carvings of 'shrews' that violence was not entirely unidirectional — is a matter of live interest today. What a pity, then, that he never thought to consider jurisdiction over marital cruelty, which we now know to have been virtually created from whole cloth in the Age of Bracton itself by the very English church courts whom he condemned for their meddling.[40]

---

[37] As R. H. Helmholz has shown both in his *Marriage Litigation in Medieval England* (Cambridge, 1975) and in his contribution to the present volume. Also C. Donahue in N. Adams and C. Donahue, eds., *Selected Cases from the Ecclesiastical Province of Canterbury, c. 1200–1301* (Selden Soc., 95, 1981), the volume envisaged in *Letters*, ii no. 189!

[38] *Letters*, ii no. 328.

[39] Pollock and Maitland, ii 436, 511, 532; and cf. ii 406–7 incl. n. 1 for a coy explanation of the phrase 'coverte de baron'.

[40] Helmholz, *Marriage Litigation*, pp. 100–5; J. Brundage, *Law, Sex and Christian Society in Medieval Europe* (Chicago, 1987), p. 455.

Testamentary disposition was another aspect of matrimonial relations to demand attention in the church courts. Maitland guessed where we now know that men put up a prolonged resistance to church calls for married women to be allowed the freedom to make wills for the good of their souls.[41] Since salvation was and long remained the major goal of last wills, it is perhaps not surprising that written testaments were slow to include express provision for widows (and children). Though Maitland drew attention to this fact (ii 339–40), he made no more of it. Yet behind lay an important issue of property that must frequently have pitted fathers-in-law, concerned for their daughters' economic security in the event of their surviving their husbands, against the husbands themselves and their expectant heirs. Custom doubtless filled the gap some of the time. We know something of the widow's share on intestacy, and I have argued elsewhere that we should read the early chapters of Magna Carta as the outcome of a contested redrawing of family custom. My point, briefly put, was that a plethora of private charters during the twelfth century represent bargains driven between family members over their shares in the family property. They attest to a prolonged struggle between the conflicting claims of different family members in their various lifetime roles. Without this pre-history, the draftsmen of 1215 could hardly have struck so satisfying a balance.[42] Over-enthusiastic endowment weakened the heir and his line. To leave a widow without adequate provision, on the other hand, disgraced both her and her kinsmen; it constituted a disparagement almost as sharp as marriage beneath one's rank. Yet it was apparently *dampnum sine iniuria;* certainly I have noticed no litigation. On the other hand, Maitland was certainly very much aware of the volume of dower litigation concerning land and the dramatic expansion of litigation on the subject from the years surrounding 1215. Recent studies have begun to bring out some very interesting patterns of development with serious social as well as legal implications.[43] Had Maitland chosen to approach his law here in a slightly more overtly

[41] Compare Pollock and Maitland, ii 428–9 with M. M. Sheehan, *The Will in Medieval England* (Toronto, 1963), pp. 234–9. He noted women's bequests en passant, ibid., ii 317, n. 5, 329, n. 1.
[42] Hyams, 'The Charter as a source', 173 sq.
[43] J. Loengard, ' "Of the gift of her husband": English dower and its consequences in the year 1200', in J. Kirschner and S. F. Wimple, eds, *Women of the Medieval World: Essays in Honour of J. H. Mundy* (Oxford, 1985), pp. 215–55; idem, 'Legal history and the medieval Englishwoman revisited: some new directions', in J. T. Rosenthal, ed., *Medieval Women and the Sources of Medieval History* (Athens GA and London, 1990); J. Biancalana, 'For want of justice: legal reforms of Henry II', *Columbia Law Review*, 88 (1988), 433–536 at 514–34; idem, 'Widows at Common Law: the development of Common Law dower', *Irish Jurist*, ns 23 (1988), 255–329; S. S. Walker, ed., *Wife and Widow in Medieval England* (Ann Arbor, MI, 1993).

sociological fashion, he might well have led the way. We are after all dealing here with the consequences of the negotiations that preceded all propertied marriages, and Maitland had himself remarked on the way that Old English betrothal texts advise that the future bride's 'kinsmen ... should stipulate on her behalf for an honourable treatment as wife and widow' (ii 365). Though he understood the problem, he did not alas find reason to pursue it in the Age of Bracton.

Crime is another aspect of women's legal history where Maitland's account retains the power to stimulate research today. His observation that 'by a maxim of later law' no woman can be outlawed, 'for a woman is never in law' (i 482; ii 437) is basic and somewhat shocking in its own right. Noting analogues from Scandinavian laws and on the authority of the great Brunner, Maitland hopefully suggested that this anomaly 'may point to a time' when all women were under the *mund* of some man. I can find no later scholar taking the statement up for critical examination.[44] Reasonably enough, Maitland cited no cases, for his treatise evidence seemed to make the point. As *Fleta* put it at the end of the century, waiver of a woman 'utlagarie equipollet quo ad poenam', which was the material point.[45] For *Bracton* and his followers the logic followed from the exclusion of women (and boys under twelve years of age) from frankpledge; ergo they lacked law. That the lack of law was true in this one context only did not give them pause.

Proof of a negative is always hard. Here, however, any presumption for the Age of Glanvill can be rebutted by clear proof that the outlawry of a female was rare but not unheard of in the early part of the period covered by the *History of English Law*.[46] The Common Law had a special term for a female outlaw, 'weyve', as still noted in lawyers'

---

[44] R. Hunnisett, *The Medieval Coroner* (Cambridge, 1961), p. 62 registers and illustrates the dictum. Cf. Hunnisett, ed., *Bedfordshire Coroners' Rolls* (Beds. Hist. Records Soc., 41, 1961), no. 338 (1386).

[45] *Fleta*, ed. H. G. Richardson and G. O. Sayles (Selden Soc., 72, 1953), p. 70. Cf. *Bracton*, f. 125b, Thorne, ii 353; *Britton*, I. xiii. 3, ed. F. M. Nichols (2 vols, Oxford, 1865), i 50. Maitland presumably knew the dictum in *The Eyre of Kent, 6 and 7 Edward II*, ed. F. W. Maitland, L. W. V. Harcourt, and W. C. Bolland (Selden Soc. Year Books of Edward II ser., Selden Soc., 24, 1910), p. 106 (15), and *BNB*, pl. 1266 (Worcs. 1238–9), which he indexed s.v. 'waif', ibid., i p. 201. This last turns out to be a fascinatingly complex set of disputes; cf. *Rolls of the Justices in Eyre for Lincs. and Worcs.*, ed. D. M. Stenton (Selden Soc., 53, 1934), no. 1298; *CRR*, xiii 115 (=*BNB*, pl. 250); *CRR*, xvi 117S, 138B (1221, 1227, 1237–8).

[46] *PR 27 Henry II*, p. 155 (perhaps from an 1180 eyre of Belet, Murdac and Peak, *pace PKJ*, iii pp. lxiii–lxv); *29 Henry II*, p. 90 (Derby eyre of 1185). Another possible example is *PR 28 Henry II*, p. 80 (Worcester eyre 1182). The silence of *Glanvill*, bk. XIV is to be expected. For possible Anglo-Saxon outlawries of women, see below n. 55.

companions much later.[47] The first appearance of the Latin verb to 'waive' in this special sense, from 1203, seems to show the rule already fully formed; the arsonist son is outlawed and his mother 'waivetur'.[48] Its interesting extension of the existing meaning (as in 'waifs and strays', wandering beasts) looks like some lawyer's conscious neologism, and perhaps resulted from the reaffirmation of the Assize of Clarendon on frankpledge and the sheriff's tourn in 1166. Clearly there is something here still worth pursuing.

The primary purpose of outlawry was to make up for the inability of the Common Law, like most other laws in societies lacking an adequate police force, to guarantee the appearance in court to answer charges of an accused offender. Frankpledge and its associated institutions were supposed to commit respectable men to produce their adult male neighbours and dependants on such occasions. Perhaps they did when the accused was sure of acquittal. But when we can see the system in action on thirteenth-century plea rolls, the overwhelming majority were conspicuous by their absence only, and were recorded as fugitives. It can hardly have been much different in earlier ages. Outlawry was the penalty of final resort in such cases. It was especially the characteristic consequence of an appeal in which the appellee failed to answer four summonses at consecutive county courts.[49]

To question the applicability of outlawry to women offenders is therefore to raise the broader, much more intriguing and equally neglected question of the degree and nature of the criminal responsibility of women at the time. Maitland said very little indeed on this subject. Apparently his reading of rolls and reports failed to raise the question for him. Almost the only relevant remark I have noticed in the *History* is his observation *en passant*, that husbands were never hanged for their wives' felonies (ii 532). Women were not in frankpledge.[50] One would not expect to find them at the sheriff's tourn, the major annual

---

[47] Cf. Oxford English Dictionary s.v. 'Waive' sb. and v¹ 1. Unfortunately *The Middle English Dictionary* has yet to reach the letter 'W'. An earlier sense denoting stray animals is clearly documented in the Latin dictionaries, e.g. R. E. Latham, *Revised Medieval Latin Wordlist* (Oxford, 1965).

[48] *PKJ*, iii no. 687 (Shrewsbury eyre 1203). It may be material to note that the junior justice sitting was Simon of Pateshull. I owe this reference and other help in the matter to Dr Richard Sharpe.

[49] This is not the place to discuss the nature of the appeal, the validity of its usual labelling as 'appeal of felony', or its origins within a culture that had yet to adopt from Roman Law a clear distinction between civil and criminal law. I hope to deal with at least some of these matters in my forthcoming book, *Rancor and Reconciliation in Medieval England*.

[50] W. A. Morris, *The Frankpledge System* (London, 1910), p. 81. *Britton*, I, xiii. 1 (Nichols, i 48–9) includes 'femmes' among those who swear the closely associated fidelity oath to the king.

meeting of the hundred court designed to check tithings and the whole functioning of frankpledge. But Maitland also noticed among the shrieval abuses condemned in 1259 the coercion of 'mulieres' to attend the tourn.[51] Again, the issue is of some significance, since tourns were occasions for much local business and the private equivalent, view of frankpledge, was among the commonest of seignorial liberties. But on the general question Maitland says nothing, and so, as usual, no one else does either!

We do have good studies of women's restricted right to bring appeals, a significant disadvantage even in the thirteenth century when male appeals were in a decline that looked likely to be terminal.[52] There has been curiously little work on female plaintiffs in trespass and other forms of action for wrong.[53] Married women could, indeed had to be joined in actions for redress of wrongs to them and their husbands. Moreover their incapacity to serve on juries barred them from the other main legal means of avenging a grudge in the Age of Bracton, the provision of an indictment to a jury of presentment. They may occasionally have been the source for some of the information behind indictments, but overall their potential to obtain recourse other than through their menfolk still seems very inadequate and of sufficient significance to merit discussion in any modern *History of English Law*.

But this says nothing at all about women's criminal liability. Modern studies of women's liability to outlawry or some equivalent and of 'criminal' appeals and indictments against them are rare or non-existent. Women certainly figure among those delivered from gaols and presented by grand juries, though the numbers are small.[54] Women clearly are criminally liable in principle and law.[55] This being so, there

---

[51] Pollock and Maitland, i 483–4, where the enactment is cited as Provisions of Westminster, c. 10. R. F. Treharne and I. J. Sanders, eds and trans, *Documents of the Baronial Movement of Reform and Rebellion, 1258–1267* (Oxford, 1973), p. 140 place it in c. 4. Most later commentators ignore the point. Two who picked it up are Morris, *Frankpledge*, p. 81 and H. Cam, *The Hundred and the Hundred Rolls* (London, 1930), p. 119.

[52] C. A. F. Meekings, *The 1235 Surrey Eyre*, vol. I, (Surrey Record Society, 31, 1979), pp. 123–5 and J. M. Kaye, *Placita Corone* (Selden Society Suppl. Series 4, London, 1966), pp. xxix–xxxii are authorities on women's appeals. Cf. also B. A. Hanawalt, *Crime and Conflict in English Communities, 1300–1348* (Cambridge, Mass., 1979), pp. 54, 115–25, 152–4.

[53] The otherwise excellent investigation of early trespass of A. Harding, *The Roll of the Shropshire Eyre of 1256* (Selden Soc., 96, 1981), pp. xxxii sq. does not examine questions of gender.

[54] Information from my student Amy Phelan, who is currently at work on violence in the decades around 1300.

[55] Patrick Wormald kindly brought to my attention relevant Old English materials from his 'A handlist of Anglo-Saxon lawsuits', *ASE*, 17 (1988). In no. 75 (1012), a sister came to the aid of her brother, an ealdorman exiled for rebellion, and was for her pains herself made *exheredem*. Neither here (A. Campbell, ed., *Charters of Rochester*, London 1973, no. 33) nor

must have been process available for the attempt to secure their appearance in court, to justice the recalcitrant and to secure execution against them. Most women would be numbered within the mainpast of some male, which explains their exclusion from frankpledge. But there must have been exceptions, *femmes soles* who really were 'in their liege power' as widowed heiresses. Were accused women subject to the same rules as the men or different ones? Were they treated differently from the men (e.g. by being burned instead of hanged or having their sentences deferred for pregnancy etc.) and if so, how often? Did women, in short, combine like villeins effective civil rightlessness at Common Law with full 'criminal' liability? I do not know the answers to these really rather important questions, and if the experts do, they have yet to tell the rest of us. This looks to be the kind of inquiry into women's history that will materially advance our general understanding.

Patently, we have no reason to criticise Maitland for what he did not do here. On the contrary, he might experience some pride that his *aperçus* retain their power to provoke further study. How we should feel about questions unraised so long after the publication of the *History* is another matter.

I have one further point to make about Maitland's treatment of Women in the *History*. This is to emphasise his view of his task in essentially expository terms. His working method was top-down; he planned what he was going to say, then said it.[56] The hard-headed way he stuck to his self-imposed brief, combined perhaps with an ability to compartmentalize data in his mind, prevented him from passing on much that his wide reading of sources and literature had taught him. One can usefully illustrate this by glancing at just a few of the texts he knew and actually cited in the *History*.

Consider first, childbirth, a topic of keen importance to both the women who suffered it and the men who waited anxiously for healthy

in 'Handlist', no. 71 are either she or her husband specifically said to be outlawed. Other charters ('Handlist', nos 58, 68, 70, 72a, 73) certainly demonstrate that women were liable to forfeit lands and rights for offences committed both by themselves and their husbands, but they never refer specifically to outlawry as far as I can see. There is no reason to doubt that women were in principle subject to the same penalties, including outlawry, as their menfolk. However, the terminological laxity is striking: Maitland would certainly have remarked upon it. It surely carries important implications for our reading of related *leges*, such as *IV As.*, 3, 6, 6.4, 6.7 relating to woman thieves. I am most grateful to Mr Wormald for his guidance on these matters, even or especially where our views do not coincide.

[56] Cf. *Letters*, ii no. 174: 'According to my habit I made a rush at it [his chapter on the Anglican Settlement for the C. M. H.], writing chiefly from memory, in order that I might see the general outlines...' Milsom in *Haskins Society Journal*, 7 (forthcoming) has some good observations on this.

male heirs. Maitland might have taught us from a charter of Earl
Gilbert de Gant's of the 1150s that founders' rights at the Augustinian
priory of Bridlington extended to hospitality for their patron's wife
when she was ready to give birth. Gilbert promised that he would take
the habit there if anywhere and that he would be buried there where
he was born and brought up.[57] Neither the apparent right nor the fact
that male monks perhaps attended the woman in her labour rather
than women was, however, enough to persuade Maitland to quote
more than a few lines of the document.

My other childbirth text appears in the context of curtesy, the
custom by which a widower might enjoy his deceased wife's lands for
his lifetime, if and only if he had sired a live child by her. The required
evidence, Maitland described as 'this quaint demand for a cry within
four walls'.[58] The 1277 holding he cited in support (ii 416) is worth
quoting at length. The husband in the case failed

> because women are not admitted to make any inquisition in the king's court,
> and (because) the court cannot be sure whether the boy was born alive or
> not unless he was seen by males or heard by them calling out, and (because)
> he was never seen by males nor could be, because it is not permitted that
> males be present at *secreta* of this kind.

It is manifestly clear that this dictum is of at least as much legal interest
as the discussion of the nature of the four walls which was perhaps
responsible for its exclusion from the book. Contemporary interest in
the definition of separate spheres by gender needs no emphasis.[59]

One more text demands admission at this point. It relates to the
crime of rape and the requirements for pardon in homicide cases. In
1259 a woman was presented for killing a would-be rapist with her
knife. She had already fled, presumably in the fear that her plea of
self-defence might commend itself no better to thirteenth-century justices than it has on occasion to their twentieth-century successors. Her
father, however, by a proffer of 40/- to the justices secured her return
to the peace together with a promise that the justices would speak to
the king on her behalf. The outcome of this case is unknown.[60] The
issue of self-defence which must have been at its core is a very emotive
one in our own day. Women's advocates argue with some force that

---

[57] *EYC*, ii no. 1138 (1150/56), cited Pollock and Maitland, ii 325 from the *Monasticon*.

[58] He was already intrigued by the 'four walls' problem in 1880, *Letters*, ii no. 3.

[59] Another case cited Pollock and Maitland, ii 399 illustrates a related matter. It shows that
sometimes women not only delivered the child but also arranged his baptism and naming,
all presumably in the father's absence. Names were important enough that contemporaries
would, one imagines, have been shocked by this, even with a babe not expected to live.

[60] Pollock and Maitland, ii 479 n. 2. N. D. Hurnard, *The King's Pardon for Homicide Before
A.D. 1307* (Oxford, 1969), the standard work on the subject, did not notice this case.

the criteria that underlie the definition of crimes of violence including rape and the defences permitted in them assume a male pattern of aggression which may not be, and in some instances demonstrably is not, applicable to women.[61] There is a prima facie case to pursue here, and the trail leads back into our and Maitland's period. We know that statutory definitions of crime began only at the very end of the thirteenth century.[62] Before then, offences (to call them crime is in a serious sense anachronistic) were customary in that they were what judges and juries thought they were, when convicting or acquitting. Many of these definitions, generated in a fashion at which we can only guess blindly, lasted on into Maitland's day with very little modification. If male jurors understood self-defence in terms of reasonable male behaviour patterns, who can blame them? Maitland's presentment is evocative in that it just might, in a more precedent-sensitive system than the thirteenth-century pleas of the crown contained, have led to a rape defence rule less inappropriate to the needs of complainants. I for one would much like to know whether this was the only father able to save his daughter from death or exile by a personal intervention.

I doubt that any of this would have surprised my contemporary, Maitland. He had, of course, read the texts to which I refer, and would certainly have taken on board more of their wider implications perhaps than I can. My suggestions are simply not the kind that he set out to make in the *History* or, for the most part, anywhere else in print. This is in the end an index of his very Victorian character. Each of us too can expect to be outflanked in our turn as historical change outdistances our creeds. I offer one final illustration both as further confirmation and to serve as a bridge to the next section. Maitland very happily discussed, again without moral or other comment on the implications for the women themselves, marriage controls on villeins (the deliberately nasty custom of merchet) as a restriction on male rights of disposal over their womenfolk (ii 372–3). Maitland did not see it as any part of his task to try to view through female eyes the system of villeinage to which I now turn.[63]

---

[61] I find the account of this matter in Anne Campbell, *Men, Women and Aggression* (New York, 1993), chs 6–7 very compelling.

[62] A. Harding, 'The origins of the crime of conspiracy', *TRHS*, 5th ser. 33 (1983), 89–108.

[63] For seignorial control over the marriage of heiresses at a higher social level, see Pollock and Maitland, i 318–21.

Rich Man, Poor Man, Serf and Villein

There is no question that Maitland was acutely sensitive to the protection of free subjects from the arbitrary treatment that accompanied tyranny and servility. This was for him a major function of law, the very glory of our Common Law. This liberal believed in firm government and legislative simplicity as the best guarantees of Anglo-Saxon freedoms.[64] Law conferred liberty; the law as an instrument of oppression was not a theme that slid easily from his pen. Hence when he mentions the processual origins of the phrase Habeas Corpus,[65] he hopes that this may promote 'our interest in the liberty of the subject' (ii 586). And when he remarks as from a lofty height that 'no law . . . has ever been able to ignore the economic stratification of society' (ii 533), his point was not the difficulty of protecting the poor against the rich and powerful. It addressed the problem posed for king and legal system by overmighty families like those referred to in Athelstan's laws or for that matter the commercial magnates, the Melmottes, of his own day. He was commenting on the scope of the doctrine 'Respondeat superior', not protection for the powerless.

In fact he evinces throughout rather little interest in the way that power relations worked through the courts as opposed to the courts' work to impose and maintain peace and order. This is curious in a way. He had a better sense of the raw fear which Norman and Angevin kings sometimes cast on their subjects than many moderns. But still he bequeathed us here a weakness not yet fully remedied. Professor Milsom has indeed shown us how the injection of lordship and social stratification into twelfth-century legal history changes our whole picture of the early Common Law.[66] What has been done to document the power of wealth in the Age of Bracton, however, remains little enough to surprise colleagues from other historical periods.[67] We still await, for example, a study of the real meaning of the myriad proffers, routine and otherwise, so lovingly recorded on pipe, oblate and fine rolls. When is a bribe not a bribe, the outside observer must wonder?[68] Maitland palpably understates the clout of the powerful and the pull of money within his beloved Common Law.

---

[64] Pollock and Maitland, i 135, 406; ii 274, 631. My friend David Eastwood contends that this combination of libertarian views with central direction is much more characteristic of Victorian liberalism than popular belief would have it.

[65] On which see Paul Brand above pp. 71–2.

[66] Milsom, *Legal Framework*.

[67] One laudable exception, R. V. Turner, *The King and his Courts, 1199–1240* (Ithaca NY, 1968), primarily documents royal power-mongering.

[68] See J. T. Noonan jr., *Bribes* (New York, 1984).

With no hint in his writings of any interest in Marx, class was for
him neither a tool nor a topic for treatment. He certainly knew enough
to situate himself socially, though. His letters show him meticulous
about the proper forms of address, including titles for his corres-
pondents. He was quick to congratulate recipients on honours and
preferments. We should be getting him wrong to infer any serious
radicalism from the occasionally ironical references to peers. Though
himself a modest landowner, a distinction whose significance a
Gloucestershire neighbour once brought home fairly brutally to his
wife, he never gained genuine financial security. Even so, he lived a
good middle-class Victorian life in houses of comfortable dimensions
and furnishing, predicated upon the uncriticised existence of servants.
He never once speaks in his letters about paupers or the slums in
which they dwelt.[69]

None of this diminishes his account of villeinage law, which remains
serviceable today. Its strength is his firm recognition that villeinage is
a lawyers' artefact. He foresees in part (i 360), and would clearly have
no difficulty with, my hypothesis of an Angevin origin for the doctrine
as an unintended by-product of the Common Law's own birth.[70] Nor,
I feel sure, would he have experienced any difficulty with the analytical
distinction between 'serfdom' (as the answer to socio-economic
questions) and 'villeinage' (answering good lawyer's questions) on
which my exposition stands.[71] Maitland grasped that Common Law
villeinage had quite significant implications for the whole legal system,
and might almost serve as a test of its character during that first period
of its existence.

Villeinage is a subject that well illustrates Maitland's feel for the
concrete. The passage in which he sought to show the physical reality
behind the legal definition of the manor (i 596 sq.) is one really rather
extraordinary example.[72] His knowledge of manorial court rolls and
other records enable him to relate Common Law doctrine to the
manorial context in which the dramas mostly played out. By this I
mean less the conflicts of everyday life than the realities of the power

---

[69] I base these impressions mostly on the two volumes of *Letters*. For the Gloucestershire
manor and the revealing snub made in ignorance of it, see Fifoot, *Life*, pp. 171 sq., *Letters*,
ii, pp. 3–4 examines finances. I fancy that G. Raverat, *Period Piece: a Cambridge Childhood*
(London, 1960), esp. ch. VI 'Propriety' might be a good place to start a real attempt to place
Maitland socially.
[70] I refer to my own *King, Lords, and Peasants*, ch. 13.
[71] Ibid., pp. vii, 232–3.
[72] Compare this with Pollock and Maitland, i 168, surely a most odd use for time-travel!

balance in the manor court itself.[73] He saw well how the content of custom turned on who controlled the court that administered it.

It apparently amused him to illustrates the way the doctrine of villeinage encouraged lords to treat their peasants as human property, 'agricultural capital', even an incorporeal hereditament, but not, as he dryly observes, an object that could be stolen (ii 145, 150, 363, 499)! Although he sees with lawyer's eyes that the crux of the system is the very limited extent to which a villein had rights (by which he mostly meant rights enforceable at Common Law), he also understands that tenure has much more practical importance than status. He locates the institution's conceptual essence in the lord's desire for cheap labour. In identifying 'certainty' as the significant test (i 369–76) — the serf with his obligation to labour for his lord always knows for certain in the evening what he must do the next day, and the week after Hoketide too — he is only partly right as to the developing law. Yet a comparison of his account with that of Vinogradoff, who is the source of most of its ideas, leaves the reader in no doubt as to the superiority of Maitland's intellect and analytical abilities.[74]

The law of villein status he brilliantly reconstructs after *Bracton* on the basis of seisin. For *Bracton*, and the lawyers who imbibed his view from Edward I's day on,[75] the villein was free as regards everyone save his lord. The disabilities thus bit less deep, a fact that is perhaps underrated in accounts of the eventual and much later disappearance of serfdom.

It is surely legitimate to ask once more what he may have thought about all this. Villeinage law remains, when all is said and done, a doctrine designed to curtail not just the rights but the humanity of one very large portion of the population in the interests of another very small minority. We can detect through the lawyer's inscrutable objectivity hints of moral criticism. He distances himself and his reader from the system with the timely reminder that 'the religion of the time saw nothing wrong' with the exploitation of serfs (i 77, 379). He reminds his reader that *Bracton* used 'the worst word he had got' to denote

[73] There has been remarkably little empirical study of the balance of power between lord and villagers in 'their' court since Maitland's day. I discount the assertions, made on the basis of one ideology or another, of seignorial oppression or the manor as the villagers' court. See very briefly *King, Lords, and Peasants*, pp. 49–50.

[74] See on all this *King, Lords, and Peasants*, chs 8 (iii), 11. Maitland read and praised P. Vinogradoff, *Villainage in England* (Oxford, 1892), but for purpose of comparison his essay on 'Agricultural Services', reprinted in his own *Collected Papers* (Oxford, 1928), i ch. III is still more enlightening.

[75] I underestimated the eventual triumph of the Bractonian 'relativity of villeinage' view in *King, Lords, and Peasants*.

villeins, the same word as for chattel slaves (i 412), and very possibly exaggerates the nastiness of the word 'sequela' as used for the villein's 'brood', or issue (i 381).[76] That the liberal should show his colours in this context more than elsewhere is quite understandable. Slavery was in his day an issue far more live than it seems now, and had within the memory of Maitland himself been a fiercely disputed one in his own circles.[77]

My own preference is to cast my moral gaze in a slightly different direction. Villeinage being hereditary, it seems appropriate to analyse it for once from the viewpoint of the women from whose bellies villeins emerged. I have recently tried to do this.[78] My most spectacular if hesitant finding was the almost complete absence of the sexual exploitation of female villeins by their lords. This is in sharp contrast to what we are told, for example, about slavery in ante-bellum America. I had expected to find some evidence at least, and had in my doctoral days made a vigorous and prurient search for the reality behind the *Ius primae noctis*. I found nothing of substance, and I think I now understand the reason. Lords, who were in any case mostly resident far from the manor, possessed too little actual control over the physical persons of their villeins to have much opportunity. In other words, even the serfdom behind legal villeinage is very different from slavery. This, if I am right, and the point is so unwelcome to some as to be heavily disputed, is an interesting conclusion to say the least, though one that might easily have been reached by a less sordid route. And if serfdom is not slavery, Maitland, the good Victorian liberal, is similarly no emotional twentieth-century do-gooder.

Heretics, Homosexuals, Maitland, and the 'rest of us'

In this paper, I have chosen to focus on a rather miscellaneous set of social groups with little in common beyond their imperfect represen-

---

[76] The alternative form 'secta' suggests to me a less emotive reading. *Sequela* is certainly found in more respectable contexts than the famous clause of Magna Carta. W. Croft Dickinson, 'What were *Sequels*?', *Juridical Review*, 52 (1940), 117–25, an article Maitland would have enjoyed, neatly illustrates the point from Scotland, where breweries could have their *sequela*. A villein's children follow him in his hereditary obligations, much as other tenants must do suit to mill or court as a function of their tenure. *Letters*, i no. 422 suggests that Maitland might not have been too hard to persuade.

[77] Cf. *Letters*, i no. 86; Pollock and Maitland, i 430 n. 2.

[78] I presented my arguments in a Ralph Karrhas Lecture at the College of Law, Syracuse in December 1994 under the portentous title 'Toward a Feminist View of Common-Law Villeinage', and earlier in less developed versions to audiences at Harvard Law School and the International Medieval Studies Congress at Kalamazoo, MI.

tation by the mainstream of English law. I set out to learn something of Maitland and his approach to law by scrutinizing the Law's border territory. This is not, it is true, the best route to a full understanding of the subject's heartland. Outlawry, to give only an example already used, obviously does define a certain aspect of that law which it withdraws from its object. But no study of outlawry can convey much of the richness and potential of the Common Law or any other legal system. Even so, I feel that I at least have learned something new from writing this paper both about Maitland and the law that unites us.

I should hate to end on any note of disrespect or unfairness to a great man. Historical characters, as Maitland now assuredly is, were what they were in their lifetime. That they were not as we should like to be *now* is not just beside the point; it is literally pointless. I therefore close with some reflections on the territory as our man saw it in his still great *History*. Maitland made no bones about his position despite all the reservations with which he habitually clothed his uncertainties. Law was a good thing. On the whole the more of it a people enjoyed, the better it fared. He looked down upon his law from the highest pinnacle of its capital city, in the way a legislator might, or at least through the eyes of judge and jurist. He identified most of the time with those who purveyed its benefits, peace and prosperity, much less with 'the rest of us' at the receiving end, rather more often sharp and painful than comforting.[79]

The legal borderland, or marcher areas, which I have surveyed here, exist only in an outwards perspective proceeding from the nation and its capital. It is thus natural and very forgivable in a way that Maitland should expend but little of that enviable stock of intellectual energy and creativity on the effort to empathise with Women or Jews or the 'Lower Classes'. This was just not his thing. And that is why the real borderers, as it were, make such brief entries onto his scene.[80]

My final subject doublet offers an instructive contrast. I referred to Maitland at the outset as an insider figure. Like many of us, he liked to think of himself more as a sceptic and maverick. He had had hopes of becoming, in the nicest possible way, a reforming thorn to prick the establishment of his younger days on its proper road. Something of this must explain why he allotted nearly ten pages of his second volume to heresy (ii 534–52). Why so lavish? To all intents and purposes, medieval England had no heresy; heresy presented few or no pressing

---

[79] See above n. 1 for telling remark to Dicey.
[80] Women are a partial exception, due to their inevitable involvement in marriage, a matter whose legal consequences to men and property were undeniable.

problems to practising English lawyers, canon or common. Of course, the topic gave him licence to expatiate on one of his favourite leit-motivs, the situation of the English Church squarely within the canoni-cal legal culture of a western Christendom that had constructed for itself very good reasons to think hard about heresy. But Maitland is less objective here than elsewhere; his sympathies are throughout thoroughly on the heretic's side. It is hardly too much to discern a self-identification as heretic, which it is amusing to compare with that of his most acute critic two generations later.[81] He even went out of his way and beyond his period by much the same two generations to express 'some satisfaction' at the fate suffered by a fourteenth-century Franciscan heresy-hunter who found himself accused in his turn (ii 549–50).

Contrast, if you will, this favour to heresy with the miserable para-graph grudgingly permitted to something entitled 'Unnatural Crime' quite close by (ii 556–7). This he glosses unhelpfully in the text as 'the crime against nature', secure in the confidence that his readership would neither require nor wish for further detail. The major point he makes is probably correct. He reads the 1553 statute on the subject as an indication that the various authorities took little interest in prose-cution of the offence during the later middle ages.[82]

We may recall that 1895 was not just the year that saw the publi-cation of the first edition of Pollock and Maitland and a new periodical called *The American Historical Review*.[83] It was also, to most people more obviously, the year of the trials of Mr Oscar Wilde, among various 'headline' events. This ought to give Maitland's readers pause. One is bound to be struck by the total absence from our man's letters and other papers not just of the whole Decadence phenomenon of the

---

[81] See Milsom in Pollock and Maitland (1968 reissue), i pp. xxv, xxvii, lxxiii. Several of the symposium participants gave eloquent personal testimony to the continuing attractions to intellectuals of the heretic persona in a society that conducts no burnings! See further *Letters*, i no. 337; *Letters*, ii no. 251 and *Collected Papers*, iii 191–2.

[82] The account of the treatment of homosexuals in medieval laws and culture in R. I. Moore, *The Formation of a Persecuting Society* (Oxford, 1987) may usefully be compared with the independent and intelligent summary of recent literature in S. Katz, *The Holocaust in Historical Context*, vol. I (Oxford, 1994). There is precious little indication of Maitland's own feelings on this subject beyond tiny scraps such as those in *Letters*, i p. 337 n. 3, *Letters*, ii no. 282.

[83] The rambling review of Pollock and Maitland by M. M. Bigelow, *American Historical Review*, 1 (1895), 112–20 is not mentioned in 'History language, and reading: waiting for Crillon', contributed to the anniversary issue ibid. 100 (1995), 799–828 by my Cornell col-league, Dominick LaCapra.

'naughty nineties' but of virtually every other stirring happening in his lifetime, war and politics excepted.[84]

Let us compare him briefly to a fictional contemporary, Ibsen's 'Enemy of the People'. Can anyone seriously believe that Frederic William Maitland would have taken up any cause so sordid and unpopular as public hygiene and the provision of sewers? Would he ever have situated himself so far ahead of the respectable opinion of the day as to constitute a minority of one? Surely not.

Were he to return to us today from Clio's compound in Elysium, he would at once regain his rightful place as our intellectual peer and superior. He would reign once more as the last surviving Founding Fellow of the British Academy, the 'Tribe of Israel' as he liked to call it.[85] He would devour with genuine enjoyment the legal history written since his time, to castigate its gaps and failings politely and without mercy. He would be enthralled, astounded and horrified by much that he saw.[86]

I imagine that he would be much keener to read all than to see all. He would not, I should wager, press to be permitted to join the throbbing, multicultural crowds at, say the Notting Hill Carnival or a Lords Test Match. Yet historians have something to learn from every quarter of their culture, even from the least unlikely corners. Lords or the Notting Hill Carnival might have helped in the understanding of one passage cited from the early thirteenth-century Civilian, Azo, on the supposed etymology of the Latin word 'Pactum', meaning agreement: '. . . vel dicitur [pactum] a percussione palmarum; veteres enim consentientes, palmas ad invicem percutiebant in signum non violandae fidei.' Maitland's understanding of this as 'that mutual grasp of hands . . . whereby men were wont to bind a bargain' must be an error. It is not possible to read *percussio* as part of any gentlemanly handshake. It makes much more sense as part of the grand, percussive gesture of the 'high (or low) five' with which Afro-Caribbean Britons

---

[84] Maitland's letters are a very incomplete source for his interests. Many are business communications. Very few are personal, as one can see from the fact one alone in *Letters*, ii is to a first-name correspondent; see ibid., no. 275. (I owe this observation to John Gillingham.) I am well aware of the great need for expert guidance as to what one may legitimately deduce from the content of such letters at this time, but have nevertheless used the leters heavily.

[85] *Letters*, i nos 353, 372.

[86] I like to think that he might be less puzzled than we are by Russia, having missed both 1917 and 1989.

and their African-American fellows have enriched our culture.[87] This trivial slip may well serve as an apt if unfair symbol of the distance that now divides our divine contemporary, Maitland, from 'the rest of us' today.[88]

[87] Pollock and Maitland, ii 194 cited Azo, *Summa Codicis*, tit. de pactis (2, 3); cf. ibid., 189–90. D. Ibbetson, 'From Property to Contract: the transformation of sale in the Middle Ages', *Journal of Legal History*, 13 (1992), 1–22, esp. 5–6; Mr Ibbetson is certainly right to doubt that the Civilian 'five' was as high and enthusiastic as today's tastes dictate.

[88] I should like to remember here an old tutor, Lady Rosalind Clay, to whom I owe my copy of Pollock and Maitland. I also wish to thank Professor Reba Soffer, author of the fine forthcoming volume on *Discipline and Power: the University, History and the Making of an English Elite, 1870–1930* (Stanford U. P., 1995) for much help (including a copy of page proofs) and encouragement.

Proceedings of the British Academy, **89**, 243–259

'Pollock and Maitland': a Lawyer's Retrospect

S. F. C. MILSOM

MANY YEARS AGO, mailing the typescript of a tentative and theoretical paper, I tempted providence by congratulating myself on not having to say exactly what it was about. When the thing had been published there came a demand from a journal of social science abstracts for a 200-word summary. I should have remembered the episode when backed into a corner by Professor Holt and handed my present assignment. Even if I were sure I had rightly digested the papers we have enjoyed, they are too diverse in aim and character for summary or synthesis.

Any such attempt would also court the special irritation felt by insiders when an outsider reinterprets their work. The initiative for this occasion came from the medieval history section of the British Academy; and although the legal section gave its enthusiastic blessing, it is essentially a conference of historians. Professor Helmholz and I are the only speakers to be or have been law teachers rather than history teachers; and it will be one of my themes that the regular medievalist and the lawyer kind of legal historian are often looking for different things in different ways, and that some of the things both would like to find are lost between them. I believe the very fact of the present gathering must be a symptom of that loss. For a work of history to retain any authority after a hundred years, and not just be read as one might read Gibbon or Macaulay,[1] testifies to some extraordinary quality in its author: also to some failure in those who have come after, including ourselves.

So instead of risking attempts at summary or synthesis, this retrospect will first pick out observations about Maitland's book which have been common to more than one of the papers, and will then take the

---

© The British Academy 1996

[1] See above, Wormald, p. 1.

greater risk of expressing some lawyerly discontent with the present state of the subject. The first common feature is the proportion of their topics in which our contributors have found that Maitland was not really interested. Neither the Anglo-Saxon nor the Anglo-Norman period was central to his concerns, nor were the learned laws, nor was the family as such, nor for the most part were Professor Hyams's underdogs. The top dog was another matter: Maitland was certainly interested in kingship and would I think have specially appreciated Dr Garnett's analysis, not least for the only sustained piece of legal argumentation which the subjects have elicited.

This catalogue of our topics in which Maitland was not really interested has an obvious corollary. His central concern in 'Pollock and Maitland' is clearly stated: 'We shall speak for the more part of the law as it stood in the period that lies between 1154 and 1272'.[2] Two points need making. The first is about Maitland: the connotations of 'the law is as it stood' are both unitary and static. The second is about us: our period papers on the ages of *Glanvill* and *Bracton* have dealt with matters of great interest and importance, but not with the law of those periods as such. For the Anglo-Saxon and Anglo-Norman periods, for which 'Pollock and Maitland' clearly cannot now be regarded as definitive, Mr Wormald and Dr Hudson have indeed concerned themselves with the law and told us much about it: in the hands of historians, the legal history of those periods is on the move. For periods after Edward I, the density of legal technicality has mostly persuaded historians to leave the subject to lawyers. But it is not only in our centenary studies that the subject central to Maitland's interest has become something of a no-go area; and so he lives on.

Why did Maitland write about things not central to his concerns? For the Anglo-Saxon period of course one answer is that he did not write about it because Pollock got in first. But Mr Wormald has given us reasons for thinking that he did not substantially dissent from what Pollock had written;[3] and perhaps this is the place to make a quite different point. Both Mr Wormald and Dr Hudson have examined the chronological relationship between Maitland's work on *Domesday Book and Beyond* and on the *History of English Law*;[4] and I am left marvelling even more than before at the speed with which the *History* was written: five years from conception to delivery to the press, and much of *Domesday Book* as well as the infant Selden Society thrown in. It is a fact to bear in mind when swearing on the book.

[2] Pollock and Maitland, i 232.
[3] See above, Wormald, p. 3.
[4] See above, Wormald, p. 4 and Hudson, pp. 27 *et seq.*

If Maitland underestimated the Anglo-Saxon legacy, and saw the Anglo-Norman period as mainly important for leaving enough royal power for Henry II to work with, and if neither period offered sufficient materials with which he felt at home, still he could hardly alter the agreed plan and leave them out; and perhaps that is all there is to it. But Mr Wormald's discussion of presenting juries introduces another feature of Maitland's work which I at least had not fully taken in, and which these papers have brought out in a striking way. He was *against* things, in Mr Wormald's case anything that 'left the taste of legal legend';[5] and perhaps he relished the chance to say so. Similarly his concern for individualism as against communalism, and therefore his hostility to theories which had seen the family rather than the individual as the original legal unit, is a principal theme of Professor White's paper.[6] In both cases his antipathy seems to have led Maitland astray.

Among our topics the most striking example of this characteristic is Maitland's treatment of the learned laws. That the Common Law had become strong enough to rule out any reception of Roman Law must be the most important single outcome of the period covered by his book. But during that period (or any other) was anybody thinking in those terms?[7] Dr Hudson and Professor Hyams both draw attention to Maitland's use of the word 'foreign'; and Professor Hyams sees patriotic pride at work.[8] The emotional charge seems to affect the question as well as the answer. Professor Helmholz sees both Maitland and the common lawyers about whom he wrote as not very interested in the learned laws and as attaching no great importance to them for their own sakes:[9] but there was an important reaction in Maitland's mind. Here he was not fighting just other scholars. He saw the Common Law as under threat, and joined up for a war which never happened. Of the treatment in 'Pollock and Maitland' Professor Helmholz says 'The smell of something very like a battle rises from the pages'.[10]

His daughter Ermengard believed that Maitland rarely wrote in

[5] See above, Wormald, p. 13.
[6] See above, White, pp. 92 *et seq.* Cf. below, p. 256, n. 57. For another aspect, see above, Summerson pp. 120–1.
[7] On Maitland's Rede Lecture, see e.g. J. H. Baker, 'English Law and the Renaissance', reprinted in *The Legal Profession and the Common Law* (London, 1986), p. 461. See also G. R. Elton, *F. W. Maitland* (London 1985), pp. 79 *et seq.*
[8] See above, Hudson, p. 25 and Hyams, p. 217, n.6.
[9] Even when Maitland saw Roman influence in a point of detail, he thought it malign, e.g. (of a curious theory about why the termor was not seised): 'English law for six centuries and more will rue this youthful flirtation with Romanism'; Pollock and Maitland, ii 115.
[10] See above, Helmholz, p. 156.

silence: he spoke aloud the words flowing from his pen.[11] If she were still here, one might ask her how often the voice coming under the study door sounded as though her father was arguing rather than just speaking. The sense of involvement must sharpen a historian's vision: I shall never forget Helen Cam pointing indignantly to a case in her typescript of the *Eyre of London* with the words 'Just look at the scoundrel. *And* he is going to get away with it.'[12] But, as these papers have suggested, a vision so sharpened may turn out on closer examination of the evidence to be just more sharply wrong.

Another of Maitland's enemies was feudalism. I have referred before to his jibe about its being introduced into England in the seventeenth century and reaching its most perfect development in the eighteenth;[13] and there is an obvious likeness to the reaction seen by Mr Wormald against what Maitland thought another 'legal legend'.[14] The language is sometimes that of contempt. ' "Feudalism" is a good word, and will cover a multitude of ignorances'.[15] '[W]e are tempted to pronounce [certain rules] quite unintelligible, and therefore presumably "feudal" '.[16] But for Maitland the enemy is not just sloppy language: it is the idea that tenure had any importance in the development of the law about property in land. For him the personal relationship between lord and man was never more than an add-on extra to a system turning on abstract relationships between man and land. To say that the man owns or possesses the land is to make a statement to which no lord can be relevant; and 'Ownership and Possession' is the title of his chapter and the essence of his vision.[17]

It would be ironical if Maitland's reaction against his feudal enemy was stealthily abetted by his Roman enemy. Dr Brand, who has concentrated on the dating and authorship of *Bracton*, points out that the book itself cannot have affected the law in the period covered by Maitland's book; and for what it is worth I share his doubt about the extent to which it is reliable evidence for any thirteenth-century law.[18] Things often look different in the plea rolls. But the *Bracton* kind of man may have been a carrier who in his own day passed on Roman infections with his Roman terms. And more importantly, to use Plucknett's words, 'Maitland's

[11] Ermengard Maitland, *F. W. Maitland, A Child's-Eye View* (Selden Soc. pamphlet, 1957), p. 8.
[12] Recollected in *Eyre of London*, ii (Selden Soc., 86, 1969), p. ix.
[13] *Constitutional History*, pp. 142–3. Cf. *Collected Papers*, i 489.
[14] See above, Wormald, p. 13.
[15] *Collected Papers*, i 175.
[16] *Collected Papers*, i 410.
[17] Pollock and Maitland, ii 1 *et seq*.
[18] See above, Brand, p. 86.

great work is essentially Bractonian'.[19] For legal historians the important influence of *Bracton* was on Maitland himself. And the important influence of Maitland on the history of property law (a puny name for the social and economic core of things) is the assumption of abstract ideas of ownership and possession — both untidy by Roman standards, but abstract still. It was some unitary system of law rather than a controlling person or authority that said 'this is yours'.

The implications of this touch several of the foregoing papers. If somebody is an owner, but faces some difficulty in transferring his ownership, you are driven to the assumptions behind another of Maitland's headings, 'Restraints on Alienation'.[20] Maitland assumes once-for-all transfers of 'ownership' for which some once-for-all consent may be required, especially of heirs. Professor White, if I have understood him rightly, sees a sale of land as indeed a once-for-all alienation, but a gift in alms as a continuing exchange of land for prayers in which a kinship group may have a continuing non-legal interest; and their assent is recorded largely to register that interest.[21]

The difference may be more in emphasis than in substance but my own vision is more 'legal' than Professor White's, though closer to Thorne's than to Maitland's. Any grant creating a tenure was a continuing arrangement and not a once-for-all alienation. The prototype of the sale for money was an exchange of the land for the service attributable to it. The grantor took homage, and this bound his heir to continue the arrangement; but since it provided for the proper proportion of his own obligation of service the heir was in principle not harmed. For grants which did not reserve compensating service, *Glanvill* describes arrangements in which the donor should not bind his heirs by taking homage. But custom still obliged the heirs to continue certain of those arrangements, particularly gifts in *maritagium* and free alms, provided they were limited to an appropriate proportion of the whole inheritance. Other gratuitous allocations within the inheritance would be continued, or not, at the unfettered discretion of the heirs.[22]

For the younger son there is no customary equivalent of the daughter's *maritagium* which the heir must honour, presumably because fathers were easily persuaded by later wives to divert resources from heirs by earlier marriages. But of course the father can make such an

---

[19] T. F. T. Plucknett, *Early English Legal Literature* (Cambridge 1958), p. 105.
[20] Pollock and Maitland, i 329.
[21] See above, White, p. 106.
[22] *Glanvill*, vii 1, Hall, pp. 69 *et seq*.; S. E. Thorne, 'English feudalism and estates in land', reprinted in his *Essays in English Legal History* (London, 1985), at pp. 24 *et seq*, especially, for the difference from Maitland's view, p. 25 n. 42.

allocation and hope that his heir will choose to continue it. *Glanvill* does not say that a father cannot or must not benefit a younger son, only that he cannot easily do so 'beyond' the consent of the heir;[23] and the word *preter* does not seem to be just an elegant variation of *sine*.

When the father died the heir would often elect not to continue an arrangement now at his will, with dismal consequences. A determined father could lock his heir out by taking the younger son's homage. Since this would carry service it would not have been seen as a gratuitous benefit in the older framework reflected in *Glanvill*'s account, and the father's seemingly new expedient must mark a change in economic perception: what matters is increasingly absence of money price rather than freedom from service. But homage within the family attracted the subversive consequences associated with 'lord and heir': if the younger son died childless the homage would require the eldest to admit such other heirs of the younger as other brothers. All would have been well if only the younger son had been a bastard, who could have no heirs except his own legitimate issue.[24] So the father took to making him an honorary bastard, confining the grant to heirs of his body; and the end of that was to be the fee tail.

So there was no rule against the younger son: there was just no customary provision like the daughter's *maritagium* or the church's alms which would stop the heir resuming this part of his inheritance. And even those customary provisions were not so secure as those guarded by the bar of homage. Even when royal jurisdiction is established, heirs can often be seen trying to undo such gifts; and all such grants had been even more precarious so long as their continuation depended upon decisions made by the heir in his own court. It is all still the heir's inheritance. So, with the emphasis of a lawyer rather than a family historian, I would be more inclined that Professor White to see kin joining in or confirming English grants primarily as potential heirs binding themselves not to discontinue the gift rather than as family recording their stake in the spiritual benefit. And if different kin seem to be recruited for different gifts by the same donor,[25] I would remember that for different inheritances, perhaps mother's rather than father's, the potential heirs might be entirely different.

What is in issue in all this, of course, is how far people were thinking in terms of some ownership as against a genuinely dependent tenure. Dr Hudson sees a truly tenurial structure in Anglo-Norman England.

---

[23] *Glanvill*, vii 1, Hall, p. 70.
[24] *Glanvill*, vii 1, Hall, pp. 70–1 juxtaposes the bastard and the legitimate younger son.
[25] See above, White, p. 112, n. 127. If it was donee rather than donor who instigated the recruiting, the legal element would be even clearer.

His tenant in fee 'had considerable security of tenure within his life-time, provided he fulfilled the services which he owed his lord. His heir, particularly if a close relative, would normally succeed him'.[26] The reader who manages to put *Bracton* (and Maitland) out of his mind will recognize the same terms of thought in *Glanvill*, although the lord's discretions are now much confined by royal power: tenure is still conditional on the fulfilment of obligations; and inheritance still involves the lord's acceptance.[27] What is more, those words of Dr Hudson's would equally describe the situation of the unfree tenant until centuries later, when he too will get a different royal protection and become another kind of owner.

By contrast, Dr Garnett's paper does at one point envisage an early idea of ownership. Comparing an ecclesiastical vacancy with the death of a lay tenant-in-chief, he sees the heir of the latter as somehow owner even before he (or in the case of a woman, her husband) has been seised by the king. This pushes to its logical conclusion a common reading of the possessive adjectives in Henry I's Coronation Charter. Two linguistic points may be made. First, Maitland was wary of possess-ives, pointing to a frequent misunderstanding of 'my money in the bank'.[28] He saw the *praecipe* writ of debt as making a proprietary claim; but one can more easily see the writ of right as about an obligation on the lord to deliver the land to the heir, which suggests a different possible sense for the Charter's possessives.

Secondly, ordinary grammar may be overruled by the obvious, so that a possessive may refer to the person under discussion in the main sentence.[29] The Charter purports to address tenants-in-chief; and when c. 2 says that on the death of one of them *haeres suus non redimet terram suam* it may have seemed obvious that the *suam* like the *suus* referred to the dead man (though you would still have to allow for ellipsis in the closing sentence). And on the death of one of them leaving only a daughter, is the promise of c. 3 to give her to a suitable man with 'her' (the daughter's) inheritance, or with 'his' inheritance, that of the tenant-in-chief who will die and to whom the promise is made? To give full weight to 'her' is hard to reconcile with the much later attitude of the *Dialogus* to even the male heir of a tenant-in-

---

[26] See above, Hudson, p. 43.

[27] Cf. below, p. 256, at n. 56; p. 258, at n. 66.

[28] Pollock and Maitland, ii 205. If you are in the red you owe the bank, if in the black the bank owes you. Both are personal obligations dependent on the solvency of the debtor; and in neither case is the money owned.

[29] One of the difficulties of legal history is that legal writers were addressing persons who knew what they meant. *Glanvill* sometimes goes for the obvious, once to the editor's puzzlement: vii 3, Hall, p. 76 n. 2.

chief.[30] And to treat the male or female heir as 'owner' immediately does not make sense in the law of *Glanvill*'s time or later. Suppose the dead man's widow is with child. Or suppose the heir having this 'ownership' dies before seisin is delivered: whoever succeeds will do so not as his or her heir but as heir of the original dead man.

Related doubts arise over any view of a grant in alms as a transfer of everlasting ownership. Of course there will be no inheritance on the side of the donee. But unless it is waived the donor's heir will still have to do the service owed in respect of the land; and *Glanvill*'s limitation of such gifts to an appropriate proportion of the inheritance is reflected when the mortmain problem seems suddenly to spring from nowhere. The earliest concern is not with the lord's incidents, but with his services when the tenant gives away too much.[31] The problem has arisen with the disappearance of *Glanvill*'s sanction, namely that the heir might discontinue a precarious tenure he could not in that sense afford. It is probably the assize of novel disseisin that now prevents the heir resuming land so given; and so a tenure in principle precarious has become a kind of ownership.[32]

To a small extent this line of thought might affect one of Professor Holt's quantitative conclusions. He attributes the disparity between the proportions of lay to ecclesiastical beneficiaries in his *acta* on the one hand, and in the Chancery rolls on the other, entirely to the preservative qualities of ecclesiastical institutions; and that must be the principal explanation.[33] But if *Glanvill*'s account is taken seriously, the beneficiaries of any such gifts, even those guarded by the heavy artillery of the Church, would feel a measure of insecurity: they might suffer if their benefactor's heir, perhaps through later acts of generosity, might default on his obligations to king or intervening lords; and this might lead them to seek any assurance they could get. By the time of the Chancery rolls, though they might worry about their chattels being distrained for service owed by their donor's heir, they were safe from their tenure being discontinued by the heir himself.

The main thrust of Professor Holt's paper is the exciting promise of more evidence for the 'Age of Glanvill'. But there will still be a need to attend more closely than Maitland did to the 'larger building-

---

[30] *Dialogus*, p. 94.

[31] *Magna Carta* 1217, c. 39.

[32] A mark of dependence had been the need to join the donor or his heir in litigation. There may be traces in the earliest rolls of warrantors suing on behalf of grantees in alms. For *Glanvill* (vii 18, Hall, p. 94) the warrantor of *maritagium* might have to be joined like the warrantor of dower. See Milsom, *Legal Framework*, pp. 50–1, 144–5.

[33] See above, Holt, pp. 60–1.

blocks' available to him.[34] He could not have described the development of property law as he did if he had immersed himself in *Glanvill*
as he had in *Bracton*, or even if he had discussed c. 4 of the Assize of
Northampton in his text, alongside his characterization of mort d'ancestor as a general possessory remedy against equals, instead of remarking
in a footnote that it was first aimed to protect heirs against their lords.[35]

And here the lawyer feels uncomfortably bound to note another
reservation. Whether or not so intended, Professor Holt's insistent
images of supply and demand and of justice as a commodity may be
understood as endorsing the hypothesis that novel disseisin and mort
d'ancestor were the beginnings of an essentially competitive scheme
of supply, which would draw litigation from lords' courts into the king's.
Professor Thorne, even though he was thinking in Maitland's terms of
the assizes as possessory remedies, judged that incredible; and he saw
'possessory' sources of demand generated by endemic disorder.[36] I
believe the assizes arose out of order rather than disorder, being
conceived as direct protection for tenants against abuses of power by
their lords; and it is worth remarking that the abuses were in precisely
the matters picked out by Dr Hudson in the sentence quoted above:
security of tenure for the living tenant and succession of his heir on
death.[37] But the evidence suggests that they were happening at a very
different level of society. Professor Hyams's villeins were excluded, but
the main beneficiaries seem to have been small free peasants; and the
earliest plea rolls sometimes show them bringing great lords to book.
If so, and whatever the immediate political motive, justice was something more than a commodity in which King Henry II saw profit.

Professor Holt's contrast between a vertical view of history, following something through in time (whether backwards or forwards) and
a 'lateral or panoramic view of all the evidence at a particular point
in time', prompts other lawyerly observations.[38] The first is that legal
history is by definition largely vertical, concerned with change through
time rather than the still snapshot of one moment. And since it is
almost a function of law to hide change, few developments other than
those made by explicit legislation can be pinned down and dated. The
same rule works differently. The same word changes its meaning.
The same action is put to a fresh purpose. The same situation is

[34] See above, Holt, p. 47.
[35] Pollock and Maitland, ii 57 and n. 1. Cf. i 147: 'the practice of the courts soon left those
words behind it'. But it is the words and not the later practice that show the original
intention.
[36] S. E. Thorne, 'Livery of seisin', in his *Essays in English Legal History*, p. 44.
[37] See above, Hudson, p. 43, quoted above p. 248–9.
[38] See above, Holt, p. 49.

analysed in a new way. It follows that there will be few conclusions that are securely established as one can establish a regular historical fact. One can go badly wrong, and perhaps Maitland sometimes did. But that is the nature of the subject.

At least to a lawyer, it seems to follow that understanding how law works is relevant to legal history. There has been misunderstanding of Maitland's well-known remark about a lawyer having to be orthodox and orthodox history being a contradiction in terms.[39] He was adamant that history should play as small a part as possible in modern legal affairs, and that a good lawyer might have no interest in history. 'But . . . a thorough training in modern law is almost indispensable for any one who wishes to do good work on legal history'.[40] He went further: 'There are large and fertile tracts of history which the historian as a rule has to avoid because they are too legal'.[41] Maitland was himself a lawyer, a practising barrister turned law teacher. He was of course offered a chair of history and declined, not I think out of modesty. He had no great opinion of the history faculty of the time, and was comfortable with his lawyer colleagues. But historians are a persistent lot and they got him in the end. Geoffrey Elton made him their patron saint.[42] And when, in hard times from which Professor Holt's 'March windfall' seems sadly remote,[43] it was necessary to make a case for filling the chair of medieval history, the case made was based on Maitland as having given Cambridge a special place in medieval studies. That he had been in the law faculty, was hardly relevant. He was 'really' a historian.

Even on that basis, Mr Wormald notes that he did not write 'in quite the idiom of modern histories'.[44] Indeed. For one thing, of course, he was of an age in which historians generally believed in narrative or 'vertical' history. Not until long after his death did they restrict themselves to panoramic views of specific topics in short periods, or concentrate on the doings of individuals whose names would take over their indexes. There are not all that many personal names in the index of 'Pollock and Maitland', nor do many of its basic propositions rest on

[39] See *Collected Papers*, i 491. The misunderstanding may stem largely from Plucknett, *Early English Legal Literature*, pp. 13–14. Plucknett was a pure historian who spent his working life in law faculties but never felt at home with his lawyer colleagues; and as a legal historian he was not at his best with legal reasoning.

[40] *Collected Papers*, i 493.

[41] *Collected Papers*, i 486.

[42] Elton, *F. W. Maitland*, p. 97.

[43] See above, Holt, p. 51.

[44] See above, Wormald, p. 1.

the kind of evidence with which today's historians work. They rest on the authority of Maitland himself.

Maitland was also 'really' a lawyer; and the longevity of 'Pollock and Maitland' has a paler legal counterpart. Some law teachers still try to persuade students to start their study of trusts by reading Maitland's *Equity*. The subject has since been transformed, but his lectures magically elucidate a conceptual basis that was hard to come to terms with in his own day, and is even harder to make out behind later incrustations of detail. In the same spirit Maitland tried to persuade his law students to start their study of property law by reading Blackstone before they turned to the standard work. That was the text-book by Joshua Williams which was first published a few years before Maitland's birth and held sway until the property legislation of 1925; and Maitland told his students he himself had found it hard going at first (hence the recommendation to start with Blackstone) but had always seen further into the subject with each successive reading.[45]

The most obvious thing that historians miss if they disregard the fact that Maitland was a lawyer is the contents of his mind. Dr Hudson refers to one of Maitland's papers as linking 'at least rhetorically' property law in the nineteenth century to that of the middle ages.[46] But there seems nothing rhetorical about the linkage in 'Pollock and Maitland': 'English law both medieval and modern seems to accept to the full this theory: — Every title to land has its root in seisin; the title which has its root in the oldest seisin is the best title'.[47] So the basic principle of the Common Law of property, a principle still alive and most clearly visible today in connection with the finding of chattels, is carried back from Joshua Williams to *Glanvill* and beyond; and there of course it links up with Maitland's vision of proprietary and possessory remedies.

This was one of two great 'vertical' leaps which for Maitland conjured up a phantom continuity in English legal history.[48] The other is less important in the sense that it does not carry the same implications of social and economic continuity. He saw the 'forms of action' as 'the core of English law'.[49] This vision, which long dominated the subject

[45] 'Two Lectures delivered by F. W. Maitland . . . in 1889', [1966] *CLJ*, 54–74, at 59, 65–8.
[46] See above, Hudson, p. 33, n.53.
[47] Pollock and Maitland, ii 46. Cf. *Collected Papers*, i 174–5.
[48] Cf. authors' introduction to Pollock and Maitland, i, p. xxxiv (p. civ in 1968 reissue): 'So continuous has been our English legal life during the last six centuries, that the law of the later middle ages has never been forgotten among us . . . Therefore a tradition, which is in the main a sound and truthful tradition, has been maintained about so much of English legal history as lies on this side of the reign of Edward I'.
[49] *Collected Papers*, i 484.

and which seems from some of our papers to be staging yet another resurrection, saw the original writs as the basis of the law. A particular factual mischief was remedied by a particular writ which dictated everything about the lawsuit including the mode of proof. This vision is more or less consonant with the law of the eighteenth and early nineteenth centuries; and Maitland carried it back into much earlier times. For some actions his lecture audience was provided with a phylogeny indeed, a diagram as of the evolution of living things.[50] The framework he thus imposed governed the subject until facts began to emerge which did not fit, one of the smaller of them coincidentally mentioned by Dr Brand in connection with the dating of *Bracton*. A sub-tenant's chattels are taken in distraint by the superior lord for a failure of service by the intervening lord. For a time the sub-tenant suing the intervening lord uses one writ if he has a charter, another if not.[51] Proof here determined the choice of writ rather than being determined by it.

So if, as Professor Holt says, Maitland largely avoided the dangers of working vertically backward on the small scale, he may have gone wrong on a scale too large to be visible to historians working within limited time periods. Legal history is about how people were thinking and can rarely reach a secure 'panoramic' conclusion: mostly it must proceed by hypothesis. In a sense, law itself proceeds by hypothesis. Historians worry about single facts — true or not. A practising lawyer may of course worry about facts like whether his client did it. But a lawyer concerned with the law is dealing with combinations of facts that are given, assumed to be so; and he postulates an analysis which will bring them within this rather than that legal principle. For example, different legal consequences follow if the same words are taken as a statement rather than a promise. The lawyer chooses between alternative perceptions of the same facts. Similarly the lawyer legal historian is not so often concerned with single facts which can be proved or disproved as with the way in which combinations of facts were perceived and rationalized; and here Maitland the lawyer was supremely convincing.

Let me vary the 'panoramic' analogy of a still snapshot at a particular moment. Imagine that some kink in time throws up video recordings of successive heirs of the same tenurial unit doing homage to successive lords through the centuries after the Conquest. You can be sure that

---

[50] *The Forms of Action at Common Law* (with *Equity*, Cambridge, 1909), p. 348; (separate publication, Cambridge, 1936), p. 54.
[51] See above, Brand, p. 72. Cf. Milsom, *Legal Framework*, pp. 63, 128: there are 'overlaps' between *warrantia carte, de fine facto, ne vexes,* and mesne.

actual observers saw the earliest as dispositive acts: custom indicated the disposition and was by definition nearly always followed, but here was this inheritance happening. The latest were seen as mere ceremonies, required by unimportant custom to follow upon an inheritance which had already happened by operation of a disembodied law. But your videos would not show you when the change of perception came about, and there was surely a period during which actual observers could not have given a clear answer. The change was not in facts which people at the time could see, or which historians now can pin down and date: it was in assumptions and perceptions. It happened in the same hiding-place as that in which Dr Hudson sees the Normans as smuggling their customs into England: peoples' heads.[52]

Although he did not discuss the matter in those terms, this was the essence of Thorne's published lecture about Feudalism and Estates in Land. I heard him read it to a group of historians in Oxford. Whoever was presiding said at the end that it had been very interesting and they looked forward to the footnotes. But the footnotes that came were not of a kind to satisfy historians who want to see things actually happening: they assumed that the end position had always been so, and thought it wicked of Thorne to suggest otherwise without giving actual examples of heirs not inheriting. But he was not supposing a change in what happened, only in perceptions.[53]

The same point can be made in terms which may seem whimsical. Both Dr Hudson and Mr Wormald remark on Maitland's use of fictitious characters as though it was strange (and Mr Wormald generously shows fellow-feeling by himself hanging an Anglo-Saxon Doe and a 12th-century Roe).[54] But lawyers and law teachers do it all the time. They have to. Even if life were so simple that you always started with a paradigm case establishing a principle which would be refined from precedent to precedent, and even if the paradigm would not have been too obvious to litigate, it would have been cluttered with distractions which you would have to tell your listeners to ignore. Tom, Dick and Harry are more amenable (and safer than my own rash habit of naming colleagues or members of my audience). But for the historian there is more to swallow than that: a fictitious case has no date. The paradigm may never have happened, being no more than a lawyer's backward rationalization from some later tangle: often you cannot say exactly when your principle was consciously recognized. But you can still be sure that it mattered for a time.

---

[52] See above, Hudson, p. 39.
[53] Thorne 'English feudalism', in his *Essays in English Legal History*, p. 13.
[54] See above, Wormald, pp. 11–12, and Hudson, p. 34.

The lawyer legal historian's version must be panoramic in another
sense. It must be consistent in itself and with all the known facts: but
it does not normally depend on a single fact. Arguments focused on
particulars do not necessarily work with generalisations, and the law is
always a generalisation. Again I will make the points in my own terms.
One of the things in *Glanvill* that Maitland did not mention (and so,
to borrow an observation from Professor Hyams,[55] nobody else did
either) is the power of a lord in various circumstances to deprive a
defaulting tenant by process of his own court without the king's writ.[56]
This is dependence: the tenant has tenure, but he is not an owner. Early
plea rolls have some entries, which also Maitland did not mention,[57] in
which a deprived tenant brings novel disseisin against his lord, who
admits the taking and relies on the due process of his own court. The
correlation between that process and the words of the writ is compelling: for example, the writ uniquely orders the replacement of chattels;[58]
and this fits a due process which distrained on chattels before any
taking of the tenement itself. So I suggested that this specific protection
of tenants against their lords, and not Maitland's abstract possessory
remedy, was the original purpose of the assize.[59]

As with Thorne when he questioned Maitland on inheritance, out-
rage ensued; and single-fact objections were made to the points of
correlation between writ and process. The most revealing (of the difference between the disciplines) concerns the writ's order to summon the
defendant's bailiff. Two separate historians pointed out that any lord
has a bailiff. Of course: and the appearance of the defendant's bailiff
in a single case would not show (though it might still suggest) that the
defendant was the plaintiff's lord. But we are concerned with what in
effect was a piece of general legislation: a carefully thought-out writ
assumes that its defendant will always have a bailiff and so always be
a lord. Can it have been aimed at irrelevant lords? The usual plaintiff
in the early rolls is a free peasant: so was the common mischief that
the lord of one manor, as it were, sought out and annexed the scattered
strips of a tenant in another manor? What would he do with them?

---

[55] See above, Hyams, p. 230.
[56] *Glanvill*, ix 1, Hall, esp. pp. 104–5; ix 8, esp. p. 112. Cf. vii 12, esp. pp. 85, 86; vii 17, pp. 90–1.
[57] The only use of novel disseisin by tenant against lord discussed by Maitland concerned
pasture, forced upon his attention by the 'statute' of Merton; Pollock and Maitland, i 622–3.
The pre-Merton situation is dramatised in ten lines of imaginary speech by an imaginary
tenant, which serves as another outlet for the antipathy to communalism noted by Professor
White. Maitland does not consider what would have been the situation before the assize was
introduced.
[58] The uniqueness of this order is noted in *Glanvill*, xiii 38, Hall, p. 170.
[59] Milsom, *Legal Framework*, pp. 8–35.

And who would tender the service and suit of court due to the victim's lord from the tenement so taken?[60]

A similar objection was that if the assize were directed against the lord it might have said so. Perhaps: and perhaps it did. The lawyers' equivalent of reckoning with all the facts at a particular time is that all the assumptions at a particular time must have been consistent. My heresy about novel disseisin goes with another about seisin: by definition it had been a lord who seised and might disseise a tenant.[61] Only as lord was marginalized by king did seisin become a kind of abstract possession connoting just one person, not two.

In fact Maitland's carrying back of ideas of ownership and possession is irreconcilable with many things in the early sources which he either ignored or swept aside. Some have been mentioned in this paper. These and others were discussed in a paper read in November 1994 to the Haskins Society, and to be published in its Journal. The title of that paper refers to what is perhaps the most striking. The nature of the writ of right was assumed by Maitland rather than discussed;[62] and in the grand assize, an alternative to trial by battle, he saw the knights as declaring which of the two parties had the greater right in the Joshua Williams sense of title derived from the earlier seisin. But in more than forty per cent of all grand assizes on the early rolls, the question for the knights is not abstract but tenurial: whether one of the parties has greater right to hold the land of the other or the other to have it in demesne. In *Bracton's Note Book*, which Maitland himself edited, the proportion is nearer fifty per cent. But he never mentions them. A possible explanation looks to his speed of working and his dependence on *Bracton* itself, from which the part treating such issues is missing. The extraordinary concentration of his mind produced a compelling picture. But the facts which lay outside the field of that concentrated vision remain; and there is no way of adjusting his account so as to accommodate them. Either you accept Maitland's authority and ignore that other evidence; or you work on a different picture.

Who cares about lawyers' concepts? Maitland did, but ironically his vision of basic concepts which did not change between King Henry II and Queen Victoria has suppressed questions. He provides historians with an all-purpose set of answers, including a glossary of legal terms

---

[60] And would the victim's lord accept service from a stranger, when that acceptance would bind him to warranty? See *Glanvill*, iii 7, Hall, p. 42.

[61] As usual (cf. Wormald, above p. 15, and Elton, *Maitland*, p. 54), Maitland had himself thought of this; *Collected Papers*, i 365. But he did not at that time consider the effect on the concept itself of the shift from seignorial to royal jurisdiction. That thought came to him later, but was not pursued; Pollock and Maitland, ii 38.

[62] There is just one paragraph: Pollock and Maitland, ii 62–3.

apparently valid for all periods: sources are read as though words such as 'wardship', 'seisin' and (for a long time) 'trespass' had always meant the same. And it seems to follow that historians need not worry too much about the law. A small symptom is a tendency to emphasise non-legal elements in a legal situation. In these papers, for example, Professor White sees a strictly legal understanding of the participation of kin in grants in alms as trivialising the matter;[63] and Dr Hudson reminds us of the trend toward consideration of disputing outside the legal process.[64] But the latter always goes on, and always largely in the shadow of what is likely to happen if the dispute does come to court. As long as many lawsuits ended in oaths, jeopardising your soul and earthly reputation (or indeed your opponent's) would often have seemed an unacceptable non-pecuniary cost.

But one's understanding of the legal concepts in peoples' heads must affect one's understanding of the world in which they lived. If you see King Henry II as providing new possessory protection for people you think of as landowners, you necessarily see land as already just property like a villa in the Roman world or in Victorian England: property without strings that you can just take, perhaps hoping that your taking will give you a Joshua Williams title. A tenement owing service and suit would not come away like that. At the very least the strings have to be dealt with; and Maitland overlooked the considerable ancillary apparatus which royal intervention necessitated. Except in a table showing the relative frequency of 'forms of action',[65] for example, he never mentions the action *de homagio capiendo*. But it is an important ingredient in *Glanvill*'s account of inheritance, to which the lord's acceptance of the heir is still essential;[66] and without it mort d'ancestor (on any view of that remedy) could have produced mere deadlock.

Nor is it just 'legal' matters that are affected, like lawsuits, inheritance, alienation. To carry back later proprietary ideas seems to a lawyer to risk anachronism in matters which are certainly not a lawyer's business, such as governmental and social structure and economic motivation.[67] So long as land was not property without strings, for example, you cannot think of a sale of land as a simple exchange of this area for money, or therefore rest too much weight on the idea of a land market. But the lawyer has done enough to lose friends without

[63] See above, White, p. 106.
[64] See above, Hudson, pp. 34 *et seq.*
[65] Pollock and Maitland, ii 565–7.
[66] *Glanvill*, ix 4–7. Hall, pp. 107–11; cf. i 3, Hall, p. 4.
[67] Cf. T. F. T. Plucknett, *The Mediaeval Bailiff* (London 1954, Creighton Lecture 1953), p. 2: 'It is only in text-books that constitutional, economic and legal history are set apart from one another. In real life they are simultaneous, and one man lives all his histories concurrently'.

trespassing further. I have tried to make my point in terms of matters which I think I understand. But for legal history the proposition is general and serious; and I hope I shall not be thought disrespectful either to the memory of Maitland or to my historian friends if I put the matter plainly. The methods of today's historians work with the institutional hedgerows of the law: but they do not work well in the legal field itself, where one is looking not so much for hard datable facts as for shifting assumptions, analyses, perceptions. There indeed Maitland's compelling vision has become an orthodoxy, almost beyond question.[68] And if we go on as we are, we can look forward to our successors celebrating the bicentenary of 'Pollock and Maitland' as still the last word on the history of English law in its most crucial period. I wonder whether he would be pleased.

---

[68] See above, Wormald, p. 10. Cf. Elton, *Maitland*, pp. 32–3: 'The history he wrote concerned itself with highly technical issues and used materials and terms of art that are not accessible to the general reader; indeed too few historians have bothered to master them since. In Maitland's hands they created lasting orthodoxies ... A hundred years of teaching have anchored them in concrete so well set that every effort of doubt or modification calls for dynamite'.

Proceedings of the British Academy, **89**, 261–278

Bibliography of the Writings of F. W. Maitland

MARK PHILPOTT

Introductory Note[1]

THIS IS NOT THE FIRST ATTEMPT to list Maitland's publications, nor will it be the last. Perhaps the first was that made by H. A. L. Fisher in the immediate aftermath of Maitland's death. It is clear that Maitland left no complete list of his own publications, since Fisher, who seems to have been acting on behalf of his sister, Mrs Maitland, found it necessary to ask editors whether Maitland had written for them.[2] We know that Maitland wrote articles anonymously — several are included in this bibliography[3] — and in the absence of an authoritative list it is unlikely that all of them will ever be identified. For example, it has not proved possible to identify any of the contributions he is said to have made to the *Pall Mall Gazette* as a young man.[4] A number of biblio-

[1] In this bibliography the following abbreviations are used:
Maitland Reader: Frederick (sic) *William Maitland Reader,* ed. V. T. H. Delany (New York, 1957);
 Roman Canon Law: Roman Canon Law in the Church of England: Six Essays (London, 1898);
Selected Historical Essays: Selected Historical Essays, ed. H. M. Cam (Cambridge, 1957);
Selected Essays: Selected Essays, eds H. D. Hazeltine, G. Lapsley, and P. H. Winfield (Cambridge, 1936); *Sketch: A Sketch of English Legal History,* ed. J. F. Colby (New York and London, 1915).

[2] Many of the results of this search, which seems to have been connected with Fisher's research for his *Frederick* (sic) *William Maitland, Downing Professor of the Laws of England. A Biographical Sketch* (Cambridge, 1910), and for *Collected Papers,* can now be found in Bodleian Library, Fisher MSS 143–145.

[3] See, for example, 'The law of real property', *Westminster Review,* 122 (ns, 56) (1879), 334–57; 'The Shallows and Silences of real life', *The Reflector,* 1 (1888), 113–17; and 'Round's "Commune of London" ', *The Athenaeum,* 3756 (21 October 1899), 547–8.

[4] Fisher, *Biographical Sketch,* p. 18, although Maitland's old teacher, Oscar Browning, suggested that Maitland was no great success as a journalist, Bodleian Library, Fisher MS 145, f. 1.

graphies of Maitland have been published, each with its faults as well as strengths.[5] This version attempts to avoid the former as far as possible and to build on the latter.

This bibliography is organized chronologically by year of publication, items are then arranged alphabetically within each year. Reviews are listed by the title of the work reviewed. Second or subsequent editions have not been listed unless they seem of particular interest or importance, but I have indicated where an item is reprinted in one of the four chief anthologies of Maitland's writings.

Bibliography

1869

'A solemn mystery', *The Adventurer*, (Eton, 4 June 1869).

1875

Historical Sketch of Liberty and Equality as Ideals of English Political Philosophy from the Time of Hobbes to the Time of Coleridge (Cambridge, 1875) (reprinted in *Collected Papers*, i 1–161).

1879

Review of A. J. Balfour, *A Defence of Philosophic Doubt, being an Essay on the Foundations of Belief* (London, 1879), *Mind* 4, (1879), 576–9.

'The law of real property', *Westminster Review*, 122 (ns, 56) (1879), 334–57 (reprinted in *Collected Papers*, i 162–201 and partially in *Maitland Reader*, pp. 45–8) (anonymous).

1880

'*In re* Morton and Hallet', Maitland argues for the purchaser, *Law Reports: Chancery Division*, 15 (1880), 145 and 147–9.

'The relation of punishment to temptation', *Mind*, 5 (1880), 259–64.

1881

'*In re* Cope', a speech attributed to Chitty QC and B. B. Rogers,[6] *Law Reports: Chancery*, 16 (1880–1), 50–2.

---

[5] Chief among them A. L. Smith, *Frederic William Maitland. Two Lectures and a Bibliography* (Oxford, 1908), pp. 59–67; *Maitland Reader*; and J. R. Cameron, *Frederick* (sic) *William Maitland and the History of English Law* (Norman, 1961), pp. 169–84.

[6] 'not one word of which was ever spoken by either of us. It was an opinion of Maitland's on the case laid before us which I gave to Chitty to assist him in his argument . . .' (B. B. Rogers quoted by Fisher, *Biographical Sketch*, pp. 16–17.)

'The laws of Wales — the kindred and the blood feud', *Law Magazine and Review*, 4th Ser. 6 (1880–1), 344–67 (reprinted in *Collected Papers*, i 202–29).

1882

'The criminal liability of the hundred', *Law Magazine and Review*, 4th Ser. 7 (1881–2), 367–80 (reprinted in *Collected Papers*, i 230–46).

1883

'The early history of malice aforethought', *Law Magazine and Review*, 4th Ser., 8 (1882–3), 406–26 (reprinted in *Collected Papers*, i 304–28).

'From the old law courts to the new', *The English Illustrated Magazine*, 1 (1883), 3–15 (reprinted in *CLJ*, 8 (1942), 2–14).

'Mr Herbert Spencer's theory of society. I The ideal state', *Mind*, 8 (1883), 354–71 (reprinted in *Collected Papers*, i 247–303).

'Mr Herbert Spencer's theory of society. II The law of equal liberty', *Mind*, 8 (1883), 506–24 (reprinted in *Collected Papers*, i 247–303).

1884

(ed.) *Pleas of the Crown for the County of Gloucester before the Abbot of Reading and his Fellow Justices Itinerant, A. D. 1221* (London, 1884).

1885

Justice and Police (The English Citizen; London, 1885).

'The seisin of chattels', *LQR*, 1 (1885), 324–41 (reprinted in *Collected Papers* i 329–57).

Review of *Year Books of the Reign of King Edward the Third, Years XII and XIII*, edited and translated L. O. Pike, (Rolls Series, 31; London, 1885), *LQR*, 1 (1885), 373–4 (signed 'F. W. M.').

1886

'Breton, John le (d. 1275)', in L. Stephen, ed., *Dictionary of National Biography*, 6, (London, 1886), p. 275.

'Cambridge in the thirteenth century' (Letter to the Editors), *Cambridge Review*, 7 (1885–6), 213–14.

'The deacon and the jewess, or apostasy at Common Law', *LQR*, 2 (1886), 153–65 (reprinted in *Collected Papers*, i 385–406, and *Roman Canon Law*, pp. 158–79, thence in *Maitland Reader*, pp. 62–79).

'The mystery of seisin', *LQR*, 2 (1886), 481–96, (reprinted in *Collected Papers*, i 358–84, thence in *Maitland Reader*, pp. 158–78; also reprinted in *Essays in Anglo-American Legal History*, 3, (Cambridge, 1909), 591–610).

Untitled note concerning a case of fornication between a Jew and a Christian, *LQR*, 2 (1886), 525–6 (signed 'F. W. M.').

1887

(ed.) *Bracton's Note-Book: a Collection of Cases decided in the King's Courts during the Reign of Henry III, annotated by a Lawyer of that Time, seemingly by Henry of Bratton*, (3 vols, London, 1887).

'Historical note on the classification of the forms of personal action', Appendix A to F. Pollock, *The Law of Torts* (London, 1887), pp. 467–74.

Regulations for Law Degrees, contributions to the meeting of Senate (20 May 1887) to discuss the amended report of the Special Board for Law, printed in *Cambridge University Reporter*, 17 (1886–7), 719–20 and 720–1.

1888

'The beatitude of seisin', *LQR*, 4 (1888), 24–39 and 286–99 (reprinted in *Collected Papers*, i 407–57).

Review of T. E. Scrutton, *Commons and Common Fields* (Cambridge, 1887), *EHR*, 3 (1888), 568–70.

(ed.) *Select Pleas of the Crown, I, 1200–1225* (Selden Soc., 1 for 1887; London, 1888).

'The Shallows and Silences of real life', *The Reflector*, 1 (1888), 113–17 (reprinted in *Collected Papers*, i 467–79) (anonymous).

'The suitors of the county court', *EHR*, 3 (1888), 417–21 (reprinted in *Collected Papers*, i 458–66).

Untitled note concerning the lord of the manor's right to enclose common land before the Statute of Merton, *LQR*, 4 (1888), 230 (signed 'F. W. M.').

Why the History of English Law is Not Written (London, 1888) (reprinted in *Collected Papers*, i 480–97 and *Maitland Reader*, pp. 48–62).

The Yorke Prize, a contribution to the meeting of Senate (18 October 1888) to discuss the report of the Special Board for Law, printed in *Cambridge University Reporter*, 19 (1888–9), 107.

1889

'Domesday measures of land', *Archaeological Review*, 4 (1889–90), 391–2.

'Fleta', in L. Stephen, ed., *Dictionary of National Biography*, 19, (London, 1889), p. 290.

'The history of the Register of Original Writs', *Harvard Law Review*, 3 (1889–90), 97–115, 167–79 and 212–25 (reprinted in *Collected Papers*, ii 110–73 and *Select Essays in Anglo-American Legal History*, 2, (Cambridge, 1908), 549–96).

'The introduction of English law into Ireland', *EHR*, 4 (1889), 516–17 (reprinted in *Collected Papers*, ii 81–3).

'The materials for English legal history', *Political Science Quarterly*, 4 (1889), 496–518 and 628–47 (reprinted in *Collected Papers*, ii 1–60, and *Select Essays in Anglo-American Legal History*, 2, (Cambridge, 1908), pp. 53–95).

'Possession for a year and a day', *LQR*, 5 (1889), 253–64 (reprinted in *Collected Papers*, ii 61–80).

(ed.) *Select Pleas in Manorial and Other Seignorial Courts. Volume I; Reigns of Henry III and Edward I* (Selden Soc., 2 for 1888; London, 1889) (The second part of the introduction (pp. xxvii–xxxviii) is reprinted in *Selected Historical Essays*, pp. 41–51, as 'Leet and Tourn').

'The surnames of English villages', *Archaeological Review*, 4 (1889–90), 233–40 (reprinted in *Collected Papers*, ii 84–95).

Review of *Year Books of the Reign of King Edward the Third, Year XIV*, edited and translated L. O. Pike, (Rolls Series, 31; London, 1888), *LQR*, 5 (1889), 82–3 (signed 'F. W. M.').

1890

Constitutional Law for pollmen, a contribution to the meeting of Senate (27 November 1890) to discuss the report of the Pass Examinations Syndicate, printed in *Cambridge University Reporter*, 21 (1890–1), 277.

'Glanville, Ranulf de', in L. Stephen, ed., *Dictionary of National Biography*, 21, (London, 1890), pp. 413–15.

'Northumbrian tenures', *EHR*, 5 (1890), 625–32 (reprinted in *Collected Papers*, ii 96–109).

Purchase of the Middlehill Library, a contribution to the meeting of Senate (6 March 1890) to discuss the report of Council, printed in *Cambridge University Reporter*, 20 (1889–90), 532–3.

'Remainders after conditional fees', *LQR*, 6 (1890), 22–6 (reprinted in *Collected Papers*, ii 174–89).

'Slander in the Middle Ages', *The Green Bag*, 2 (Boston, 1890), 4–7.

Review of H. Brunner, *Überblick über die Geschichte der Französischen, Normannischen und Englischen Rechtsquellen* (Leipzig, 1889), *LQR*, 6 (1890), 217–18 (signed 'F. W. M.').

Review of *Year Books of the Reign of King Edward the Third, Years XIV and XV*, edited and translated L. O. Pike (Rolls Series, 31; London, 1889), *EHR*, 5 (1890), 592–3.

1891

'A conveyancer in the thirteenth century', *LQR*, 7 (1891), 63–9 (reprinted in *Collected Papers*, ii 190–201).

(and W. P. Baildon, eds)[7] *The Court Baron, being Precedents for Use in Seignorial and Other Local Courts, together with Select Pleas from the Bishop of Ely's Court of Littleport* (Selden Soc., 4 for 1890; London, 1891).

Review of *A Descriptive Catalogue of Ancient Deeds in the Public Record Office*, 1 (London, 1890), *EHR*, 6 (1891), 562–3.

'Frankalmoign in the twelfth and thirteenth centuries', *LQR*, 7 (1891), 354–63 (reprinted in *Collected Papers*, ii 205–22).

Review of C. Gross, *The Gild Merchant, a Contribution to British Municipal History*, (2 vols, Oxford, 1890), *Economic Journal*, 1 (1891), 220–4 (reprinted in *Collected Papers*, ii 223–31).

'A new point on villein tenure', *LQR*, 7 (1891), 174–5 (reprinted in *Collected Papers*, ii 202–4).

'The "praerogativa regis" ', *EHR*, 6 (1891), 367–72 (reprinted in *Collected Papers*, ii 182–9).

Provision for law students, a contribution to the meeting of Senate (28 February 1891) to discuss the report of the Perse School Buildings Syndicate, printed in *Cambridge University Reporter*, 21 (1890–1), 610–11.

Provision of a Law School, a contribution to the meeting of Senate (22 October 1891) to discuss the report of the Law School Buildings Syndicate, printed in *Cambridge University Reporter*, 22 (1891–2), 134.

Three Rolls of the King's Court in the Reign of King Richard the First, A. D. 1194–5, with an introduction and notes by F. W. M., (PRS, 14; London, 1891).

Review of E. Lamond, *Walter of Henley's Husbandry, together with an Anonymous Husbandry, Seneschaucie and Robert Grosseteste's Rules* (London, 1890), *Economic Journal*, 1 (1891), 225–6.

1892

'Court rolls, manorial accounts and extents', in R. H. I. Palgrave, ed., *Dictionary of Political Economy*, 1, 4, (London, 1892), 447–8.

Review of J. -A. Brutails, *Étude sur la condition des populations rurales du Roussillon au moyen âge* (Paris, 1891), and P. Errera, *Les Masuirs. Recherches historiques et juridiques sur quelques vestiges des formes anciennes de la propriété en Belgique* (2 vols, Brussels, 1891), *EHR*, 7 (1892), 748–54 (reprinted as 'Tenures in Roussillon and Namur' in *Collected Papers*, ii 251–65).

'Glanvill revised', *Harvard Law Review*, 6 (1892–3), 1–20 (reprinted in *Collected Papers*, ii 266–89).

'Henry II and the criminous clerks', *EHR*, 7 (1892), 224–34 (reprinted in *Collected Papers*, ii 232–50 and *Roman Canon Law*, pp. 132–47).

A lecturer in palaeography, a contribution to the meeting of Senate (26 May 1892)

---

[7] In fact Baildon's work was squeezed out and what was printed was, as the British Library Online Catalogue notes, 'rather by F. W. Maitland only', (compare Preface p. viii).

to discuss the report of the General Board, printed in *Cambridge University Reporter*, 22 (1891–2), 855.

Provision of a Law School, a contribution to the meeting of Senate (18 February 1892) to discuss the report of the Law School Buildings Syndicate, printed in *Cambridge University Reporter*, 22 (1891–2), 553–4.

'The "Quadripartitus" ', *LQR*, 8 (1892), 73–5.

Review of *Year Books of the Reign of King Edward the Third, Year XV*, edited and translated L. O. Pike (Rolls Series, 31; London, 1891), *LQR*, 8 (1892), 85–6 (signed 'F. W. M.').

1893

The accounts of the Syndics of the Press, a contribution to the meeting of Senate (9 March 1893) to discuss a grace to amend the legislation concerning the publication of the accounts, printed in *Cambridge University Reporter*, 23 (1892–3), 639.

The Corporation Aggregate: the History of a Legal Idea. A Lecture delivered at Liverpool under the Auspices of the Liverpool Board of Legal Studies and the Liverpool Law Students' Association on the 25th May, 1893 (Liverpool, 1893).

'Domesday Book', in R. H. I. Palgrave, ed., *Dictionary of Political Economy*, 1, 5, (London, 1893), pp. 629–30.

Review of C. Gross, *The Early History and Influence of the Office of Coroner* (New York, 1892), *EHR*, 8 (1893), 758–60.

'English law under Norman rule', in H. D. Traill, ed., *Social England*, 1, (London, 1893), pp. 274–84 (reprinted together with 'The history of trial by jury' (see below, *sub* 1893) in *Collected Papers*, ii 430–65 as 'Outlines of English legal history, 560–1600: English law under Norman and Angevin', and in *Sketch*, pp. 26–73 as 'English law under Norman rule and the legal reforms of Henry II, 1066–1216'. Parts also reprinted in *Maitland Reader*, pp. 92–9).

'Growth of jurisprudence 1154–1272', in H. D. Traill, ed., *Social England*, 1, (London, 1893), pp. 408–10 (reprinted in *Collected Papers*, ii 465–8 as 'Outlines of English legal history, 560–1600: The growth of jurisprudence', in *Sketch*, pp. 77–81 as 'Growth of law from Henry II to Edward I, 1154–1272', and partly in *Maitland Reader*, pp. 100–2).

'History from the Charter Roll', *EHR*, 8 (1893), 726–33 (reprinted in *Collected Papers*, ii 298–309).

'The history of trial by jury', in H. D. Traill, ed., *Social England*, 1, (London, 1893), pp. 285–98 (reprinted together with 'English law under Norman rule' in *Collected Papers*, ii 430–65 and *Sketch*, pp. 26–73).

'Maitland, John Gorham', in S. Lee, ed., *Dictionary of National Biography*, 35, (London, 1893), p. 367.

(ed.) *Memoranda de Parliamento: Records of the Parliament Holden at Westminster on the Twenty-eighth Day of February, in the Thirty-third Year of the Reign of King Edward the First, A. D. 1305*, (Rolls Series, 98; London, 1893), (The Introduction is reprinted in *Selected Historical Essays*, pp. 52–96, and, as edited by G. Lapsley, partly so in *Selected Essays*, pp. 1–72).

A new Statute for Private Hostels, contributions to the meeting of Senate (9 May 1893) to discuss the report of the Council of Senate, printed in *Cambridge University Reporter*, 23 (1892–3), 826.

'Old English law', in H. D. Traill, ed., *Social England*, 1, (London, 1893), pp. 164–73 (reprinted in *Collected Papers*, ii 417–30 as 'Outlines of English legal history, 560–1600: Old English law', *Maitland Reader*, pp. 80–91, and *Sketch*, pp. 1–10 and 13–23 as 'Early English law, 600–1066').

Prostitution and soliciting, contributions to the meeting of Senate (3 June 1893) to discuss the report of the Council of Senate on the University Jurisdiction Bill, printed in *Cambridge University Reporter*, 23 (1892–3), 1026 and 1027.

The recognition of lecturers, a contribution to the meeting of Senate (18 May 1893) to discuss the report of the General Board, printed in *Cambridge University Reporter*, 23 (1892–3), 866.

Review of L. Huberti, *Studien zur Rechtsgeschichte des Gottesfrieden und Landfrieden*, 1 (Ansbach, 1892), *EHR*, 8 (1893), 328–31 (reprinted in *Collected Papers*, ii 290–7, as 'The Peace of God and the Land-Peace').

Review of H. C. Lea, *Superstition and Force: Essays on the Wager of Law, the Wager of Battle, the Ordeal, Torture* (4th edn, Philadelphia, 1892), and F. G. La Mantia, *Ordines Iudiciorum Dei nel Missale Gallicano del XII° Secolo della Cattedrale di Palermo* (Palermo, 1892), *EHR*, 8 (1893), 755–6.

'The survival of archaic communities: I The Malmesbury case', *LQR*, 9 (1893), 36–50 (reprinted in *Collected Papers*, ii 313–37).

'The survival of archaic communities: II The Aston case', *LQR*, 9 (1893), 211–28 (reprinted in *Collected Papers*, ii 337–65).

'Taltarum's case', *LQR*, 9 (1893), 1–2 (reprinted in *Collected Papers*, ii 310–12).

'Trial by jury', in H. D. Traill, ed., *Social England*, 1, (London, 1893), p. 285–99.

Review of *Yorkshire Inquisitions of the Reigns of Henry III and Edward I*, 1, ed. W. Brown (Yorkshire Archaeological and Topographical Association, Record Series, 12, 1892), *EHR*, 8 (1893), 555–7.

1894

Review of F. Zinkeisen, *Die Anfänge der Lehngerichtsbarkeit in England* (Berlin, 1893), *EHR*, 9 (1894), 600 (signed 'F. W. M.').

Review of F. Liebermann, *Consiliatio Cnuti, eine Übertragung Angelsächsischer Gesetze aus dem Zwölften Jahrhundert* (Halle, 1893), *EHR*, 9 (1894), 137–8.

The Financial Board's 'more than papal authority', a contribution to the meeting of Senate (15 November 1894) to discuss the report of the Cavendish Laboratory Syndicate, printed in *Cambridge University Reporter*, 25 (1894–5), 230.

Review of H. Brunner, *Forschungen zur Geschichte des Deutschen und Französischen Rechtes* (Stuttgart, 1894), *EHR*, 9 (1894), 593–4.

'The history of a Cambridgeshire manor', *EHR*, 9 (1894), 417–39 (reprinted in *Collected Papers*, ii 366–402 and *Selected Historical Essays*, pp. 16–40).

'The history of English law 1307–1600', in H. D. Traill, ed., *Social England*, 2, (London, 1894), pp. 476–89 (reprinted in *Collected Papers*, ii 477–96 as 'Outlines of English legal history, 560–1600: English law (1307–1600)'; and *Sketch*, pp. 103–28 as 'Growth of Statute and Common Law and rise of the Court of Chancery, 1307–1600').

'Legal reform under Edward I' in H. D. Traill, ed., *Social England*, 2, (London, 1894), pp. 32–8 (reprinted in *Collected Papers*, ii 468–76 as 'Outlines of English legal history, 560–1600: Legal reform under Edward I', and in *Sketch*, pp. 90–1 and 92–101 as 'Legal reform under Edward I and the system of writs').

The LLM, a contribution to the meeting of Senate (10 May 1894) to discuss the report of the Special Board for Law, printed in *Cambridge University Reporter*, 24 (1893–4), 761.

Review of E. A. Bryan, *The Mark in Europe and America* (Boston, 1893), *EHR*, 9 (1894), 598–9.

'The Origin of Uses and Trusts', *Harvard Law Review*, 8 (1894–5), 127–37 (reprinted in *Collected Papers*, ii 403–16).

Review of F. Liebermann, *Über die Leges Anglorum Saeculo XIII. Ineunte Londoniis Collectae* (Halle, 1894), *EHR*, 9 (1894), 741–2.

1895

Review of *Cornelii Taciti de Germania*, ed. H. Furneaux (Oxford, 1894), *EHR*, 10 (1895), 779–81.

Review of H. M. Luckock, *The History of Marriage, Jewish and Christian, in Relation to Divorce and Certain Forbidden Degrees* (London, 1894), *EHR*, 10 (1895), 755–9 (reprinted in *Collected Papers*, iii 21–30 and partly in *Maitland Reader*, pp. 102–10).

(F. Pollock and F. W. M.) *The History of the English Law before the Time of Edward I* (2 vols, Cambridge, 1895; see also below, 1898)

'Introduction', A. Horne (attrib.), *The Mirror of Justices*, ed. W. J. Whittaker, (Selden Soc., 7 for 1893; London, 1895), pp. ix–lv.[8]

'The murder of Henry Clement', *EHR*, 10 (1895), 294–7 (reprinted in *Collected Papers*, iii 11–16).

Printing prize exercises and dissertations, a contribution to the meeting of Senate (6 June 1895) to discuss the report of the Council of Senate, printed in *Cambridge University Reporter*, 25 (1894–5), 963.

---

[8] This is the extent of Maitland's involvement according to the title page, but it is clear from his correspondence that he took a substantial part in the production of the volume, see *Letters*, i nos 112, 140, 155.

Regulations for the Law Tripos, a contribution to the meeting of Senate (21 February 1895) to discuss the report of the Special Board for Law, printed in *Cambridge University Reporter*, 25 (1894–5), 583.

(ed.) *Selected Passages from the Works of Bracton and Azo* (Selden Soc., 8 for 1894; London, 1895).

Review of F. Seebohm, *The Tribal System in Wales* (London, 1895), *Economic Journal*, 5 (1895), 589–94 (reprinted in *Collected Papers*, iii 1–10).

Review of *Two Chartularies of the Priory of St Peter at Bath*, ed. W. Hunt (Somerset Record Society, 1893), *EHR*, 10 (1895), 558–60 (reprinted in *Collected Papers*, iii 17–20).

1896

'Canon Law in England: I William Lyndwood', *EHR*, 11 (1896), 446–78 (reprinted in *Roman Canon Law*, pp. 1–50).

'Canon Law in England: II Church, State and decretals', *EHR*, 11 (1896), 641–72 (reprinted in *Roman Canon Law*, pp. 51–99).

Review of O. J. Reichel, *A Complete Manual of Canon Law*, 1, *The Sacraments* (London, 1896), *LQR*, 12 (1896), 181–2.

Review of *The Crawford Collection of Early Charters and Documents (Analecta Oxoniensia)*, eds A. S. Napier and W. H. Stevenson (Oxford, 1895), *EHR*, 11 (1896), 557–8.

The degrees of LLM and LLD, a contribution to the meeting of Senate (7 May 1896) to discuss the report of the Special Board for Law, printed in *Cambridge University Reporter*, 26 (1895–6), 731–4.

Deputies for professors, a contribution to the meeting of Senate (27 February 1896) to discuss the report of the Council of Senate on a Repealing Statute, printed in *Cambridge University Reporter*, 26 (1895–6), 554.

' "Execrabilis" in the Common Pleas', *LQR*, 12 (1896), 174–80 (reprinted in *Collected Papers*, iii 54–64 and *Roman Canon Law*, pp. 148–57).

The Law School and Library, a contribution to the meeting of Senate (13 February 1896) to discuss the report of the Special Board for Law, printed in *Cambridge University Reporter*, 26 (1895–6), 509.

The MC degree, a contribution to the meeting of Senate (23 January 1896) to discuss the report of the Special Board of Medicine, printed in *Cambridge University Reporter*, 26 (1895–6), 426.

The New Electoral Roll Statute, a contribution to the meeting of Senate (23 January 1896) to discuss the Statute, printed in *Cambridge University Reporter*, 26 (1895–6), 425.

'The origin of the Borough', *EHR*, 11 (1896), 13–19 (reprinted in *Collected Papers*, iii 31–42).

The Professorship of Surgery, a contribution to the meeting of Senate (3 December

1896) to discuss the report of the General Board of Studies, printed in *Cambridge University Reporter*, 27 (1896–7), 335.

'A song on the death of Simon de Montfort', *EHR*, 11 (1896), 314–18 (reprinted in *Collected Papers*, iii 43–9).

'Wyclif on English and Roman Law', *LQR*, 12 (1896), 76–8 (reprinted in *Collected Papers*, iii 50–3).

1897

'Borough English', in A. W. Renton, ed., *The Encyclopaedia of the Laws of England*, 2, (London, 1897), 216–17.

'Burgage tenure', in A. W. Renton, ed., *The Encyclopaedia of the Laws of England*, 2, (London, 1897), 302–3.

'Canon Law', in A. W. Renton, ed., *The Encyclopaedia of the Laws of England*, 2, (London, 1897), 354–9 (reprinted in *Collected Papers*, iii 65–77).

'Canon Law in England: III William Drogheda and the Universal Ordinary', *EHR*, 12 (1897), 625–58 (reprinted in *Roman Canon Law*, pp. 100–31).

'Court Baron and Court Leet', in A. W. Renton, ed., *The Encyclopaedia of the Laws of England*, 4 (London, 1897), 3–7.

Degrees for women, contributions to the meeting of Senate (13–16 March 1897) to discuss the report of the Degrees for Women Syndicate, printed in *Cambridge University Reporter*, 27 (1896–7), 748–51, 788, 792 and 802.

Review of J. B. Thayer, *Development of Trial by Jury*, 1 (Boston, 1896), *EHR*, 12 (1897), 147–8.

Domesday Book and Beyond: Three Essays in the Early History of England (Cambridge, 1897; 2nd edn, 1907), (reprinted with an introduction by E. Miller (Cambridge, 1960); with a foreword by J. C. Holt (Cambridge, 1987); and fragments in *Maitland Reader*, pp. 110–11 and pp. 144–5).

The Historical Tripos, a contribution to the meeting of Senate (28 January 1897) to discuss the report of the Special Board for History and Archaeology, printed in *Cambridge University Reporter*, 27 (1896–7), 505–6.

Law prizes, a contribution to the meeting of Senate (10 June 1897) to discuss the report of the Special Board for Law, printed in *Cambridge University Reporter*, 27 (1896–7), 1189–90.

Review of H. Pirenne, *Le Livre de l'Abbé Guillaume de Ryckel: Polyptyque et comptes de l'Abbaye de Saint-Trond au milieu du treizième siècle* (Ghent, 1896), *EHR*, 12 (1897), 552.

(ed.) 'Magistri Vacarii Summa de Matrimonio', *LQR*, 13 (1897), 133–43 and 270–87 (issued separately London, 1898, and partly reprinted in *Collected Papers*, iii 87–105).

'A plea for the codification of English Law, IX', *New Century Review*, 2 (1897), 52–3.

The Special Board for Indian Civil Service Studies, a contribution to the meeting of Senate (25 February 1897) to discuss the report of the General Board of Studies, printed in *Cambridge University Reporter*, 27 (1896–7), 655.

Review of *Year Books of the Reign of Edward III, Year XVI (First Part)*, edited and translated L. O. Pike (Rolls Series, 31; London, 1896), *EHR*, 12 (1897), 350–1.

1898

Review of C. Gross, *Bibliography of Municipal History, including Gilds and Parliamentary Representation* (New York, 1897), *EHR*, 13 (1898), 816 (signed 'F. W. M.').

Review of P. Fournier, *Les Collections canoniques attribuées à Yves de Chartres* (Paris, 1897), *EHR*, 13 (1898), 815–16 (signed 'F. W. M.').

(F. Pollock and F. W. M.) *The History of English Law before the Time of Edward I* (2 vols, revised 2nd edn, Cambridge, 1898) (reprinted with an introduction by S. F. C. Milsom, Cambridge, 1968; extracts in *Maitland Reader*, pp. 111–15).

Review of E. Besta, *L'Opera d'Irnerio* (2 vols, Turin, 1896), *EHR*, 13 (1898), 143–4.

'A prologue to a history of English Law', *LQR*, 14 (1898), 13–33, (reprinted in *Essays in Anglo-American Legal History*, 1 (Cambridge, 1907), pp. 7–33, also as Chapter I in the second edition of *The History of English Law* (Cambridge, 1898)).

Review of *The Records of the Honourable Society of Lincoln's Inn. The Black Books, Volume I, from A. D. 1422 to A. D. 1586* (London, 1897), *EHR*, 13 (1898), 576–8 (reprinted in *Collected Papers*, iii 78–83 as 'Records of the Honourable Society of Lincoln's Inn I').

Roman Canon Law in the Church of England: Six Essays (London, 1898).

Township and Borough, The Ford Lectures for 1897, (Cambridge, 1898) (Lecture 1 is reprinted in *Selected Historical Essays*, pp. 3–15).

The Whewell Scholarships, a contribution to the meeting of Senate (10 March 1898) to discuss the report of the Council of Senate, printed in *Cambridge University Reporter*, 28 (1897–8), 617.

Review of *Yorkshire Inquisitions of the Reigns of Henry III and Edward I*, 2, ed. W. Brown (Yorkshire Archaeological and Topographical Association, Record Series, 23, 1898), *EHR*, 13 (1898), 775–6.

1899

'Canon MacColl's new convocation', *Fortnightly Review*, 72 (66) (1899), 926–35 (reprinted in *Collected Papers*, iii 119–36, and *Selected Historical Essays*, pp. 247–58).

Review of G. des Marez, *Étude sur la propriété foncière dans les villes du moyen âge et spécialement en Flandre* (Ghent and Paris, 1898), *EHR*, 14 (1899), 137–41 (reprinted as 'Land holding in medieval towns' in *Collected Papers*, iii 106–14).

'Round's "Commune of London" ', *The Athenaeum*, 3756 (21 October 1899), 547–8 (reprinted in *Selected Historical Essays*, pp. 259–65) (anonymous).

'An unpublished "revocatio" of Henry II', *EHR*, 14 (1899), 735–7 (reprinted in *Collected Papers*, iii 115–18).

1900

'The Corporation Sole', *LQR*, 16 (1900), 335–54 (reprinted in *Collected Papers*, iii 210–43 and, as edited by P. H. Winfield, *Selected Essays*, pp. 73–103).

Review of G. Fagniez, *Documents relatifs à l'histoire de l'industrie et du commerce en France* (Paris, 1898), *EHR*, 15 (1900), 142–3.

'Elizabethan gleanings. I "Defender of the Faith, and so forth" ', *EHR*, 15 (1900), 120–4 (reprinted in *Collected Papers*, iii 157–65 and *Selected Historical Essays*, pp. 211–16).

'Elizabethan gleanings. II Queen Elizabeth and Paul IV', *EHR*, 15 (1900), 324–30 (reprinted in *Collected Papers*, iii 165–77 and *Selected Historical Essays*, pp. 216–24).

'Elizabethan gleanings. III Pius IV and the English church service', *EHR*, 15 (1900), 530–2 (reprinted in *Collected Papers*, iii 177–80 and *Selected Historical Essays*, pp. 224–6).

'Elizabethan gleanings. IV Thomas Sackville's message from Rome', *EHR*, 15 (1900), 757–60 (reprinted in *Collected Papers*, iii 180–5 and *Selected Historical Essays*, pp. 226–9).

Henry Sidgwick, a speech to a meeting (26 November 1900) to discuss a memorial to Henry Sidgwick, printed in *Cambridge University Reporter*, 31 (1900–01), 317–18 (quoted extensively in *Henry Sidgwick. A Memoir*, by A. S[idgwick] and E. M. S[idgwick], (London, 1906), pp. 304–6, and Fisher, *Biographical Sketch*, pp. 7–9).

(translated by F. W. M.) O. Gierke, *Political Theories of the Middle Age* (Cambridge, 1900), Maitland's Introduction is pp. vii–xlv, (reprinted Boston, 1958).

Review of *The Records of the Honourable Society of Lincoln's Inn. The Black Books, Volume II, from A. D. 1568 to 1660* (London, 1898), *EHR*, 15 (1900), 170–1 (reprinted in *Collected Papers*, iii 83–6 as 'Records of the Honourable Society of Lincoln's Inn II').

The Salomons Lectureship in Russian, a contribution to the meeting of Senate (10 May 1900) to discuss the report of the Council of Senate, printed in *Cambridge University Reporter*, 30 (1899–1900), 874.

1901

'Canon Law in England: a reply to Dr MacColl', *EHR*, 16 (1901), 35–45 (reprinted in *Collected Papers*, iii 137–56).

(and Mary Bateson, ed.) *The Charters of the Borough of Cambridge* (Cambridge, 1901).

'The Crown as Corporation', *LQR*, 17 (1901), 131–46 (reprinted in *Collected Papers*, iii 244–70 and, as edited by P. H. Winfield, *Selected Essays*, pp. 104–27).

English Law and the Renaissance, The Rede Lecture (Cambridge, 1901) (reprinted in *Select Essays in Anglo-American Legal History*, 1 (Cambridge, 1907), pp. 168–207, *Selected Historical Essays*, pp. 135–51, and *Maitland Reader*, pp. 211–28).

'Introduction', W. A. J. Archbold, ed., *Essays on the Teaching of History* (Cambridge, 1901), pp. ix–xx (reprinted as 'The teaching of history', in *Collected Papers*, iii 405–18).

Roofing the East Quadrangle of the Library, a contribution to the meeting of Senate (31 October 1901) to discuss the report of the Library Syndicate, printed in *Cambridge University Reporter*, 32 (1901–2), 186–7.

'A survey of the century. II Law', *The Twentieth Century*, 1 (1901), 164–9 (reprinted in *Collected Papers*, iii 432–9).

'William Stubbs, Bishop of Oxford', *EHR*, 16 (1901), 417–26 (reprinted in *Collected Papers*, iii 495–511 and *Selected Historical Essays*, pp. 266–76).

1902

'English Law (History of)', *Encyclopaedia Britannica*, 28 (10th edn, Edinburgh and London, 1902), pp. 246–53 (also 11th edn, 9 (London, 1910), pp. 600–7; reprinted in *Selected Historical Essays*, pp. 97–121, and *Maitland Reader*, pp. 125–30).

Review of G. des Marez, *La Lettre de foire à Ypres au treizième siècle* (Brussels, 1901), *EHR*, 17 (1902), 555–6.

'Lord Acton', an obituary, *Cambridge Review*, 24 (1902–3), 7–9 (reprinted in *Collected Papers*, iii 512–21, and E. Homberger, W. Janeway and S. Schama, eds, *The Cambridge Mind: Ninety Years of the Cambridge Review, 1879–1969* (London, 1970), pp. 69–74).

Review of R. J. Fletcher, *The Pension Book of Gray's Inn, 1569–1669* (London, 1901), *EHR*, 17 (1902), 613–14.

1903

Review of *Court Rolls of the Manor of Ingoldmells in the County of Lincoln*, translated W. O. Massingberd (London, 1902), and *Yorkshire Inquisitions*, 3, ed. W. Brown (Yorkshire Archaeological Society, Record Series 31, 1902), *EHR*, 18 (1903), 780–2 (reprinted in *Collected Papers*, iii 440–6 as 'Lincolnshire Court Rolls and Yorkshire Inquisitions').

'Elizabethan gleanings. V Supremacy and uniformity', *EHR*, 18 (1903), 517–32 (reprinted in *Collected Papers*, iii 185–209 and *Selected Historical Essays*, pp. 229–58).

Review of W. S. Holdsworth, *A History of English Law*, 1 (London, 1903), *LQR*, 19 (1903), 335–7.

The new Tripos in Economics and Political Science, a contribution to the meeting of Senate (7 May 1903) to discuss the report of the Economics and Political Science Syndicate, printed in *Cambridge University Reporter*, 33 (1902–3), 772.

'The oldest code of laws', Review of *The Oldest Code of Laws in the World*, translated by C. H. W. Johns (Edinburgh, 1903), *Journal of the Society of Comparative Legislation*, ns 5 (1903), 11–13.

(ed.) *Year Books of Edward II: volume I, 1 and 2 Edward II, 1307–9*, (Selden Soc., 17, Year Books Series 1; London, 1903), (Extracts from the introduction were reprinted as 'The Anglo-French law language', in A. W. Ward and A. R. Waller, eds, *The Cambridge History of English Literature*, 1 (Cambridge, 1907), pp. 408–12. Others were reprinted in *Maitland Reader*, pp. 145–8 as 'The value of the Year Books').

1904

'The Anglican Settlement and the Scottish Reformation', in A. W. Ward, G. W. Prothero and S. Leathes, eds, *Cambridge Modern History*, 2 (Cambridge, 1904), pp. 550–98, (reprinted in *Selected Historical Essays*, pp. 152–210, and partially in *Maitland Reader*, pp. 142–4).

Compulsory Greek, a contribution to the meeting of Senate (1 December 1904) to discuss the report of the Studies and Examinations Syndicate, printed in *Cambridge University Reporter*, 35 (1904–5), 372–3.

(rev.) L. Stephen, *Hobbes* (English Men of Letters; London, 1904).[9]

'The laws of the Anglo-Saxons', *Quarterly Review*, 200 (1904), 139–57 (reprinted in *Collected Papers*, iii pp. 447–73).

Regulations for the Squire Law Library, a contribution to the meeting of Senate (3 November 1904) to discuss the report of the Special Board for Law, printed in *Cambridge University Reporter*, 35 (1904–5), 187.

'Sir Leslie Stephen', *Proceedings of the British Academy*, 1 (1903–4), 316–20, (reprinted in *Collected Papers*, iii 522–30).

The Squire Law Library and Law School, a contribution to the meeting of Senate (19 May 1904) to discuss the report of the Special Board for Law, printed in *Cambridge University Reporter*, 34 (1903–4), 856.

(ed.) *Year Books of Edward II: volume II, 2 and 3 Edward II, A. D. 1308–9 and 1309–10* (Selden Soc., 19, extra volume for 1904, Year Books Series 2; London, 1904).

1905

Letter on depositing books in the Squire Law Library, read in the meeting of Senate (2 February 1905) to discuss the report of the Library Syndicate, printed in *Cambridge University Reporter*, 35 (1904–5), 558–9.

'Moral personality and legal personality', (The Sidgwick Lecture for 1903, delivered at Newnham College), *Journal of the Society of Comparative Legislation*, ns 6

---

[9] Maitland claimed (p. 237) his involvement in the book was confined to making 'those small changes that must always be made whenever a book is printed', but it is clear that he edited the book with some considerable care, see *Letters*, i nos 380–1, 384–5, 388.

(1905), 192–200 (reprinted in *Collected Papers*, iii 304–20, and, as edited by H. D. Hazeltine, in *Selected Essays*, pp. 223–39).

'Trust und Korporation', *Zeitschrift für das Privat- und Öffentliche Recht der Gegenwart*, 32 (Vienna, 1905), 1–76 (English version in *Collected Papers*, iii 321–404 and, as edited by H. D. Hazeltine, *Selected Essays*, pp. 141–222).

(ed.) *Year Books of Edward II: volume III, 3 Edward II, A. D. 1309–10* (Selden Soc., 20, Year Books Series 3; London, 1905).

1906

'Preface', Thomas Smith, *De Republica Anglorum. A Discourse on the Commonwealth of England*, ed. L. Alston (Cambridge, 1906), pp. vii–xi.

'Henry Sidgwick' (A review of *Henry Sidgwick. A Memoir*, by A. S[idgwick] and E. M. S[idgwick], (London, 1906)), *Independent Review*, 9 (1906), 324–31 (reprinted in *Collected Papers*, iii 531–40).

'In Memoriam: Mary Bateson', *The Cambridge Review*, 28 (1906–7), 136.

The Life and Letters of Leslie Stephen (London, 1906) (reprinted Bristol, 1991).

'The making of the German Civil Code', *Independent Review*, 10 (1906), 211–21 (reprinted in *Collected Papers*, iii 474–88).

'Miss Mary Bateson', *The Athenaeum*, 4128 (8 December 1906), 736[10] (reprinted in *Collected Papers*, iii 541–3 and *Selected Historical Essays*, pp. 277–8).

Review of T. F. Tout and H. Johnstone, eds, *State Trials of the Reign of Edward I, 1289–93* (London, 1906), *EHR*, 21 (1906), 783–6 (reprinted in *Collected Papers*, iii 489–94, as 'State trials of the reign of Edward I'[11]).

1907

'Introduction', *Liber Memorandum Ecclesie de Bernewelle*, ed. J. W. Clark (Cambridge, 1907), pp. xliii–lxiii.

(F. W. M. and G. J. Turner, eds) *Year Books of Edward II: volume IV, 3 and 4 Edward II, A. D. 1309–11* (Selden Soc., 22, Year Books Series 4; London, 1907).

1908

The Constitutional History of England, a Course of Lectures, ed. H. A. L. Fisher (Cambridge, 1908) (reprinted 1909, 1950, and 1961 [a photographic reproduction of the 1909 edition]).

1909

Equity, also the Forms of Action at Common Law. Two Courses of Lectures, eds A. H. Chaytor and W. J. Whittaker (Cambridge, 1909) (reprinted 1932, and reissued

---

[10] The manuscript is held by Newnham College, Cambridge.
[11] Where it is said to be from *English Historical Review*, 1896.

in 1936 in two parts *Forms of Action at Common Law. A Course of Lectures*, (reprinted, 1968); and *Equity. A Course of Lectures* revised by J. Brunyate).[12]

1910

'Bracton, Henry de', in *Encyclopaedia Britannica*, 4 (11th edn, London, 1910), p. 369.

(F. W. M., L. W. V. Harcourt and W. C. Bolland, eds) *Year Books of Edward II: volume V, The Eyre of Kent, 6 and 7 Edward II, A. D. 1313–1314, volume 1* (Selden Soc., 24 for 1909, Year Books Series 5; London, 1910).[13]

1911

The Collected Papers of Frederic William Maitland, Downing Professor of the Laws of England, ed. H. A. L. Fisher (3 vols, Cambridge, 1911).

'The Body Politic', *Collected Papers*, iii 285–303[14] (reprinted, as edited by P. H. Winfield, in *Selected Essays*, pp. 240–56).

'Law at the universities', *Collected Papers*, iii 419–31[15] (partially reprinted in *Maitland Reader*, pp 115–25.

'The Unincorporate Body', *Collected Papers*, iii 271–84 (reprinted, as edited by P. H. Winfield, in *Selected Essays*, pp. 128–40, partially reprinted in *Maitland Reader*, pp. 130–42).

1912

(W. C. Bolland, F. W. M., and L. W. V. Harcourt, eds) *Year Books of Edward II: volume VII, The Eyre of Kent, 6 and 7 Edward II, A. D. 1313–1314, volume 2* (Selden Soc. 27, Year Books Series 7; London, 1912).

1915

A Sketch of English Legal History, edited with notes and appendices by J. F. Colby (New York and London, 1915), contains reprints of the work of F. C. Montague and F. W. M., in Maitland's case from *Social England* and *The History of the English Law*.

---

[12] The Squire Law Library in Cambridge has a Japanese translation of the 1909 edition published at Kyoto, 1991, and the Bodleian Law Library an Italian translation, *L'equità* by A. R. Borzelli with 'presentazione' by C. Geraci (Milan, 1979).

[13] According to the preface (p. xiii), Maitland made a rough transcript, dated 27 January 1901, of one of the MSS, which was the basis for further work.

[14] Winfield notes, *Selected Essays*, p. 240, 'The date of this paper is probably 1899. Maitland's note on the MS is "Read to the Eranus Club".'

[15] Fisher notes, *Collected Papers*, p. 419 n. 1, 'A paper read to the Cambridge Law Club, 1901.'

1936

Selected Essays, eds H. D. Hazeltine, G. Lapsley, and P. H. Winfield (Cambridge, 1936).

1957

Frederick (sic) *William Maitland Reader*, ed. V. T. H. Delany (New York, 1957).

Selected Historical Essays, ed. H. M. Cam (Cambridge, 1957).

1960

Frederic William Maitland, Historian. Selections from his Writings, edited with an introduction by R. L. Schuyler (Berkeley and Los Angeles, 1960).

1965

The Letters of Frederic William Maitland, ed. C. H. S. Fifoot (Selden Soc. Supplementary Series, 1; London and Cambridge, 1965).

1966

'Two lectures delivered by F. W. Maitland, Downing Professor of the Laws of England, in the Easter Term, 1889', as edited by C. H. S. Fifoot, in *CLJ*, 24 (1966), 54–74.

1976

F. W. Maitland. Letters to George Neilson, ed. E. L. G. Stones (Glasgow, 1976).

1995

The Letters of Frederic William Maitland. Volume II, ed. P. N. R. Zutshi (Selden Soc. Supplementary Series, 11; London, 1995).

Note I am grateful to all those who have helped in the preparation of this bibliography, especially Dr John Hudson and Professor John Baker. But, above all, thanks are due to the staff of the Bodleian Library for their helpfulness, courtesy and patience without which it would have been impossible to complete this task.

Index

Prepared by Nora Bartlett

abbatia, 194
Abelard, Peter, 148
Abingdon Abbey, 62–3, 192n.; abbot of, 37, 210n.; chronicle of, 14, 47
abjuration, 124–5, 127, 128, 141
Accursius, 162
accusation, false, 132–4; public, 123
acquittals, 121
Adam Roules, 124–5
Adams, Henry, 6, 9
advowsons, 164
Aelfgar, earl, 188n.
aethelings, 187
Africa, 9
aids, 26
Alfred, king, 2–3nn., 13–15, 17n., 18–19, 45, 186n.
Algar of Charton, 136–7
alienability of land, 42n., 102, 105–6, 198, 258; *see also kinship; land grants; retrait lignager*
alms, 40, 42n., 192n., 199–200, 247, 250, 257–58; alms tenure, 208–9; in Normandy, 193n.; perpetual, 193, 211
amercements, 6, 15, 45, 100n., 132, 149
American Historical Review, The, founding of, 239–40
Angevin kings, as law-makers, 10, 15–16, 21, 28, 53–4, 56–7, 59, 95, 234. *See also Henry II, Richard I, John*
Anglo-Saxon charters, 5, 21, 102n., 104, 186n.; forged 202
Anglo-Saxon kings, and royal demesne, 186n.
Anglo-Saxon law, 1–6, 8–20, 23, 25, 43–6, 172, 173, 184–91, 208; compared with Anglo-Norman, 39–44; concept of penalty, 13–17, 44–5; Frankish influence on, 8–10, 13; law-making, 17–19; pleas of the Crown, 6–7
Anjou, 54, 55, 56, 58, 62
Anselm, archbishop of Canterbury, 174–83, 191
Anstey case, 47–8, 50–1, 57–8
antecessor, concept of, 184–91
anthropology, 112
appeal of felony, *see felony*

Aquitaine, 54, 55, 62; dukes of, 54
arrest, 135–6, 139–40, 141–2; difficulty of, 123; *see also hue and cry*
arson, 117, 140, 229
Arthur of Brittany, 59–60
assarting, 129
assault, 117, 142
assizes, 47, 69, 156, 251; grand, 257; of Clarendon (1166), 10, 46, 229; assizes of cloth and wine, 133; of Northampton (1176), 46
Athelstan, king, laws of, 101, 234
attaint, writs of, 69
Augustinians, 232
Austin, John, 33n., 34n.
Aylesbury (Bucks), 122, 138
Azo, 147–8, 240

Badgeworth (Glos.), 138
bailiffs, powers of, 135–6, 138–9, 256–7
bailments, law of, 153n.
baptism, 166n, 232n.
Barking Abbey, 210n.
Barnwell Priory, 19–20n.
Bartlett, R., 36n.
Bartolus, 147
bastardy, 84, 164, 248n.; *see also legitimacy*
Bates, D., 178n.
Bath (Somerset) 184n.; Henry of, 88; Walter of, 137; church of, 192n.; Robert Burnel, bishop of, 74
Battersea (Surrey), 203
Battle Abbey, 62–3, 200; chronicle of, 47, 200, 206, 209n.; forgeries, 200–1, 205–10
Bayeux Tapestry, 174n.
Beachampton (Bucks), 133–4
Bec, abbey of, 174
Beccles (Suffolk), 210n.
Becket, Thomas, chancellor, archbishop of Canterbury, 61–3, 74, 157, 159–60; controversy involving, 154, 157, 159–60
Becontree hundred (Essex), 210n.
Beddingham (Sussex), 187n.
Bedfordshire, 126, 228n.
Beeding (Sussex), 187n.
beneficia, in Normandy, 25n.
Beowulf, 7

Berkeley (Glos.), 129
Berkshire, 138
Bermondsey Priory, 211
Bibliothèque Nationale, 53
Biddlesden Abbey, 211
Bigelow, M. M., 28, 31n., 35n. 40, 47–49, 239n.
birth-rights, 103–5
Blackpool (near Burton, Staffs.), 36
Blackstone, William, 13, 33, 217n., 218, 253
Bloch, M., 110–11
blodwite, 201
blood-feud, 3, 6, 14, 16–17, 95–6n., 97–101, 112, 131
Blythburgh (Suffolk), 192n.
bocland, see book-land
Boer War, 223
book-land, 6, 42, 103–4
Booth, Charles, 219n.
Bordeaux, 54
borough, 120–1; and Domesday survey, 184n.; *see also* towns
bót, 14, 16, 44, 45
Bracton, 9n., 11, 21, 25–7, 34, 43, 46, 49, 65–90, 115–23, 131, 154–8, 162, 212, 220–1, 225–30, 234, 236–7, 244, 246–51; authorship of, 65, 66, 73–9; dating of, 65–73, 254; *Note Book*, 27, 34, 66n., 79–83, 257; ms. of 79–80; *see also* Henry of *Bracton*
Bramber (Sussex), 138
Bramford (Suffolk), 192n.
breach of faith, law concerning, 150
bribery, 135–6, 234
Bridgnorth (Shropshire), 141
Bridlington Priory, 232
brigands, 126–7, 129, 142.
Brightlingsea (Essex), 188n.
Bristol (Glos.), 126, 135; St Augustine's Abbey, 211
British Academy, 240
British welfare state, origins of, 120
Brittany, 69
Britton, 115
Briwerre, William, 82
Browning, Oscar, 261n.
Brunner, H., 8n., 10, 11, 12, 15n., 27, 39, 171n., 217n., 228
Bruns, Carl, 155n.
Buckland (Herts.), 139
Bunstey (Bucks.), 133–4
burglary, 136, 142
Burnel, Robert, 74
Burrow, J., 94, 95–6, 97
Burton Abbey, 36
Bury St Edmund's, abbey of, 195n., 199–201, 207–8, 210n.; Baldwin, abbot of, 200

Caen, abbey of St Etienne, 188n., 202n., 203; La Trinité, 202n., 203n.

Cam, H. M., 7, 27, 134, 230n., 246
Cambridge, 252; University Press, 29
Canon Law, 145–69, 178–9, 182, 190–3; and custom, 166–69; and private life, 162; of possession, 159n.; *see also* ius commune
canon lawyers, 238–9
Canterbury, archbishopric of, 62–3, 160n., 174, 177–8, 181, 193n., 195n., 201n.; *see also Anselm, Becket, Lanfranc, Hubert Walter*
Capetian kings of France, 213
Carolingian elements, in law, 11, 15
Carolingian empire, 9
cartularies, ecclesiastical, 42n.
cases, referred to higher courts, 40n.
Casus et Judicia, 81
cattle-rustling, 140, 141
cessavit per biennium, 153n.
Chadwick, H. M., 5
Chamberlain, Joseph, 223
chancery, 160n.; clerks, 87–8; rolls, 52, 59, 250
Chaplais, P., 204–5, 206–7n.
Charles the Bald, 11
charter chronicles, monastic, 38
charters, 7, 27n, 40, 42–64 *passim*, 72–3, 104, 107n.; consent, clauses in, 107n.; French, 111; *see also Anglo-Saxon charters*
Chartres, 111n.
chattels, 253; separated from realty, 150–1
Cheltenham (Glos.), 26n.
Cheviot Hills, 54
Chichester bishop of, 193, 205
childbirth, and male heirs, 231–2
children, as oathworthy, 11, 15
Chinon, 59, 60
Church, and criminal law, 150–1; as landholder, 43n., 105, 151, 171–214 *passim*; as sovereign power, 168; churches, as corporations, 192–4
Cirencester, abbot of, 131
Clairvaux, 56
clan, 97n., 99, 101
Clarendon, Assize of see Assize
Clarendon, Constitutions of (1164), 46n.
Clementia de Fougères, Countess, 225
clerics, charged with felony, 116, 159; in litigation, 40; tried for homicide, 127
close rolls, 115–16
'Clovesho', 3n.
Cluny, 189n.
Cnut, king, 7, 11, 15, 18–19, 45, 174n., 201n., 208
Coke, Edward, 13, 147, 171n., 217n.
Colchester (Essex), 205; abbey, 210
Commentaria in Decretalium libros, 164n.
commodatum, 148
Common Law, 4–5, 25, 26, 39–46, 58–9, 63, 84, 86–7, 108, 146, 148–52, 154–62, 199,

215, 217, 221–2, 228–9, 231, 234–6, 238, 245; in Normandy, 58
comparative law, 32, 149–50, 154
compensation, 46, 99–101; for homicide, 98; in Anglo-Saxon codes, 99–100; see also bót
compurgation, 151
confession, sacrament of, and justice, 140
contract law, 149, 150, 155; and ecclesiastical courts, 160–1
corona, see crown
coroner, 124, 131, 133, 135, 228n.; coroners' inquests, 122; coroners' rolls, 126
corporation, 97, 98n., 101, 154–5, 171–214 passim; corporations sole, 199; ecclesiastical, 171n.
Corpus iuris canonici, 146, 225–6
Corpus iuris civilis, 146
corruption, see bailiffs, bribery, sheriffs
Cotswolds, 128
courts, 3n., 34–5, 234; abbot's 200; bishop's 40; Common Bench, 71, 78–9, 88; Common Pleas, 53; county, 6, 40–1, 43n., 68, 86, 122, 123, 229; ecclesiastical, 76–7, 116, 142, 148, 150–70, 226; hundred, 6, 40–1, 43n., 122, 229–30; king's, 10–11, 15–16, 23, 31, 33, 37, 40, 55, 56–7, 65, 76, 83–6, 117–18, 179; King's Bench, 53, 79, 87, 88; lord's, 6–7, 8, 39–41, 73; manor, 235–6; papal, 180–1; Sheriff's tourn, 122, 134–5, 229–30
Coventry (Warw.), 138
crime, 13–15, 93, 115–43; and sin, 140–1; acquittals, 121; community response to 121–43; of violence, 121–2, 124, 126, 127–30, 232–3; rate, and civil wars, 126; statutory definitions of, 233; see also arson, brigands, homicide, murder, rape
crown, corona, 171–214; and immunities 202–8; and kingship, 172, 198–9, 201, 204–5, 211–13; as physical object, 201–4; as symbolic object, 171–6, 181–90, 198–9, 202–8, 212–13; see also pleas of the crown
Curia Regis rolls, see plea rolls
curtesy, 218n., 232

De iniusta vexacione, 173–91
de homagio capiendo, 258
death penalty, 44, 100n., 117, 118, 121, 125, 127, 141; among Anglo-Saxons, 14; by burning 226; cemeteries, 14
death, accidental, 133
debt 93; and royal succession, 197; writs of, 50
Decretales Gregorii IX, 159
decretals, papal, 159, 163–4
Deerhurst (Glos.), 130–1
demesne, 184–5, 187n., 196n., 206n.
Denham (Suffolk), 192n.
Deville, Achille, 53
Dialogus de Scaccario, 47, 249–50

Dicey, Edward, 12n., 215–16, 218n.
Digest, 146
diplomatic, 52; Norman, 189–90n.
disinheritance, 108; of younger sons, 109–10
dispute settlement, 36–9
distraint, 85–6, 250, 254, 256; districciones Scaccarii, 86
divine intervention, in disputes, 36–7
divorce law, 150
Domesday Book, 7, 14n., 21, 27ff., 41–5, 183–97, 206; as geld-book, 31; scribe of, 185–6; Little Domesday, 186, 192, 194
Domesday Book and Beyond, see Maitland, F. W., works
dominus rex, 189–90
Dove, P. E., 120, 143
dower, 67, 82, 227–8
Duby, G., 111
Duckworth, George, 219n.
Dudstone (Shropshire), 131
Duggan, C., 159
Durham, 173, 182

Eadmer, 173–99, 207, 212, 213–14
Ealdred, archbishop of York, 173n., 174n., 177n.
earls, Domesday records of, 186
Eastbourne (Sussex), 133, 187n.
ecclesiastical vacancies, 209, 249–50; seized by king, 195–6
Ecole des Chartes, 9n.
Edgar aetheling, 187
Edgar, king, 202n.
Edith, queen, 187n.
Edlesborough (Bucks.), 136
Edward the Elder, king, 14
Edward the Confessor, king, 7, 14, 23, 31–2, 39, 174n., 184, 185, 187, 190, 199–200, 202–3, 206n.; crown and regalia, 202; estates of, 187–8n.; William's antecessor, 185–7
Edward I, king, 31, 88, 135, 147, 156, 158, 212n., 222, 236, 244, 253n.
Edward II, king, 228n.
Edwardstone (Suffolk), 192n.
Eleanor of Aquitaine, queen, 52–4, 56, 62
Elton, G. R., 252
Ely, church of, 210n.
Encyclopaedia Britannica, 2–3n., 22, 34n.
enfeoffment, 104
Engels, Friedrich, 91
England, relations with papacy, 159–60, 163; see also Stubbs
English Historical Review, 30
English, as language of private justice, 8
episcopatus, episcopium, 190–91, 194
Ermenfrid of Sion, 209
escheat, 195–8
espousals, by verba de futuro, 164–5
Essex, 119, 125–6, 138, 188n.

essoin, 71; *de malo lecti*, 84; rolls, 213n.
Ethelred, king, 10–11
Evesham Abbey, 192n.; Aethelwig, abbot of, 177–8
evolutionary theories, of history, 21n.; of law, 16, 94–8; *see also Maine*
exceptio spolii, 190–1, 198; influence on novel disseisin, 152
Exchequer, of England, 55, 86; of Normandy, 55; of the Jews, 220n.
excommunication, 140–1, 154, 164–5
execution, *see death penalty*
Exeter, 185n.; Henry, bishop of, 142
Exon Domesday, 185–6, 190
eyre, 68, 70, 115–43; Buckinghamshire (1227), 122, (1262), 133–4; Cornwall (1201), 142; Devon, (1238), 117, 132–3, 137; Durham (1242/3), 140; Essex (1235), 133; Hertfordshire (1248), 139; Kent (1227), 71, (1231), 136–7, (1262/3), 139; Leicestershire (1232), 68n.; Norfolk (1250–1), 137; Shropshire (1203), 229n., (1256) 230n; Surrey (1235), 118–19, 125–6, 230n., (1241) 137, (1255) 117; Sussex (1248), 133; Warwickshire (1232), 138; Wiltshire (1249), 118–19

family, family history *see kinship*
Faversham hundred (Kent), 136
fealty 96n., 175, 180, 183
Fécamp Abbey, 126n.
fee, *feudum*, 40, 42, 43; *see also fief*
felony, 14, 15, 116, 119–43, 128, 140; appeal of, 117, 119, 123–4, 136–7, 141, 229; husbands and wives, 226, 229
Ferme, Brian, 165
feud *see blood-feud*
feudal law, concept of, 33
'feudalism', 6, 8, 17, 19, 27n., 32, 39–40, 102n., 107n.
fief, 42–3, 104; in Normandy, 25n.
Fifoot, C. H. S., 18n. 215, 224, 235n.
final concords, 48–9
fine rolls, 57
Fisher, H. A. L., 9n., 16n., 261
Fleta, 115–17, 228
Fontevrault, 54
'fore-oath', 3n.
forest of Dean, 126
forfeiture, 6; among Franks, 15; of chattels 13–14; *see also escheat*
forgery, of papal documents, 204; of William I's seal, 205; of witness lists, 203n.; *see also Osbert of Clare*
Fossier, 111
Fouracre, P., 9n.
Framsden (Suffolk), 192n.
France, 62, 109–11, 149; feud in, 100n.; legal history of, 102
Franciscans, 239

Frankish influence, on English law, 9–10, 13, 15, 22, 24
frankpledge, 10, 11–13, 116, 127, 129, 140, 228–31; children and women excluded from, 117, 228; *see also tithing*
Freebridge hundred (Norfolk), 137
freehold land, 76
Freeman, E. A., 23n.
fugitives, 128, 229; *see also arrest, difficulty of; outlawry*
Fulks, Robert, 88n.
Fustel de Coulanges, N.–D., 9n., 92

gage, 27n., 222
Ganelon, 35n.
gaol, 70, 136, 132, 136, 137–8, 230
geld, exemption from, 184n., 187–8, 210
gens, 97n., 101
Geoffrey de Mandeville, earl of Essex, 63, 210–11
Geoffrey fitz Peter, 57–8
Geoffrey of Anjou, 62
Geoffrey of Sutton, 118
Germany, 56, 149; influence of Roman law, 157; law, 5n.
Gervase of Canterbury, 201n.
Gibbon, Edward, 1, 243
Gierke, Otto von, 4–5, 8n., 154–5, 171
Gilbert de Gant, 232
Gilbert of Seagrave, 138
Gillingham (Dorset), 174
Given, J. B., 126
Gladstone, William, 120, 223
'Glanvill', *Tractatus de Legibus*, 4, 15–16n., 18–19, 26, 27n., 47, 49, 115, 158, 209, 228, 244, 247–51, 253, 255–6, 258; *see also Ranulf de Glanville*
Glastonbury (Somerset), 192n.
glossa ordinaria, 155
Gloucester, Gloucestershire, 117, 118, 121, 130, 194n., 203, 235; Crown Pleas (1221), 119, 125–32, 135, 140; *see also Maitland, works*
Gloucester, earl of, 131
Godwine family, 185
Goebel, Julius, 4
Grace, W. G., 20
grants, in alms, 250, 257–58; in perpetuity, 193, 201; of jurisdictional rights, 23, 200; royal grants, of liberties, 206–7; *see also alienability*
Gratian, 147
Great Baddow (Essex), 188n.
Green, J. R., 219n.
Green, T. A., 118
Gross, C., 29
guardianship, 96, 160; *see also wardship*

habeas corpus, 71–2, 234
Hale, Matthew, 217n.

Hamo Petch, 139
hanging, *see death penalty*
Harcourt (Anjou), 57, 58
hard cases, 43
Harold Harefoot, 174n.
Harold, king, 25, 174n., 186n., 187, 187–8n.
Harvey, B., 204
Hastings, battle of, 23, 25,
Henbury hundred (Glos.), 135
Henry I, king, 6, 13–14, 24n., 40, 41n., 44n.
    45n., 48, 62, 176, 178n., 184n., 196–212;
    coronation charter, 196–8, 249–50
Henry II, king, 10–11, 22, 24–6, 35n., 40, 41,
    46, 47–55, 57, 60–5, 69, 85, 88, 120, 126,
    157, 159–60, 178n., 200n., 205–6, 211–13,
    244–5, 251, 257, 258
Henry III, king, 83–9, 126n., 134,
Henry of Bracton / Bratton, 65, 71, 73–9,
    83, 87–9; *see also* Bracton
Henry of Huntingdon, 201n.
Hereford, Herefordshire, 125, 184n., 188n.,
    194; *terra regis*, 184n.
heresy, heretics, 151, 155, 216, 238–9
heriot, 44n.
Herlihy, D., 111
Hervey de Glanville, 19
hide, 30–1, 100n., 188n.
Historische Rechtsschule, 4–5
History of English Law, see Maitland, works
Holt, J. C., 178
homage, 96n., 247; within family, 248;
    clerical, 176–8
homicide, 14n., 96n., 117–19, 120–2, 124,
    129, 131, 136, 139, 140, 142, 226, 247; and
    circumstantial evidence, 139; and murder
    125; and pardon, 232–3; as sin, 140; by
    unknown hand, 129; compensation for,
    98; in self-defence, 232–3; punishment
    for, 123–27; rates of, 125–6
homosexuality, homosexuals, 149, 216, 239
Horsepools (Glos.), 31n.
Hospitallers, 122
Hostiensis, 147–8, 155, 165n.
Hoyt, R. S., 187–8
Hubert Walter, 78
hue and cry, 122, 124–5, 130, 136, 138, 141
Hugh le Seler, 139
hundred, 7, 10, 12, 40, 120–1; serjeants, 141;
    see also courts
Hurnard, N., 4

Ibsen, Henrik, 240
immunities, Anglo-Saxon, 9; Frankish, 9;
    from episcopal jurisdiction, 204–6
imprisonment, 138
indictment, 230
infancy, as legal concept, 96, 102n.
Ingelrann fitz Ilbert, 189n.
inheritance, 35–6, 42–3n., 67, 76, 96, 101–3,
    105, 193n., 196–7, 247–8, 254–5, 258; and

alienation, 103, 105–9, 247; and re-
    marriage, 35; by infants, 102n., 196–7; by
    parents, 45n.; by women, 196–7, 231,
    249–50; in France, 35n.; modern right of
    105; *see also primogeniture*
Innocent II, pope, 202n., 204
inquest, 24, 136–7, 141, 142
interdict, personal, 164n.
interregnum, and homage, 197–8
intestacy, 96, 155; and widow's share, 227
investiture contest, in England, 176–8, 190n.
Ireland, 59–60, 69, 126, 218
itinerant workers, 127–8
Ius primae noctis, 237
ius commune, 16, 145–6, 150–69 *passim*; 245
ius patronatus, 164
ius proprium, 146
Ivo de Clifford, 117
    Milisent, his wife, 117

Jewish Historical Society of England, 224
Jews, 218–23, 238; accused of killing
    children, 222–3; and gage, 222; expulsion
    of, 221; landholding in fee, 222; legal
    disabilities, 221; legislation concerning
    (1269–75), 221; massacre of, 222–3;
    special relationship with king, 220–1;
    toleration of, 223
John of Sleekburn, 140
John of Standon, 139
John, king, 57–62, 69, 213n.; as count of
    Mortain, 52
Johnson, Samuel, 4
jury, 10, 46, 86, 131–2, 217n., 230, 233; of
    presentment, 10, 230; trial, 116–18, 121,
    127, 131, 133, 141, 157
justices itinerant, *see eyre*
justices, royal, laymen as, 87–8

Kantorowicz, E. H., 212n., 213n.
Kelsale (Suffolk), 192n.
Kemble, J. M., 8
King's Bench, 53, 79, 87, 88
'king's enemy', concept of, 15
king's peace, 124, 134, 140
kingship, 15, 23–4, 39, 107n., 173–214, 257–8
kinship, 92–113, 247; and compensation, 98;
    and homicide, 98; and land-grants, 102n.,
    106–9, 111–12, 257–8; Germanic, 102n.
knight service, owed by clerics, 178
knight's fees, 31n.
Kuttner, Stephen, 159

Laga Edwardi, 39
Land Transfer Act (1897), 217n.
land grants, 41–3, 76, 185, 188–93, 247; to
    saints, 192–5, 201; and kin, 43n., 106–9,
    248; in perpetuity, 208–10; sales, 247; *see
    also alienability; tenure*

Lanfranc, archbishop of Canterbury, 177, 179–83, 190–1, 193n.
language, of legal history, 32–4
Lateran Council (1078), 177n.
laudatio parentum, see kinship
law, civil distinguished from criminal, 229n.
law, evolutionary theories of, *see evolutionary theories*
Lawford (Essex), 188n.
lawyers, as legal historians, 243; civilian terminology of, 152; education, 156; Maitland as, *see Maitland*
Leap Year, essoin in, 84; ordinance, 84
Learned Laws, *see ius commune*
legal language, 25–6, 32
Leges Edwardi Confessoris, 212
Leges Henrici Primi, 4, 7–8, 10–11, 15–16n., 17–19, 21, 24, 44, 98, 183, 207–8
Leges Willelmi, 44n., 208
legitimacy, 248n.; *see also bastardy*
lepers, 216
leuga, 205
Lewes Priory, 189n.
lex mercatoria, 146
lex talionis, and amercing, 149
Lexden (Essex), 133
Liber duo de synodalibus causis, 149
liberalism, 120
Libri feudorum, 3, 146
Liebermann, Felix, 4, 5, 8–9, 27n., 44, 196n.
'liege' widowhood, 225
Lincoln, bishopric of, 61
literacy, increase of, 46, 63
literary texts, as source for trials, 37
litis contestatio, 147
Littleton, Thomas, 147
Lodge, H. Cabot, 102n.
Lombardy, 33
London, 58, 193–4, 208; submission of 174n.; Tower of, 171; St Paul's, 78; canons of, 193–4; bishop of, 204
lords, lordship, 3n., 5–7, 8, 27n., 28, 39–42, 246, 249, 255–6, 258; and peasants, 236–7
Ludlow (Shropshire), 124–5
lunatics, 216
Lyndwood, William, 165

Macaulay, Thomas Babington, 1, 243
Magna Carta, 47, 134, 227
Maine, Henry, 2–3n., 16, 91–100, 101n., 102, 104n., 105, 108, 110
mainpast, 128, 230

MAITLAND, Frederic William
family:
    Samuel Roffey (grandfather), 18
    Florence (wife), 21n., 219n., 235, 261
    Ermengarde (daughter), 245–6
    Fredegond (daughter), 21n.
  career and temperament:

agnosticism, 140, 224
anonymous articles, 261
attitude to Jews, 219–24
attitude to moneylending, 222
careful use of language, 219
cosmopolitanism of, 8, 19
declines chair of history, 252
landowner, 235
law career, 252–4
lectures on English land law, 29
Liberal, 120
liberalism, 215–24
patriotism, 216–19, 223–4
personality and background, 120, 212, 215–16, 223–4
political attitudes, 215–24
Rede Lectures, 157
reformer, 238–9
rhetorical habits, 222
speaking whilst writing, 245–6
influence and opinions:
  admission of women to Cambridge, 224–5
  on anachronism, 32–4
  Anglo-Saxon kings, 39
  anthropology, 16, 102n., 105n.
  archaisms in family law, 96–7
  on Austin, J., 34–5n.
  blood-feud groups, 99–100
  Bracton, 65–6, 76, 246–7
  changes in view of Anglo-Saxon law, 15n.
  christens 'Bracton's note book', 79
  church and religion, 140
  church's marriage law, 150
  Common and Canon Law, 153–4
  communalism, 93–5, 120, 245
  comparative jurisprudence, 102n.
  comparative law, 217–18
  constitutional history, 34n., 134
  England's legal 'precocity', 96–7
  European scholarship, 8–9, 12, 96n., 180n., 217
  evolutionary theories, 110–11
  'family ownership', 97–104
  'feudalism', 17, 29–31, 246
  'forms of action', 253–4
  French and English customs, 96–7
  German village, 93
  Henry of Bracton, 87–9
  ignorance of English lawyers, 156
  influence on English historical study, 252–3
  influence on study of law, 253–4
  interest in Scots law, 218
  jury, 12–13
  kingship, 244
  kinship, 92–112
  Latin and vernacular, 34
  law and liberty, 234

law's 'typical person', 224–5
law-making of kings, 15
learned laws, 149–56, 157, 244–5
'legal individualism', 92–110, 112–13
on legal language, 25–6, 32–4
legal sense of manor, 30–1n.
litigation and social class, 50–1
on Sir Henry Maine, 94n.
marital property, 149
medieval criminal law, 116–43 passim
not a statistician, 42n.
on law as science, 152–3
on lords' consent to land grants, 42–3n.
on punishment, 16–17
ordeal, 38n.
'Ownership and Possession', 246
papal decretals, 163–4
parliament, 142
peasants, 34–5
pecuniary penalties, 134
primogeniture, 43n., 107
Roman terminology, 156n.
royal courts, 19, 26
tort, 13–14
use of analogy, 33–4
use of charter evidence, 107–8
use of fictitious characters, 11–12, 255,
    256n.
use of 'foreign', 245
use of ideal cases, 34n.
use of Rotuli Hundredorum, 135
use of 'trespass', 257
use of 'wardship', 257
wary of possessives, 249
women, 216, 221
works:
    Collected Papers, 2–3n., 120n.
    Constitutional History, 8n., 23n., 24n.,
        48n.
    Domesday Book and Beyond, 1, 3n.,
        4–5n., 6–9, 10n., 15, 21, 22, 26–34, 44n.,
        93, 186n., 215–17, 244
    Equity, 50n., 253
    Gloucestershire Crown Pleas, 118–19,
        121, 124–8, 130–2, 134–5, 140–1
    History of English Law, 1–5, 9–10,
        13–20, 21–35, 36n., 39–40, 43–4,
        45–6, 47–8, 50–1, 65–6, 87, 91–110,
        112–13, 115–17, 121, 123, 128, 131,
        134, 141, 145, 147–61, 163–5, 167–9,
        171–2, 184, 192, 212–13, 215–20, 224,
        225–33, 234–241, 244–7, 249, 251,
        253, 256–9
        and Bracton, 34, 65–6, 115–17, 119
        and 'the Crown', 171–2, 184, 192,
            212–13
        'Domesday' chapter, 29–31
        and learned laws, 145, 147–61, 163–5,
            167–9
        role of family in, 91–110, 112–13

    writing of, 13, 28–31
    'The Law of Real Property', 12
    Letters, 4, 18, 19, 22n., 28–9, 30, 31n.,
        33, 97n., 120, 165n., 215, 219, 220,
        222–4, 226, 227, 235, 237n., 239n.,
        240n.
    'Materials for English Legal History',
        5n.
    Roman Canon Law in the Church of
        England, 154, 225–6
    Select Pleas of the Crown, 49n., 141–2
    Selected Historical Essays, 2–4n., 10n.
    Township and Borough, 93

major pleas, 6–7
Malmesbury Abbey, 192n.
manor, 21n. 184–5, 187, 192, 194, 202n., 203;
    see also courts
maritagium, 247, 250n.
maritime law, 146
marriage, 35, 93, 96; controls on, 233; of
    heiresses, 233n.; law 161–2, 225–6; and
    property, 149
Martin of Pateshull, 69, 74, 78–9, 83–4, 87
Marx, Karl, 235
Mathilda, empress, 210–12, 213
Mathilda, queen, 201, 202n., 203n.
mayhem, 14n.
Meekings, C. A. F., 118–19, 131
merchet, 233
Merton, 'provisions' / 'statute' of (1236), 67,
    73–4, 81, 164, 256n.
military service, 42
Milson, S. F. C., 162, 234, 239n.
minor pleas, 6–7
Mirror of Justices, The, 13
moneylending, 222
monks 154; maintenance of, 193n.
mortgage, and Jewish privilege, 220
Morgan, Lewis H., 92
Morris, W. A., 13
mort d'ancestor, 69, 70, 251, 258
mund, 14
murder, of children, 126; of spouse 226; of
    women, 130; see also homicide
murdrum, 201
mutilation, 138

naming, of children, 232n.
ne vexes, 72–3, 254n.
Neilson, G., 36n., 218
Newport (Essex), 188n.
Nicholas II, pope, 202, 204
Nichols, F. M., 115
Nigel d'Oilly, 36–7
Niort (Poitou), 59, 60
Norfolk, 123
Norman Anonymous, the, 181–2
Norman conquest, impact on law, 21–8,
    39–46, 171–214 passim

Norman kings, ceremonies of, 181; crown-wearing, 181n.–182
Normandy, 15n., 25n., 55–6, 59–60, 62, 176, 201, 208–9, 218n.
Northamptonshire, 123
Northumberland, 128, 137
novel disseisin, 19n., 67, 69, 70, 75, 152, 190–1, 250, 251, 256–7
nuns, 194

oath, 11, 15, 24, 45n.; and women, 117, 229n.; *de calumnia*, 166n.; in Normandy, 15n.; *see also compurgation, fore-oath*
Odo, bishop of Bayeux, 179n., 189–90
offences, classification of, 31
Offler, H. S., 173
ordeal, 38–9, 141, 142
Orderic Vitalis, 179n.
Osbert of Clare, 202–5
Oswaldslow, 7
Otto, papal legate, 140–1
Ottonian dynasty, 14
Ousden (Suffolk), 192n.
outlawry, 3n., 101, 117, 119, 122, 123–5, 127, 137–8, 142–3, 229, 238; and exile, 123–5; and forfeiture of chattels, 125; and sanctuary, 123–5; Anglo-Saxon, 228n.; of vill, 142; of women, 228–30
ownership, 33, 247, 249–50
Oxford, 159, 210n., 255
Oxfordshire, 41

Page, William, 128
Paine, Thomas, 171n.
Pall Mall Gazette, 261
Palmer, Robert, 160n.
pancarte, 203
Panormitanus, 147, 164n.
papal decretals, enforcement of, 163–6
papal relations, with Norman kings, 174–7
parish priests, 164–5; churches, 70
parliament, 142, 164; beginnings of, 134
Paschal II, pope, 204
patent rolls, 59, 115–16, 138
peasants, 36–7, 111n., 184–5, 251; *see also villeins*
penalties, financial, 14, 16, 140; for murder of spouse, 226; *see also amercement*
Pershore Abbey, 182n.
Peter of Pinchbeck, 137–8
Peterborough Abbey, 210n.
Philip Marmion, sheriff, 137
Placita Quo Warranto, 27
plaint, 119–20
plea rolls, 72–3, 79, 86–7, 115–16, 119–20, 122, 125, 127, 128, 218, 229, 246, 251, 256
pleas of the crown, 7, 119–20, 125–32
pleas, and royal succession, 197
pledge, release on, 142
Plucknett, T. F. T., 171, 214, 246

Poitiers, 50, 54, 59
Pollock, Sir Frederick, 1–20 *passim*, 28–31, 34n., 44, 94, 96, 145–9, 217n., 244; author of introduction to *History of English Law*, 34n.; learned in Roman Law, 148; writing Anglo-Saxon chapter of *History*, 28–9
pope, unrecognised in England, 174–77, 181n.
possessives, interpretation of, 249–50
Powicke, F. M., 8, 55
prayers, as services for land, 106n.
presentment, 131–2, 138, 141
primogeniture, 43n., 104, 107–10
private justice, 3n., 8, 17, 31n.
private war, 36, 100n.
probate, *see wills*
Property Acts (1925), 217n., 253
prostitution, 142
Provinciale, 165
Pseudo-Isidorian decretals, 182, 190–1
Public Record Office, 18, 53, 115, 118
Pucklechurch (Glos.), 127
Pugh, R. B., 120
punishment, 3, 13–14, 16, 19n., 45; corporal 100n.; for petty theft, 138; *see also death penalty*
Pyrenees, 54

Quadripartitus, 17, 183

Ramsey Abbey, 40, 201, 207–8; Aldwin, abbot of, 201
Ranulf de Glanville, 19, 65
rape, 116, 140, 142, 232–3; charge, settled by marriage, 142
Reading Abbey, 209, 210
recaption, 68n.
Record Commission, 12n.–13n.
redisseisin, 67, 168
Regesta Regum Anglo-Normannorum, 52
Regino of Prüm, 149
regio, regnum, 186n., 195–8
regnal dates, 191–2
replevin, 68, 86
restitution, privilege of, 164n.
retrait lignager, 104–5
revenance, 36–7
rhetoric, in historical writing, 175
Richard de Lucy, 63
Richard I, king, 47, 50, 52–9, 69, 213n.; as Count of Poitou, 56
Richard Poore, bishop of Salisbury, 140
Richardson, H.G., 120
rights, theories of, 33
robbery, *see theft*
Robert Basset, 118
Robert de Beaumont, earl of Leicester, 11–12, 63
Robert de Castello, 137
Robert Kari, 126

Robert le Holdere, 135
Robert of Lexington, 87, 88
Robert of Limesey, bishop of Coventry, 206–7n.
Robert of Scarborough, 74
Rochester, bishopric of, 160n., 176–8
Rockingham, council of (1095), 174–5, 176, 180, 183, 191, 198
Roger de Sumery, 138
Roger le Vacher, outlaw, 123–4
Roger of Thirkleby, 88
Roger the Poitevin, count, 36–7
Rolls Series, 115
Roman Empire, 146–7
Roman inquisition, 161
Roman Law, 19, 25, 58, 217, 229n., 245–7; criminal law, 149; see also ius commune
Roman Republic, 147
Rome, 174, 179n., 204; appeals to 182
Rotuli Hundredorum, 135
Rouen, Saint-Ouen, 189n.
Round, J. H., 3, 9, 22n., 29–30, 31, 48–9, 186n., 188n.
Royston (Herts.), 139
Russia, 240n.

saints' lives, 36
sake and soke, 8, 9, 40, 188n., 199–201, 206
Salian dynasty, 14
sanctuary, 123, 141
Sandwich (Kent), 201n.
Savigniac monks, 225
Sayles, G. O., 120
Scandinavian law, 228; elements in Anglo-Saxon law, 11
Schulte, J. F. von, 154–5
Scotland, 218, 237n.; law, 218
Scott, Captain Robert, 217
Searle, E., 205–6
Seebohm, F., 28
seisin, 33n., 41, 73, 196, 220–1, 245n., 250, 251n., 253, 256–7
Selden Society, 4, 9n., 115, 120, 141, 220n., 244
seneschals, royal, jurisdiction of, 55–6, 59–60
sequela, in breweries, 237n.
serfdom, compared with slavery, 237
serfs, see villein, villeinage
servitia debita, 178
sexual offences, 14n.
Sharpe, R., 229n.
sheep-farming, 128
Sherborne, church of, 193n.
sheriff, 40, 67, 86, 122, 131–8, 141, 142; and royal interest, 137; powers of, 131–8; see also courts
sheriffs' serjeants, 141
Shropshire, 124–5
Sidgwick, H., 21–2n., 222n., 224
Simon de Montfort, 134

Simon of Pateshull, 229n.
Simon, archdeacon of Wells, 58
slavery, 237; penal, 3n.
Smith, A. L., 5, 16–17
Smith, F. E., 216–17
Sodbury (Glos.), 135–6
Somerset, 186
Southern, R.W., 4n., 12, 18n., 159
sovereignty, see kingship
St Albans Abbey, 62–3; chronicle of, 47
St Denis, 213
state, concept of, 3n., 6, 19, 25, 95–6, 108, 112, 172
Stein, P., 159
Stenton, D., 49, 228n.
Stephen, king, 25, 36, 48–9, 52, 62, 202n., 205–6, 210, 212–13
Stephen, Leslie, 219n.
Stevenson, W. H., 5
stipulatio, 148
stolen goods, traced, 142
strangers, as suspected criminals, 122–3, 126–7
Stubbs, W., 1, 4n, 6, 8, 13, 23n., 40, 48, 165, 215; controversy with Maitland, 151, 154, 163, 167–8
Suffolk, 192n.
Suger of St Denis, 213
sureties, 10
Surrey, 137
suspension ab ingressu ecclesie, 164n.

Tavistock Abbey, 194n.
taxation, and Anglo-Saxon state, 15
Templars, 210n.
tenant, unfree, 249
tenant-in-chief, status of, 196–8, 249–50
tenure, 34, 176–200 passim, 256; and services, 248–9; discontinued by heir, 250; in fee, 43
terra regis, 184–5, 187–9
testaments, law of, see wills
testimonials, 138–9
theft, 14n., 73, 116–17, 122, 124, 131, 132, 135, 138, 140, 142; by women, 230–31n.
thegn, thegnage, 11, 42n., 43–4
thieves, killed in flight, 132
Thomas, archbishop of York, 176n.
Thorne, S. E., 66–70, 73–85, 119, 247, 252, 255
Thorney (Suffolk), 192n.
tihtbysig, 11
tithes, 84–5, 157n.; law of 167n.
tithing, 10, 122, 128, 129, 142, 229–30; see also frankpledge
toll and team, 201
tonsure, to avoid trial, 141
tort, 13–14
Toulouse, 165
tourn, sheriff's, see courts

Toward the Unknown Region (R. Vaughan Williams), 21
towns, 146; and Domesday survey, 184n.; attraction of, 126; duties, 26; *see also* boroughs
treason, 15; trials for, 37
treasure trove, 138, 201
Treaty of Winchester (1153), 49–50
Trent, Council of, 167
trespass, 45, 230, 257; writs of, 50
trial by battle, 257
Twiss, Sir Travers, 9n., 115

Ullman, W., 168
undersheriffs, holding court, 135
United States, 217
universities, 146, 156
Unnatural Crime, Statute on, 239
Urban II, pope, 174–5, 180, 181n.
urban law, 146
uses, enforced in ecclesiastical courts, 160
utrum, assize brought by laity, 69–70

Vacarius, 159
vagrancy, 126; arrest for, 138; *see also* strangers
Vaughan Williams, Ralph, 21
Victoria, queen, 257
vill, 120–2, 126, 128–9, 131–2, 135, 136
villeins, villeinage, 34, 216, 231, 235–7, 251; and chattel slaves, 236–7; female, 237
Vinogradoff, P., 18n., 19n., 29, 33, 79, 93, 94n., 97n., 101n., 102n., 236

Wales 59–60, 126, 218
Walter of Bolbec, 40
Walter, bishop of Hereford, 177n.
Waltham, college of, 201n.
Wandsworth (Surrey), 203
Wantage code, 11
wapentake, 11
wardship, 26, 258; prerogative, 197n.; *see also guardianship*
warranty, 82, 257n.; of charter, 72, 254n.
watch, 122, 129
Wells, 74; canons of, 57–8
Welsh law, 16
wer, wergild, 14, 16, 44, 98–101
Westbury (Glos.), 130
Westminster, 57, 69, 83; charters, 201–5, 207, 213n.; hall, 27n.; Provisions of (1259), 84; *see also forgery, Osbert of Clare*
'weyve', 228–9
Whitman, Walt, 21n.
wife-battering, 226
Wiglaf, 7
Wilde, Oscar, 239–40

William I, king, 19n., 22–4, 25, 39, 173–8, 183–9, 200–3, 205–9; as Confessor's heir, 184–9; crown-wearing, 203
William II (Rufus), king, 173–91, 195, 197–8, 202n., 203
William de Warenne, 189n.
William des Roches, 59
William Durantis, 155
William Heron, 137
William le Sleghe, 117
    Alice, wife of, 117
William of Malmesbury, 13, 179n., 199
William Mansel, 137
William of Poitiers, 173–4
William of Raleigh, 68, 73–4, 78–9, 80n., 83, 84, 87
William of St Calais, 173–91, 195, 198–9; and Domesday survey, 183–4
Williams, Joshua, 253, 257, 258
wills, testaments, 96, 109n., 150, 155, 161, 227; bequests by women, 227; papal decretals on, 164–5; *see also intestacy*
Winchester, 201n., 203, 210–11; Treaty of (1153), 62–3, 211–12
wite, 14, 17, 44; and amercement 45
witness-lists, 63
witnesses, examination of, 133; synodal, 149
Wolverhampton, church of, 206–7n.
women, 32, 116–17, 216, 222, 225–31, 238; as attorneys, 225n.; as guardians, 225n.; capital punishment of, 116; criminal liability, 116–17, 230–1; in matrimonial role, 221; in Welsh law, 16; married, and *wer*, 98; plaintiffs in trespass, 230; protectors of, 221; right to bring appeals, 230
Woodstock code, 11
Worcester, 122, 130, 194n.
Worcestershire, 126
Worlington (Suffolk), 192n.
wounding, 142
writs, 47–64, 149, 189n., 253, 255–6; forged, 178n.; of attaint, 69; of debt, 249; of disseisin, 68; of distraint, 72; of grand distress, 72; of prohibition, 70; of recaption, 68; of right, 73, 257; of summons, 71
Writtle (Essex), 138, 188n.
Wulfstan, bishop of Worcester, 7, 177n.
Wye (Kent), 206
Wymondham Priory, 123

Year Books, 6
York, archbishopric of, 181n.; *see also Ealdred, Thomas*
York, William of, 87, 88n.
Yorkshire, 109, 111n., 117, 122